Language Ideologies and Media Discourse

Advances in Sociolinguistics
Series Editors: Professor Sally Johnson, *University of Leeds*
Dr Tommaso M. Milani, *University of the Witwatersrand*

Since the emergence of sociolinguistics as a new field of enquiry in the late 1960s, research into the relationship between language and society has advanced almost beyond recognition. In particular, the past decade has witnessed the considerable influence of theories drawn from outside of sociolinguistics itself. Thus rather than see language as a mere reflection of society, recent work has been increasingly inspired by ideas drawn from social, cultural, and political theory that have emphasized the constitutive role played by language/discourse in all areas of social life. The Advances in Sociolinguistics series seeks to provide a snapshot of the current diversity of the field of sociolinguistics and the blurring of the boundaries between sociolinguistics and other domains of study concerned with the role of language in society.

Discourses of Endangerment: Ideology and Interest in the Defence of Languages
Edited by Alexandre Duchêne and Monica Heller

Globalization of Language and Culture in Asia
Edited by Viniti Vaish

Linguistic Minorities and Modernity: A Sociolinguistic Ethnography, 2nd Edition
Monica Heller

Language, Culture and Identity: An Ethnolinguistic Perspective
Philip Riley

Language in the Media: Representations, Identities, Ideologies
Edited by Sally Johnson and Astrid Ensslin

Language and Power: An Introduction to Institutional Discourse
Andrea Mayr

Language Testing, Migration and Citizenship
Edited by Guus Extra, Massimiliano Spotti and Piet Van Avermaet

Multilingualism: A Critical Perspective
Adrian Blackledge and Angela Creese

Semiotic Landscapes: Language, Image, Space
Adam Jaworski and Crispin Thurlow

The Languages of Global Hip-Hop
Edited by Marina Terkourafi

The Language of Newspapers: Socio-Historical Perspectives
Martin Conboy

The Languages of Urban Africa
Edited by Fiona Mc Laughlin

Language Ideologies and Media Discourse

Texts, Practices, Politics

Edited by
Sally Johnson and Tommaso M. Milani

continuum

Continuum International Publishing Group

The Tower Building   80 Maiden Lane
11 York Road   Suite 704
London SE1 7NX   New York, NY 10038

www.continuumbooks.com

British Library Cataloguing-in-Publication Data
A catalogue record for this book is available from the British Library.

ISBN: 978-1-44112-967-3 (Hardback)
       978-1-44115-586-3 (Paperback)

Library of Congress Cataloging-in-Publication Data
A catalog record for this book is available from the Library of Congress.

Typeset by Newgen Imaging Systems Pvt Ltd, Chennai, India
Printed and bound in Great Britain by the MPG Books Group, Bodmin and King's Lynn

Contents

Notes on contributors

Jannis Androutsopoulos is Professor of German and media linguistics at the University of Hamburg, Germany. His research is situated on the interface of sociolinguistics and media discourse, examining language, style and discourse processes in an array of non face-to-face settings (e.g. news discourse, fiction and performance genres, advertizing, pop music, computer-mediated communication, texting) and relating these to more established issues in sociolinguistics such as language in adolescence, language and identity, code-switching, and style. He is editor of a special issue of the *Journal of Sociolinguistics* (2006) on sociolinguistics and computer-mediated communication. Email: jannis.androutsopoulos@uni-hamburg.de

Iris Bachmann is Lecturer in Hispanic Linguistics at the University of Manchester, UK. Her research interests include the history of linguistics and language ideologies, and language norms in relation to the media. She has previously published a monograph on the history of Creole Studies, *Die Sprachwerdung des Kreolischen* (Narr, 2005) and is currently working on a research project on 'Transnational Portuguese: language, space and the media'. Email: iris.bachmann@manchester.ac.uk

Richard Bauman is Distinguished Professor Emeritus of Folklore and Ethnomusicology, Communication and Culture, and Anthropology at Indiana University, Bloomington, US. His research centers on oral poetics, genre, performance, and remediation. Among his recent publications are *Voices of Modernity* (with Charles L. Briggs, CUP, 2003), and *A World of Others' Words* (2004). Email: bauman@indiana.edu

Adrian Blackledge is Professor of Bilingualism in the School of Education, University of Birmingham, UK. His research interests include the politics of multilingualism, linguistic ethnography, education of linguistic minority students, negotiation of identities in multilingual contexts, and language testing, citizenship, and immigration. His publications include *Multilingualism: A Critical Perspective* (with Angela

Creese, forthcoming, Continuum), *Discourse and Power in a Multilingual World* (2005, John Benjamins), and *Negotiation of Identities in Multilingual Contexts* (with Aneta Pavlenko, 2004, Multilingual Matters). Email: a.j.blackledge@bham.ac.uk

Bethan L. Davies is a Lecturer in Linguistics at the Department of Linguistics and Phonetics in the School of Modern Languages and Cultures at the University of Leeds, UK. Her research interests and areas of publication include: (im)politeness, critical discourse analysis and pragmatics (particularly the issue of common ground). She is currently working on texts like *The Highway Code* which are integral to the discourse of the transport debate. Email: b.l.davies@leeds.ac.uk

Astrid Ensslin is Lecturer in New Media at the National Institute for Excellence in the Creative Industries at Bangor University, Wales, UK. Her main research interests are in the areas of discourse analysis, hypertext, games studies, corpus linguistics and sociolinguistics (language attitudes and metalanguage). Her publications include *Canonizing Hypertext: Explorations and Constructions* (Continuum, 2007), *Language in the Media: Representations, Identities, Ideologies* (co-edited with Sally Johnson, Continuum, 2007), *Journal of Gaming and Virtual Worlds* (Intellect), and articles in *Language and Literature*, *Corpora*, *Sprache und Datenverarbeitung*, *Gender and Language* and *Dichtung Digital*. Email: a.ensslin@bangor.ac.uk

Vasiliki Georgiou is a doctoral student at the University of Southampton, UK. Her PhD examines how language planning, language ideologies, national identity and history are intertwined in a specific language debate in Cyprus. Her research interests include language and identification processes, language ideologies, language in history, CDA and linguistic ethnography. She is also a researcher for the European Commission funded programme *Linee*, working on language and national identity. Email: vg1@soton.ac.uk

Monica Heller is Professor at the Ontario Institute for Studies in Education, University of Toronto, Canada. Her research interests focus on the role of language (in particular multilingualism) in the globalized new economy, and in the changing shape of the nation-State, with a focus on francophone Canada. Her recent publications include *Bilingualism: A Social Approach* (Palgrave, 2007) and *Discourses of Endangerment: Ideology and Interest in the Defence of Languages* (London, Continuum, 2007 – co-edited with Alexandre Duchêne). Email: mheller@oise. utoronto.ca

Sally Johnson is Professor of Linguistics at the University of Leeds, UK. Her recent publications include *Spelling Trouble: Language Ideology and the Reform of German Orthography* (Multilingual Matters, 2005) and *Language in the Media: Representations, Identities, Ideologies* (co-edited with Astrid Enssslin, Continuum, 2007). She is currently Director of a three-year research project (with Clive Upton) funded by the UK Arts and Humanities Research Council entitled 'Whose Voices? Language ideological debates on the interactive website of the 'BBC Voices' project'. Email: s.a.johnson@leeds.ac.uk

Michelle M. Lazar is Associate Professor in the Department of English Language and Literature at the National University of Singapore. Her research interests are in critical discourse analysis, gender and feminisms, multimodality, political and media discourses, and language ideologies. She is editor of *Feminist Critical Discourse Analysis* (Palgrave, 2005/2007), is currently working on a book on discourses of gender for Palgrave, and is also the editor of the book series *Routledge Critical Studies in Discourse*. Email: ellmml@nus.edu.sg

Tommaso M. Milani is Senior Lecturer in linguistics at the University of the Witwatersrand, South Africa and was formerly a postdoctoral research fellow on the AHRC-funded 'BBC Voices' project at the University of Leeds with Sally Johnson and Clive Upton. He recently completed his PhD at the Centre for Research on Bilingualism at Stockholm University on how language politics, language ideology and national identity are intertwined in debates over Swedish. His broader areas of research encompass language politics in Scandinavia, media discourse, multimodality, and language and gender/sexuality. His publications include articles in *Language in Society, Journal of Language and Politics, Linguistics and Education* and *Language Problems and Language Planning* as well as chapters in edited collections. Email: tommaso.milani@wits.ac.za.

Spiros Moschonas is Assistant Professor of Linguistics and the Philosophy of Language in the Faculty of Communication and Media Studies at the University of Athens, Greece. His research interests include language ideologies, media discourse analysis, history of linguistics, grammatical analysis of modern Greek, bilingualism and second language acquisition. Recent publications include *Ideology and Language* (Athens: Patakis, 2005; in Greek). Email: smoschon@media.uoa.gr.

Darren Paffey teaches Spanish Linguistics at the University of Southampton, UK. He recently completed a PhD investigating language ideologies and standardization in the discourse of the Spanish Language Academy, particularly in the Spanish national press. He has published articles in *Language Policy* and in a forthcoming volume on Spanish in the US and other contexts published by Vervuert Iberoamericana. Darren is currently involved in establishing MEXSU, a centre for research and educational collaboration between Southampton and Mexico. Email: darren.paffey@soton.ac.uk

Joseph Sung-Yul Park is an Assistant Professor in the Department of English Language and Literature at the National University of Singapore. He studies issues in language and globalization, language ideology, media discourse, and interactional linguistics. Through his recent work, he has been exploring the role of global English in identity construction, with a particular focus on South Korea. Email: ellpjs@nus.edu.sg

Jürgen Spitzmüller is a Senior Research Assistant in the Department of German Language and Literature at the University of Zurich, Switzerland. His research interests include language ideological debates (particularly within Germany), discourse theory, visual communication as well as sociolinguistic issues in general. Previous publications include *Metasprachdiskurse* [metalanguage discourses] (Mouton de Gruyter, 2005), *Trends and Developments in Youth Language Research* (as co-editor, Lang 2006), *Methoden der Diskurslinguistik* [methods of discourse linguistics] (as co-editor, Mouton de Gruyter 2008). Email: spitzmueller@ds.uzh.ch

Clive Upton is Professor of Modern English Language at the University of Leeds, UK. Involved with the Survey of English Dialects for more than 30 years, he advised the British Broadcasting Corporation on its 'Voices' project, 2004–5 and is currently co-directing an AHRC-funded research project on this topic together with Sally Johnson. Consultant on pronunciation to the Oxford English Dictionary, his most recent large-scale publishing project has been as co-editor of Mouton de Gruyter's *Varieties of English* (2004–2008). Email: c.s.upton@leeds.ac.uk

Acknowledgements

This volume has its origins in a conference of the same name, which was held at the University of Leeds in September 2007. The editors of this book would particularly like to thank the following individuals for their support at that event: Susan Lacey of the Leeds Conference office, Kristine Horner, Bethan Davies, Ann Thompson and Will Turner. The conference was also funded – together with the work which appears in Chapter 12 – by the UK Arts and Humanities Research Council (AHRC) as part of the research grant (ref. AH/E509002/1) on language ideological debates on the BBC 'Voices' website.

The editors and authors of individual chapters gratefully acknowledge permission to reproduce various text extracts, images and screenshots as follows:

- Park Seyoung from KBS for use of screenshots from the Korean TV shows *Ulimal Gyeolugi* and *Sangsang Plus* in Chapter 4 by Joseph Park;
- Marcelo Espirito Santo of RBTI Network in Brazil for extracts/image from *América Légal* in Chapter 5 by Iris Bachmann;
- Serene Choo at MediaCorp TV for permission to reproduce the song lyrics of the SARS rap in Chapter 7 by Michelle Lazar;
- Joachim Gauger of the music channel www.laut.de for the extract from the news feature *Grup Tekkan: Mit 'Sonnenlischt' bei Stefan Raab*; Domenika Ahlrichs of the *Netzeitung.de* for the extract from *Sonnenlischt: Top 5 ist Pflicht*; Frank Meyer at *dradio.de* for the extract on "*Kanaksprak*"; and Silvia Iburg of *Der Spiegel* for the extract from "*Die verlorene Welt*" – all contained in Chapter 10 by Jannis Androutsopoulos;
- Sam Van Tilburgh at Microsoft for the screenshots from the computer game *Black and White 2* in Chapter 11 by Astrid Ensslin;
- Mandy Rose at the BBC for various screenshots from the BBC Voices website in Chapter 12 by Sally Johnson, Tommaso M. Milani and Clive Upton.

Every endeavour has been made to contact copyright holders but we will be happy to rectify any omissions in future editions of this volume.

The editors would also like to thank Gurdeep Mattu, Colleen Coalter and P. Muralidharan for their support in bringing the volume to publication. While our book is clearly a joint effort and we have worked closely together in its production, it should be noted that the authors of individual chapters are responsible for their own views, which are not necessarily shared by the editors.

Finally, this book is dedicated to three very special men in our lives – Ben, Frank and Carlo.

Sally Johnson and Tommaso M. Milani
Leeds and Johannesburg
April 2009

INTRODUCTION

1 Critical intersections: language ideologies and media discourse

Tommaso M. Milani and Sally Johnson

1.1 Where are we coming from . . . ?

This volume does not emerge in an academic vacuum. Specifically it has its origins in a conference of the same name that was held at the University of Leeds in September 2007 and that was itself part of a range of research events organized by the 'Language in the Media' Special Research Network set up in 2006 under the auspices of the International Association for Applied Linguistics (AILA). An early agenda for the activities of this network was set by the collection entitled *Language in the Media: Representations, Identities, Ideologies* (Johnson and Ensslin 2007a) with its particular focus on the study of (meta-)linguistic issues in the context of different media text types. That book covered a wide range of topics including: (i) metaphors of speech and writing, political apologies, and personalist ideologies in the press; (ii) debates concerning language, national identities and citizenship; (iii) contact and code-switching in broadcast media; and (iv) youth, gender and cyber-identities in computer-mediated communication. In many ways, we see this new volume as an attempt to continue the academic debates begun in that earlier collection, extending them across a wider range of socio-cultural, geographical and media-technological contexts than was previously possible. At the same time, however, we aim to take those debates around 'language in the media' significantly further in theoretical terms by focussing more strongly on the *ideological dimension* of language representation and usage in the context of late-modern *media discourse* (Giddens 1991).

1.2 Why language ideologies? Why now?

Over the past two decades, the notion of *language ideology* has gained considerable momentum in different strands of scholarship that aim to unpack the workings of language in the context of social processes. It is not our intention in this introduction to offer a comprehensive overview of the now substantial body of research that has recently been

3

informed by this approach (see e.g. Milani and Johnson 2008 for an outline). Suffice it to note here that the field of language ideology has its origins in North American linguistic anthropology as a framework within which to explore the 'mediating links between social forms and forms of talk' (Woolard 1998: 3). To put this point in the simplest possible terms, while it is axiomatic for linguists that 'all languages are equal' in terms of their meaning-making potential and their worth as objects of academic inquiry, a cursory glance at any sociolinguistic environment in the 'real world' will reveal a less equal scenario – one in which linguistic phenomena are *ranked* according to different meanings and values, so that, say, code X is posited as a 'sexist, multi-ethnic lads' slang' while 'language' Y is believed to be lexically richer, more logical and thus better suited for wider communication within a polity than, say, 'dialect' Z. Crucially, this differentiation is not random but is the result of particular processes under specific social, political, cultural and economic conditions. And it is precisely these processes of naming, signifying and valorizing linguistic practices – what one could call the *sociolinguistic imagination* – that language ideology researchers set out to investigate. More precisely, the aim of this scholarship is to show how linguistic phenomena are invested with meanings and values through the production, reproduction and/or contestation of conventional *indexical ties* between (i) perceived or presumed features, genres, styles or varieties of language and (ii) broader cultural representations of their purported speakers in terms of nationality, ethnicity, gender, sexuality, aesthetics, morality and so forth (see e.g. Woolard 1998).

At this juncture, it is important to state upfront that, inspired by scholars of language ideology, we take a materialist stance that focuses rather less on ideologies as 'mental schemata' (van Dijk 1991: 40) or 'frameworks of social cognition' (van Dijk 1995: 21). This is not to say that we totally reject any cognitive dimension of such views and ideas (see Spitulnik 1998; Blackledge, Chapter 8, this volume). However, we are ultimately more interested in understanding 'how such very deep cognitive patterns end up in people's heads, and end up there as collective phenomena' (Blommaert 2005: 162). In other words, we want to tease out the *social mechanisms* through which particular ideas or beliefs about linguistic practices are produced, circulated and/or challenged through meaning-making activities under particular conditions. And in our view, such a materialist approach cannot be fully achieved without a close scrutiny of the texts, practices, and politics of *mass mediation*. First, this is insofar as technological artefacts – newspapers, telephones, televisions, computers, iPods – have become increasingly prominent in many late-modern societies as more or less dynamic interfaces with which individuals engage in daily interactions, thereby gaining experiences of themselves and a range of different realities, including linguistic reality (Coupland 2007; Johnson and Ensslin 2007b). Second, many critical discourse analysts (e.g. Norman Fairclough, John Richardson, Mary Talbot, Teun van Dijk, Ruth Wodak – for a discussion see Milani and Johnson 2008) have systematically demonstrated over the past three decades how the media are deeply imbricated in relations of power and ideology given that 'the representation of any issue for a mass audience has implications for the way it is understood' (Cameron 2007: 268). That said, we concur with Jan Blommaert (2005) who warns against falling into the 'fallacy of internalism' (Thompson 1990: 24), thereby locating the 'power of ideologies [. . .] in the message alone' (Blommaert 2005: 163). Reasoning along similar lines, we believe that the power of language ideologies should not be treated as simply embedded within the mediated text alone, thus downplaying or even overlooking the variability in the reception of a particular text on the part of different audiences. By the same token, the power of language ideologies cannot be merely situated in the media in general or, more specifically, in their semiotic and technological affordances as part of the production processes underpinning media texts (see Androutsopoulos 2006; Constantinou 2005; Johnson and Ensslin 2007b). In practice, all of the contributors to the present volume ascribe to a greater or lesser extent to a view of the media as 'institutions of power' (Schieffelin, Woolard and Kroskrity 1998: 148). However, the various authors also show how the media are not powerful purely as a corollary to their particular institutional status; on the contrary, what emerges from the analyses undertaken by the different contributors is that the power of the media is a highly complex phenomenon that requires a great deal of detailed textual, ethnographic and social deconstruction.

Pulling together the many insights that emerge from the chapters here, we would argue that the power of the media in language ideological processes lies to a considerable extent in their practices as gatekeepers in the regimentation of 'expert systems' (Giddens 1991) on language-related issues (see also Jaworski 2007). In other words, the media, constrained or pressed by particular economic and political imperatives, open up *discursive spaces* (see also Heller, Chapter 14, this volume), thereby giving a public voice to a variety of social actors who compete with each other in staking various claims regarding what counts as *legitimate* knowledge in the domain of language (Blommaert 1999; Johnson 2001). Of course, we would not want to imply that such discursive spaces are entirely open arenas where equal contenders democratically vie for hegemony. As Teun van Dijk (1993) has noted, individuals with high social, cultural and symbolic capital (Bourdieu 1991)

5

are always likely to have greater and privileged *access* to the processes of media production (see also Blommaert 2005; Milani 2007a). Similarly, 'reference to élite people' (Galtung and Ruge 1965) has itself been singled out as a key 'news value', according to which journalists assess the newsworthiness of an issue or event (see also Mayr 2008). Nonetheless, it would be an over-simplification to reduce the media to sheer conduits of the 'voices of the dominant'. In this regard, not only have ethnographers reiterated many times that what counts as 'dominant' versus 'dominated' cannot be simply presupposed, but media practitioners have also recently observed how 'Vox pops, where the man and the woman in the street are asked to give their view on a particular issue, have become far more prevalent' (Chris Elliot, news features editor of the *Cambridge Evening News*, cited in Venables 2005: 3–11; see also Mayr 2008 and Myers 2004). By the same token, the emergence of interactive 'Web 2.0' technologies (e.g. YouTube, Facebook, Twitter) has facilitated the opening up of a range of discursive spaces to individuals and groups who may not have traditionally had access to public media fora.

Clearly, we need to be wary of over-generalizing from one journalist's statement describing a strategy adopted by many regional newspapers in the UK to try to arrest a decline in circulation figures – or, indeed, over-estimating the democratic force of web users posting snapshots of their pet dogs on Facebook. What we want to emphasize, however, is that, in the very act of choosing, citing, and 'styling' (Coupland 2007) certain voices (but not others) in particular ways, *all* media producers have the *potential* to re-scale social, cultural and symbolic capital, and thereby 're-shuffle' authority and expertise on particular issues. And these practices ultimately pay lip service to the media themselves in that they are geared to the production of newsworthiness in the name of information and public knowledge under specific economic and political conditions (Richardson 2007). It is apparent then that media practitioners have a range of vested interests in both constructing and obfuscating the boundaries between such categories as 'expert/lay' (Johnson 2001; Milani 2007b; Androutsopoulos, Bachmann, Moschonas and Spitzmüller, Paffey, this volume), 'information/entertainment' (Blackledge; Ensslin; Georgiou; Johnson *et al.*; Lazar, this volume), 'ordinary/celebrity' (Kelly-Holmes and Atkinson 2007; Davies; Park, this volume) and 'public/private' (Fairclough 1995; Hill 2001; Davies, this volume). Therefore, understanding the *strategies*, *stakes* and *constraints* on the part of the media in establishing or blurring these (and many other) dyadic oppositions becomes a crucial empirical goal if we want to grasp the relationships between language ideologies and media discourse.

6

1.3 Overview of chapters

The volume is divided into four sections. In Part I, 'Standards and standardization in national and global contexts', we begin with three chapters exploring the role of the national press and broadcast media as gatekeepers in defining what counts as 'proper' language. In Chapter 2, Spiros Moschonas and Jürgen Spitzmüller analyze so-called *corrective* practices with regard to media language in the Greek and German press, showing how such *metamedial* activity (see also Ensslin 2007; Davies, Chapter 9) differs in the two countries under investigation. In their analysis, the authors also reflect upon the ideological underpinnings of prescriptivism in relation to media language, showing how corrective utterances in both the Greek and German press are underpinned by a standard language ideology (Milroy and Milroy 1998) that treats linguistic variation as a danger that must be challenged for the sake of linguistic unity. In Chapter 3, Darren Paffey similarly examines mainstream newspaper discourse, but shifts the focus to the context of Spain. Here the author shows how the Spanish language is represented – even marketized – as an apparently diverse, but ultimately unitary, commodity 'owned' by Spain that can be exported and therefore has economic value in a global linguistic marketplace. What Paffey also highlights is the dialectic interplay between mainstream Spanish newspapers and the prestigious *Real Academia Española* in constructing authority and expertise around issues of verbal hygiene. Reasoning along similar lines, Joseph Park analyses, in Chapter 4, two game shows on the theme of language transmitted on a national television channel in Korea, showing the subtle strategies through which a broadcasting corporation presents itself as the legitimate source of 'correct' language knowledge. Here, the author also makes an important point about the relationships between media interests, linguistic nationalism and the changing conditions of globalization. According to Park, employing Korean celebrity figures as the presenters of such game shows is itself a strategic move through which a national television channel can face the dilemma of maintaining its position as the legitimate guardian of a 'correct' national language while simultaneously addressing the economic imperatives of an increasingly competitive national and international media market.

In Part II, 'Planning and policy in media programming', we continue to investigate language usage and representation on television albeit with a tighter focus on the *conditions* and *constraints* of broadcasting. In Chapter 5, Iris Bachmann discusses two television programmes targeted at the Brazilian diaspora. Bachmann illustrates how such programmes are constrained by a monoglot ideology (Silverstein 1996) that erases any *direct* representation of multilingual practices among

7

Brazilian migrants – an ideology which in turns reproduces a view of Brazilian Portuguese as a 'unitary language' mapped onto a 'unitary community' of speakers. However, Bachmann also provides evidence of alternative strategies through which migrants' multilingual experiences are *indirectly* acknowledged via, *inter alia*, representations of language schools and learners of Portuguese as a second language. In Chapter 6, Vasiliki Georgiou explores the ideas and beliefs surrounding the meaning and value of Cypriot Greek in a range of television series broadcast in Cyprus. Through a combination of detailed textual and ethnographic analyses, Georgiou highlights the changing conditions that media producers in Cyprus are facing as a result of specific economic, technological and societal developments (see also Park, Chapter 4). While acknowledging that these developments may open up new opportunities for the use of Cypriot Greek on the screen, the author also shows how the incorporation of such a variety for mainly 'humorous' purposes implicitly reproduces a minoritizing ideology that emphasizes the 'non-seriousness' of Cypriot Greek in contrast to standard Greek. The topic of 'standard' versus 'non-standard' varieties is pursued further in Chapter 7. Here, Michelle Lazar demonstrates how the 'anomalous' public usage of Singlish, rather than the more prestigious Standard Singapore English, was accorded a very particular function in the National Campaign against SARS (Severe Acute Respiratory Syndrome) organized by the Singapore Government in 2003. Lazar argues that, despite a long-standing crusade against the use of Singlish in public domains, the Singapore Government strategically capitalized on the indexical ties between Singlish and entertainment for the sake of educating the nation in a major time of crisis. As the author nicely puts it, once the threat of SARS had subsided, Singlish could be 'taken off the airwaves, quite literally' (p. 137) – given that it had lost its instrumental and symbolic value for state purposes.

The contributions to Part III, 'Media, ethnicity and the racialization of language', also consider the indexical ties between linguistic phenomena and other axes of social categorizations, but look more precisely at the ways in which such ties are created, naturalized and/or contested in three 'media firestorms' (see Hill 2007). In Chapter 8, Adrian Blackledge analyzes two news items broadcast on BBC 1 in 2006/7 that reported on the public money apparently spent (read: wasted) on translating and interpreting services for non-English speaking users of UK public services. Blackledge begins by tracing the intertextual 'chains of discourse' (Blackledge 2005: 1) that connect these television items with other political and media discourses on migration in the UK. This is followed by a multimodal analysis (Kress and van Leeuwen 2006) of the news features in question that demonstrates how the relationship between voiceover and images contributes to turning a debate that is ostensibly about *language* into an issue of broader societal concern around race, religion, gender, and ultimately social segregation (see also Gieve and Norton 2007). The links between language and race are investigated further in Chapter 9 where Bethan Davies explores a print-mediated debate on a disputed case of 'racist language' on the reality TV show, Celebrity Big Brother. Through an analysis of the British press coverage on the issue, Davies shows how metamedial pronouncements (see also Moschonas and Spitzmüller, Chapter 2) – in this case, newspaper utterances about television language – demonstrate disagreement about what counts as 'racist' versus 'non-racist' language. Through close scrutiny of those newspaper voices that were reluctant to classify the events on Celebrity Big Brother as racist, Davies highlights the existence of an underlying personalist ideology (Hill 2007) according to which we are unable to establish the racist loading of an utterance unless we can pin down the precise intentions of the speaker – a virtually impossible enterprise. However, Davies also illustrates the rhetorical moves through which some of the commentators in her data did indeed assign intentions and attempted to justify them. In the final chapter in this section, Jannis Androutsopoulos shifts the debate from race to ethnicity by looking at a particular set of linguistic representations in a combination of German media, that is, internet, national press and radio. Drawing upon Irvine and Gal's (2001) model of linguistic ideologization, the author unpacks the semiotic processes through which certain linguistic features that are perceived as 'deviant' from 'standard' German are not only portrayed as inherent *icons* of their speakers in terms of age (i.e. youth) and ethnicity (i.e. migrants) but are also devalued as 'negative' and 'foreign'. Androutsopoulos concludes his analysis with a critical reflection of the constraints placed upon media producers in searching for, incorporating, or excluding different voices of 'expert' knowledge on language-related issues.

In Part IV, 'Language ideologies in new media technologies', we conclude by re-visiting some of the topics addressed elsewhere in the volume, this time with a critical focus on 'new' media and their affordances in relation to language ideology. In Chapter 11, Astrid Ensslin discusses different examples of computer games showing a clear-cut opposition in the usage of Received Pronunciation and Standard North American, on the one hand, and non-standard accents of English, on the other. Analogous to Rosina Lippi-Green's (1997) treatment of Hollywood films, Ensslin argues that the use of 'standard' and 'non-standard' accents in computer games exploits, and at the same time reproduces, stereotypical images of their speakers with respect to morality, erudition,

9

social class, gender and race. That said, Ensslin also underscores the interactive dimension of gaming activities and their subversive potential. Thus what is most desirable and valuable in cyberspace – language included – is not necessarily the same as in the 'real' world. In Chapter 12, Sally Johnson, Tommaso Milani and Clive Upton analyze the home page of the BBC 'Voices Project' through which the national British public service provider aimed to 'celebrate' linguistic diversity in the UK. Bringing together insights from multimodal analysis and website research, the authors outline a *hypermodal* approach that aims to capture the ways in which the linguistic, visual and phonic work together in the representation of language. In their analysis, Johnson, Milani and Upton not only discuss the meanings and functions of different semiotic items on this home page but also tease out the tensions and discrepancies between an attempt to acknowledge linguistic diversity on the part of the BBC, on the one hand, and the semiotic prominence of (standard) English and (southern) England, on the other. In Chapter 13, Richard Bauman then explores the ways in which technological changes are accompanied by transformations in communicative practices and experiences. For this purpose, the author takes us back in history through an analysis of commercial sound recordings describing early encounters with the telephone in the US at the turn of the twentieth century. These data offer illuminating examples of the difficulties and anxieties in dealing with a new technological device; they also illustrate how communicative incompetence was projected onto two 'social types', the 'immigrant' and the 'rustic' for the amusement of middle-class audiences. Finally, Bauman not only reminds us that the social meaning of linguistic practices is always historically situated, but that what constitutes 'new' – technologies included – is itself always contingent and transient (Gitelman and Pingree 2003). The volume ends with an epilogue in which Monica Heller draws together a number of insights on the theme of language ideologies and media discourse, highlighting how a focus on the *practices* of the media in relation to linguistic matters is particularly pertinent for gaining a deeper insight into the processes of social change in late modernity. Following Bourdieu (1991), Heller argues that it is important to lay bare the synergy between the media and the State in regimenting what counts as 'legitimate' language within a polity. This is insofar as the media can act as discursive spaces where the *status quo* is maintained and legitimized under new guises. At the same time, however, the media can also play a key role in the opening up of new discursive spaces in order to challenge previously conventionalized social arrangements and thereby bringing about new social practices and relations. Ultimately, it remains a matter of further investigation how such change is achieved over a longer period of time.

1.4 Where are we heading? Language ideologies and multimodality

We want to conclude this introductory chapter by acknowledging that it has not been possible to address in their entirety the many theoretical and methodological challenges arising from a dual focus on language ideologies and media discourse. Moreover, it is notable how, a decade or so after the programmatic contributions to *Approaches to Media Discourse* (Bell and Garrett 1998), the chapters in the present volume still appear to privilege texts and their broader social, cultural, political and economic contexts. Accordingly, few authors are entirely able to come to grips with the multiple and varied stages of media production and reception that underpin those texts. While this bias might be seen as a researcher's choice of a particular theoretical and methodological paradigm, we believe that the institutional limitations that constrain language-ideological research into and about the media cannot be overlooked. As Peter Garrett and Allan Bell cogently point out, 'It is more difficult to research production than reception (while reception is more difficult than the text itself). That difficulty is not so much theoretical as practical and interactional. Access to and acceptance by media organizations and personnel is the central problem' (1998: 19). Having said this, the emphasis placed by many of our contributors on television and 'new-media' texts has certainly foregrounded other important issues, one of which is the imperative to go beyond *language* (in the narrow sense of written and spoken codes) in language ideology research, thereby incorporating and expanding upon recent theoretical insights into visual communication and multimodal discourse analysis.

In this respect, it is useful to remind ourselves how Fairclough argued more than a decade ago that 'written texts in contemporary society are increasingly becoming more visual [. . .], not only in the sense that newspapers, for instance, combine words with photographs [. . .], but also because considerations of layout and visual impact are increasingly salient in the design of a written page' (1995: 17; see also Machin 2007: 16). Taking an even stronger position, Gunther Kress and Theo van Leeuwen proposed that 'Language always has to be realized through, and comes in the company of, other semiotic modes' (1998: 186), concluding that 'any form of text analysis which ignores this will not be able to account for all the meanings expressed in texts' (ibid.). Against this backdrop, we would argue that if we similarly want to account for

11

the processes of *mediatization* of language ideologies, we too cannot afford to overlook the growing field of research into *multi-* or *hypermodality* (Kress and van Leeuwen 2006; Lemke 2002), that is, the dynamic interplay between the verbal, the visual and other semiotic modes in the workings of the sociolinguistic imagination (see also Gal 2008). In other words, notwithstanding the particular theoretical and methodological approaches one might want to adopt, research on language ideologies and media discourse cannot be confined to the 'purely linguistic' elements of a text. Without a serious engagement with visual and other semiotic modes, it will be difficult, nigh on impossible, to tease out the complexity of language ideologies embedded in media texts as produced in late-modern contexts. Indeed we would go so far as to suggest this to be one of the key challenges for language ideology research in the near future.

References

Androutsopoulos, J. (2006), 'Introduction: sociolinguistics and computer-mediated communication'. *Journal of Sociolinguistics*, 10(4), 514–33.

Bell, A. and Garrett, P. (eds) (1998), *Approaches to Media Discourse*. Oxford: Blackwell.

Blackledge, A. (2005), *Discourse and Power in a Multilingual World*. Amsterdam: John Benjamins.

Blommaert, J. (1999), 'The debate is closed', in J. Blommaert (ed.) *Language Ideological Debates*. Berlin: Mouton de Gruyter, pp. 1–38.

Blommaert, J. (2005), *Discourse: A Critical Approach*. Cambridge: Cambridge University Press.

Bourdieu, P. (1991), *Language and Symbolic Power*. Cambridge, MA: Harvard University Press.

Cameron, D. (2007), 'Language endangerment and verbal hygiene: history, morality and politics', in A. Duchêne and M. Heller (eds), *Discourses of Endangerment: Ideology and Interest in the Defence of Languages*. London: Continuum, pp. 268–85.

Constantinou, O. (2005), 'Multimodal discourse analysis: media, modes and technologies'. *Journal of Sociolinguistics*, 9(4), 602–18.

Coupland, N. (2007), *Style: Language Variation and Identity*. Cambridge: Cambridge University Press.

Ensslin, A. (2007), 'Of chords, machines and bumble-bees: the metalinguistics of hyperpoetry', in S. Johnson and A. Ensslin (eds), *Language in the Media: Representations, Identities, Ideologies*. London: Continuum, pp. 250–68.

Fairclough, N. (1995), *Media Discourse*. London: Arnold.

Gal, S. (2008), 'Language and space/place: implications for linguistic minorities'. Keynote address at the International Conference on Language Planning and Policy. Saltsjöbaden, Sweden, 9–10 June 2008.

Galtung, J. and Ruge, M. H. (1965), 'The structure of foreign news'. *Journal of International Peace Research*, 2(1), 64–90.

Garrett, P. and Bell, A. (1998), 'Media and discourse: a critical overview', in A. Bell and P. Garrett (eds), *Approaches to Media Discourse*. Oxford: Blackwell, pp. 1–20.

Giddens, A. (1991), *Modernity and Self-Identity: Self and Society in the Late Modern Age*. Stanford, CA: Stanford University Press.

Gieve, S. and Norton, J. (2007), 'Dealing with linguistic difference in encounters with others on British television', in S. Johnson and A. Ensslin (eds), *Language in the Media: Representations, Identities, Ideologies*. London: Continuum, pp. 188–210.

Gitelman, L. and Pingree, G. B. (eds) (2003), *New Media, 1740–1915*. Cambridge, MA: MIT Press.

Hill, J. H. (2001), 'Mock Spanish, covert racism and the (leaky) boundaries between public and private spheres'. *Pragmatics*, 5(2), 197–212.

Hill, J. H. (2007), 'Crises of meaning: personalist language ideology in US media discourse', in S. Johnson and A. Ensslin (eds), *Language in the Media: Representations, Identities, Ideologies*. London: Continuum, pp. 70–88.

Irvine, J. T. and Gal, S. (2001), 'Language ideology and linguistic-differentiation', in P. V. Kroskrity (ed.), *Regimes of Language: Ideologies, Polities and Identities*. Santa Fe, NM: School of American Research Press, pp. 35–83.

Jaworski, A. (2007), 'Language in the media: authenticity and othering', in S. Johnson and A. Ensslin (eds), *Language in the Media: Representations, Identities, Ideologies*. London: Continuum, pp. 271–80.

Johnson, S. (2001), 'Who's misunderstanding whom? (Socio)linguistics, public debate and the media'. *Journal of Sociolinguistics*, 5(4), 591–610.

Johnson, S. and Ensslin, A. (eds) (2007a), *Language in the Media: Representations, Identities, Ideologies*. London: Continuum.

Johnson, S. and Ensslin, A. (2007b), 'Language in the media: theory and practice', in S. Johnson and A. Ensslin (eds), *Language in the Media: Representations, Identities, Ideologies*. London: Continuum, pp. 3–22.

Kelly-Holmes, H. and Atkinson, D. (2007), 'When Hector met Tom Cruise: attitudes to Irish in a radio satire', in S. Johnson and A. Ensslin (eds), *Language in the Media: Representations, Identities, Ideologies*. London: Continuum, pp. 173–87.

Kress, G. and van Leeuwen, T. (1998), 'Front pages: (the critical) analysis of newspaper layout' in A. Bell and P. Garrett (eds), *Approaches to Media Discourse*. Oxford: Blackwell, pp. 186–219.

Kress, G. and van Leeuwen, T. (2006), *Reading Images: The Grammar of Visual Design* (2nd edn). London: Routledge.

Lemke, J. L. (2002), 'Travels in hypermodality'. *Visual Communication*, 1(3), 299–325.

Lippi-Green, R. (1997), *English with an Accent: Language, Ideology and Discrimination in the United States*. London: Routledge.

Machin, D. (2007), *Introduction to Multimodal Analysis*. London: Hodder Arnold.

Mayr, A. (2008), *Language and Power: An Introduction to Institutional Discourse*. London: Continuum.

Milani, T. M. (2007a), 'A language ideology in print: the case of Sweden', in S. Johnson and A. Ensslin (eds), *Language in the Media: Representations, Identities, Ideologies*. London: Continuum, pp. 111–29.

Milani, T. M. (2007b), 'Voices of authority in conflict: the making of the expert in a language debate in Sweden'. *Linguistics and Education*, 18(2), 99–120.

Milani, T. M. and Johnson, S. (2008), 'CDA and language ideology: towards a reflexive approach to discourse data', in I. H. Warnke and J. Spitzmüller (eds), *Methoden der Diskurslinguistik: sprachwissenschaftliche Zugänge zur transtextuellen Ebene*. Berlin: Mouton de Gruyter, pp. 365–88.

Milroy, J. and Milroy, L. (1998), *Authority in Language*. London: Routledge.

Myers, G. (2004), *Matters of Opinion: Talking about Public Issues*. Cambridge: Cambridge University Press.

Richardson, J. E. (2007), *Analysing Newspapers: An Approach from Critical Discourse Analysis*. Basingstoke: Palgrave Macmillan.

Silverstein, M. (1996), 'Monoglot "standard" in America: standardization and metaphors of linguistic-hegemony', in D. Brenneis and R. Macaulay (eds), *The Matrix of Language: Contemporary Linguistic Anthropology*. Boulder: Westview Press, pp. 284–306.

Spitulnik, D. (1998), 'Mediating unity and diversity: the production of language ideologies in Zambian broadcasting', in K. A. Woolard, B. B. Schieffelin and P. V. Kroskrity (eds), *Language Ideologies: Practice and Theory*. Oxford: Oxford University Press, pp. 163–88.

Thompson, J. B. (1990), *Ideology and Modern Culture*. Cambridge: Polity Press.

van Dijk, T. A. (1991), *Racism and the Press*. London: Routledge.

van Dijk, T. A. (1993), 'Principles of critical discourse analysis'. *Discourse & Society*, 4(2), 249–83.

van Dijk, T. A. (1995), 'Discourse analysis as ideology analysis', in C. Schäffner and A. Wenden (eds), *Language and Peace*. Aldershot, UK: Dartmouth, pp. 17–33.

Venables, J. (2005), *Making Headlines: News Values and Risk Signals in Journalism*. Huntingdon: Elm.

Woolard, K. A. (1998), 'Language ideology as a field of inquiry', in K. A. Woolard, B. B. Schieffelin and P. V. Kroskrity (eds), *Language Ideologies: Practice and Theory*. Oxford: Oxford University Press, pp. 3–47.

PART I

STANDARDS AND STANDARDIZATION IN NATIONAL AND GLOBAL CONTEXTS

2 Prescriptivism in and about the media: a comparative analysis of corrective practices in Greece and Germany

Spiros Moschonas and Jürgen Spitzmüller

And what should they know of England who only England know?
(Rudyard Kipling)

2.1 Introduction

Metalinguistic discourse in the media is often referred to as *prescriptivist* insofar as it appears to be a clear example of the kind of discourse whereby someone tries to tell someone else how to speak or write. Here prescriptivism is typically contrasted to *descriptivism*, that is, a 'scientific' discourse that aims to capture how people *actually* speak or write. Undoubtedly 'telling other people how to speak or write' is a central metapragmatic practice in the context of language ideological debates, and, as such, is a core topic of language ideology research. However, as has often been pointed out (e.g. Cameron 1995; Johnson 2001), the objective definition and delineation of 'prescriptivism', on the one hand, and 'descriptivism', on the other, is inherently problematic, not least since each concept is invariably subject to the linguist's self-perception of her or his own 'scientific' task. And although the definitional advantage might appear to be on the part of the descriptivist, it is rarely entirely apparent what prescriptivism is supposed to be and do, let alone how it should be accounted for in (socio-)linguistic terms. That said, one thing remains clear: if language ideology research is to be acknowledged as part of the mainstream of linguistic research, it should similarly aspire to the descriptivist ideal of explaining what it is that people actually say and do *when* they tell other people how to speak or write. In other words, definitional and methodological precision remain fundamental concerns in language ideology research, not least since they apply to notions and practices that overlap with those employed in other fields of linguistics. In this regard, a key concern is the use of large-scale comparative studies. We believe that, within the field of language ideology research, there is an urgent need to devise methodologies for the processing of large corpora, and particularly for the use of comparative corpus-based – or even corpus-*driven* – discourse analysis alongside metalinguistic, metapragmatic or folk linguistic studies (Schieffelin *et al.* 1998; Kroskrity 2000; Niedzielski and Preston 2000; Jaworski *et al.* 2004). In this chapter we therefore set out to address each of these three issues: we provide, (i) a pragmatic definition of *prescriptivism* on the basis of which we then develop (ii) a *corpus-driven* approach to prescriptivist media discourse in (iii) a *comparative* context, namely that of Greece and Germany.

We will apply our comparative approach to two corpora of metalinguistic print-media texts from a selection of Greek and German newspapers. Our corpora consist of texts that contain references to *media language* – hence our dual focus on prescriptivism *in* and *about* the media. We concentrate on the period from the mid-1990s to the year 2001, during which time both countries experienced a remarkable upsurge of public interest in media language use (Delveroudi and Moschonas 2003; Spitzmüller 2005a). In our analysis we will be focusing on metalinguistic references in newspapers only, that is a mere subset of reflexive discourse about the media that appears in the media generally. The reasons for this will be explained in section 2.2, where we will describe and contextualize the data selection process for each of the two corpora. In section 2.3, we introduce our central theoretical concept of *corrective practices*, and elaborate on why we think that prescriptivism can, and should, be approached by means of a pragmatic analysis of so-called 'corrective speech acts'. Section 2.4 then presents the results of our corpus-driven analysis of corrective repertories in Greek and German newspapers. Finally, in section 2.5, we sum up our observations on prescriptivism in each of the two discourse communities. Here we discuss differences and similarities, identify further issues for possible future research, and conclude with a tentative re-evaluation of our overall approach in the hope that this might be fruitfully adapted to the study of such issues as standardization and purism more generally together with the institutionalization and the propagation of metalinguistic discourse.

2.2 Data selection and corpus construction

2.2.1 Why the press?

It goes without saying that the press is not the only arena where language, or even media language, are discussed. In Greece, for example, since the language reform of 1976, there have been numerous radio and television programmes dealing explicitly with questions of language use (see e.g. Kriaras 1988). Moreover, media language became the subject of many written guides or manuals, some of which were specifically addressed to media professionals (Moschonas 2001, 2005: 161–62). Similarly, in Germany, the past two decades have witnessed considerable discussion about the language of the media, much of it outside the press. So, for example, the ('mis')-use of media language has been the key topic of many best-selling books (e.g. Sick 2004; Zimmer 2005). It has also been extensively discussed in talk shows both on radio and TV, in lay-linguistic Internet forums (Spitzmüller 2002) as well as in countless sites and chatrooms on the World Wide Web (Spitzmüller 2005a; Pfalzgraf 2006).

For the purposes of our study, however, there were many reasons why it was not only convenient but also appropriate to restrict ourselves to the analysis of *newspaper* texts (see also Paffey, Chapter 3, this volume). Despite what often appears to be a form of prejudice against broadcast and the new electronic media formats, the press provides us with the most representative sample of the kind of prescriptivism that is aimed at a range of media types. Moreover, the sheer volume of prescriptivist statements to be found in the newspaper texts has also to be seen in the context of a much longer tradition of 'philological' and/or 'linguistic' journalism that can be found in both countries (for Greece, see e.g. Majer 1959; for Germany, see e.g. Schiewe 1998). At the same time, the press is not just a vehicle for metalinguistic and/or metamedial commentary; it is also itself a popular *target* for prescriptivism. In Germany, newspapers were themselves branded 'corrupters of language' (*Sprachverderber*) as early as the beginning of the seventeenth century and there is a long tradition of criticizing 'newspaper German' (*Zeitungsdeutsch*). Meanwhile in Greece, criticism directed at the 'language of the newspapers' has been associated mostly with the so-called 'Language Question' (Browning 1982). Thus, while supporters of the high '*katharevousa*' variety of Greek typically blamed journalistic jargon for being too lenient towards 'foreign words', the proponents of *demotic* Greek accused the high variety of being needlessly puristic, excessively archaic, and largely incomprehensible to the wider public (Triandaphillidis 1905–07: 253–54). That said, it became clear over time that the press was itself slowly adjusting to, as well as actually promoting, a more vernacular model of literacy (Triandaphillidis 1915: 294–95). New proposals for correcting media language appeared again in the 1980s, after the official adoption of a *demotic* standard in 1976. The 1990s continued to witness widespread press criticism of the media in general for the excessive use of loan words and borrowings from other languages (Delveroudi and Moschonas 2003). Finally, within both Greece and Germany, newspapers have often been blamed for being the main propagator of (undesirable) forms of language change. In the contemporary discourse on Anglicisms in Germany, for instance, the press – and not least the electronic media – have been perceived as key driver behind the so-called 'Anglification' of the language, surpassed only by advertising and business (Spitzmüller 2005a: 262–64; for similar criticism of the Greek media see e.g. Babiniotis 1999).

Another reason for our focus on newspaper texts is that, in the context of prescriptivism, it is often (though by no means exclusively) *written* language – in particular, public written language – that is being criticized. Accordingly, the press (alongside the media in general) is very rarely cited as a purveyor of *good* language use. Instead, newspaper language is often portrayed as the prototype of *bad* usage (at the other extreme, in both countries, it is poetry that is posited as the prototypical 'high' register; for German, see Spitzmüller 2005a: 302–6; for Greek, see Moschonas 2009: 298). At this juncture it is also important to note how prescriptivism both in and about the press appears to result in an interesting paradox: those very subjects who most typically engage in metalinguistic and/or metamedial critique, namely journalists and editors, are simultaneously subject to the greatest degree of criticism themselves. Perhaps it is for this very reason that such metamedial reflexivity can be sustained over long periods of time in the form of protracted language ideological debates (Blommaert 1999).

Finally, it is impossible to overlook the sheer convenience of processing newspaper texts when engaging in this kind of research. This is insofar as metalinguistic texts are relatively easy to locate, do not require transcription and can be multiply indexed, thereby allowing us to generate the kind of large-scale corpora that can enable us to identify the differing discursive patterns and intertextual relations that are of particular interest for metalinguistic analysis.

2.2.2 The corpora: size and comparability

Having specified the type of data required, the next task in this comparative study was to build and combine two corpora of newspaper texts. Here a key requirement was that of 'comparability', that is, the two corpora had to allow for similar sets of observations. By 'the Greek corpus' we will henceforth be referring to a compilation of newspaper articles about media language that appeared in the Greek press in the three-month period between November 1999 and January 2000. This corpus consists of 80 texts on media language that were selected out of a larger set of 364 texts on several language issues (texts on media language = 22%) and was compiled via a press monitoring agency for 76 newspapers and 102 magazines, whereby no metalinguistic reference was excluded during the compilation phase.

By the 'German corpus' we refer to a similar set of texts albeit collected over a much longer period, namely January 1990 to June 2001. The German corpus was made up of 81 texts on media language that were selected from a larger corpus of 1,783 entries on a range of different language issues (texts on media language = 4.5%). This larger corpus, in turn, had been compiled manually from nine newspapers and three magazines that were archived in their entirety, and, additionally, from forty-two newspapers and nine magazines that were archived more selectively. All texts that dealt with language evaluation were included, with one notable exception: texts exclusively about the spelling reform, a major topic in the given period (see Johnson 2005), were deliberately excluded since their sheer volume meant that questions of orthography were beyond the scope of the analysis at the time of compilation. In the German corpus, most references to media language appeared during the periods 1994 (10 occurrences) to 1995 (11) and 1999 (15) to 2000 (18).

Due to the different ways in which the two corpora were compiled, the large difference in the percentages of texts on *media* language relative to *all* metalinguistic texts should not be considered to be indicative of a difference in public interest in the two countries. Moreover, we believe that the two corpora remain comparable for the purposes of this study in view of the fact that each consists of approximately the same number of texts on a range of topics (all of which, however, deal with 'media language' or contain references to it). These texts also belong to comparable genres (see Table 2.1) and were published across broadly similar periods of time. Both the Greek and German corpora were compiled from within larger corpora on various language issues and over longer periods of time that formed part of our own individual and in-depth research projects on metalinguistic issues in Greece and Germany, respectively (e.g. Moschonas 2004, 2009; Spitzmüller 2005a, 2007).

A further pre-requisite for the comparability of the two corpora was that of the criteria for the selection of individual texts. Here our operational definition was as follows: 'any text, in any newspaper genre, containing at least one reference to "media language" or "media language use"'. In this context we defined such references as occurring in metalinguistic discourse, that is, 'discourse about language', whereby we draw on the notion of the metalinguistic 'aboutness' that characterizes, following Jakobson (1957: 388), an 'autonomous mode of speech' consisting of 'overlappings' or 'messages referring to the code'. Both the larger Greek and German from which we had drawn dealt with metalinguistic aboutness at such a level of generality.

21

Table 2.1 Texts on media language – Genres

Texts on media language	Greek corpus	German corpus
letters to the editor	7	44
opinion articles	24 'usage columns'	23 commentaries [= 17 *Glossen* & 6 *Kommentare*]
	10 essays	7 essays
short comments	11	–
news articles	21	3
Features	4	–
Reviews	–	4
Interviews	3	–
Total	80/364 (22%)	81/1,783 (4.5%)

For 'usage columns' (διορθωτικές στήλες), that is, regular (bi-weekly or monthly) columns on language usage, see Moschonas (2001); 'commentaries' is the closest equivalent in the German press; *Glossen* are opinion articles with an explicit humorous/satirical aim.

Finally, for the purposes of this particular analysis, although we were interested in principle in *all* so-called message-to-code references, we proceeded to search the selected texts for occurrences of a very specific type of speech act in order to operationalize our particular approach to prescriptivism. It is to this we now turn in the next section.

2.3 Correctives: a performative theory of prescriptivism

As noted in the introduction, prescriptivism can be a somewhat vague concept and, as Deborah Cameron (1995: 5) has pointed out, is often used by linguists as a means of stigmatizing 'the threatening Other, the forbidden', thereby defining *ex negativo* the professional identity of linguists. We agree with Cameron that the binary opposition 'descriptive/prescriptive', as it typically applied in structural linguistics, is in fact itself a discursive construct (cf. also Spitzmüller 2005b). Nevertheless, we also believe that prescriptivism is an important practice in the context of metapragmatic discourse, and that we therefore need a well-defined concept of prescriptivism itself in order to achieve a greater understanding of the dynamics of prescriptivist discourse. Such a concept needs to account for the fact that, as already noted, prescriptive texts cannot easily be differentiated from descriptive ones as well as enabling us to explore the reasons why prescriptive statements so often masquerade as descriptive. Thus, a strict *ad hoc* differentiation of the texts within our corpora as 'professional' versus 'folk linguistic' (Niedzielski and Preston 2000: viii) or their categorization into 'larger systems of discourse and enterprise' (Silverstein 1979: 193) does not strike us as methodologically feasible, even though the print-media genres we have examined are undeniably good examples of such folk linguistic, popularizing accounts of linguistic phenomena.

Our approach to the concept of prescriptivism is ultimately a pragmatic one: we assume that prescriptivism is most productively conceptualized as a sum of specific metalinguistic speech acts (or meta-speech acts), that is to say, speech acts with a *corrective* function. We refer to such speech acts as *corrective instructions* or, simply, *correctives*. Accordingly, prescriptivism can be defined as sets of correctives or 'corrective repertoires' that can then be explored by means of a pragmatic analysis of corrective speech acts. Following Moschonas (2005, 2008), we define *correctives* as *directive speech acts of a metalanguage-to-language direction of fit*. Typically such correctives consist of three parts: a *prohibitive*, *normative* and *explicative* part with their 'regular' form as follows:

- one should neither say nor write X [*prohibitive*];
- instead one should say or write Y [*normative*];
- because Z [*explicative*].

For example, in Greek it has been suggested that one should avoid the use of *αποφασίζω ότι* [to decide that]. Instead, one should say or write *αποφασίζω να* [to decide to], because . . . (example from Ioanna Papazafiri 1991). Alternatively, in German, one should neither say nor write *geschockt* [shocked]; instead one should use *schockiert*, because . . . (a corrective proposed by Klaus Natorp 1996).

Of course, it is important to highlight how there is, in metalinguistic discourse, no explicit performative for a corrective ('I hereby correct you'!). That said, it is still possible to identify specific grammar and discourse markers for the various constituent parts of correctives. So, for example, prohibitives and normatives can be typically identified by deontic expressions ('must', 'should', etc.) and explicatives by their causal markers ('because', 'on account of', etc.). Moreover, explicatives, more often than not, employ an evaluation of X/Y as 'correct/incorrect', 'appropriate/inappropriate' as in 'one should not say or write X – one should say or write Y because X is incorrect and Y is more appropriate'. Of course, if we disregard the synonymy of the terms employed, the deontic and the etiological parts are often tautological. In other words, the explanation provided is typically circular: 'one should not say or write X because it is improper, incorrect, and so on, to write or to say X'. Thus in the Greek example cited, the explanation for the corrective regarding 'to decide that' (αποφασίζω ότι) goes as follows: 'the verb "to decide" requires a non-finite construction; therefore, it cannot be constructed with a that-clause' – itself a totally circular explanation (Moschonas 2008: 43). In addition, correctives – like all other speech acts – can be implicit or indirectly expressed. But even where it is not explicit, it is still possible to test each component of a corrective by paraphrasing it according to the 'regular' form. Each part should also be defined relative to the other. In some cases, of course, it is the illocutionary force (the 'import') not of particular expressions but rather of the whole context that determines the prescriptiveness of a given corrective. In this sense, it is worth noting how correctives are often mistaken for constatives, that is, descriptive speech acts. Notwithstanding, such ambiguity need not deter us since, for the purposes of classification, the overlap between prescriptivist and descriptivist uses is, as already noted above, itself taken for granted. Moreover, no part of a corrective is mandatory, and when all parts appear in a text, they are usually dispersed across the text as opposed to within the same sentence or statement.

A range of examples of correctives in the Greek corpus can be found in Moschonas (2005, 2008). Here, by contrast, is an example from the German corpus:

Hated word of the week

Unkosten [= *expenses*, literally: 'un-costs']

Never let it be said that the German language is logical (no one says this? er, never mind). Anyway, there's a persistent little fad that gives rise to the suspicion that the Germans are masters of obscuration, not to say of self-deception. What other explanation could there be for placing the unobtrusive negating prefix *un-* in front of certain quantities, leading to total confusion about the dimension of the cause? Costs [*Kosten*] incurred? No, un-costs [*Unkosten*]. What amounts [*Mengen*] are stored? Huge amounts [*Unmengen*], not to say huge masses [*Unmassen*], which is according to the Duden dictionary equivalent to a 'very big amount'. But why, the layman keeps asking, does one use a negation of all things in German, if one wants to highlight – for example – something really huge? Obviously, the urge is to use an unobtrusive prefix in order to make what are actually very big things small in front of the outside world which does not understand anything about all this. It must have something to do with an inexplicable depth [*Untiefe*] in the national character. To make matters worse, *Untiefe* can refer both to 'depth' and to 'shallow'. Preposterous [*ein Unding*]. (AW 1996; our translation)

This example is taken from a series of columns called 'Haßwort der Woche' ('Hated word of the week'). The text argues that the prefix *un-*, which can be used as a negating particle, but also as an intensifying morpheme, can only have one function (i.e., negating) since language should be 'logical' (i.e., the relation between form and function should be one-to-one). Consequently, words that employ the prefix *un-* as an intensifier run counter to the language's inner logic. All three parts of the corrective can be located in specific areas of the text although some of them are implicit. We have the prohibitive: 'there's a persistent little fad . . . ' (namely the use of *Unkosten* and similar word forms); the normative: 'do not use the prefix *un-* in such a way' (implied by phrases such as 'producing total confusion . . . '); and the implicit explicative: '. . . *un-* is a negating prefix [and thus it must not be used to denote anything else]' (' . . . why does one use a negation of all things in German, if one wants to highlight something really huge?'), which includes an explicit reference to a usually implicit topos, namely 'the German language should [ideally] be logical in itself' ('never let it be said that the German language is logical (no one says this? Er, never mind)').

As becomes clear from this example, prohibitives and normatives can be more easily located in a text than explicatives. This is because explicatives are often implicit; they depend on a text's overall meaning and force, relying on what are often hidden presuppositions that have to be provided by the reader. In what follows, we consider prohibitives and normatives as indices to a corrective practice (exemplified through corrective repertoires such as the ones discussed in section 2.4 below). By contrast, we take explicatives (expressed or implied) to index a more general conceptual scheme, a set of beliefs, a complex of shared presuppositions or what might be called 'ideology proper'. Roughly speaking, prohibitive-normative pairs belong to what Niedzielski and Preston (2000: 302–14) call 'Metalanguage 1', while explicatives belong to 'Metalanguage 2' (or 'Metalanguage 3', according to Preston 2004; cf. Johnson and Ensslin 2007: 6–11). The following analysis concentrates on 'Metalanguage 1'. At the present time, we are unable to suggest a definite methodology for identifying explicatives, given that there is no precise means of predicting textual interpretation. However, it is highly likely that corrective practices will differ significantly across languages, periods and linguistic forms, that is, they vary in the 'courte durée', to use Fernand Braudel's well-known phrase (Braudel 1969). On the other hand, conceptual schemes tend to be long-term phenomena of wider (even supra-cultural) scope that persist in the 'longue durée' of the history of linguistic ideas. In other words, we expect patterns of German and Greek prescriptivism to be characterized by differing corrective practices operating nonetheless under similar conceptual schemes.

At this juncture it is important to stress that correctives do not appear in isolation. Rather, they form part of '*répertoires correctifs*' (Moschonas 2008: 45), that is, sets of correctives that occur repeatedly within a text and/or across a group of texts. Specific kinds of corrective repertories, we can assume, will then prevail within certain circles, in certain genres or registers, or in a particular period of time. In what follows, we will take a closer look at some specific examples of these phenomena.

2.4 Corrective repertories in the Greek and German corpora

On the basis of the theoretical and methodological reflections outlined above, we proceeded to count all examples of prohibitive/normative pairs (henceforth: 'X/Y-pairs') from within our two corpora. By concentrating on X/Y-pairs, our approach to prescriptivism becomes at least partially *corpus-driven* in the sense that 'the discourse itself, and not a language-external taxonomy of linguistic entities [. . .] provide[s] the categories and classifications' (Teubert 2005: 5) of our analysis. This means that the actual practices to be classified as prescriptivist emerge from within the data as opposed to either prefiguring the corpus or being applied post hoc. In this section, we present the results of this procedure starting with some general findings before turning to more specific phenomena.

2.4.1 Initial findings

In total, we counted 328 X/Y-pairs in the Greek corpus (an average of 4.10 pairs per text) and 239 X/Y-pairs in the German corpus (2.95 per text). X/Y-pairs can be distinguished into *token pairs* and *type pairs*. 'Token pairs' refer to specific phrases, words, morphemes or other grammatical or discourse units (e.g., 'Do not use the English word "media"; use the Greek phrase *μέσα μαζικής ενημέρωσης* instead'). 'Type pairs' meanwhile refer more generally to classes of words or other units (e.g., 'Do not use foreign words, use Greek words instead'). In many texts, an X/Y-type is often exemplified by several X/Y-tokens although this is not strictly necessary. Accordingly, both type and token references had to be counted.

In addition to complete X/Y-pairs, we also encountered several X/Ø-references, that is, references to a particular X-token that is not followed by any suggestion for a Y-replacement. There are 162 X/Ø-references in the Greek corpus (2.03 per text) and 388 X/Ø-references in the German corpus (4.79 per text), whereby it is interesting to note that the Greek corpus contains more 'real' X/Y-pairs while in the German data X/Ø-references predominate. This is due to the fact that texts about Anglicisms (and perhaps puristic texts in general) generally favour X/Ø-references (a point to which we will return later). The Greek corpus also contains a few instances of Ø/Y-references, that is, 'descriptive', extensional references to word classes, exemplifying a particular linguistic phenomenon (e.g., 'such and such a noun appears only in the singular'). Such references were not counted, unless they could be reconstructed as X/Y-pairs (e.g., 'the [hypothetical] plural of such and such a noun should not be used; this noun should only appear in the singular'). Overall, there are 490 X/Y-pairs or X/Ø-references in the Greek corpus (6.13 per text) and 627 in the German corpus (7.74 per text).

The highest concentration of correctives in the Greek corpus was found in a single text, which contains 31 X/Y-pairs and 20 X/Ø-references (Charis 2000 – incidentally an author who does not consider himself a prescriptivist). Zero occurrences were found in 34 texts, which suggests that it is a particular genre, that is, 'usage columns', that shows the highest concentrations of correctives (the Greek corpus also contains 21 news articles about 'Greek in the new media' containing general references to media language but no X/Y-pairs). In the German corpus, by contrast, the highest concentration of references was found in Natorp (1998: 38 pairs) and of real X/Y-pairs in another text by the same author (Natorp 1999: 23 pairs). Finally, there are seven texts on media language that contain no correctives. The results are summarized in Table 2.2.

The next step was to categorize all metalinguistic references according to one of the seven types of grammatical or discourse phenomena to which they referred as follows: 1. Lexicon, 2. Discourse/Pragmatics, 3. Semantics, 4. Morpho-syntax, 5. Phraseology, 6. Orthography and 7. Miscellaneous. The percentage values for both corpora can be found in Figure 2.1, whereby it should be noted that the differences between the two corpora for each major category were found to be statistically

Table 2.2 Occurrences of correctives

Greek corpus		German corpus	
	490 (6.13 per text)		**627 (7.74 per text)**
X/Y-pairs	328 (4.1 per text)	X/Y-pairs	239 (2.9 per text)
token pairs	252 (3.14 per text)	token pairs	221 (2.73 per text)
type pairs	76 (0.95 per text)	type pairs	18 (0.22 per text)
X/Ø-references	162 (2.03 per text)	X/Ø-references	388 (4.79 per text)

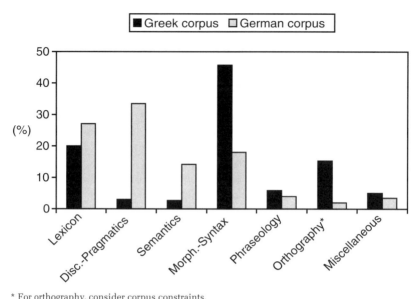

* For orthography, consider corpus constraints.

Figure 2.1 Major categories of correctives

significant (with the exception of Phraseology, which can nevertheless be subsumed under Morpho-syntax – see section 2.4.5; Orthography and Miscellaneous were not tested for statistical significance).

As it becomes clear from Figure 2.1, German prescriptivism predominates in the fields of Lexicon, Discourse/Pragmatics and Semantics, while Greek prescriptivism is concentrated in Morpho-syntax, Phraseology and Orthography (as noted earlier, however, the issue of the orthographic reform was not exhaustively covered in the German corpus). After outlining the various types of correctives in each category in the following sections, we will go on to suggest that this difference is in fact significant in relation to the particular models of prescriptivism typical of the print-media in each of the two countries.

2.4.2 Lexicon

Words – in the sense of individual lexical items – are the most popular target of prescriptivism. Loanwords, in particular Anglicisms, are a recurrent topic in the German corpus (see Table 2.3), where we find 157 references to English loans (25%). Here the percentage would have been considerably lower (11.2%) had we counted only complete X/Y-pairs

28

Table 2.3   Lexicon

Greek corpus		German corpus	
	98 (20%)		170 (27.1%)
foreign words	30 (6.1%)	foreign words	169 (27.1%)
English loans	24 (4.9%)	English loans	157 (25.0%)
loans from other languages	3 (0.6%)	loans from other languages	9 (1.4%)
loan translations	3 (0.6%)	loan translations	3 (0.5%)
marked *demotic* forms	17 (3.5%)	vulgarisms	1 (0.1%)
marked archaic forms	38 (7.8%)		
dialectal	6 (1.2%)		
translation of archaisms	7 (1.4%)		

(z-test = 2.691, p-value = 0.070)

but, as noted above, both measures are important since many texts about Anglicisms list only a number of undesirable words albeit without offering suggestions for replacements. In complete X/Y-pairs, by contrast, translated loans are often devised as substitutes for a 'foreign word' in both the Greek and German corpora, suggesting that translation is the preferred method of adaptation.

In addition to loanwords, there are many references in the Greek corpus to either archaic or modern *demotic* words suggesting ongoing concern about the diglossic situation in Greece. By 'marked' archaic or *demotic* forms, we mean words that are often referred to as 'extreme' (ακραίοι) or as belonging to a 'wooden language' (ξύλινη γλώσσα). Finally, it is interesting to note how in the German corpus there is only one corrective relating to a 'vulgarism' (or colloquialism).

2.4.3 Discourse/Pragmatics

The use of stereotypical expressions, phrases or metaphors is another recurrent topic in the German corpus. Correctives in this category frequently refer to the overuse of certain expressions (e.g., idioms, metaphors, formulaic expressions, superlatives or fillers) at the expense of available alternatives, or their inappropriate use in a given context. It is for this reason that such items are placed here in the category of Discourse/Pragmatics rather than Phraseology. In such cases it is not the expression itself that is criticized but rather its careless or 'unthinking

Table 2.4 Discourse/Pragmatics

Greek corpus		German corpus	
	15 (3%)		**210 (33.5%)**
media discourse		'overused'/	
structure	13 (2.7%)	inappropriately	
	[+ 21 articles	used words	110 (17.5%)
	on 'Greek in	metaphors	64 (10.2%)
	the new	formulaic expressions	30 (4.8%)
	media']	superlatives	4 (0.6%)
		fillers	2 (0.3%)
euphemisms	1 (0.2%)		
politeness	1 (0.2%)		

(z-test = 12.508, p-value = 0.000)

use' (see for instance, Natorp 1994, entitled *Gedankenlos dahergeredet* ['talking thoughtless rubbish']). In the Greek corpus, it is interesting to note how most metalinguistic references in this category refer not to the usage of particular words or set phrases but rather to the structure of media discourse more generally (i.e. how the journalists' discourse should be organized in order to be intelligible to a wider public). In addition to correctives found in various texts, there are also 21 articles concerning the standing of 'Greek in the new media', which contain no specific correctives. The results for Discourse/Pragmatics are given in Table 2.4.

2.4.4 Semantics

Table 2.5 presents the results for the field where prescriptivism in the German corpus appears to predominate: semantics. The correctives in these cases focus on the 'meaning' of a given word or expression, whereby meanings are imagined within the discourse as clear, distinctive and context-free. Many of these correctives seek to show what an allegedly 'incorrectly' used expression 'really' means, that is, in its 'original' domain (in the case of a technical term) or language (in the case of loans). This 'topos of logicality' (Spitzmüller 2005a: 294–98) is evident in the popular notion of semantics as needing to be 'logical' (examples criticized include pleonasms and the use of reflexive verbs such as *sich bedanken* 'to thank' – literally 'to thank oneself'). This is then underpinned by the conviction that every object that can be perceived should be denoted by a single and distinct expression (and, vice

Table 2.5   Semantics

Greek corpus		German corpus	
	13 (2.7%)		89 (14.2%)
obscurity of learned/		incorrectly used foreign	
archaic forms	7 (1.4%)	words	29 (4.6%)
semantic differentiation		loss of semantic	
or change	6 (1.2%)	differentiation	26 (4.1%)
		'illogical' semantics	18 (2.9%)
		'contaminated'	
		expressions	9 (1.4%)
		misapplications of	
		technical terms	6 (1.0%)
		'odd' metaphors	1 (0.1%)

(z-test = 6.539, p-value = 0.000)

versa, in the sense that the semantic extension of an expression results in a loss of perceptibility) as well as in the fear that words can be contaminated by past usages (a particularly sensitive topic in Germany). By contrast, several instances of correctives in the Greek corpus concern the *obscurity* of learned or archaic forms, whereby it is implied that such forms should be avoided or replaced by corresponding vernacular and/or demotic expressions. Other instances concern the loss of semantic differentiation due to changes in meaning.

2.4.5 Morpho-syntax/Phraseology

Correctives in the fields of Morpho-syntax and Phraseology are presented together in Table 2.6, although it should be noted that Morphology and Syntax is not applied here in any of the modern senses of the terms. In other words, by 'Morpho-syntax', we mean that part of traditional grammar that deals with parts of speech, inflection ('τυπικό') and compounding. Syntagms, in this traditional conception, are understood on the basis of prototypical constructions. Accordingly, there is no real boundary between Morpho-syntax and Phraseology from the point of view of our corpora.

Most correctives in the Greek corpus occur in these two fields: if we add the number of phraseological to morpho-syntactic correctives, the total amounts to 228 occurrences (51.6%). According to Moschonas (2001: 61–64), this increase in phraseological and syntactic correctives is a relatively recent development in the evolution of Greek prescriptivism.

31

Table 2.6 Morpho-syntax and Phraseology

Greek corpus		German corpus	
Morpho-syntax			
199 (45.7%)			**113 (18.0%)**
violation of archaic rules	27 (5.5%)	wrong inflection	43 (6.9%)
agreement/ attraction	12 (2.4%)	Wrong prepositions	15 (2.4%)
demotic adv. ending (-α)	29 (6.0%)	agreement	3 (0.5%)
stress mov. in declension	25 (5.1%)	code-switching	3 (0.5%)
wrong affix	36 (7.3%)	word order	2 (0.3%)
augmented imperative	6 (1.2%)	Wrong conjunction	1 (0.1%)
prep + relative clause	1 (0.2%)	wrong tense 'foreign' syntax	1 (0.1%)
nouns with no		'illogical' morphology	34 (5.4%)
plural/sing.	60 (12.2%)	Foreign word morphology	11 (1.8%)
loan adaptation	25 (5.1%)		
mixed Greek-foreign			
compounds	2 (0.4%)		
foreign word morphology	1 (0.2%)		
Phraseology			
29 (5.9%)			**25 (4%)**
formulaic expressions	21 (4.3%)	foreignisms	25 (4%)
αφορά σε [to concern/be			
about]	8 (1.6%)		

(Morpho-syntax: z-test = 8.283, p-value = 0.000; Phraseology: z-test = 1.352, p-value = 0.176; Sum of percentages for Morpho-syntax and Phraseology: z-test = 8.6, p-value = 0.000)

Before the language reform of 1976, the traditional model for correctives had been almost entirely morphological.

Although 'violation of archaic rules' is categorized separately, most of the corrective instructions under the heading of Morphology/Syntax are in fact concerned in one way or another with the correctness of archaic forms. For example, agreement or attraction phenomena are only stigmatized with respect to learned forms, such as archaic participles: *των υπαρχόντων προβλέψεων* ['of the existing (masculine) predictions (feminine)']. The *demotic* adverbial ending -α (*απλ-ά* instead of *απλ-ώς*) is, by contrast, like a red rag to a bull for the prescriptivists, who in turn criticize 'extreme' *demotic* standards provoking a plethora of different correctives. Stress movement in declension is also subject to the archaic-*demotic* dichotomy and is generally prescribed according to the more traditional rules. Of the formulaic expressions, the distinction αφορά σε N ('it concerns N') versus αφορά το N ('it is about N') seems to have become something of a puzzle for the prescriptivists (the αφορά σε construction is actually an internal calque, based on the archaic αφορά εις + accusative).

In the German corpus, we find correctives in relation to the notion of typical grammatical 'infringements' ('wrong inflection', 'agreement', etc.) as well as a critique of foreign influences on grammar and word formation. Again we find the notion of 'logicality', which manifests itself particularly with respect to 'illogical' morphology, that is, word formations where 'wrong' or 'misleading' constituents are used (as in the *Unkosten* case discussed in section 2.3 above). Such forms are criticized primarily because they infringe the 'internal logic of German', which dictates that the semantics of the word should be derived from the semantics of its constituents (a folk linguistic principle of compositionality).

2.4.6 Orthography

Orthography (i.e. spelling and punctuation) is a huge topic in both Greece and Germany and, as many sociolinguists have pointed out (Jaffe 2000; Johnson 2005; Sebba 2007), is widely and popularly perceived to be an integral part of language, notwithstanding the linguistic division between speech and writing typically foregrounded by linguists.

In Greece, the central subject of the relevant discussions is the writing system itself (Greek vs. Roman alphabet) as well as its varieties (monotonic vs. polytonic). The orthographic reform of 1982 sanctioned a monotonic ('single-accent') system which, although widely used now, has still not been adopted by many prestigious publishers, nor has it prevailed in the 'high register' of poetry. Within the Greek corpus, there are five occurrences of X/Y-types in favour of the monotonic system versus four against it. Meanwhile, there are only three references in favour of the Roman script in some registers (such as e-mails) versus ten against the Roman script in any register (see Table 2.7).

In Germany, by contrast, the spelling reform that was introduced during the period of our analysis in the mid-1990s was one of the main metalinguistic issues in the media, and certainly fuelled a high level of prescriptivism in and about the media. Which spellings a newspaper preferred became a crucial question that threatened the very implementation of the reform. A striking example of this was the return of the

Table 2.7 Orthography/Spelling

Greek corpus			German corpus	
	75 (15.3%)			13 (2.0%)
in favour of monotonic	5	(1.0%)	spelling reform*	9 (1.4%)
against monotonic	4	(0.8%)	spelling of loanwords	1 (0.1%)
in favour of the Roman			miscellaneous	3 (0.5%)
script in some registers	3	(0.6%)		
against the Roman script				
in any registers	10	(2.0%)		
loan transliteration	7	(1.4%)		
'final -v' rule (assimilation)	5	(1.0%)		
CC clusters (dissimilation)	1	(0.2%)		
punctuation	2	(0.4%)		
misspellings	38	(7.8%)		

(* For orthography, see discussion of corpus constraints in 2.2.2)

Table 2.8 Miscellaneous

Greek corpus		German corpus	
	25 (5.1%)		22 (3.5%)
pronunciation	2 (0.4%)	pronunciation	1 (0.1%)
pronunciation of loans	7 (1.4%)	pronunciation of loans	9 (1.4%)
false etymologies	6 (1.2%)	typos	12 (2.0%)
blunders/boners	10 (2.0%)		

Frankfurter Allgemeine Zeitung to the 'old' orthography in 2000, itself a clear attempt to initiate a counter-reform (Johnson 2005: 81).

2.4.7 Miscellaneous

Finally, Table 2.8 presents the results for a number of cases that do not belong to the previous categories and have therefore been classified as 'Miscellaneous'. Here it is interesting to note those correctives that refer to the *pronunciation of loans* (1.4% in either the Greek or the German corpus) – something which might be classified as a kind of 'inverse purism'. In other words, although the purists' concern is to prevent foreign words from intruding into their native language, those self-same purists are nevertheless criticizing, for example, the apparently 'incorrect' pronunciation of non-adapted loan words (urging a kind of pronunciation closer, say, to the original English), the 'incorrect' semantics of translated loans (where meanings do not match those of the original English words) as well as the 'incorrect' use of such loans (in those cases where their meaning differs from their English counterparts).

2.5 Discussion and conclusions: prescriptivism and standardization

At the beginning of this chapter, we proposed that the analysis of prescriptivism, in general, and the use of correctives, in particular, may well be able to tell us much about processes of language standardization – or *re*-standardization. This is insofar as the form and function of any language are to a considerable extent shaped both in and by public (and typically media) discourse about language. So, for example, the perennial 'Language Question' in Greece has meant that the diglossic situation in general has given rise to two conflicting and competing standards, the archaic or puristic standard, on the one hand, and the *demotic* or vernacular standard, on the other. Arguably, there is also a variety of standards between these two extremes. Standard Modern Greek is supposed to be based on the *demotic* model, permitting nevertheless a certain number of archaisms, especially in the higher registers of the language. And here it is interesting to observe how, as vernacular forms have gradually become accepted as standard, it is the archaic forms in turn that have been seen to be in need of corrective instruction and guidance. The new morpho-syntactic/phraseological model that corresponds to the 'mixed' standards of Standard Modern Greek is therefore supposed to be *comprehensive* (encompassing virtually any expression in the language), *historical* or *pan-chronic* (including all stages in the development of the language, as opposed to *synchronic*), *conventional* (based on the obligatory and arbitrary nature of lexical forms), and *internal* (i.e. concerned with internal rather than external purism).

In Germany, there has also been a long tradition of prescriptivism in relation to the process of standardization. In this regard, the 1990s saw particular efforts towards forms of re-standardization in relation to: (a) purism directed at Anglicisms and (b) the spelling reform, whereby the latter can be also been seen as a battle over who, in particular, has 'the right to prescribe' (Johnson 2005). Similarly the pragmatic–semantic model that corresponds to these processes of re-standardization is meant to be *all-embracing* and *pan-historical*. Unlike the Greek model of re-standardization, however, the German approach favours a more *logical* topos (based on a 'regularized' semantics of expressions and a 'tight' pragmatics of language use). The German model of purism is also largely *external* (i.e. preoccupied with external rather than internal purism).

These differences in the conception and process of (re-)standardization can be seen clearly in practices that can be described as purist. If we count the total number of X/Y-pairs and X/Ø-references to loans in all major categories (Lexicon, Semantics, etc.), we find a total of 62 correctives (12.7%) in the Greek corpus and a total of 254 correctives (40.5%) in the German corpus (z-test = 10.191, p-value = 0.000). Meanwhile references to diglossia in the Greek corpus amount to 158 (32.2%). It is apparent therefore that prescriptive practices in the Greek press are primarily concerned with, and shaped by, the diglossic situation in Greece as opposed to questions of borrowing or language contact. In the German press, on the other hand, Anglicisms have become a major focus for corrective practices.

Despite their differences, however, both the Greek and German models of standardization share certain presuppositions in relation to the kind of correctives (i.e. the speech acts) observed. For a corrective to be issued, it is presupposed – at the very least by those who do the issuing – that there is variation between the linguistic forms X and Y, and it is the task of those engaging in such corrective repertoires to try to promote language awareness of that variation to a wider public. Such variation is thereby conceived to be 'transitional', that is, correctives (X/Y-pairs) raise awareness of X and Y with the aim of ultimately *replacing* X by Y. The underlying presupposition of such corrective processes is therefore that variation is *not* considered to be the 'norm' (as it is widely held to be in, say, sociolinguistics). Instead, as a 'transitional' stage between two exclusive uses – X *or* Y – variation is like a pendulum in motion. Could correctives have a lasting impact under particular circumstances? Could an increase in awareness of X/Y in favour of Y stop the pendulum swinging towards X? This seems to be the prescriptivist's main concern in the corpus data we have been analysing.

In this chapter, we have only been able to touch upon the idea that shared presuppositions about the (undesirable) nature of language variation are what underpin corrective suggestions, in particular, and prescriptivism, in general. It will therefore be the task of future research to categorize more comprehensively the kinds of correctives and corrective practices that will allow us to access the ideologies of, say, prescriptivism at a higher meta-level. However, we genuinely believe – and indeed aim to have shown here – that corpus-driven procedures of classifying and categorizing those practices in order to access such underlying ideologies can be especially productive for language ideology research more widely. This is not least if we wish to avoid engaging in what Jan Blommaert (2008: 261) refers to as merely 'symptomatic discourse analysis that just confirms what we already knew or what we believe to be the case', a criticism directed particularly at some strands of Critical Discourse Analysis (but see Milani and Johnson 2008, for further discussion). It is our conviction that the kind of corpus-driven comparative approach that we have presented here, together with the concept of correctives, constitute one way of fleshing out what other-wise remains a rather vague concept of 'prescriptivism'. This in turn will allow us to go some way towards an analysis of prescriptivism that manifests itself at the level of actual discourse – in this case, print-media discourse – and can thereby be subject to the discursive analysis of actual linguistic performance that can and should, in our view, be an integral part of language ideology research.

Acknowledgements

Both writers wish to thank Sally Johnson for her meticulous editing and proofreading of an earlier version of this chapter.

Spiros Moschonas would particularly like to acknowledge the support of a grant from the University of Athens (research grant 70/4/4131).

Primary sources cited

AW (1996), 'Haßwort der Woche: Unkosten'. *Süddeutsche Zeitung*, 10 August 1996.

Babiniotis, G. (1999), 'Τα θετικά και αρνητικά για τη γλώσσα' ['Positive and negative aspects of (media) language']. *Ethnos*, 29 November 1999.

Charis, J. I. (2000), 'Αυτοί και οι εαυτοί τους' ['Them and themselves']. *Ta Nea*, 29 January 2000.

Kriaras, E. (1988), 'Τα πεντάλεπτά μου στην ΕΡΤ και άλλα γλωσσικά' [*My 5-minute broadcasts in the Greek national radio-television and other linguistic articles*]. Thessaloniki: Malliaris.

Natorp, K. (1994), 'Gedankenlos dahergeredet'. *Frankfurter Allgemeine Zeitung*, 12 March 1994.

Natorp, K. (1996), 'Verarmt und verwildert. Kleines Lamento über den Umgang mit der Sprache'. *Frankfurter Allgemeine Zeitung*, 3 August 1996.

Natorp, K. (1998), 'Jeden Tag dieselbe fade Sauce, gnadenlos. Wie der Wortschatz der deutschen Sprache immer mehr zusammenschrumpft'. *Frankfurter Allgemeine Zeitung*, 20 June 1998.

Natorp, K. (1999), 'Alles auf dem Prüfstand. Klagelied über die tägliche Sprachschändung'. *Frankfurter Allgemeine Zeitung*, 6 November 1999.

Papazafiri, I. (1991), 'Αποφασίζω . . . ότι' ['To decide . . . that']. *Ta Nea*, 2 March 1991.

References

Blommaert, J. (1999), 'The debate is closed', in J. Blommaert (ed.) *Language Ideological Debates*. Berlin: Mouton de Gruyter, pp. 425–38.

Blommaert, J. (2008), Review of 'Norman Fairclough, Language and Globalization'. *Discourse & Society*, 19(2), 257–62.

Braudel, F. (1969), 'Histoire et sciences sociales: la longue durée', in *Écrits sur l'histoire*. Paris: Flammarion, pp. 41–83.

Browning, R. (1982), 'Greek diglossia yesterday and today'. *International Journal of the Sociology of Language*, 35, 49–68.

Cameron, D. (1995), *Verbal Hygiene*. London: Routledge.

Delveroudi, R. and Moschonas, S. (2003), 'Le purisme de la langue et la langue du purisme'. *Philologie im Netz*, 24, 1–26.

Jaffe, A. (2000), 'Introduction: non-standard orthography and non-standard speech'. *Journal of Sociolinguistics*, 4(4), 497–513.

Jakobson, R. (1957), 'Shifters and verbal categories', in L. R. Waugh and M. Monville-Burston (eds), *On Language*. Harvard, MA: Harvard Universtity Press, pp. 386–92.

Jaworski, A., Coupland, N. and Galasiński, D. (eds) (2004), *Metalanguage: Social and Ideological Perspectives*. Berlin: Mouton de Gruyter.

Johnson, S. (2001), 'Who's misunderstanding whom? (Socio)linguistics, public debate and the media'. *Journal of Sociolinguistics*, 5(4), 591–610.

Johnson, S. (2005), *Spelling Trouble? Language, Ideology and the Reform of German Orthography*. Clevedon, UK: Multilingual Matters.

Johnson, S. and Ensslin, A. (2007), 'Language in the media: theory and practice', in S. Johnson and A. Ensslin (eds), *Language in the Media: Representations, Identities, Ideologies*, London: Continuum, pp. 3–22.

Kroskrity, P. V. (ed.) (2000), *Regimes of Language: Ideologies, Polities, and Identities*. Oxford: James Currey.

Majer, K. (1959), *Ιστορία του ελληνικού τύπου* [*History of the Greek Press*], vol. 2: *Αθηναϊκαί εφημερίδες 1901–1959* [*Athens Newspapers 1901–1959*]. Athens.

Milani, T. M. and Johnson, S. (2008), 'CDA and language ideology: Towards a reflexive approach to discourse data', in I. H. Warnke and J. Spitzmüller (eds), *Methoden der Diskurslinguistik: sprachwissenschaftliche Zugänge zur transtextuellen Ebene*. Berlin: Mouton de Gruyter, pp. 365–88.

Moschonas, S. (2001), 'Οι διορθωτικές στήλες στον ελληνικό τύπο' ['Columns on language usage in the Greek press']. *Journal of Applied Linguistics* [Thessaloniki], 17, 49–68.

Moschonas, S. (2004), 'Relativism in language ideology: on Greece's latest language issues'. *Journal of Modern Greek Studies*, 22(2), 173–206.

Moschonas, S. (2005), 'Διορθωτικές πρακτικές' ['Corrective practices'], in *Χρήσεις της γλώσσας* (Scientific Colloquium, 3–5.12.2004). Athens: Εταιρεία Σπουδών Νεοελληνικού Πολιτισμού και Γενικής Παιδείας, pp. 151–74.

Moschonas, S. (2008), 'Vers une théorie performative du purisme', *Le français moderne*, 76(1), 38–50.

Moschonas, S. (2009), 'Language issues after the Language Question: on the modern standards of Standard Modern Greek', in A. Georgakopoulou and M. Silk (eds), *Standard Languages and Language Standards: Greek, Past and Present*. London: Ashgate, pp. 293–320.

Niedzielski, N. A. and Preston, D. R. (2000), *Folk Linguistics*. Berlin: Mouton de Gruyter.

Pfalzgraf, F. (2006), *Neopurismus in Deutschland nach der Wende*. Frankfurt am Main: Peter Lang.

Preston, D. R. (2004), 'Folk metalanguage', in A. Jaworski, N. Coupland and D. Galasiński (eds), *Metalanguage: Social and Ideological Perspectives*. Berlin: Mouton de Gruyter, pp. 75–101.

Sebba, M. (2007), *Spelling and Society. The Culture and Politics of Orthography Around the World*. Cambridge: Cambridge University Press.

Schieffelin, B. B., Woolard, K. A. and Kroskrity, P. V. (eds) (1998), *Language Ideologies: Practice and Theory*. New York: Oxford University Press.

Schiewe, J. (1998), *Die Macht der Sprache. Eine Geschichte der Sprachkritik von der Antike bis zur Gegenwart*. Munich: Beck.

Sick, B. (2004). *Der Dativ ist dem Genitiv sein Tod. Ein Wegweiser durch den Irrgarten der deutschen Sprache*. (29th ed. 2006). Cologne: Kiepenheuer & Witsch.

Silverstein, M. (1979), 'Language structure and linguistic ideology', in P. Clyne, W. Hanks and C. Hofbauer (eds), *The Elements: A Parasession on Linguistic Units and Levels*. Chicago, IL: Chicago Linguistic Society, pp. 193–247.

Spitzmüller, J. (2002), 'Selbstfindung durch Ausgrenzung. Eine kritische Analyse des aktuellen Diskurses zu sprachlichen Entlehnungen', in: R. Hoberg (ed.), *Deutsch – Englisch – Europäisch. Impulse für eine neue Sprachpolitik*. Mannheim: Duden-Verlag, pp. 247–65.

Spitzmüller, J. (2005a), *Metasprachdiskurse: Einstellungen zu Anglizismen und ihre wissenschaftliche Rezeption*. Berlin: Mouton de Gruyter.

Spitzmüller, J. (2005b), 'Das Eigene, das Fremde und das Unbehagen an der Sprachkultur. Überlegungen zur Dynamik sprachideologischer Diskurse'. *Aptum*, 1(3), 248–61.

Spitzmüller, J. (2007), 'Staking the claims of identity: purism, linguistics and the media in post-1990 Germany'. *Journal of Sociolinguistics*, 11(2), 261–85.

Teubert, W. (2005), 'My version of corpus linguistics'. *International Journal of Corpus Linguistics*, 10(1), 1–13.

Triandaphillidis, M. (1905/1907), *Ξενηλασία ή ισοτέλεια: Μελέτη περί των ξένων λέξεων της νέας ελληνικής* [*Banishment or equality? A study of foreign words in Modern Greek*], in *Άπαντα Μανόλη Τριανταφυλλίδη*

39

[*M. Triandaphillidis' Complete Works*], vol. 1. Thessaloniki: Institute of Modern Greek Studies, pp. 1–297.

Triandaphillidis, M. (1915), 'Η γλώσσα μας στην κοινωνική ζωή' ['Our language in social life'], in *Άπαντα Μανόλη Τριανταφυλλίδη* [*M. Triandaphillidis' Complete Works*], vol. 4. Thessaloniki: Institute of Modern Greek Studies, pp. 284–99.

Zimmer, Dieter E. (2005), *Sprache in Zeiten ihrer Unverbesserlichkeit*. Hamburg: Hoffmann und Campe.

3 Globalizing standard Spanish: the promotion of 'panhispanism' by Spain's language guardians

Darren Paffey

3.1 Introduction

The aim of this chapter is to consider and analyse the way in which language ideologies are present in the Spanish print media. In particular, I explore articles from two of Spain's leading daily newspapers, arguing that they represent examples of how media are discursive sites in which language ideological debates take place. These debates deal with the status and role of the Spanish language in a world marked by the processes of globalization, and in which the language itself is being re-conceptualized as it is subjected to those processes.

I chart the rise of one crucial institution, the Spanish Language Academy (*Real Academia Española*, RAE), which throughout its history has been the principal agent in standardizing the Spanish language. For centuries now, the number of Spanish speakers in the world has far outranked the population of Spain itself, but in recent years, the Madrid Academy (one of 22 Spanish language academies worldwide) has engaged in an increasing number of debates about Spanish as an essentially unified global language.

My investigation considers how a critical analysis of news discourse can reveal more about the ideological underpinnings of the Academy's Panhispanic Language Policy (PLP), developed in collaboration with the other Spanish Academies and commercial partners, but led by Madrid. I reflect on the discursive features and strategies employed in press coverage of the PLP which reinforces and legitimizes the authoritative voice of the Madrid Academy in the definition, management and guidance of the Spanish language and related language debates in a globalized world.

3.2 Language ideologies and the media

In line with the works of Rosina Lippi-Green (1997), Bambi Schieffelin *et al.* (1998), and Jan Blommaert (1999), I take language to be ideological in both how it is used, and in how it represents and is represented by the linguistic choices that users make. Kathryn Woolard, in her introduction to the seminal volume by Schieffelin *et al.*, explains that:

> Representations, whether explicit or implicit, that construe the intersection of language and human beings in a social world are what we mean by 'language ideology'. (Woolard 1998: 3)

Woolard goes on to suggest three specific contexts where we might identify these representations: (i) language practices, (ii) explicit metalinguistic discourse, and (iii) implicit metapragmatic strategies (1998: 9–11). In the first siting, *language practices* inform and shape ideology by taking the status quo and reifying it through repetition and naturalization, which in turn justify existing linguistic configurations. The second context, *metalinguistic discourse*, includes explicit discussion, evaluation, and planning about how speakers both *use* language and *ought* to use it. Such discourse usually takes place within circles of so-called 'experts', and often through deliberations and 'language ideological debates' (Blommaert 1999) which are then made public through the media (Johnson and Ensslin 2007). The third siting that Woolard suggests is *implicit metapragmatics*, the strategies that are 'part of the stream of language use in process and that simultaneously indicate[s] how to interpret that language-in-use' (Woolard 1998: 9). Through employing implicit metapragmatic strategies, language users – whether 'expert' or 'lay' – reinforce social relations and their corresponding forms of talk.

Language ideological debates – while often addressing language structure itself – tend to focus largely on the historical (and current) role, usefulness, value and quality of a language variety. This focus on the context of language use demonstrates that 'ideologies of language are not about language alone' (Woolard 1998: 3), and that language not only carries functional meaning, but also indexes characteristics and values common to groups of speakers, such as educational experience, social background, moral instruction, political persuasion and authority structures.

Language ideologies, which reflect some of these asymmetrical social relations, are – as Norman Fairclough writes – often expressed in institutional discourse where assumptions about the relative authority of different interlocutors and their roles/rights within discourse are well established and ritualized (2001: Chapter 2). One particular linguistic ideology that has been well embedded in institutions such as Academies, the education system and the press is 'standard language ideology', a term first coined by James and Lesley Milroy (1985, 1999) and defined by John E. Joseph as a belief in the 'planned and centralized regulation of language' (1987: 14). In particular, he writes that:

> The interaction of power, language, and reflections on language, inextricably bound up with one another in human history, largely defines language standardization. (Joseph 1987: 43)

Joseph recognizes here the multiplicity of interests and their related representations of language which yield differing discourses on standardization (see also the chapters by Moschonas and Spitzmüller, Chapter 2; Park, Chapter 4; Androutsopoulos, Chapter 10; Ensslin, Chapter 11, this volume). This recognition is crucial, given that discourse about language is more than just descriptive: as the underlying ideology takes root and is manifested either in habitual linguistic practice or in further evaluative metalinguistic discourse, the reciprocal and dialectical nature of discourse and ideology means that the former affects the latter, and vice versa.

Terry Eagleton's analysis is that 'ideology creates and acts in a social world whilst it masquerades as a description of that world' (Eagleton 1991: 19), suggesting that ideologies become 'naturalized' through repetition of certain discourses to the point that the values represented become 'common sense'. If a particular view is considered to be common sense, further scrutiny of its basis is deemed to be unnecessary, and the belief becomes embedded in society (Milroy and Milroy 1999: 135). These authors go on to explain how:

> Such an appeal to common sense is powerful, as it engages an audience at a gut level at which it can readily respond. It also implies that the experts (who may raise objections to 'common sense') can be ignored; if we apply common sense our problems will be solved. (Milroy and Milroy 1999: 135–6)

'Common-sense' arguments about standard language are frequently based on the premises of: sharing a common linguistic variety for the perceived benefit of all members of a society; the prestige of the particular variety; its literary production, and its presence in influential spheres of education, commerce, government and other powerful domains. Whatever the recognizable benefits of linguistic standardization, its foundations are ideologies masquerading as descriptions of an idealized world which all too often become the unquestioned dominant view of language in society. Consequently, the ideology of standardization in fact *creates* the vision of standard language and *acts* to make its realization in society a goal of its proponents. Nonetheless, standardization can only ever fully be an ideology and not a measurable reality due to variation and evolution of languages, one of the 'linguistic facts of life' (Lippi-Green 1997: 11–14).

Deborah Cameron's (1995) notion of 'verbal hygiene' is useful for understanding one of the predominant metaphors used in standardization processes, that to standardize language is to 'cleanse' it of impurities brought in by (unnecessary) variation. Verbal hygiene functions as a language ideological debate and practice in that 'verbal hygienists' (i.e. writers, editors, educationalists and Academies as well as non-linguists and members of the public) claim to represent widely held or authoritative views of language, masking the fact that their views are actually 'derived from, rooted in, reflective of, or responsive to the experience or interests of a particular social position' (Woolard 1998: 6). Cameron argues that the practices of verbal hygienists represent more than a desire simply to shape language; they represent 'the struggle to control language by defining its nature' (1995: 8). As can be seen from the above examples of verbal hygienists, those who hold most power to define language, and who have significant 'voice' in doing so, are writers of published books and articles, editors who filter media content, teachers who shape the experiences of language learners and Academies that produce the 'pillars of language': dictionaries, grammars and orthography guides. What these linguistic 'role models' have in common is that they represent institutions – media, the education system, government and other contributors to public life – who are involved in what Lippi-Green calls 'the ordering of social groups in terms of who has authority to determine how language is best used' (1997: 55 – see also Ensslin, Chapter 11, this volume, on computer game discourse as a further example of this phenomenon).

In recognizing this concept of social ordering, it is necessary to also recognize that (language) ideologies work more forcefully to act and create in the social world when they do so through the discourse of institutions with all their associated prominence, prestige and influence. Media can be considered such an institution – certainly in Western societies – because of its purpose of providing a public information service, its well established position in influencing (and reflecting) public opinion, and its tradition of particular practices, coverage and format. If 'ideology is pervasively present in language' (Fairclough 2001: 2), then the influential position of, say, newspapers to inform and influence readers is a particularly interesting vehicle of ideological transmission – a point that numerous scholars have recognized and explored (see Cameron 1995; Fairclough 1995; Fowler 1991; Richardson 2007; van Dijk 1998). Fairclough's view is that:

> [. . .] media discourse should be regarded as the site of complex and often contradictory processes, including ideological processes.

[. . .] Media texts do indeed function ideologically in social control and social reproduction, but they also operate as cultural commodities in a competitive market [. . .], are part of the business of entertaining people, are designed to keep people politically and socially informed, are cultural artefacts in their own right, informed by particular aesthetics; and they are at the same time caught up in – reflecting and contributing to – shifting cultural values and identities. (Fairclough 1995: 47)

Spanish newspapers – as in the majority of democratic nation-states – reach a large readership across a wide geographical and social territory, now even beyond Spain's national borders via the internet. As Fowler notes, the scale of production and dissemination of newspaper discourse, along with the economic and political positions and perspectives of individual papers are what give the press a particularly crucial role as a site of ideological diffusion (Fowler 1991: 121–22). These media texts function ideologically in society because journalists' writings do not simply recount facts about interesting events within (and beyond) that society. Journalists and editors first make decisions about what is 'newsworthy' or important enough to include for their readers (and/or express for their patrons); they then decide how these articles should be presented in terms of the space allocated to them and the section titles under which new items should be categorized (e.g. national, international, culture, business, etc). Linguistic decisions are also made at the writing stage about how news should be framed, described, interpreted and 'delivered' for the consumption of a readership which both is subject to, and generates, the 'shifting cultural values and identities' Fairclough identifies.

John E. Richardson believes that 'journalism exists to enable citizens to better understand their lives and their position(s) in the world' (2007: 7) and, in favour of this idealist vision, shuns the idea that entertainment, propaganda or mere profit-making can be primary goals or end products of newspaper journalism:

When the work of journalists emphasizes entertainment, or the activities and opinions of the powerful, or the pursuit of profit in themselves or above the primary function of journalism – to help citizens understand the world and their positions in it – it stops being journalism. (Richardson 2007: 8)

The seemingly noble goal of journalism that Richardson proposes does not exclude the possibility – or indeed the inevitability – of ideological underpinnings permeating the news-producing process. In seeking to help citizens to understand their lives, it is common for a newspaper to reinforce views of what 'their' citizens' lives are like, and should be like: the reproduction of the model citizen or reader. The relation

45

between the 'consuming' reader and the 'producing' newspaper sets the latter up as an institution, and thus its ideological foundations and output can be seen as institutional ideologies, as Teun van Dijk claims:

> [. . .] the ideologies and opinions of newspapers are usually not personal, but social, institutional or political. (van Dijk 1998: 22)

The institutional ideologies reflected in the press are not, however, solely those of the particular publication; Fairclough points out that there are other institutions – economic, political and cultural – who already possess power in their own domains, and who furthermore exercise a degree of control over media output through their often privileged access to the processes of its production (Fairclough 1995: 40). The ideologies then that underlie – and are transmitted through – media discourse are (i) embedded in the structural choices made by the editors as well as the linguistic choices made by writers and their sources, and (ii) naturalized through the variety of textual features and discursive strategies employed by writers. The institutional nature of press discourse often obscures the particular interests of the view being presented by anonymizing individual agency, thus achieving a more powerful influence as an 'official' or 'authentic' view. Thus we see that the press is a particularly rich and important site for propagating (and locating) many different ideologies, but particularly those ideologies and representations of the world which are institutional and even hegemonic.

3.3 The Spanish context

Throughout the history of the Iberian Peninsula, the Castilian language has repeatedly been employed as a tool for achieving political and cultural hegemony: language spread accompanied the overthrow of foreign occupiers (Romans, Visigoths, Moors, Napoleon) and ethnic groups (Jews) as well as the establishment of Spain's overseas empire.

The standardization of Castilian dates from the thirteenth century with a Royal decree that the language of Toledo's upper classes should be used in science, literature and administration. Castilian gained prestige, which was further enhanced by Nebrija's *Gramática de la lengua castellana* (1492), an important work that used the print medium to reify and spread the official language of the newly unified Spanish kingdom. The Spanish literary 'Golden Age' did much to level variation and consolidate the standardized code and linguistic culture of educated Castilian-speakers. By the nineteenth century, a definite sense of 'Spanish-ness' existed, and with the Napoleonic invasion in 1808, local linguistic and cultural identities were further obscured for the cause of defending Spain as a whole. National crisis followed the loss of Spain's last colonies in 1898, refuelling a belief that cultural and linguistic unification would lead to national progress through reviving a sense of Spain's greatness (Mar-Molinero 2000b: 25–27).

So by the start of the twentieth century, ideologies of linguistic unification and standardization had existed in Spain for centuries. The anticipated revival of Spanish greatness never materialized: on the whole, political upheaval and economic strife gripped Spain well into the Franco dictatorship. Strong state centralization ensued, with repressive measures towards non-Castilian 'peripheral' communities and their languages.

Upon Franco's death, a Constitution was drafted, cementing Spain's return to democracy. Article 3 (Constitution 1978) recognizes Castilian as the official language of the one, indivisible state, with citizens having a *duty* to know the language as well as the right to use it. While this initially shows little progress from Francoist language policy, legislation does now exist for use of what the Constitution calls the 'other languages of Spain' – a huge leap towards acceptance of the multilingualism and multiculturalism present in some of Spain's autonomous communities (e.g. Catalonia and the Basque Country). However, Castilian has maintained its position of hegemony as the 'official Spanish language of State', because the use and promotion of other languages are limited to their respective, well-defined geographical regions.

In Spain today, language ideological debates regarding the importance, use and current state of Spanish (and the other Peninsular languages) are commonplace, and come from the variety of sources that Cameron (1995) predicts: the general public, politicians, writers, critics and media representatives. One such body of 'craft professionals' is the *Real Academia Española* (Spanish Language Academy, hereafter: RAE). Based on the Italian and French models, this Academy brought together scholars, politicians, religious men and aristocrats, and – by royal appointment – sought to purify Castilian Spanish of 'all errors in its construction, style and vocabulary which have been brought about by ignorance, careless habits, neglect and too much liberty to innovate' (*Fundación y Estatutos de la RAE* 1715. Cited in Zamora Vicente 1999: 35 – all translations are my own). Evident here is the purism of these founding Academicians, linking variation with socially undesirable traits such as ignorance and carelessness for the 'correct' structure of Castilian.

Madrid was then the centre of a vast American colony as well as an emerging unified Spanish state. Consequently, Castilian and the prestigious discourse of the Court, commerce and Academy had spread and become widely (though not universally) received as *the* authentic and legitimate form of a standard national language. The function of the RAE in its early years – and arguably since – was clear: it contributed to the forming of a common national and political identity based on a harmonious vision of the Spanish nation, state and language (Castilian): *linguistic nationalism* as it has become known (see Lodares 2002, 2005; Mar-Molinero 2000a).

The relationship between Castilian and the 'other languages of Spain' has been well documented and analysed (see Salvador 1987; Siguan 1992; Castillo Lluch and Kabatek 2006). Suffice it to say here that although the privileged position of Castilian is assured (in legislation at least), it does face internal 'competition' from the co-official regional languages and their association with Basque independence, Catalan nationalism, and so on. Hence the contemporary Academy perceives the 'threat' to Spanish to be more a question of relative *status* rather than of 'infiltration' of influences from regional languages. The RAE is particularly concerned with maintaining and developing Spanish as the language of official national (and international) affairs, and so RAE members often promote Castilian as an identity factor which crosses barriers, unifies communities and facilitates communication and understanding, with regional languages representing cultural artefacts of the Spanish 'nation' rather than internationally important languages.

In terms of Spain's 'external' language policies, the status planning of Spanish in the world is primarily implemented through the activities of the *Instituto Cervantes* – the government organization set up in 1991 responsible for the promotion overseas of Spanish language and Hispanic culture (see Mar-Molinero 2006). However, in recent years, the Academy itself has increasingly focused on the global position and status of Spanish. The RAE has been a member of the Association of Spanish Language Academies since it was formed in the 1950s to promote greater collaboration between the individual academies. Moreover, changes were made to the Madrid Academy's statutes in 1995 which state that its:

> [. . .] principal mission is to ensure that the essential unity of the Spanish language maintained across the Hispanic world is not fractured by the changes which the language experiences in its constant adaptation to the needs of its speakers. (Artículo 1°, Real Academia Española 1995)

This reflects the Academy's response to the contemporary sociolinguistic situation of Spanish, in that it acknowledges linguistic change according to the needs of its speakers. However, underlying this is the assumption that the 'essential' unity of language is of greater importance than the innovative function of a language to meet the diverse communicative/symbolic needs of its users. Linguistic change should not be allowed to 'break' that unity, of which the RAE sees itself (and is seen widely and publicly) as guardian and guarantor.

In this way, the latest Statutes indicate that the RAE perceives fragmentation across the Spanish-speaking world to be a 'threat'. It also perceives lexical and grammatical borrowings (particularly from English) as threatening to the integrity of Spanish, particularly when these are 'excessive' or 'unnecessary' (Torrent-Lenzen 2006: 48). A third threat is the absence of Spanish in key global domains such as science, information technology and international diplomacy.

The original motto of the Academy ('cleanse, fix and give splendour') has now given way to a renewed endeavour to 'unify, cleanse and fix' Spanish. A particularly visible response to this is the emergence of the Panhispanic Language Policy, driven by the current linguistic climate in which, one commentator writes:

> The Spanish language is enjoying one of the finest moments in its history: more than 440 million people speak it and it is an official language in 21 countries, now also consolidating its position in the US and Brazil . . . However, the growth of Spanish has until this point been a natural process, without the intervention of any official policy – a policy which only now is arising. (Miguel Ángel Noceda, *El País*, 05.11.06)

This 'newly arising policy' was actually created in 2004 by the RAE and the Association of Academies (ASALE 2004) as a guiding policy for the activities of the latter, whose President – Víctor García de la Concha – is also director of the former. The *Política lingüística panhispánica* (PLP) finds expression in standardizing publications, media discourse, collaborative projects and conferences such as the International Spanish Language Congress at which it was launched. The publications – dictionaries, grammars and orthography guides – serve the entire Spanish-speaking world with a definition of the Spanish language, that is, *what it looks like* and what shape it takes. Consequently I suggest that these publications represent part of 'the struggle to control language by defining its nature' (Cameron 1995). Furthermore, the inclusion of a list of all 22 participating Academies, as well as explicit reference in its foreword to the Academies' collaborative efforts, points towards the panhispanic authority and reach of the publications and their producers. The PLP – which shapes these publications – also responds (and contributes) to a 're-scaling' of relations between the RAE and Spanish-speakers in which the global scale is 'an ultimate horizon for action' (Fairclough 2006: 34) for nation-states and multinational organizations.

49

This re-scaling is taking place for the RAE, and its domain of activity is no longer limited to nation-states, nor its activities to those of 'cleansing, fixing and giving splendour' to a territorially based variety of Spanish. Instead, and perhaps above all, the PLP pursues global linguistic unity, or a standardized 'total Spanish' (del Valle 2007). As such, the PLP is at least in part externally-focused. However, Clare Mar-Molinero and I argue elsewhere that it is also internally-focused, insofar as the RAE maintains a leading position in this policy as *primus inter pares,* and seeks to ensure that Spain benefits (in terms of prestige as well as economically) from the global expansion of Spanish as a first, second and foreign language (Paffey and Mar-Molinero 2009).

3.4 Panhispanism in the Spanish press: a critical analysis

Upon exploring and considering the context of Spain's language debates, it is clear that the media – and the print media in particular – is one of the vehicles in which RAE policy is published, commented upon and diffused. To my earlier general discussion of media discourse can be added the following observation made by a Spanish professor of journalism *in* the press *about* the press:

> Audio-visual media have a high popular consumption in Hispanic culture, and without doubt the impact they have on the linguistic system, and on society in general, are the most common and persistent. However, the press still plays an important role in processes of standardization and control, a role that corresponds specifically to the leading quality or influential newspapers which are characterized by their ability to set standards for social and cultural renewal, in keeping with the evolving thoughts and trends of a given time. (Bernardo Díaz Nosty, *El País*, 07.04.97)

In a previous article, I critically analysed the Academy's discourse in the Spanish press to show how textual features construct a vision of the Spanish language as transnational and unified, while simultaneously being under threat of impoverishment and invasion from Anglicisms as well as exclusion from influential fields of technology and diplomacy (Paffey 2007). My analysis here – based on a selection of newspaper texts taken from my doctoral corpus – brings to light various other aspects of standardization discourse. The texts come from the two top-selling quality daily newspapers in Spain – the centre-left national *El País* and the Madrid-based right-wing *ABC* – and are articles which relate to language debates in which the RAE is either a contributing voice or an object of the coverage. The articles appeared between 1997 and 2007, a time-frame chosen firstly because during this period the series of international Congresses began which now play an important role in the PLP's development and promotion, and secondly because of the renewal of the three 'pillars' of Spanish which took place by means of new editions of the Academy's Dictionary, Grammar and Orthography.

In my critical approach to these texts, I seek to show their 'hidden agendas' (Cameron 2001: 123–41), that is, the way the texts are produced with both explicit and implicit meaning, which requires a more detailed consideration of the text within its contexts of production and consumption. This means that, having acknowledged the importance of *denoted* meanings and perspective, I will consider the *connoted* meaning by analysing and critiquing the ideological assumptions which construct certain representations of language (and other topics). Of interest are the ways in which the subject content is framed within broader discourses and social contexts, and also the way in which the texts themselves encode decisions about the way in which standardization is conceived and presented by the RAE to the newspaper-reading public.

Richardson (2007) discusses the value of Critical Discourse Analysis (CDA) as a theory and method for uncovering the hidden ideological agendas of newspaper discourse. In his particular application of this approach to journalism, he writes that:

> [C]ritical discourse analysts: offer *interpretations* of the meanings of texts rather than just quantifying textual features and deriving meaning from this; situate *what* is written or said in the *context* in which it occurs, rather than just summarizing patterns or regularities in texts; and argue that textual meaning is *constructed* through an interaction between producer, text and consumer rather than simply being 'read off' the page by all readers in exactly the same way. (Richardson 2007: 15)

In seeking to offer interpretations of textual meaning in relation to its contextual consumption, Richardson and many other critical discourse analysts adopt a number of different approaches, the most prominent being from writers such as Fairclough (1995, 2006), Ruth Wodak and Michael Meyer (2001) and van Dijk (1998, 2001). The works cited here certainly serve as guides for the analysis that follows, but I have not adopted any one single approach mainly because these scholars emphasize that CDA is not simply a methodological blueprint. A number of analytical questions from CDA are useful as I critique the debates; my focus, however, remains the exposure of ideological representations of the Spanish language in the press, particularly related to the context of globalization and the developing panhispanic policies of the RAE and associated Academies.

3.5 Data analysis

Language ideological debates regularly figure in both *El País* and *ABC* through the devotion of space within the 'Culture' sections to the voices of language 'experts'. A selected number of experts – mostly members of the Academy and the *Cervantes*' director – either write articles or are interviewed and have their statements cited in articles. In particular, there is evidence of the way that in this metalinguistic discourse, verbal hygienists not only define the nature and activities of the panhispanic language policy but also define the Spanish language itself. These definitions are presented for public consumption and their objectives are often achieved through vocabulary choices which represent the text producer's experience and evaluation of the social world, that is, how the RAE and *Cervantes* – as 'establishment' agencies – view the Spanish language and its role in national and international relations through their ideological frameworks. There are also repetitions of set phrases which in turn generate a process of naturalization; these terms come to represent the dominant 'common sense' perspective of panhispanic language and culture. Two particularly salient categorizations of Spanish to emerge from the data corpus are (i) Spanish as a unitary language, and (ii) Spanish as a commodity with economic benefits.

3.5.1 Spanish as a unitary language

In spite of its considerable variety across the Spanish-speaking world, the Spanish language is repeatedly described as being just one language. This is a point of view reinforced by experts in the press on many occasions, and little if any space is given over to the exploration of dissenting views. Take for example this extract from an interview with the Academic and philologist José Manuel Blecua, published during the Zacatecas International Congress:

> Interviewer: But there are different 'Spanishes', and the Spanish of an Ecuadorian farmer is more beautiful than that spoken on the television.
>
> Blecua: Yes, but the Spanish language, in the end, is but one language, which unites us to the world, which designates life, love, death and the little things of life. (*El País* 19.10.01)

Challenged with the perspective that there are numerous, distinct varieties of Spanish, and that a Latin American variety might be valued more than the variety used in TV media, Blecua first makes an 'apparent concession' (van Dijk 2000: 40) that this is the case, then immediately introduces a contrary argument that actually it is 'the' Spanish language, and that after all is said and done, there is only one Spanish. Blecua's use of the definite article implies consensus and authority, and the indicative mood indicates a truth claim suggesting that there is no need for a more measured or modalized response. The article itself took as its title part of his phrase: 'El español, al final, es uno' (the Spanish language, in the end, is but one language), representing the choice of the journalist/editor to foreground this particular point of Blecua's interview, and establishing an 'expert view' on the Spanish language at a time when press coverage of language matters was increased due to the International Congress.

Another example is this quotation from an interview with the Secretary General of the *Asociación de Academias*:

> '80% of the vocabulary is common to the Spanish-speaking world' assured López Morales. (*El País*, 14.11.06)

Here, the use of statistics to legitimize López Morales's point together with strong verbs such as 'assure' and the indicative mood 'is' all point to a projected certainty of the truth claims being made, and serve to reinforce the authority of the interlocutor in texts such as this.

Representative voices of the Academies further emphasize the unity of Spanish varieties, not least through repetition and naturalization of the phrase 'Total Spanish' (*español total*):

> '**A complete vision** of Spanish.' (*El País*, 10.11.05)

> '[. . .] its innovative feature is that it considers not only the grammar of peninsular Spanish from Spain, but of **total Spanish**.' (*ABC*, 29.11.05)

> *The Fourth Congress of the Spanish Language will analyse the diversity of Spanish*: 'It is an innovation. For the first time we will have a grammar of **total Spanish**, not only of peninsular Spanish.' (*El País*, 29.03.06)

> 'a grammar of **total Spanish**, not only from Spain.' (*ABC*, 01.09.06)

> 'it will be the first **total Spanish** grammar.' (*El País*, 01.03.07)

> '"[The New Grammar] is descriptive and normative. It tackles **total Spanish** and has been developed on the basis of equality throughout the world" indicated García de la Concha.' (*ABC*, 02.03.07)

In RAE discourse, this 'total Spanish' is seen to be supported by panhispanic norms and publications which are legitimized through a claim of egalitarian values in their production ('not only from Spain'; 'developed on the basis of equality throughout the world'). Moreover, the all-encompassing vision of a globally unified Spanish, the panhispanic projects which promote and advance it together with the standardizing publications which define its form appear as accessible and applicable to all speakers:

> [Reference to the Panhispanic Dictionary of Doubts] 'a unified response to **any** Spanish-speaker.' (*El País*, 22.11.01)

> 'a unified response agreed upon by **all the Academies** of the Spanish language.' (ASALE 2004: 9)

> The Academies of the Spanish language today clear up the doubts of **all speakers** worldwide. (ABC, 13.11.04)

> *The Spanish language: 21st century industry:* '. . . we have been working on a normative and descriptive grammar which, for the first time, is common to all [Spanish-speaking] countries. (*El País*, 02.03.07)

Indeed, the New Spanish Grammar launched in 2007 is described frequently using the metaphor of a 'map of the whole language', emphasizing that there is a definite shape and territory of Spanish, which can – and indeed should – be navigated using a trustworthy guide: the Academies' normative, panhispanic publications.

Statements regarding the unity of Spanish are often collocated in the press with a positive evaluative discussion about the context of an overall panhispanic community, as can be seen in these extracts:

> 'The Director of the Spanish Language Academy assured that "we believe that with this [Panhispanic Dictionary of Doubts] we are providing a **service** that goes beyond the strictly linguistic and which has **great value** in the integration of the Ibero-american Community of Nations. We believe too that this is being realized as the **highest service** towards the **strengthening** of the unity of Spanish, yet with the greatest **respect** for the varieties which that united Spanish has in each of the regions."' (*El País*, 15.09.05)

> *The living essence of what we speak*: 'The panhispanic policy, which does not pronounce one norm or definition without room for debate but opens up the meaning of each word to multiple varieties according to its geographical use, provides for many variations in this *Essential Dictionary*. (*El País*, 14.11.06)

The two quotations above show evidence of how discourse on total Spanish co-exists with another policy line which emphasizes *unity in diversity* – a further concept which throughout contemporary Spanish language debates has been naturalized into the common ground of linguistic beliefs through repetition in influential media. However, it is worth noting that even in contexts where linguistic diversity is acknowledged, it is generally given little prominence and discussed in scant detail. Furthermore, this topic is recurrently collocated with discourse on the 'essential unity' of Spanish, and 'unity in diversity' which are in turn foregrounded topics, suggesting that these are the more pressing and prominent themes for communication.

3.5.2 Spanish as a commodity with economic benefits

Following the notion that Spanish can be considered a single, unified language, it is hardly surprising that another recurring strand of language ideological discourse employs the metaphor of language as a commodity, classifying Spanish as a profitable economic resource or industry:

> *The Spanish language: 21st century* **industry** . . . 'It is the biggest **industry** of the 21st century, our main raw material.' (*El País*, 02.03.07)

> 'Our language [. . .] can serve as the basis of a common cultural, economic and **labour trade**.' (Director of RAE) (*El País*, 30.03.97)

> *The wealth of the language*: [. . .] 'language tourism is the most clean, non-polluting and prosperous **industry** of the coming years' (Director of Cervantes) (*ABC*, 19.12.06)

> 'It is obvious that the **multinational enterprise** awaiting us is the promotion of Spanish in terms of profitability, statistical base and strategic demand.' (*ABC*, 23.10.06)

These metaphors of 'language as commodity' and 'language as business' are supported by other linguistic features and strategies. By referring to the Spanish language industry as 'our main raw material', the use of inclusive 'our' by the directors of both the RAE (*El País*, 30.03.97) and the *Cervantes* (*El País*, 02.03.07) points again to the linguistic nationalism consolidated in previous centuries. 'Nation' and 'language' are bound inextricably to each other, and there is an apparent ownership of this commodified language by Spain. Here there is also an assumption – based on contemporary capitalist economic models – that Spain as the 'producer' of the Spanish commodity should receive the benefits of the raw materials it 'owns'. The metaphor is employed to define the profitability of Spanish, that is, 'the oil of the Spanish language' (*ABC*, 23.10.06), from whose rich well Spain 'extracts' approximately 15 per cent of its Gross Domestic Product (*El País*: 27.10.06, 27.03.07; *ABC*: 28.10.06, 29.10.06, 31.12.06). As important as what is included in discourse is what is excluded from it, and no mention is made within the corpus of the economic benefit of Spanish as a commodity/industry to any country other than Spain, reinforcing not only the Euro-centric and even Spain-centric perspective of the Spanish press, but also making clear the similar concerns of the language guardians in their public discourse.

The commodification of language taking place in Spanish newspaper discourse is one of what Nikolas Coupland recognizes as the key processes of globalization which impact on language: interdependence, compression across time and space, disembedding and commodification (2003: 467; for discussion of these processes in the Spanish context, see Paffey and Mar-Molinero, 2009). If ideological brokers are able to define the nature of Spanish as, among other things, a 'multinational enterprise' (*ABC*, 23.10.06) and to widely and influentially promote this definition, then they are also able to apply the norms of international commerce to language. These norms include unquestioned capitalist approaches to advancing language teaching and cultural propagation from Spain as the symbolic 'oil of the Spanish language'; they also include defining the context and shaping the conditions under which other interest-laden business organizations become involved in language standardization practices, i.e. private business or government sponsorship of publications (i.e. the Panhispanic Dictionary of Doubts – Telefónica), ongoing projects (Historical Dictionary of Spanish – Government of Spain) or conferences (International Spanish Language Congresses, International Seminar on the Economic Value of Spanish – numerous communications, financial and energy companies). There is an increasing amount of transnational commerce which takes place *through* the medium of the Spanish language, and as the number of Spanish speakers and Spanish-speaking areas increase around the world through high birth-rates, migration and language learning, commercial opportunities also increase. Spain-based multinationals that invest in opening doors for linguistic spread and explicit policy activities therefore find the largest economies in the Americas being opened up to them. Spanish does indeed function as a commodity and a tool in a globalized world.

3.6 Discussion and conclusions

In this chapter, I have explored the Spanish print-media as a discursive site in which language ideological debates take place, and in which the Spanish Language Academy reinforces various aspects of an ideology of 'global standard Spanish'. Woolard's (1998) concept of metalinguistic discourse has usefully characterized the way in which ideologies can be expressed *through* and *about* language. Furthermore, I have discussed how critical analysis is useful in revealing hidden agendas of

RAE discourse in the press as well as the more implicit ideologies embedded within press coverage of language matters. These ideologies are often institutional in that they belong to and are put forth by socially, economically or politically powerful organizations such as the Academy, *Cervantes* and their commercial partners. The authority of these organizations lends prestige and legitimacy to the views they express in the media. Of particular importance to this study has been the notion that these verbal hygienists are involved in 'the struggle to control language by defining its nature'. One way of controlling public beliefs about language is through maintaining good relationships with prestigious newspapers deemed to use 'good Spanish', and by using these vehicles of dissemination whose 'ideological power stems from their ability to say the same thing to millions of people simultaneously' (Fowler 1991: 122).

Spanish as a global language has been developing through the processes of globalization defined by Coupland (2003), and Spain's government agencies, Academies, cultural and commercial bodies have actually been very astute in recognizing this re-scaling of language, and in seeking to guide, mould, influence and enshrine this in the Panhispanic Language Policy. I have sought to show how language debates and discourse in the press focus on key aspects of policy, in particular those which highlight language as a commodity, skill, and source of cultural and economic capital, through which Spain is able to access more global markets (beginning with language tourism and teaching but also communications, energy and financial markets).

The promotion of panhispanism, then, and the re-conceptualisation of Spanish as a global commodity is more than just a linguistic phenomenon: it opens the way for language guardians to follow more commercial practices and to collaborate with Spain-based multinational companies such as Telefónica, BBVA, Repsol, Endesa, and Mapfre (among others). Hence Spain's transnational industries are expanding too, for example, through the investment opportunities opened up in the regions (usually Latin American) where the International Congresses are hosted. The benefits of the spread of Spanish, the subsequent re-scaling of discursive and social practices of language guardians, and the increasing collaboration with commercial entities are first and foremost going to Spain. As the *Cervantes'* director has suggested, it is *Spain* that is present in the world through Spanish, and there is evidence that media discourse is used to propagate the panhispanic language ideology of which these trends are a part.

Throughout the present chapter, I have sought to show that there is a conscious effort on the part of the RAE to maintain its place of leadership as *primus inter pares* in relation to the other academies in the

Panhispanic Language Policy. The RAE's primary approach to achieving this is discursive, appearing in the print media as the 'natural' commentator and authority on debates regarding Spanish, even beyond Spain. This confirms Fairclough's claim that news production displays 'an overwhelming reliance [. . .] on a tightly delimited set of official and otherwise legitimized sources which are systematically drawn upon [. . .] as sources of "facts"' (Fairclough 1995: 49).

Finally, the discourse of Spanish language guardians on aspects of the Panhispanic Language Policy in the majority of language-related articles reinforces and legitimizes their place as authorities, and validates their discourse as prestigious and worthy of print space and therefore serious consideration in the definition, management and guidance of the Spanish language and related language debates in a globalized world.

References

ASALE: Asociación de Academias de la Lengua Española (2004), *La nueva política lingüística panhispánica*. Madrid: Real Academia Española.

Blommaert, Jan (ed.) (1999), *Language Ideological Debates*. Berlin: Mouton de Gruyter.

Cameron, D. (1995), *Verbal Hygiene*. London: Routledge.

Cameron, D. (2001), *Working with Spoken Discourse*. London: Sage.

Castillo Lluch, M. and Kabatek, J. (eds) (2006), *Las Lenguas de España: Política lingüística, sociología del lenguaje e ideología desde la Transición hasta la actualidad*. Madrid/Frankfurt: Vervuert Iberoamericana.

Coupland, N. (2003), 'Introduction: sociolinguistics and globalization'. *Journal of Sociolinguistics*, 7(4), 465–72.

Del Valle, J. (2007), 'Embracing diversity for the sake of unity: linguistic hegemony and the pursuit of total Spanish', in A. Duchêne and M. Heller (eds), *Discourses of Endangerment: Ideology and Interest in the Defence of Languages*. London/New York: Continuum, pp. 242–67.

Eagleton, T. (1991), *Ideology: An Introduction*. London: Verso.

Fairclough, N. (1995), *Media Discourse*. London: Edward Arnold.

Fairclough, N. (2001), *Language and Power*. Harlow: Longman.

Fairclough, N. (2006), *Language and Globalization*. London/New York: Routledge.

Fowler, R. (1991), *Language in the News: Discourse and Ideology in the Press*. London: Routledge.

Johnson, S. and Ensslin, A. (2007), 'Language in the media: theory and practice', in Johnson and Ensslin (eds), *Language in the Media: Representations, Identities, Ideologies*. London/New York: Continuum, pp. 3–22.

Joseph, J. E. (1987), *Eloquence and Power: The Rise of Language Standards and Standard Languages*. London: Pinter.

Lippi-Green, R. (1997), *English with an Accent: Language, Ideology, and Discrimination in the United States*. London: Routledge.

Lodares Marrodan, J. R. (2002), *Lengua y patria: Sobre el nacionalismo lingüístico en España*. Madrid: Taurus.

Lodares Marrodan, J. R. (2005), *El porvenir del español*. Madrid: Taurus.

Mar-Molinero, C. (2000a), 'The Iberian peninsula: conflicting linguistic nationalisms', in S. Barbour and C. Carmichael (eds), *Language and Nationalism in Europe*. Oxford: Oxford University Press, pp. 83–104.

Mar-Molinero, C. (2000b), *The Politics of Language in the Spanish-Speaking World: From Colonisation to Globalization*. London/New York: Routledge.

Mar-Molinero, C. (2006), 'The European linguistic legacy in a global era: linguistic imperialism, Spanish and the *Instituto Cervantes*', in C. Mar-Molinero and P. Stevenson (eds), *Language Ideologies, Policies and Practices: Language and the Future of Europe*. Basingstoke/New York: Palgrave Macmillan, pp. 76–91.

Milroy, J. and Milroy, L. (1985, 1999), *Authority in Language: Investigating Language Prescription and Standardization*. London: Routledge and Kegan Paul.

Paffey, D. (2007), 'Policing the Spanish language debate: verbal hygiene and the Spanish language academy (Real Academia Española)'. *Language Policy*, 6(3-4), 313–32.

Paffey, D. and Mar-Molinero, C. (2009), 'Globalization, linguistic norms and language authorities: Spain and the panhispanic language policy', in M. Lacorte and J. Leeman (eds), Español en Estados Unidos y otros contextos de contacto: Sociolingüística, ideología y pedagogía / Spanish in the United States and other contact environments: Sociolinguistics, ideology and pedagogy. Madrid/Frankfurt: Vervuert Iberoamericana, pp. 159–73.

Real Academia Española. (1995), *Estatutos y reglamento de la Real Academia Española*. Madrid: Real Academia Española.

Richardson, J. E. (2007), *Analysing Newspapers: An Approach from Critical Discourse Analysis*. Basingstoke: Palgrave Macmillan.

Salvador, G. (1987), *Lengua española y lenguas de España*. Barcelona: Ariel.

Schieffelin, B. B., Woolard, K. A. and Kroskrity, P. V. (eds) (1998), *Language Ideologies: Practice and Theory*. New York/Oxford: Oxford University Press.

Siguan, M. (1992), *España plurilingüe*. Madrid: Alianza Tres.

Torrent-Lenzen, A. (2006), *Unidad y pluricentrismo en la comunidad hispanohablante: Cultivo y mantenimiento de una norma panhispánica unificada*. Titz: Axel Lenzen Verlag.

van Dijk, T. (1998), 'Opinions and ideologies in the press', in A. Bell and P. Garrett (eds), *Approaches to Media Discourse*. Oxford: Blackwell, pp. 21–63.

van Dijk, T. (2000), 'New(s) racism: a discourse analytical approach', in S. Cottle (ed.), *Ethnic Minorities and the Media*. Milton Keynes: Open University Press, pp. 33–49.

van Dijk, T. (2001), 'Multidisciplinary CDA: a plea for diversity', in R. Wodak and M. Meyer (eds), *Methods of Critical Discourse Analysis*. London: Sage, pp. 95–120.

Wodak, R. and Meyer, M. (eds) (2001), *Methods of Critical Discourse Analysis*. London: Sage.
Woolard, K. A. (1998), 'Introduction: language ideology as a field of inquiry', in B. B. Schieffelin, K. A. Woolard and P. V. Kroskrity (eds), *Language Ideologies: Practice and Theory*. New York/Oxford: Oxford University Press, pp. 3–47.
Zamora Vicente, A. (1999), *La Real Academia Española*. Madrid: Espasa.

4 Language games on Korean television: between globalization, nationalism, and authority

Joseph Sung-Yul Park

4.1 National media and the challenges of globalization

The media are one of the most powerful forces involved in the shaping of national identity. As Benedict Anderson has noted, publicly accessible media that can potentially reach the entire population of a nation-state inculcate in their consumers a 'remarkable confidence of community in anonymity which is the hallmark of modern nations' (1991: 36). At the same time, it is precisely through participation in this process that national media establish themselves as institutions of authority. As those institutions mediate this fundamental sense of community, the legitimacy that is conferred upon the nation-state is naturally projected onto them. Thus, national media typically invest significantly in valorizing essential symbols of the 'imagined community', ranging from the flag and the national anthem to devoted patriots and model citizens, but most importantly, the national language – the ultimate key to unity that represents the indelible essence of a people (Gal and Woolard 2001). National media accomplish this in multiple ways, not only by reaching their audience in the standard, national, official variety of language and through policies that inscribe hierarchical orders of legitimacy among different language varieties (Spitulnik 1998), but also through explicitly promoting the importance of using the standard variety in the 'correct' way, as we will see throughout this chapter. By engaging in such work, the media simultaneously reinforce the importance of the national language and present themselves as the guardians of language and national identity (see also Moschonas and Spitzmüller in Chapter 2 and Paffey in Chapter 3 of this volume).

This status of the media, of course, is not without challenges, as the ideology of a homogeneous, unified imagined community is necessarily mired with slippages and contradictions due to the multiplicities and diversities that define our lives. Indigenous and resistant media in various forms, for instance, constantly contest the dominant linguistic order by creating alternative spaces within the public mediascape laid out by mainstream national media (e.g. Ginsburg 1991; Jaffe 2007; Urla 2001). But it is not only in the struggles of linguistic and ethnic minority groups against domination that the ideological ground for mainstream media is challenged. Construction of national identity, as is the case for any type of identity, is never a finalized product (Bucholtz and Hall 2004, 2005), and even in the absence of overt resistance such discursive constructs are necessarily located within a space filled with a multiplicity of ideologies such that they must be 'dynamically responsive to ever-changing forms of opposition' (Kroskrity 2004: 503). In the ever-shifting landscape of language ideologies, then, media discourse must constantly invent new modes of rationalizing the construct of the language community, erasing elements in the sociolinguistic field that do not fit with the dominant vision of national identity (Irvine and Gal 2000; see also Androutsopoulos, Chapter 10, this volume).

Social changes brought about by globalization, in particular, highlight this need for constant ideological work. As the postmodern condition problematizes assumptions of essentialism and authority, conveying the message of a unified community mediated by a single language requires greater discursive work than ever. Increased awareness of and familiarity towards other languages and cultures, hybrid identities, and new ways of articulating those identities cast a critical light upon the state-based narratives of language that support the authority of media institutions. For instance, in Europe, issues such as immigration and the changing notions of citizenship (Milani 2007) and the restructuring of the educational system linked to the expanding infrastructure of the European Union (Horner 2007) have led to heated debates about national identity across many national contexts. The fact that the media served as central sites for such debates is hardly a coincidence. As 'ideology brokers' that not only act as powerful forces in shaping dominant language ideologies but also have a great stake in the reproduction of those ideologies (Blommaert 1999), the media clearly constitute a highly interested party in those debates that must seek to re-establish the imagined community of the nation-state and defend its authority.

As we have learned through ongoing debates over whether globalization undermines the authority and culture of the nation-state (see Guillén 2001), transculturation and hybridity of the global do not necessarily lead to disintegration of local structures of cultural identity but to their re-formulation and re-signification in terms of modernity. From the perspective of authoritative institutions such as national media, then, the challenge posed by globalization is how the authority of those institutions can be re-told and re-framed in response to shifting language ideologies. Of course, we may see this problem as an extension of the ideological work of imagining the community that defined the formation of modern nation-states albeit within a new domain of postmodernity that is constantly in flux. As Tomlinson notes, 'the really interesting cultural-political question that emerges is of how nimble and reflexively attuned state apparatuses are capable of becoming in response to these changes' (2003: 276). In this chapter, I will explore this question in greater detail through an analysis of how Korean television strategically aligns itself with linguistic nationalism in the face of shifting media environments.

4.2 Television in Korea: dilemmas of linguistic nationalism

In South Korea (henceforth Korea), linguistic nationalism has played a central role throughout the country's modern history. Its strong monolingualism in Korean and wider cultural homogeneity are considered a source of great national pride. Moreover, the Korean language, as a language that is (believed to be) spoken by all Koreans and only by Koreans, is often taken to symbolize the pure essence of a people, bringing all Koreans under the wings of a highly naturalized Korean nationhood. Such linguistic nationalism is reproduced on many levels of society with the support of many powerful actors, including a national language academy and the circle of Korean scholars positioned in institutions of higher education (Go 1995) as well as the media, particularly Korean television.

Television in Korea plays a major role in reproducing the imagined purity and cultural value of Korean not only by broadcasting in the standard Korean language, but also by explicitly promoting 'correct' ways of using it. For instance, all three of the major broadcasters in Korea have aired short but regular prescriptive language programmes: Korean Broadcasting System (KBS)'s *Baleunmal Gounmal* ('Correct Language, Beautiful Language'), Munhwa Broadcasting Corporation (MBC)'s *Ulimal Nadeuli* ('An Excursion in Our Language'), and Seoul Broadcasting System (SBS)'s *Salanghaeyo Ulimal* ('We Love You, Our Language').[1] As these titles indicate, the shows instruct the viewers in the usage of Korean, warning them against incorrect grammar, non-standard usage, and foreign loanwords. While SBS cancelled its programme in 2005, KBS and MBC both continue to run their shows as of 2009. It is through such processes of authorization (Bucholtz and Hall 2004) that Korean television thereby derives its authority as a public institution;

that is, by projecting itself as a guardian of language which promotes the use of 'standard' and 'correct' Korean, and thus as an institution that contributes to the protection and upholding of national values.

But the changing conditions of Korean society present challenges for the authority of the institution of television. Globalization heightens Koreans' familiarity with other languages, particularly the global language of English, with foreign loanwords and code-mixing penetrating Koreans' language use. New, mediated modes of communication such as online interaction and text messaging also introduce new conventions of using the Korean language. These changes clearly highlight – and make salient – the artifice of the imagined purity of Korean as promoted through linguistic nationalism. In this context, the vision of a unified and pure language may appear increasingly outdated, and the institution of television, which depends on such imagination for its authority, may face greater risk of being seen as a backward, patronizing institution, which in turn can potentially have a negative impact on ratings due to viewers who are accustomed to on-demand content from new-media channels such as cable television and the internet.

This poses a dilemma for Korean broadcasters given that the material constraints of broadcasting companies require that they must compete within a market, thereby pressing them to focus more on entertainment programmes with higher viewer ratings. In the Korean television market, the three broadcasting companies each occupy a distinct position with respect to its public and financial status. KBS is a public broadcasting company which relies mostly on television licence fees and government funds; MBC is another public broadcaster, though unlike KBS, it derives its funding almost entirely from commercial advertising. In contrast, SBS is a privately-owned corporation. While this configuration is meant to provide a system that ensures public interest and prevents total commercialization of broadcasting, it nonetheless leads to competition among the companies and the need to appeal to viewers through entertainment-oriented content. Being relatively free from the responsibility to pursue public interest content, SBS invests heavily in income-generating programmes with high entertainment value to overcome its lack of government support, but this leads the other broadcasters to see their public status as a restriction in creative licence and to attempt to secure their share in more commercial content (Jeong 2002). In other words, competition for ratings is a highly important matter for all three companies despite the structural separation of public and privately-owned television.

This means that Korean television companies must pursue entertainment value and make connections with notions of hybridity and popularity, and that essentialist conceptions of the Korean language

64

may be in conflict with this need – and this may be one possible reason why SBS, the most entertainment-oriented broadcaster, cancelled its prescriptive language programme in 2005. However, Korean broadcasters cannot simply abandon the linguistic essentialism and purism that define Korean linguistic nationalism. This is not only because they serve as an important basis for their authority, as we discussed above, but also because viewers in fact expect the broadcasters to serve the role as guardians of language and are strongly critical of possible deviations from standard language use that appear on television. For instance, uses of foreign loanwords and slang in the language of broadcasting (e.g. in the form of English-mixed programme titles; Lim 2004) receive much criticism from the viewing public. In other words, Korean broadcasters find themselves in a complicated dilemma; they must open themselves up to hybridity and transculturation in order to connect with audiences living in the modern age, but they must also maintain their image as an authoritative institution that represents the legitimacy of the national language.

Thus, the Korean situation is a good illustration of the tensions that national media face in the context of globalization, and understanding how Korean broadcasters deal with such a dilemma can present us with some clues regarding the ways in which local institutions of authority may work to re-signify and reformulate older semiotics of nationalism in order to adapt to changing conditions of modernity. In this regard, it is interesting to note that there have recently been several popular game shows with the Korean language as their subject matter. Quite strikingly, these shows take an explicit stance of viewing language as a fundamental basis for national identity, appealing to sentiments of an imagined community to engage the viewers and promoting the legitimized standard language. How do these programmes fit within the broader picture of the current Korean situation, and what do they imply for a re-imagination of linguistic nationalism? In the rest of this chapter, I present an analysis of two of these language-related game shows, *Ulimal Gyeolugi* and *Sangsang Plus*, based on 20 episodes of each show that aired between November 2006 and April 2007, in order to understand to what extent these programmes effectively balance the dual pressures towards linguistic nationalism on the one hand and towards hybridity and entertainment on the other, and what this implies for the construction of television as an institution of authority more generally.

4.3 Rearticulating authority: *Ulimal Gyeolugi*

The first programme I discuss is *Ulimal Gyeolugi* (henceforth UG), whose title can roughly be translated as 'Our Language Competition', a

65

show that airs on KBS1, a KBS channel that specializes in news, educational and cultural content. *Ulimal Gyeolugi* is a traditional quiz show. In each week's episode there are five contestants, who compete with each other to gain greater points; the top contestant then answers an additional set of five questions which determines the final prize money to be won. What makes this show different from other shows is that it quizzes the contestants on their knowledge of the Korean language. The specific content of the questions on UG underlines how the programme highlights not simply the generic Korean language per se but a specific institutionalized variety of Korean. Although some questions rely on cognitive-linguistic skills (e.g. guessing a word based on syllable-initial sounds of a word, identifying a superordinate term for a group of lower-level terms, etc.), most questions test highly specific prescriptive knowledge of the Korean language, many aspects of which are codified by the national language academy, The National Institute of the Korean Language (NIKL: *Guklip Gukeowon*) which itself comes under the Ministry of Culture and Tourism.

A selection of these questions is listed in Table 4.1. For instance, question (a) asks the contestant to identify whether the given expression is part of the 'standard language' (*pyojuneo*) as opposed to a 'dialect' (*satuli*), a distinction which ultimately boils down to whether the item has been codified in dictionaries as legitimate or not. Question (b) asks whether an expression is 'correct', which in this case is defined through a highly specific logic that problematizes semantic redundancy – even though the expression in question is frequently used in everyday contexts. Question (c) is essentially a question regarding correct orthographic representation of the phrase meaning 'welcome' as prescribed in official regulations on orthography (*majchumbeop*) given that either representation could be pronounced in the same way. Finally, (d) distinguishes 'pure Korean expressions' (*sun ulimal*) from Sino-Korean expressions, which are often considered to derive from Chinese and can be expressed with Chinese characters, and from loanwords from other languages. This highlights how UG displays very strong continuity with prescriptive language programmes, as it is precisely this type of knowledge that is the subject matter of those shows.

UG has in fact a close relationship with NIKL. NIKL researches language policy issues relating to the Korean language, proposing regulations on such matters as the standardization of orthography and lexicon together with the representation of foreign words, and is thus the official authority on the Korean language. The connection between NIKL and UG is indicated, for instance, on UG's accompanying website.[2] This website not only provides information regarding the show, but also presents itself as a portal for information on the Korean language

Table 4.1 Examples of questions on *Ulimal Gyeolugi*

Question	Answer and explanation	*Source*
(a) Is *gudakdali* ('an outdated person') standard language?	Yes: it is part of the standard lexicon	episode 156 (12 March 2007)
(b) Is *jamuneul guhada* ('ask for advice') a correct expression?	No: *jamun* already means 'ask for advice', so the verb *guhada* 'to ask for' is redundant	episode 156 (12 March 2007)
(c) Which of the following is incorrect: *eoseo osipsiyo* ('welcome') or *eoseo osipsio* ('welcome')?	*eoseo osipsiyo* is incorrect	episode 159 (9 April 2007)
(d) Is *yudoliga issda* ('to be flexible') a pure Korean expression?	No: *yudoli* comes from Japanese	episode 148 (15 Jan 2007)

more generally. Thus, one of the prominent links titled 'Korean language information search' (*gukeo jeongbo geomsaek*) takes the viewer to the online version of the Standard Korean Dictionary (SKD: *Pyojun Gukeo Daesajeon*) on the NIKL's own website[3]. This dictionary is a major work on Korean compiled and published by NIKL, which is the only dictionary based on the official regulations of standard Korean as established by NIKL, and is thus by definition an official, authoritative source on 'correct' language use. The SKD in fact plays an important role in the show itself. For instance, some questions ask the contestants to demonstrate their knowledge of a word by filling in the blanks of a definition provided on screen. In such cases, those definitions are always taken verbatim from the SKD, so the contestant must provide the definition exactly as it is worded in the dictionary – and answers that reasonably approximate the meaning of the word but do not match SKD's definition are not accepted.

But it is not the case that UG only passively recognizes the authority of NIKL; it actively uses the information provided by NIKL to construct its own authority. For example, definitions of words are never explicitly attributed to NIKL or SKD within the show (while there are hypertext links to NIKL on UG's website, no overt reference is made to NIKL or SKD in the show itself); that is, the voice of NIKL and the voice of the institution are merged, as it were, so that the legitimate knowledge emanating from NIKL is presented as being in fact pronounced by the institution of television (Bakhtin 1981; Briggs and Bauman 1992).

In this way, television constructs itself as an institution with the authority to guide, correct, and comment on the language life of ordinary citizens, rather than as a mere conveyor of legitimate knowledge sourced from elsewhere.

Another important mediating link in this process of authorization is the host of UG, Han Seokjun. In UG, the host is a central character who produces the questions and also gives the verdict on whether a contestant's answer is right or wrong. In carrying out such tasks, the host contributes to the grounding of the media institution's authority by serving as an embodiment of legitimate knowledge. While the regulations for standard Korean put forth by NIKL take the form of impersonal (and perhaps impenetrable) guidelines and lists of acceptable forms, prescriptive knowledge explained through the mouth of UG's host speaks directly to the viewers – thus making it more approachable, reasonable, and natural. Therefore, the host serves as a visible index that connects the authority of standard language with the institution of television, for he is seen as the representative of that institution, a human face that narrates the flow of the show and instructs the viewers in the correct way of using the Korean language.

But in the case of UG, the host also plays a crucial role in re-framing the semiotics of linguistic nationalism, since the host, Han Seokjun, is one of the most popular male announcers on KBS. On Korean television, announcers are professionally trained speakers who work as news readers, emcees, or programme narrators. As is the case in other contexts, they are considered to have great skills in diction, memory, poise, and also be highly unflappable and extemporaneous, capable of smoothly hosting events and dealing with live broadcasts. In the spe-cific case of Korea, however, they are also assumed to be highly skilled in the Korean language, able to know the correct way of speaking the language, and to speak it with good and clear pronunciation. In fact, this is an important part of announcers' identity construction. Announcers overtly present themselves as guardians of the Korean language and are perceived by the public as such. For instance, KBS announcers form an organization called the 'Korean Language Research Group' (*Hangukeo Yeonguhoe*), which actively engages in the promotion of the Korean language; a guidebook that introduces the craft of announcing to future announcers published by this group devotes many pages to explaining the standard pronunciation of Korean (KBS Hangukeo Yeonguhoe 2005). And this is part of the reason why Han's presence on UG contributes to the authorization of the institution of television.

But another important aspect of announcers' identities is the fact that many of them have recently gained the status of highly popular media celebrities. While the hosting of entertainment programmes had traditionally been a role reserved for celebrity entertainers (who may have originally been comedians, singers, or actors), from 2005 KBS started to use their announcers to host entertainment shows. Reportedly, this was initially a measure to save on production costs (because they are employees of the broadcasting company, the casting of announcers does not require a separate contract), but this had the unforeseen effect of transforming announcers into top stars (Seo 2006). Many of the young announcers were talented and good looking and, due to their previous training as announcers, already had a positive image of being intelligent and articulate; for this reason, many of them became instant stars with broadcasting companies attempting to bank on their popularity by placing them as hosts of entertainment shows in addition to those programmes that have been their traditional domain such as the news.

Han Seokjun is one of these popular young announcers. Born in 1975, he started to work with KBS in 2003, hosting various entertainment shows and documentaries, winning an award given to the most successful new television presenter in 2007. Han's popularity no doubt contributes to the success of UG, for his celebrity status increases the show's appeal to a wider audience. But more importantly, his presence allows UG to frame the show's content as not grounded on older images of linguistic nationalism but on ones that are embraced by the younger, interactive generation; embodied by the popular Han, prescriptive knowledge of Korean can be framed as cool and hip, without sacrificing the linguistic authority it signifies. That is, Han's young and attractive image, combined with his background as an announcer, has much potential for re-framing the institution's authority in terms of entertainment, making it approachable and appealing to an audience with great awareness of the hybridity of contemporary culture, and it is this image of Han that is foregrounded in UG. To be sure, shows like UG are typically hosted by announcers anyway, as is the case with prescriptive language programmes that were discussed above. But while one's status as an announcer does not re-frame traditional modes of linguistic nationalism in itself, Han's position as a top celebrity does indeed allow UG to present itself as a show with greater mass appeal, and thus manages to convey the message of linguistic nationalism in a more entertainment-based frame.

This is not the only context where celebrity presenters play important roles in shaping the audience's conception of language. Helen Kelly-Holmes and David Atkinson (2007), for example, discuss how the popular Irish television presenter Hector Ó hEochagáin has been a major influence in changing the younger generation's attitudes towards Irish. As a non-native speaker of Irish who adopts frequent codemixing with English in his speech, Ó hEochagáin has been able to popularize the language among audiences who do not feel so competent in Irish and thus may have felt distanced from the Irish-language media. In cultural contexts where consumption and circulation of information on, and images of, celebrities have become a central element of popular culture (Turner *et al* 2000), the power of celebrities to draw and mobilize the interest of potential audiences is clearly a key to transforming or reinforcing the perception of language varieties.

In the case of UG, of course, the celebrity status of Han works to give a renewed sense of attractiveness to the hegemonic standard variety of Korean, and this is ideologically the reverse of the Irish case where celebrity provides some sense of legitimacy to varieties that were previously considered impure and socially inappropriate. This means, then, that despite the image of celebrity employed in the show, UG does not actually incorporate any element of the hybridity of contemporary Koreans' linguistic life in its representation of the Korean language. Instead, the merging of entertainment with linguistic nationalism is done without any sacrificing of the authority of the institution. Han still embodies the traditional authority of the media through his knowledge and skills as a professional announcer, and the prescriptive rules for standard Korean that he communicates to the viewers remain as rigid as ever. Thus we can argue that linguistic nationalism is not compromised in UG, but is in fact strongly maintained. While there is engagement with popular entertainment, there is no relaxation of the strict assumptions of linguistic essentialism and linguistic purism – and no opening up of the institution's authority that is grounded in linguistic nationalism. In the next show to be discussed, by contrast, hybridity and diversity in language use are given much more room.

4.4 Experiments with hybridity: *Sangsang Plus*

Sangsang Plus ('Imagination Plus' – henceforth SP) is another show on KBS which has enjoyed great popularity since its debut in November 2004. The show itself is composed of several smaller segments, but the segment for which it has become best-known is *Sedae Gonggam Old and New* (SGON), which can roughly be translated as 'empathy of generations old and new'. In this segment, which aired from 2005 to 2007, celebrity entertainers would engage in a game whose objective was to identify a Korean word based on several clues given by an announcer. The segment was widely perceived as contributing to viewers' knowledge of the Korean language, and in this sense is comparable to UG.

However, UG and SP are also different in many ways. To begin with, unlike UG, which aims for entertainment value but is nonetheless classified by KBS as a 'cultural programme' (*gyoyang peulogeulaem*), SP is considered an 'entertainment programme' (*yeonye olak peulogeulaem*) and is aired on KBS2, the company's entertainment channel. This difference is also reflected in the shows' cast. In contrast to UG, in which lay people participate as contestants and Han Seokjun is the sole host, SP's cast is composed predominantly of celebrity entertainers. In SP, four male comedians present the show, along with a female announcer, and they chat and gossip with weekly celebrity guests (a defining feature of many Korean entertainment shows) as well as engaging in games together. In other words, SP explicitly orients towards entertainment, while UG pursues entertainment with a greater emphasis on information.

But SP is also different from UG in that there is greater openness towards non-authorized forms of language. From its inception, SP explicitly aimed to incorporate aspects of culture associated with younger people in order to be able to connect with potential youth audiences. So, for instance, realizing that the younger generation relied heavily on communication through new media, SP adopted a format that would allow viewers to participate in the programme through the internet. In this way, viewers could ask questions to celebrity guests and send in photos they found on the internet that resembled the celebrities, which in turn formed a central element of the show.

Another way in which SP tried to incorporate the perspective of younger audiences was by focusing on the linguistic differences between the younger and older generations. The assumption here was that inter-generational communication was becoming more and more difficult, with the younger generation developing a new language through electronic communication, and words associated with traditional culture losing currency (Oh 2005; see also Thurlow 2007, on English youth language and new media). SP attempted to address this issue through SGON, which later evolved to become the main event and the defining segment of SP until the format was abandoned in late 2007. In this part of the show, a 'word of the week' was selected, which was either a 'teenagers' word' (that is, a neologism typically used by teens) or an 'adults' word' (that is, a traditional word with which teenagers are unfamiliar). The objective of the game was to figure out what this word is, based on a series of clues given by the announcer (who was always female, in contrast to the hosts, who were all male). This premise is most succinctly expressed in the comment that the announcer would make at the end of every episode: 'Until the 48 million Koreans can talk to each other freely, *Sedae Gonggam Old and New* will go on. *Sedae Gonggam Old and New*'.

This shows that, instead of being equated with deviant forms of language, the language of the younger generation was given an official space for representation in SP. While prescriptive language programmes and shows like UG condemned or ignored such language, SP treated them as being merely different rather than illegitimate, a rare instance in which public media endowed such varieties with formal recognition (cf. Moschonas and Spitzmüller, Chapter 2, this volume). In this sense, SP can be seen as embracing more openness towards linguistic creativity and hybridity, rather than insisting on an essentialist view of language and identity. This openness is reflected in the title of the show and of the segment SGON, which are combinations of Sino-Korean words (*sangsang* – 'imagination', *sedae* – 'generation' and *gonggam* – 'empathy') and English ones (*plus, old and new*); while such language-mixing is common in other entertainment programmes (Lim 2004), the difference between the titles of SP and UG (the latter of which is in 'pure' Korean, excluding even Sino-Korean words) illustrates the contrasting stances of the two shows towards hybridity and creativity in language use.

This contrast in stance between the two shows is in part a reflection of their difference in genre (i.e., cultural vs. entertainment programme). Alexandra Jaffe (2007) notes in her study of prescriptivism in the Corsican broadcast media that Corsican programmes would be subject to different pressures towards linguistic purism depending on their degree of formality. Thus, the news, as a highly formal genre, was delivered with visible effort to minimize the influence of French through novel adoptions of loan translations and neologisms, while more informal programmes such as radio call-in shows demonstrated considerable tolerance towards codeswitching and language mixing. Likewise, due to its status as a show that is explicitly oriented toward entertainment, SP is subject to less pressure to adhere to a stricter sense of prescriptivism in the form of linguistic purism.

At the same time, however, important differences from the Corsican situation should also be noted. In contrast to the informal genres of Corsican broadcasting, which aimed to capture and represent the shifting relations between dominant language ideologies and affective dimensions of local linguistic practices by emulating the 'language of the street', the embracement of hybridity in SP had more apparent limits. This can be seen from several facts. First, 'teenagers' words' and 'adults' words' were not given equal coverage in SP. In more than 80 episodes of SGON, the ones that dealt with 'teenagers' words' were fewer than a dozen (many of which were clippings such as *yeolgong*, derived from *yeolsimhi gongbuhada*, that is, 'study hard', or *dochwal*, that is, 'surreptitious video recording', from *doduk* –'thief' and *chwalyeong* –'video recording') with most of them concentrated in earlier episodes aired in 2005. Of course there is a practical reason for this bias; it is simply more difficult to produce episodes based on 'teenagers' words' – there are relatively few neologisms with established meaning that are not already widely known, while it is easy to look up a less-known traditional word in a dictionary.

But it may be argued that it is not just these practical constraints that lead to this bias. For instance, the show was still based upon a strong essentialist view of the Korean language, as evidenced by the fact that it drew heavily upon various imageries of traditional Korean culture. The show's set uses a motif from traditional Korean architecture whereby the stage resembles an open area of a traditional Korean house with the hosts and announcer sitting on the floor with their legs crossed in front of a small tea table (see Figure 4.1). The signature tune that opens the show is reminiscent of traditional Korean music, and the male hosts and the guests (but not the female announcer) all wear the same shirt, the printed design of which is based on traditional Hangeul orthography (itself often used as an iconic image that represents Koreans' pride in their language). When the show begins, the hosts and the announcer also exchange deep bows, an act that is marked as quite traditional by today's standards. Finally, the hosts and guests all use what may be called a 'mock courtly register', modeled on the language of historical television dramas; for example, they use older terms of address such as *daegam* or *manim* (roughly 'sir' and 'ma'am') and speak in a marked intonation contour. All of this clearly index traditional Korean culture, giving the impression that the Korean language – the subject matter of the show – is really the version of the language that is associated with this tradition. In effect, then, it is implied that newer forms of language, which are commonly *not* associated with traditional Korean culture, are not really part of the Korean language. In fact, given the premise of SGON, which claims that the languages of the younger and older generations are becoming increasingly divergent, the equation of the older generation's language with a Korean essence treats the younger generation's language as maximally removed from that essence. In other words, despite apparent attempts to acknowledge and incorporate the internet culture and new varieties of language, traditional linguistic purism and essentialism serve as dominant ideological underpinnings for SP, just as was the case in UG.

SP also bears great similarity to UG in the way that it deploys the knowledge and skills of the announcer as a resource for constructing linguistic authority.[4] Among the predominantly male cast, the female announcer in SP often plays a noticeably gendered role; for instance, the hosts and guests frequently comment on, or tease her about, her appearance. But at the same time, the announcer also plays a highly authoritative role insofar as she is the only person within the cast

Figure 4.1 The set of *Sangsang Plus* (see colour plate section)

who knows the answer as well as controlling the distribution of clues. In addition, the announcer does not merely police the flow of the show. As is expected from her status as an announcer, she is also constructed as a language expert, embodying all proper knowledge of the Korean language. So, for example, while chatting with each other, the male hosts occasionally ask the announcer whether something they just said is 'correct', to which she always provides an answer. In fact, the announcer's gendered positioning and her status as language expert are deliberately brought together at several junctures of the show. In a striking example, when the hosts and guests make a guess at the word of the week, they must whisper it into the announcer's ear using a large red cone, upon which the announcer will announce whether they are right or wrong; if they are wrong, she hits them on the head with the cone and says *gongbuhaseyo* ('go study!') – an expression that became a widely circulated catchphrase. Apparently borrowed from a stereotypical scene between a female teacher and unruly students, such playful, gendered interactional routines serve as prominent images of the show and contribute to its popularity. At the same time, they also clearly symbolize the authority that the show attributes to the female announcer as a language expert.

Thus again, as in UG, the framing of the announcer as authoritative guardian of language reproduces the authority of the standard Korean language. Linguistic knowledge as presented by the announcer is not framed as contestable knowledge, or knowledge that comes from a particular position, despite its discursively constructed origins. Instead, such knowledge is presented as the 'correct' way of using Korean, and prescriptive rules for the use of the language become naturalized, uncontestable knowledge that viewers should heed and follow. In other words, as in UG, the announcer embodies the authority of institutionalized language, imbuing the show with a sense of institutional authority. Against this backdrop, SP's acknowledgement of hybridity and creativity in language use and its playful gendering of the announcer's role have only limited power to subvert linguistic nationalism. Despite being incorporated in the show, such elements are treated as residing outside the domain of pure Korean language, as images of traditional Korean culture employed in the show remind the viewers that true Korean language derives from the 'words of the older generation'. While SP departs in certain ways from the reiteration of traditional linguistic nationalism apparent in UG, it nonetheless maintains and reproduces essentialist views of linguistic nationalism.

4.5 Conclusion

To return to the question of how the tension between globalization and nationalism is addressed by media institutions, we can see how the two shows discussed in this chapter employ a range of strategies to present linguistic nationalism as attractive and relevant by placing it within the context of entertainment – but that the fundamental assumptions of essentialism and purism are largely left unrevised. Thus, even though there is greater openness towards what constitutes 'pure' Korean language in the case of SP, the boundary of legitimate language remains intact, rather than being opened up towards alternative language ideologies.

That the institution of television continues to defend the integrity of the standard Korean language is not surprising, given our discussion above of the importance of linguistic authority in constructing the legitimacy of national media. Thus, strategies on the two shows focus on highlighting the entertainment value of the shows rather than negotiating the authority of the Korean language. The deployment of famous announcers as central figures, a major component of both shows' strategies, is perhaps a natural choice in this regard. Foregrounding the star power of popular announcers and their linguistic capital – a strategy comparable to commodification of linguistic skills in other domains (Heller 2003; Cameron 2005) – allows the media institution to make the authority of legitimate language work for their own particular material goals. The announcer, who, due to the peculiarities of the current Korean media market, simultaneously embodies linguistic authority *and* contemporary celebrity culture, is indeed a perfect link that can

75

resolve the Korean broadcasters' dilemma – a link that those companies do not fail to exploit.

This, of course, does not mean that linguistic nationalism cannot be challenged, but it also shows us that it does not necessarily become any less stable under the new conditions of media production and consumption. In a sense, as the politics of identity becomes more salient in the context of globalization, there are not only many possible ways in which media institutions may protect their link to legitimate language, but also very good reasons why preserving such links would further support their authority (see also Paffey, Chapter 3; Blackledge, Chapter 8; and Androutsopoulos, Chapter 10, this volume). In the Korean context, where globalization is not necessarily seen as being at odds with national identity, but as a new arena in which visions of nationalism may potentially be realized (Shin 2006), the imagination of a homogeneous national community can still be a useful resource – though it also brings new risks. The two television shows that we observed in this chapter illustrate how institutions of power may continue to find ways to rationalize and naturalize ideologies of linguistic nationalism even in the face of pressures that question those ideologies.

However, the discussion above also shows that such ideologies must be continuously re-constituted and re-articulated into new forms. The current Korean television system manages to popularize linguistic nationalism through the 'celebrification' of presenters and announcers, a strategy that works due to the current conditions that push for competition among broadcasters. But as the trends of popular culture change over time, new ways of articulating linguistic nationalism will have to be sought. And it is through such processes that linguistic nationalism may be supported or challenged (see e.g. Ensslin, Chapter 11, this volume on computer game discourse). For this reason, the maintenance or weakening of linguistic nationalism cannot be taken for granted, or presumed to be a simplistic function of shifts in globalization; it must be recognized as a process that is embedded in the choices and strategies of institutions and individuals as they interact with the material and ideological constraints that surround them.

Notes

1 Transliteration of Korean in this chapter follows the Revised Romanization system. All translations are my own.
2 www.kbs.co.kr/1tv/sisa/woorimal/index.html
3 www.korean.go.kr/06_new/dic/search_input.jsp
4 Three announcers have hosted SP during the run of SGON: No Hyeonjeong, Baek Seungju, and Choi Songhyeon – all of whom are highly popular stars. No Hyeonjeong, in particular, is often credited with igniting the boom in the

popularity of announcers, and SP was the show that solidified her celebrity status.

References

Anderson, B. (1991), *Imagined Communities: Reflections on the Origin and Spread of Nationalism.* London: Verso.

Bakhtin, M. M. (1981), *The Dialogic Imagination: Four Essays.* Austin, TX: University of Texas Press.

Blommaert, J. (1999), 'The debate is open', in J. Blommaert (ed.) *Language Ideological Debates.* Berlin: Mouton de Gruyter, pp. 1–38.

Briggs, C. L., and Bauman, R. (1992), 'Genre, intertextuality, and social power'. *Journal of Linguistic Anthropology*, 2(2), 131–72.

Bucholtz, M. and Hall, K. (2004), 'Language and identity', in A. Duranti (ed.), *A Companion to Linguistic Anthropology.* Malden: Blackwell, pp. 369–94.

Bucholtz, M. and Hall, K. (2005), 'Identity and interaction: a sociocultural linguistic approach'. *Discourse Studies*, 7(4-5), 585–614.

Cameron, D. (2005), 'Communication and commodification: global economic change in sociolinguistic perspective', in G. Erreygers (ed.), *Language, Communication, and the Economy.* Amsterdam: John Benjamins, pp. 9–23.

Gal, S. and Woolard, K. A. (eds) (2001), *Languages and Publics: The Making of Authority.* Manchester: St. Jerome Publishing Ltd.

Ginsburg, F. (1991), 'Indigenous media: Faustian contract or global village?' *Cultural Anthropology*, 6(1), 92–112.

Guillén, M. F. (2001), 'Is globalization civilizing, destructive, or feeble? a critique of five key debates in the social science literature'. *Annual Review of Sociology*, 27, 235–60.

Go, G. (1995), *Uri Sidaeui Eoneo Geim.* Seoul: Todam.

Heller, M. (2003), 'Globalization, the new economy, and the commodification of language and identity'. *Journal of Sociolinguistics*, 7(4), 473–92.

Horner, K. (2007), 'Global challenges to nationalist ideologies: language and education in the Luxembourg press', in S. Johnson and A. Ensslin (eds), *Language in the Media: Representations, Identities, Ideologies.* London: Continuum, pp. 130–46.

Irvine, J. T. and Gal, S. (2000), 'Language ideology and linguistic differentiation', in P. V. Kroskrity (ed.), *Regimes of Language: Ideologies, Polities, and Identities.* Santa Fe, NM: School of American Research Press, pp. 35–83.

Jaffe, A. (2007), 'Corsican on the airwaves: media discourse in a context of minority language shift', in S. Johnson and A. Ensslin (eds), *Language in the Media: Representations, Identities, Ideologies.* London: Continuum, pp. 149–72.

Jeong, J. (2002), *Telebijyeon Bogi: Sicheongeseo Bipyeongeulo.* Seoul: Chaeksesang.

KBS Hangukeo Yeonguhoe. (2005), *Anaunseo Bangsongin Doegi.* Seoul: Hanguk Bangsong Chulpan.

Kelly-Holmes, H. and Atkinson, D. (2007), '"When Hector met Tom Cruise": attitudes to Irish in a radio satire', in S. Johnson and A. Ensslin (eds),

Language in the Media: Representations, Identities, Ideologies. London: Continuum, pp. 173–87.

Kroskrity, P. V. (2004), 'Language ideologies', in A. Duranti (ed.), *A Companion to Linguistic Anthropology*. Malden: Blackwell, pp. 496–517.

Lim, G. (2004), 'Hanguk tellebijyeon bangsongui oelaeeo peulogeulaem ileume daehan eoneohakjeok bunseok', *Hangeul*, 263, 157–88.

Milani, T. M. (2007), 'A language ideology in print: the case of Sweden', in S. Johnson and A. Ensslin (eds), *Language in the Media: Representations, Identities, Ideologies*. London: Continuum, pp. 111–29.

Oh, H. (2005), 'Deunadeulmgwa hwakjangui jinhwa, Sangsang Plus', in Bangsong Munhwa Jinheunghoe (ed.), *2005 Bangsong Munhwa Jinheunghoe Joheun Bangsongeul Wihan Siminui Bipyeongsang Susangjip*. Paju: Hanul, pp. 9–16.

Seo, B. (2006, 14 March), 'Jisangpa 3sa, yeoja anaunseodo maenijimeonteu sidae dolip?' *Heleoldeu Gyeongje*, Retrieved 26 March, 2006 from www.heraldm.com/

Shin, G. (2006), *Ethnic Nationalism in Korea: Genealogy, Politics, and Legacy*. Stanford, CA: Stanford University Press.

Spitulnik, D. (1998), 'Mediating unity and diversity: the production of language ideologies in Zambian broadcasting', in B. B. Schieffelin, K. A. Woolard and P. V. Kroskrity (eds), *Language Ideologies: Practice and Theory*. Oxford: Oxford University Press, pp. 163–88.

Thurlow, C. (2007), 'Fabricating youth: new-media discourse and the technologization of young people', in S. Johnson and A. Ensslin (eds), *Language in the Media: Representations, Identities, Ideologies*. London: Continuum, pp. 213–33.

Tomlinson, J. (2003), 'Globalization and cultural identity', in D. Held and A. McGrew (eds), *The Global Transformations Reader: An Introduction to the Globalization Debate* (2nd edition). Cambridge: Polity Press, pp. 269–77.

Turner, G., Bonner, F. and Marshall, P. D. (2000), *Fame Games: The Production of Celebrity in Australia*. Cambridge: Cambridge University Press.

Urla, J. (2001), 'Outlaw language: creating alternative public spheres in Basque free radio', in S. Gal and K. A. Woolard (eds), *Languages and Publics: The Making of Authority*. Manchester: St. Jerome Publishing Ltd., pp. 141–63.

PART II

PLANNING AND POLICY IN MEDIA PROGRAMMING

5 *Planeta Brasil*: language practices and the construction of space on Brazilian TV abroad[1]

Iris Bachmann

5.1 Introduction

Planeta Brasil is a television show directed at the Brazilian diaspora that is broadcast on the international satellite channel of Brazil's largest television network, TV Globo. While *telenovelas* have long been a successful Brazilian media export product, shows like *Planeta Brasil* represent a relatively recent phenomenon in the transnational programming of so-called ethnic channels that offer 'global narrowcasting' (Sinclair and Cunningham 2000) to niche audiences, in this case, Brazilians living abroad. The programmatic title *Planeta Brasil* seems to suggest that Brazil can be anywhere on the planet as long as you have Brazilians there – or, of course, simply access to TV Globo. Ethnic channels are thus part and parcel of the transnational media flows that characterize globalization. In view of the ever increasing numbers of migrants, this international narrowcasting connects such people in new ways to the wider mediascape (Appadurai 1996) of their 'home' country, while such channels claim at the same time to cater specifically to their needs as *emigrants* via shows such as *Planeta Brasil*.[2] Departing from James Collins and Stef Slembrouck's claim (2005: 191) that 'language use contributes to the production of space', I explore in this chapter the architecture of space created by language practices on ethnic channels and ask a number of questions. How does the diasporic space appear in these channels? How does it relate to respective national spaces, and what are the contours of those spaces? How are language varieties used to structure these spaces and how does such usage relate to dominant language ideologies in the countries between which the media flows are channelled? I am particularly interested in analysing how multilingualism – an everyday experience for migrants but one that is rarely on display on television – appears on two programmes that specifically address the Brazilian diaspora community. I will argue that while these language practices initially appear to conform to monolingual language

81

ideologies, a closer inspection reveals that they do in fact give a glimpse of the multilingual reality of Brazilians abroad. However, the language practices on display on the two shows construe different spatial and linguistic practices of belonging, which situate them in different frames of reference with respect to language norms.

5.2 Language, space and media

The image of 'flows' has become almost emblematic for processes of globalization and media products have played a prominent role in the description of the transnational flows of people and goods (García Canclini 1999). The concept of flows is also interesting in that it indicates their uneven spread across the globe, a phenomenon that is nicely illustrated by advertisements on Brazilian satellite TV in the US for products catering to the prime audience of those channels, namely Brazilians living in that country. Here there are a number of advertisements, for example, for money remittances, that visualize the streams of dollars indicated by arrows originating from places in the US such as Miami, New York, Boston with sizable Brazilian populations to the southeast of Brazil where the bulk of the migrants originate (cf. Amaral and Fusco 2005). Arjun Appadurai (1996) has fittingly described such flows as different 'scapes' as in the sense of 'ethnoscape' or 'mediascape', thus indicating their structured nature. In addition to the aspect of selective distribution of flows, Appadurai's metaphor of scapes introduces an 'imaginary' aspect in relation to 'constructed' landscapes as opposed to a natural, physical environment in order to point out human actions as vital to the processes of globalization. Similarly, we can think of the circulation of language – be it via media or through the dislocation of speakers – as flows of language varieties, textual genres and linguistic repertoires that create structured spaces of communicative practices, where these varieties are being re-evaluated in new contexts and thus acquire different currencies (Blommaert 2005).

While there is now a small body of research on the global flow of mass-market media products and their different local contextualization such as Latin American *telenovelas* (Martín-Barbero 2002) or women's magazines such as Cosmopolitan (Machin and van Leeuwen 2003), rather less attention has so far been directed at the phenomenon of ethnic channels (but see Sinclair and Cunningham 2000). Moreover, whereas global mass-market media products such as *telenovelas* reach for the widest possible audience and overcome language barriers by dubbing or subtitling, ethnic channels use new technologies to bring media products to globally dispersed niche audiences with language typically constituting their unique selling point in a highly segmented

TV market. In this context, Arlene Dávila (2000), for example, analyses
how TV networks directed at Latinos in the US tend to present themselves as guardians of the Spanish language and thus make little attempt
to depict the often multilingual reality of their target audience.[3] She
argues that marketability is the biggest driving force behind these monolingual language policies since they allow for a clear delineation of
'Hispanic' as an undivided, significant market segment (see also Paffey,
Chapter 3, this volume). This is reminiscent of Monica Heller's (2003)
notion of the commodification of language and identity in the new
global economy whereby language practices are also linked to struggles
over who gets to define what counts as an authentic product – in this
case Spanish-language TV in the US – in order to secure privileged
access to audiences within highly competitive markets. However, Heller
(2003: 475) also notes the paradox that while language-related services
and products in the new economy typically build on notions of authenticity related to essentialized concepts of ethnonationalism, the market
ultimately requires inauthentic processes of standardization in order to
create a recognizable product, itself a prime example of Allan Bell's
(1984) notion of 'audience design' whereby radio and TV programmes
streamline their language practices according to the targeted audience.

5.3 Ethnic channels, diaspora populations and monolingual language ideologies

The research to be discussed in this chapter was undertaken during
a period spent at New York University, which is why the data to be
discussed was all collected from US television. When trying to order
Brazilian satellite TV from within the US, I was confronted with the
marketing strategies of ethnic channels as distributed by a local provider. According to this logic, 'language' determines access and thus
Brazilian and Portuguese channels were marketed under the same
rubric of 'Portuguese language channels'. On offer were the Brazilian
channels TV Globo Internacional, Record Internacional, RBTI (*Rede
Brasileira de Televisão Internacional*) and PFC (*Premiere Futebol
Clube*), a Globo channel for Brazilian football. In addition, one could
access three Portuguese channels: the international channel of the public network RTP and the private SPT (part of the SIC network) as well
as the more recent addition of SIC News, a 24-hour news channel.[4]

These channels are enmeshed in a whole set of spatial relations, not
least that of creating their own communicative space (Hofmann 2006).
The international channels of the two major Brazilian networks, Globo
and Record, transmit their programmes to countries and regions with
sizable Brazilian populations such as the US, Western Europe and Japan,

but they are also established in other lusophone countries such as Angola, Mozambique and Portugal. They broadcast a selection of their Brazilian programmes and in that sense try to replicate national Brazilian TV. However, due to licensing conflicts in the US and other countries of transmission these channels have to omit parts of the national broadcasting output such as international sports programmes or US movies. Ironically, it is this very process that makes these international channels more 'national' in that all the programmes shown are produced in Brazil. An exception is RBTI, which has a more mixed output consisting of low-budget community TV productions, dubbed US movies and shows bought from Brazilian TV networks such as Gazeta. However, all three Brazilian channels have programmes that are specifically produced for the satellite channels that transmit abroad.

After a period of ethnographic study of the programmes available, I chose to focus on two shows which deal directly with the life of Brazilians abroad: the personal interest show *Planeta Brasil* (TV Globo) and the legal advice programme *América Legal* (RBTI).[5] Given that the Portuguese language is of utmost importance for the design of these channels, I will analyse extracts from the two shows to see if and how they deal with multilingualism, an everyday reality for migrants. I will then look at how the language practices on display in these shows construe spatial frames that situate them within value systems that contribute to their subsequent interpretation. Here I will be drawing on Jan Blommaert's (2005: 102) distinction between macro-level orders of discourse, which he calls 'regimes of language' following Paul Kroskrity (2000) and the notion of indexicality and indexical orders. The latter refer to the embedding of language variation at the micro-level in the social norms and values that are themselves invoked by linguistic differences over and above the denotational level of an utterance.

In this chapter, I will also discuss the importance of *monolingualism* as a language regime in Brazil as a background against which the analysis of alternative strategies on diaspora programmes will gain a sharper profile. For example, Gladis Massini-Cagliari (2004: 3) identifies as a myth the widespread belief 'that the Portuguese language in Brazil is characterized by an astonishing unity'. According to Ana Maria Zilles (2001: 150), this belief neglects the existence of 180 indigenous languages (from around 1,500 existing prior to Portuguese colonization in the sixteenth century) as well as the languages of immigrants and the Spanish that is spoken in many border regions. Moreover, Zilles (2001: 152) points out how such apparent unity is in fact a euphemism for what was not a Pentecostal miracle but an imposition enforced by legal instruments beginning with a law issued by the Marquês de Pombal in 1757. This law declared Portuguese to be the official language and prohibited the use of the widespread 'língua geral' (*general language*), a Tupi variety spoken along the coastline. But despite such monolingual policies, the nineteenth century and first half of the twentieth century continued to see an influx of people speaking different languages. Once again, therefore, the twentieth century witnessed the introduction of further legislation aimed at curbing the use of migrant languages during the authoritarian New State (1937–45) under Gétulio Vargas, whereby the use of the native languages of the numerous European immigrants, particularly Italian and German, was prohibited in conjunction with the take-over of their schools (Massini-Cagliari 2004: 12–13). Here Zilles (2001: 153) notes the waves of immigrants beginning in 1820 and the most intense phase of the slave trade between 1830 and 1850. Combined with a high degree of illiteracy (around 85% at the beginning of the twentieth century – ibid.: 154), this situation points to a further linguistic divide still pertaining today and thus continuing to under-mine the myth of unity, namely that between educated and uneducated speakers, the latter often unable to read or write and hence with little access to the standard language. Marcos Bagno (2000) in fact character-izes the Brazilian situation as one where a written standard largely based on European Portuguese is very far removed from even the edu-cated norm, which makes the task of teaching the written standard very difficult and leads to widespread linguistic prejudice.

At first glance, monolingualism appears to predominate on television, with programming almost exclusively in Portuguese. Massini-Cagliari (2004: 4) points towards economic reasons for this, given that the other languages are spoken by marginalized minorities, and furthermore presupposes an ideological embrace of linguistic homogeneity on the part of the media. While it is certainly true that some high-profile shows such as the evening news (*Jornal Nacional*) on TV Globo have been characterized by the presenters' deliberate use of a variety of Portuguese that is more neutral with respect to salient features of the two major urban norms from Rio de Janeiro and São Paulo (Massini-Cagliari 2004: 5),[6] even a cursory look at TV broadcasting in Brazil reveals that programming is far from homogeneous. On the one hand, TV Globo and other major channels have undergone a process of region-alization by setting up and entering into cooperation with local net-works (Brittos and Bolaño 2005: 234–38). On the other hand, different programmes exhibit a variety of linguistic styles and registers depend-ing on format and targeted audience (Bell 1984; Hofmann 2006). Finally, the end of Globo's quasi monopoly in the free-to-air sector and the introduction of satellite and cable have led to a certain degree of segmen-tation of the national audience. Thus the major Brazilian TV channels may be monolingual but they are not mono-*varietal* and the globalization of media flows has also meant the introduction of foreign language channels to the Brazilian market. Multilingualism on television under these conditions is determined by audiences who have the option to switch channels. This is also true of course for Brazilians abroad who might receive the Portuguese language channels together with, at least, the free-to-air channels of their respective country of residency. The monolingualism of the individual channels is similarly embedded in a variety of language-specific programmes. The question that arises is therefore as follows: do TV abroad break away from 'channelled mono-lingualism' in an attempt to reflect the multilingual experience of migrants or do they tend to follow national programming practices in this regard? In order to explore this question, I now turn to an analysis of the two shows on Brazilian satellite TV in the US, *Planeta Brasil* and *América Legal*.

5.4 *Planeta Brasil*: multilingual practices undercover

Planeta Brasil is an entertainment/news show that deals with the life of Brazilian migrants in various countries. It is produced for TV Globo in the US and hosted by their New York studio. In the shows I recorded between June and September 2007, the programme was presented by the TV journalists César Augusto Gomes and Luciana de Michelli in New York together with the producer, Tanira Lebedeff, who presented episodes from California. The show features a mix between thematic episodes (voluntary work, family abroad, language maintenance, foreign-ers who love Brazil) and country-specific episodes (Argentina, Mexico, Japan). The introduction to the programme stages the international set-ting insofar as we see a globe spinning around (Figure 5.1) displaying well-known landmark buildings ranging from St. Basil's cathedral in Moscow, the Statue of Liberty in New York, Big Ben in London and the Eiffel Tower in Paris to the Cheops Pyramid in Egypt. Even if the images represent a slightly dated notion of internationalism, the message antic-ipates the headline and title of the programme that is flagged up at the end of the introduction: *Planeta Brasil*. The spinning globe is seen at the end to be embedded in an image that looks like the graphics of the Brazilian flag, thus seemingly implying that the whole world is con-tained in Brazil or that the world is seen through the eyes of Brazilians in this show.

Thus from the beginning *Planeta Brasil* establishes the connection between Brazilian migrants – the protagonists of the show – both with respect to one another and to their Brazilian 'homeland'. The presenters make frequent use of the terms *a nossa comunidade* ('our community')

Figure 5.1 Introductory image from *Planeta Brasil* (see colour plate section)

or *a comunidade brasileira* ('the Brazilian community') and it is people from this transnational community that are shown on the programme. Consequently, Brazilians are generally seen alongside other Brazilians speaking in Portuguese in line with the monolingual pattern of other television programmes. If another language is used on the programme, the tone is often silenced or backgrounded by voice-over. In an episode on voluntary work (7 July 2007), for example, we see an interview with the English-speaking boss of a Brazilian, who volunteers as a fireman in New York. At first, the tone is cut and then voice-over is used to briefly summarize in Portuguese what the volunteer fireman has to say in English. (Interestingly, he is also referred to only as 'Steve' and not by his full name as in the case of the Brazilians.) In another episode, Brazilian voluntary workers in an orphanage in Mexico are seen playing with the Mexican children living there, but conversation is edited so as to become inaudible. The images are seemingly considered to be sufficient to portrait the good deeds of these Brazilian women who care for the orphans. We do not hear how they speak to the children and can only assume that conversation probably takes place in Spanish or Portuguese. The Spanish-speaking woman in charge of the orphanage is interviewed with the aid of Portuguese voice-over and in that case not even her name is mentioned – she is simply referred to as the director of the orphanage.

These examples clearly demonstrate who is at the centre of the show: the Brazilian migrants who are individually singled out by a tag line including their names, location and time of residence abroad. It is interesting to compare these findings to the strategies of incorporating foreign-language use in UK television programmes dealing with travel and lifestyle filmed abroad as identified by Simon Gieve and Julie Norton (2007). These authors describe the mediation of foreign-language usage as a complex three-way interaction that includes the protagonists (hosts, travellers abroad), the foreign-language speakers and the audience, before

87

going on to identify eight editorial strategies for the representation of such encounters that range from the complete omission of linguistic difference to the overt inclusion of foreign-language material under specific conditions. In the Brazilian data mentioned above, such editorial strategies fall primarily into the category of mediated interaction where post-production (voice-over and narrator's summary) are used to introduce foreign-language contributions by speakers other than the protagonists while minimizing the effect of linguistic difference (ibid.: 199–200). The exact pattern in the Brazilian data is, however, slightly more complex. While on the travel shows analysed by Gieve and Norton, the interaction takes place primarily between the traveller-presenter and locals inhabitants, in *Planeta Brasil* we have to distinguish between *four* potential groups: the hosts (Globo reporters), the Brazilians living abroad, other locals from the respective countries of residence, and the target audience. The base language is therefore shared by the hosts and the principal interviewees (i.e. members of the Brazilian diaspora) but foreign-language use is evident in certain interactions between Brazilian migrants and locals in their respective countries of residence. However, since *Planeta Brasil* focuses primarily on interviews with Brazilians abroad undertaken by the show's Brazilian hosts, it necessarily foregrounds Brazilians interacting with *other* Brazilians rather than showing Brazilians abroad in what are likely to be much more mixed-language environments where they deal with speakers from different backgrounds and nationalities. In addition, we never see any direct exchanges between Brazilians (be it the hosts or Brazilians who are interviewed) and speakers of other languages, which is again different from what Gieve and Norton (2007) observe on some of the travel shows they analysed. Having said this, there are still, as I will show in the next section, alternative language practices on display that give a glimpse of the multilingual reality of the Brazilian migrants. These practices fall broadly into the category of *foreigners* (i.e. non-Brazilians) speaking in the main language of the programme, namely Portuguese (ibid.: 197). While Gieve and Norton pay little attention to this strategy in view of the relative lack of linguistic difference it displays, I will argue that this phenomenon nonetheless plays a significant role in the depiction of linguistic difference, and hence the multilingual reality, of Brazilian migrants in both shows analysed in this chapter.

5.4.1 Language maintenance: young Brazilians abroad

One of the multilingual sites depicted in *Planeta Brasil* appears to be the display of language learning, even if the show's overall monolingual bias limits its representation. Thus we find examples of Argentines learning Portuguese in Argentina in order to prepare for jobs offered by Brazilian firms operating in the Mercosul country (*Planeta Brasil*, 19 May 2007). That said, language learning is not introduced as an issue for the young Brazilians who are shown to come to Buenos Aires attracted by the lower cost of studying in Argentina. In fact, the only Brazilians we see in my sample of recordings as learning a language are second-generation Brazilians in the US attending a Portuguese language school in the home of another Brazilian emigrant, who has started the project in order to maintain her daughter's fluency in her first language, which she had been rapidly losing following the move to the US with her family at age 7. The daughter, Bruna, is now 11 years old and explains on the show (*Planeta Brasil*, TV Globo, 23 June 2007) why she likes her Portuguese classes (all translations are my own):

> [tagline: Bruna Carvalho. 11 anos. 4 anos nos EUA] *Eu achei legal porque quando . crescer eu quero fazer . em . eu quero trabalhar com coisa de model . e eu quero falar português porque eu vou morar no Brasil e mandar as coisas pra cá.*

> [Bruna Carvalho. 11 years old. 4 years in the USA] I thought it was cool because when . I get older I want to do . em . I want to work with something like *model* . and I want to speak Portuguese because I will live in Brazil and send things over here.

Bruna comes across as an eloquent young girl who is making plans for a future that includes Brazil. She seems to know quite well what she wants to get out of the Portuguese classes in that she is envisaging a life that takes advantage of her familiarity with both the US and Brazil. In this respect, she seems to embody a theme that runs through the episode about second-generation Brazilians abroad, namely that keeping the language alive is also a way of keeping children in touch with modern Brazilian society. This is the reason for the teacher's emphasis not only on the spoken language but also on teaching her students to read and write in Portuguese, a point that is emphasized visually by showing the children reading out texts in class before being interviewed. The importance of writing is further underscored by references to modern computer communication, which is also frequently shown in other episodes where we see Brazilian migrants communicating with family 'back home' with the help of new-media technologies. Interestingly, this emphasis on writing corresponds to an observation made by Alexandra Jaffe (2007) in her analysis of Corsican media discourse in a situation of minority language shift. Here Jaffe demonstrates how the display of *literacy* in Corsican in a TV programme about a bilingual school is similarly used to lend linguistic authority to the minority language. Given that the Brazilian migrant communities depicted are themselves often living in a context of language shift, the attempt to depict Portuguese as a language of literacy and modern communication technologies seems to serve a similar aim to that described by Jaffe. Moroever, for Globo – as a Portuguese-language TV network – there is of course a vested market interest in keeping the young migrants tuned in to Portuguese and it is not therefore surprising that they present themselves as both advocates of, and a vehicle for, language mainte- nance abroad.[7]

In the same episode of 23 June 2007, we have another example of a young Brazilian called Diego participating in the Portuguese classes, who represents a very different dimension of language maintenance:

> [tagline: Diego Silva. 8 anos. Nasceu nos EUA] *E meu mãe quere eu . vá . no Brasil . . . mas eu . no . sei muito português . . . hm . . eu . . hm . . agora eu vai . no esse aula e . . agora . . eu sei muito português.*

> [Diego Silva. 8 years old. Born in the USA] My mother want I . go . to Brazil . . . but I . don't know much Portuguese . . . hm . . I . . now I go in to this class and . . . now . . I know much Portuguese.

It is almost painful to see Diego struggling on screen to get his sentence across with his clearly limited ability to express himself in Portuguese. He hesitates frequently, his speech displays mismatches of agreement and a lack of preposition-article contraction, and he reverts to a very simple structure of short clauses in order to report on his mother's moti- vation for his learning Portuguese, namely to be able to go to Brazil. With his stuttering speech, he unwittingly represents the popular ste- reotype of the immigrant characterized by an incomplete mastery of the dominant language (Collins and Slembrouck 2005: 192). Seeing Diego struggle with his Portuguese evokes that image of the immigrant as a language learner with all its attendant difficulties, even though Diego is, of course, learning his mother's language as opposed to the language of their adopted country. This episode thus indirectly gives a glimpse of the sometimes precarious multilingual language practices of foreigners with which the audience can be assumed to have a degree of familiarity.

5.4.2 Estrangeiros abrasileirados – the Brazilianized foreigners

Another example that allows us to see through the seemingly smooth veneer of monolingual language practice is that of *foreigners* shown on *Planeta Brasil* and on 30 June 2007, an entire episode was dedicated to the topic of *estrangeiros abrasileirados* ('Brazilianized foreigners'). It is interesting to see how these people are introduced on the show: there is Patricia Leão, a Bolivian married to a Brazilian, and living together in the US. According to the reporter, '*O Berto deve ter o maior orgulho da esposa boliviana de alma brasileiríssima*' ('Berto must be very proud of his Bolivian wife with a super-Brazilian heart') (ibid.). Hal Rubin, meanwhile, a Wall Street banker looking for a job in Rio is said to have a *coração abrasileirado* ('Brazilian heart') and Alexa Burneikis, a Lithuanian-American who practises *Gafieira*, a Brazilian ballroom dance, *renasceu brasileira* ('was born again Brazilian') (ibid.). According to the Globo journalist: '*Não tem Brasil no sangue, mas deve ter na alma*' ('Brazil is not in her blood, but it must surely be in her soul') (ibid.). It is as if the presence of foreigners to whom a whole programme is dedicated must be justified by making them appear quasi-Brazilian, if not by lineage then by choice. In view of the typical structure of the programme, these Brazilianized foreigners take the place of the Brazilians abroad who are usually interviewed and this prominent position (compared to the traditionally backgrounded status of 'locals') is in fact in need of an explanation. What all these foreigners therefore have in common, apart from their affiliation with Brazil, is that they speak Portuguese. In order to have a voice on Brazilian TV and not be voiced-over (as is the case with other locals), they must be capable of conversing in Portuguese. Moreover, throughout the programme, there is a correlation between the fluency of the speakers and their airtime given to them on the show. Thus language clearly indexes the bond with Brazilian culture whilst at the same time reinforcing the monolingual set-up of the show.

I will now take a closer look at one of the interviews with Wall Street banker, Hal Rubin, who talks about his experiences in Brazil on previous trips together with his plans to seek work in Brazil some time in the future. Rubin explains that he had to return to the US after his last prolonged stay on a tourist visa emphasizing that he did '*tudo diretinho com as regras*' ('everything super correct following the rules') (*Planeta Brasil*, TV Globo, 30 June 2007). The Globo journalist makes the obvious connection for the diaspora audience introducing Hal as follows (ibid.):

> [Luciana de Michelli:] *A maioria dos brasileiros quando vem pro exterior, vem pra fazer dinheiro, ter uma vida melhor. Tem um americano que trabalha onde o dinheiro está, aqui em Wall Street, o centro financeiro do mundo. E adivinha para onde ele quer ir?*

> [Luciana de Michelli:] The majority of Brazilians, when they go abroad, come to make money, have a better life. There is an American who works where the money is, here on Wall Street, the world's financial center. And guess where he wants to go?

Hal, with his desire to find a job in Rio, is compared to Brazilians going abroad. But while these emigrants look for a better life and to make more money, Hal's workplace on Wall Street epitomizes financial success. He then gets his say as to why he nonetheless wants to immigrate to Brazil (ibid.):

> [tagline: Hal Rubin executivo, nasceu nos EUA] *Tem muita coisa na vida, tem uma carreira, tem o dinheiro, tem o amor, tem carinho, tem família. E e cada um tem uma ordem dessas coisas. Eu acho que o americano, a ordem está com . completamente diferente. E uma coisa com o dineiro eh . emprego, carreira, tá no topo, entendeu. Mas aqui no Brasil acho que é uma coisa com familia, com carinho, com amor, as coisas mais importantes eu acho. Fica fica no tal ponto lá. Eu a . acho que .. comigo eu ligo mais pra isso. Acho que no Brasil tem balanço de tudo.*

> [Hal Rubin manager, born in the USA] There are many things in life, there is a career, there is money, there is tenderness and love, there is a family. And everyone has their priorities with these things. I think that [for] Americans, the priorities are com . completely different. It's the thing with money, eh . a job, a career, that's on top of the list, you know. But, here in Brazil, I think it's to do with family, with tenderness, with love, the more important things, I think. It stays there at a certain level. I th . think that .. for me I connect better to this. I think that in Brazil everything is more balanced.

Hal is set up to mirror the Brazilian immigrant who is trying to get a visa and find a job, except that he has not tried (and probably never would try) to enter the country illegally contrary to the experience of many Brazilians. Hal echoes the journalist by characterizing the US as a country that values work and money above all other things, a lifestyle he then juxtaposes with a more 'balanced' Brazilian society, which in his view values family and emotional well-being more highly. This juxtaposition of two different sets of values correlates with the images of Hal in the US wearing a suit close to his place of work on Wall Street as opposed to the photos from Brazil, on which he is always seen surrounded by his Brazilian friends in a leisurely atmosphere. Hal Rubin is therefore the foreigner, who is pointing out the *disadvantages* of the supposed golden land of emigrant dreams with its materialistic culture, while at the same time portraying Brazilian values in a favourable light. By showcasing well-off foreigners such as Hal and Alexa with a desire to live in Brazil, TV Globo is therefore signalling to the mostly Brazilian diaspora audience that Brazil is not in fact doing so badly itself in terms of the global popularity scale. Contrary to Gieve and Norton's generalization (2007: 197) about a *lack* of linguistic difference contrasting with the foreignness of the location, we find here instead a complex juxtaposition of images from the Brazilian 'home country' (and foreigners' adopted country) and the US as a destination for Brazilian migration (and foreigners' country of origin). This is then illustrated by the differing levels of linguistic fluency that appear to index the degree of voluntary assimilation of the brazilianized foreigners. Here the audience is implicitly invited to make comparisons with their own situation and degree of assimilation to a US culture that has been painted as materialistic and emotionally somewhat deprived.

5.5 *América Legal:* mediating for the Brazilian immigrant

We now turn to another programme on US satellite TV catering specifically for the Brazilian diaspora community, but one with a markedly different setting and possibly a different target audience to *Planeta Brasil. América Legal* is a legal advice programme linked to an immigration service website called www.guiadoimigrante.com (accessed 20 December 2007), on the home page of which the programme's presenter, Moisés Apsan, is shown in his legal office and some personal and professional background details are provided. Apsan is himself Brazilian and emigrated to the US in 1955 at the age of 7. His family went back to Brazil when he was 12 but quickly returned to the US due to their children's difficulties in re-adapting to the Brazilian school system. Apsan has been active in the Portuguese and Brazilian immigrant community in the US, which is obviously helpful for his business as well. In an interview originally given to the immigrant website MUDABRASIL[8], he insists on the importance of being able to speak the languages of his clients:

> [Moisés Apsan:] *Eu gosto muito de trabalhar com a comunidade brasileira, a cultura que eu entendo. Gosto de trabalhar com brasileiros, espanhóis e portuguese (sic) de Portugal. Eu não gosto de trabalhar com outros países porque eu penso que advogado da imigração tem que falar a língua do país que conhece.*
>
> *Existem muitos advogados que tem uma secretária que faz tradução, eu acho ruim porque se eu não posso falar direitamente com o cliente eu prefiro não pegar o caso.*
>
> [Moisés Apsan:] I very much like to work with the Brazilian community, the culture I understand. I like to work with Brazilians, Spanish, and Portuguese from Portugal. I don't like to work with other countries because I think that an immigration lawyer must speak the language of the country he knows.

> There are many lawyers who have a secretary to do the translating,
> I think that's crap because if I cannot talk to the client directly,
> I prefer not to take on the case.

Once again language is seen as the primary means with which to gain access to certain groups of people, who are in this case also Apsan's potential clients. However, language is not portrayed as a neutral business skill, which can be bought in through a secretary. Indeed, Apsan goes to great lengths to point out that his own ability to speak his clients' languages gives him a more direct access to their culture and therefore putting him in a position to help them more effectively. Interestingly, the group of potential clients to which he claims privileged access is not confined to the 'Brazilian community'. It includes 'Brazilians, Spanish, and Portuguese from Portugal', thus appealing to a transnational Latino community which has become a clearly demarcated market segment in the US (Dávila 2001). Even though Apsan refers to the 'Spanish', however, it is clear from his narrative of growing up in the Bronx and learning Spanish from the 'kids on the block' that he uses the term to refer to US Latinos whose culture he similarly associates with the Portuguese language and whose language – in this case, Spanish – is singled out as the key to access that community and consequently market segment.

Despite the pan-Latino scope of Apsan's law practice, the show *América Legal* aims only at a Portuguese-speaking audience in the US as the respective Brazilian, Portuguese and US flags in the studio set-up make clear. In comparison to *Planeta Brasil* with its interview-based approach, dynamic camera, and many outdoor shots, this programme is a rather static low-budget production. There is only one camera position showing the young female presenter, Cintia Martins, and the older lawyer, Moisés Apsan, sitting behind a desk with shelves filled with law books in the background and the flags in front of them on the table (see Figure 5.2).

The programme invariably revolves around questions from the audience, either transmitted by telephone or read out by the presenter if received by email. Moreover, we also find a number of pertinent topics concerning immigrants' lives taken up by co-presenter Martins and evaluated, in legal terms, by lawyer Apsan. While Martins exhibits a fairly standard urban variety of Brazilian Portuguese (probably from São Paulo), Apsan himself displays a language practice that does not sit squarely with what one would expect of a Brazilian lawyer. In what follows, I will discuss two examples to show how his language practices stray from the expected monolingual pattern. In the first example, Apsan talks about an initiative to amend the US constitution so that

Figure 5.2 Screenshot from *América Legal* (see colour plate section)

US American citizenship would no longer be automatically given to anyone simply born in the country (in accordance with the principle of *jus soli*):

> *[Moisés Apsan:] E isso não é uma nova proposta . . Cada ano tem um maluco desse tipo que quer muDAR a constitução americana. A constitução americana dá direito para tudo mundo que nasce em esse país para receber a cidadania automático. Ele não vai poder mudar isso. Ele crê que ele pode mudar, mas ele nunca vai mudar, porque o povo americano nunca vai deixar ele mudar a constitução americana em em jeito tão dramático. E . e . então isso . bom se esquecer que ele está falando. É uma loucura. [. . .] (América Legal, RBTI, 11 June 2007)*

> [Moisés Apsan:] And this is not a new proposal . . Every year there is a nut-head like that who wants to change the American constitution. The American constitution gives everyone who is born in this country the right to be given American citizenship. He will not be able to change that. He thinks that he can change it, but he will never change it, because the American people will never allow him to change the American constitution in in such a drastic way. And . and then this . it's best to forget what he is talking about. It's nuts.

The Portuguese used by Apsan here is fluent, with a recognizable Brazilian accent that has not undergone the more recent changes of pervasive palatalization of /ti/ and /di/ originating in the southeastern regions of the country, particularly Rio de Janeiro (Carvalho 2004). His speech on the show is marked by a relatively high degree of informality as can be seen by the high frequency of full subject pronouns as well as the use of the stigmatized full direct object pronouns, both of which are typical of unmonitored speech (Tarallo 1991; Kato 2000). This casual speech style is further underlined by the use of lexical choices such as *maluco* ('*nut head*') or *jeito* ('*way*') as opposed to the more formal *maneira*. Relatively frequent mismatches of agreement as well as a number of non-standard choices for pronouns bear witness to the way in which his Portuguese has in fact been superseded by American English as his first language. This is further underlined by a slight American accent in what is nonetheless his recognizably Brazilian Portuguese.

The next citation shows another characteristic of Apsan's speech pattern displayed on *América Legal*, where he answers an audience query concerning the deportation of parents with children who have no legal right to residency in the US:

> [Moisés Apsan:] *Tem uma lei que chama* **cancellation** *of* **removal** . . *Pode parar a deportação e receber o* **grccn card** *sc tcm uma criança que nasceu aqui já conta dez anos de idade.* (*América Legal*, RBTI, 11 June 2007)

> [Moisés Apsan:] There is a law called *cancellation of removal* . . It can hold up deportation and receive a *green card* if you have a child who was born here and is already 10 years old.

Throughout the programme, Apsan uses legal terms in English where the equivalent technical term in Portuguese is not given. Instead he chooses to explain the legal concept and its implications as in the case above. In this case, the term 'green card' does not even require explanation since it is the objective for many who come to the US and thus forms part of their basic vocabulary. This language practice of inserting legal terms in English which are then explained in Portuguese is, of course, perfectly well suited to Apsan's role as counsel on legal matters. However, in this context there is a double mediation at work. Not only does Apsan 'translate' as a lawyer the technicalities of a complex legal system to his potential clients: he also translates a social system that functions in English into his clients' native language Portuguese. His language practice thus points at the double marginalization of illegal immigrants who might find themselves not only struggling to understand the language of the country they have entered but also to comprehend the implications of a complex legal system on which their ability to remain in the US nonetheless depends.

In sum, we see how the language practice of the lawyer Apsan exhibits an interesting criss-crossing of indexical orders. While his Portuguese is clearly sufficiently fluent and sophisticated to express himself well on television, he nevertheless lacks a command of the register that would typically be expected of a Brazilian lawyer in the relatively formal setting of this legal advice programme. However, the dominant indexical order here is the English language and US legal practice as evidenced by the use of legal terms in English. The Brazilian immigrants are therefore interpellated as being dependent on Apsan's mediating services in order to overcome the obstacles of their potentially insufficient knowledge of, and their marginal status within, that system. Here, Brazilian language and culture are not the relevant indexical order. If at all, Brazil appears in questions from the audience as the space to which they must return should their attempts to achieve legal status in the US fail. With his informal style, Apsan therefore embodies the American self-made man who speaks the language of the people despite his law degree. He also shows little respect for US politicians, whom he often criticizes for their opportunistic anti-immigration slogans, as evident in the first quote above. At the same time, should he try to evoke sympathy with, and closeness to, his potential clients, that sentiment is overshadowed by the demonstration of their ignorance of a legal system for whose navigation they will need (his) professional support and advice.

5.6 Conclusions

Ethnic channels offer rich material for the exploration of the construction of spaces in diaspora language use. In this chapter, I have shown how such language practices are represented and negotiated in two television programmes aimed at a Brazilian diaspora audience. The language practices on display are underpinned by specific constraints that have their roots in a language ideology of monolingualism within audiovisual media (in the sense of monolingual channels) as well as being designed for a specific audience (here: the migrant community). Generally speaking, this monolingual bias tends to prevent a direct display of Brazilian migrants engaged in multilingual language practices. However, we have also seen how, indirectly, alternative strategies such as the representation of language schools, foreigners speaking Portuguese, or the insertion of legal terms in English nevertheless construct spatial relations that are tied to the migrants' multilingual experience. In *Planeta Brasil*, for example, these strategies emphasize the monolingual performance of the migrants' 'home' language by language learners (second generation and foreigners) in a way that mirrors their own experiences of multilingualism. This compares to Jaffe's discussion of the seemingly monolingual bias to be found on a TV documentary on a bilingual school in Corsica, where the focus was 'on the bilingual *individual* as a product of schooling, rather than on bilingual practice as a central element of pedagogical practice or social interaction' (Jaffe 2007: 167 – emphasis in original). Likewise, as argued at the beginning of this chapter, in the case of narrowcasting, with its necessary focus on a single diaspora language (here: Portuguese), it is not difficult to see how exhibiting multilingual practices would in fact run counter to the creation of a recognizable Portuguese-language product. By contrast, in the case of *América Legal*, bilingual practices are brought into being by means of English legal terms that themselves index the threatening experience of marginalization through linguistic difference. In this case, one can argue that the programme even capitalizes on that very threat by offering mediating legal services.

By way of conclusion, it is interesting to note how, in one of the episodes of *Planeta Brasil* (22 September 2007), there was indeed a more comprehensive depiction of migrants' interaction with their host societies in a programme that focussed on the failed proposal for new immigration laws in the US. In this episode, we saw US citizens who have contact with Brazilian communities in the States, as well as Brazilians themselves, talking openly about the illegal status of many Brazilians in the US. It is, in fact, possible that this episode was a direct response to criticism posted on internet forums and various contributions to 'YouTube' directed at the apparently elitist view of migration presented by TV Globo.

Notes

1 I would like to thank the British Academy for its financial support and the audiences at New York University, at the conference on 'Language Ideologies and Media Discourse' at the University of Leeds, and at the Centre for Latin American Cultural Studies at the University of Manchester for their comments on papers presented on this topic.

2 I am using the terms 'emigrant' and 'immigrant' whenever there is a clear distinction of perspective from the point of view of those employing the term, such as the TV networks in this case, since this attests to the spatializing practices engrained in these very terms. In other contexts, I will use the unspatialized term 'migrant'. The notion of diaspora, of course, carries a heavy spatial weight as well in that it creates a bond between an ethnic group and their country of 'cultural belonging' (Sinclair and Cunningham 2000: 12).

3 The Spanish-speaking market is certainly a special case since it encompasses more than a niche audience in the US. However, its target audience is attracted and approached through the Spanish language so as to appeal to an inclusive transnational Hispanic culture. This strategy is comparable to other ethnic channels.

4 The following link shows the available channels in Portuguese language as well as other ethnic channels available through Dish Satellite TV: www.allsat.com/international/portuguese.php (accessed on 20 December 2007).

5 I started ethnographic study for this research in March 2007 until end of May when I began recording. *Planeta Brasil* is a weekly 30-minute programme and I recorded the episodes in the period from June to September. *América Legal* is also a 30-minute programme but runs on all weekdays and, given the repetitious nature, I only analysed two programmes from 11 and 12 June 2007 for this work.

6 The *Globo* news presenters receive special speech training to help them acquire this standardized variety and early attempts on the part of the TV network even included the suggestion to avoid plurals, which end in /s/, so as to avoid the palatalized /s, z/ that are commonly associated with the speech of Rio (Memória Globo 2004: 63; also Bortoni 1991: 54).

7 The *Globo* website makes explicit reference to being a resource for language maintenance: '*Entendemos que a TV Globo Internacional é um meio de manter o contato das criancas com a língua Portuguesa (sic)*' (We understand that TV Globo Internacional is a way of maintaining children's contact with the Portuguese language). Available at: http://tvglobointernacional.globo. com/AProgramacao.aspx?id_submenu=9 (accessed 18 January 2008).

8 www.guiadoimigrante.com/artigo.php?idPublicacao=1821 (accessed 18 January 2007).

References

Amaral, E. F. and Fusco, W. (2005), 'Shaping Brazil: the role of international migration' (available online at www.migrationinformation.org/Profiles/display.cfm?ID=311, accessed 19 December 2007).

Appadurai, A. (1996), *Modernity at Large: Cultural Dimensions of Globalization*. Minneapolis, MN: University of Minneapolis Press.

Bagno, M. (2000), *Drámatica da lingual portuguesa: Tradição, mídia & exclusão social*. São Paulo: Edições Loyola.

Bell, A. (1984), 'Language style as audience design'. *Language in Society*, 13(2), 145–205.

Blommaert, J. (2005), *Discourse: A Critical Introduction*. Cambridge: Cambridge University Press.

Bortoni, S. M. (1991), 'Dialect contact in Brasília'. *International Journal of the Sociology of Language*, 89, 47–59.

Brittos, V. C. and Bolaño, C. R. S. (eds) (2005), *Rede Globo: 40 anos de poder e hegemonia*. São Paulo: Paulus.

Carvalho, A. M. (2004), 'I speak like the guys on TV: palatalization and the urbanization of Uruguayan Portuguese'. *Language Variation and Change*, 16(2), 127–51.

Collins, J. and Slembrouck, S. (2005), 'Editorial. multilingualism and diasporic populations: spatializing practices, institutional processes, and social hierarchies'. *Language and Communication*, 25(3), 189–95.

Dávila, A. (2000), 'Mapping Latinidad: language and culture in the Spanish TV battlefront'. *Television and New Media*, 1(1), 75–94.

Dávila, A. (2001), *Latino, Inc.: The Marketing and Making of a People*. Berkeley, CA: University of California Press.

García Canclini, N. (1999), *La globalización imaginada*. México: Paidós.

Gieve, S. and Norton, J. (2007), 'Dealing with linguistic difference in encounters with others on British television', in S. Johnson and A. Ensslin (eds), *Language in the Media: Representations, Identities, Ideologies*. London: Continuum, pp. 188–210.

Heller, M. (2003), 'Globalization, the new economy, and the commodification of language and identity'. *Journal of Sociolinguistics*, 7(4), 473–92.

Hofmann, S. (2006), 'Spanisch im Massenmedium Fernsehen: Sprachliche Variation, sprachliches Design und mediale Räume in Lateinamerika'. (unpublished) Frankfurt am Main, Habilitationsschrift.

Jaffe, A. (2007), 'Corsican on the airwaves: media discourse in a context of minority language shift', in S. Johnson and A. Ensslin (eds), *Language in the Media: Representations, Identities, Ideologies*. London: Continuum, pp. 149–72.

Kato, M. A. (ed.) (2000), *Brazilian Portuguese and the Null-Subject Parameter*. Madrid/Frankfurt am Main: Iberoamericana/Vervuert.

Kroskrity, P. (ed.) (2000), *Regimes of Language: Ideologies, Politics and Identities*. Santa Fe, NM: School of American Research Press.

Martín-Barbero, Jesús (2002), 'Medios y culturas en el espacio latinoamericano'. *Iberoamericana*, 6, 89–106.

Machin D. and van Leeuwen, T. (2003), 'Global schemas and local discourses'. *Journal of Sociolinguistics*, 7(4), 493–512.

Massini-Cagliari, G. (2004), 'Language policy in Brazil: monolingualism and linguistic prejudice'. *Language Policy*, 3(1), 3–24.

Memória Globo (2004), *Jornal Nacional: A notícia faz história*. Rio de Janeiro: Jorge Zahar Ed.

Sinclair, J. and Cunningham, S. (2000), 'Go with the flow: diasporas and the media'. *Television and New Media*, 1(1), 11–31.

Tarallo, F. (1991), 'Major sociolinguistic patterns in Brazilian Portuguese'. *International Journal of the Sociology of Language*, 89, 9–24.

Zilles, A. M. S. (2001), 'Ainda os equívocos no combate aos estrangeirismos', in C. A. Faraco (ed.), *Estrangeirismos: Guerras em torno da língua*. São Paulo: Parábola Editorial, pp. 143–61.

6 Circularity in the reproduction of language ideology: the case of Greek Cypriot TV series

Vasiliki Georgiou

6.1 Introduction[1]

In the last fifteen years the television scene in Cyprus has changed dramatically[2]. Until the early 1990s the only channel had been the semi-state RIK (Cyprus Broadcasting Corporation) set up in 1957. However, the lifting of the state monopoly in 1992 quickly led to the launch of a number of new television channels (Sophocleous 1995) and, in the following three years, six other Cyprus-wide channels began broadcasting: a second state-run channel (RIK 2), three private channels (LOGOS (relaunched as MEGA in 1999), ANTENNA and SIGMA), a subscription channel (LTV) and ET (Greek Television Corporation) via satellite, as well as a number of smaller local channels.

This proliferation of TV channels has led to an increasing number of locally produced programmes including series which use the Cypriot Greek (henceforth: CG) language variety. However, the novelty did not lie in the use of CG in television series per se, but in their sheer quantity (more than thirty between 1997 and 2007) and their overall makeup. As Nayia Roussou observes, series produced by the state channel, RIK, up until that time had dealt more with Cypriot history, traditions, customs and village life. They were 'in a theatrical style with simple scripts, uncomplicated characters and autochthonous, extended narratives' and 'generally portrayed a countryside lifestyle' (Roussou 2006: 92). But while the state channel still seems to favour this kind of production, the private channels, being more commercially orientated, have introduced series which draw on scenarios from everyday life. The settings have changed from rural to urban, as have the stories, the characters and their language use. Keeping up with changes in Cypriot society, another new element in these series is the inclusion of characters/actors who are foreigners, using either actors invited from Greece or immigrants in Cyprus. In sum, the increase of Cypriot series using the CG dialect brought about its increased visibility on television and by extension in the public sphere. However, this increase was restricted to use in series, not other types of programmes, notably in comedy series rather than other genres, and only for certain functions. Only six of more than thirty series produced in ten years were, for example, dramas.

Roussou also observes how there was a shift between mid-1990s and 2000 in audience viewing patterns (based on survey results) from watching mainly English-language to watching Greek-language programmes (Greek *and* Cypriot productions). She argues that this occurred in conjunction with 'the crystallization of the national (or ethnic) identity in Cyprus society, more especially after 1974, with the territorial consolidation of the ethno-cultural identity of the Greek-Cypriot population' (Roussou 2000: 56). This kind of analysis suggests that this shift reflects a change in audience *preferences* over these five years. However, a key issue here seems to be a conflict between the audience as a *producer* (the power of the customer) or as a *product* of television programming, a conflict to which I will return when discussing television as a mirror of, or a model for, social and linguistic practices.

The aim of this chapter is to outline the relationship between language practices, policies and television representations in the context of the current media landscape in Cyprus. The main argument here encompasses three key points: (i) television representations of linguistic varieties both reflect *and* feed back into language practices and attitudes; (ii) this relationship is framed by factors related to the politics of television, which contribute to the quantity, quality and type of programmes that are produced using the Cypriot Greek variety; and (iii) the complex relationship between these factors seem to reproduce a language ideology that holds Cypriot Greek to be a 'non-serious' language variety. These practices, policies, representations and ideology are caught up in a cyclical process that to an extent both legitimates and reproduces them as described in Figure 6.1.

6.2 Theoretical frameworks and data collection

The critical pool for this chapter is Linguistic Anthropology (LA) – especially the field of Language Ideology – and Critical Discourse Analysis (CDA). Although these two traditions have developed more or less independently over the past two decades, there are now a number of scholars who draw selectively on both in their work (e.g. Blackledge 2005; Meinhof and Galasiński 2005; Milani 2008), arguing that each has something to gain by engaging critically with the other (also Milani and Johnson 2008; Blommaert *et al.* 2001). As Tommaso Milani and Sally Johnson argue, CDA might well benefit from the incorporation of a more reflexive and historiographical approach to data collection and

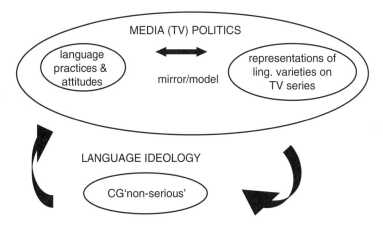

Figure 6.1 Circularity in the reproduction of language ideology

analysis (see also Blommaert 2005), while language-ideological work could be enhanced by the kind of closer textual analysis that is characteristic of CDA. In line with this argument is also the work and ideas of a group of scholars within the 'UK linguistic ethnography forum'. In a special issue of the *Journal of Sociolinguistics*, Ben Rampton *et al.* (2007) argue that a close dialogue between linguistic and ethnographic approaches in research will help both in 'tying ethnography down' and 'opening linguistics up'. Against this backdrop and along with a number of other chapters in this volume, the theoretical and analytical approach adopted here is very much an attempt to combine insights, analytical concepts, and tools from both linguistic anthropology and CDA (see also Paffey, Chapter 3, Lazar, Chapter 7, Blackledge, Chapter 8; and Johnson *et al.* Chapter 12, this volume).

More specifically, from language-ideological work, I take the notion that ideas about language are invested with social, economic, political and moral values, and that these have implications for actual linguistic practices and policies (and vice versa) (see e.g. Blommaert 1999; Jaffe 1999; Kroskrity 2000; Schieffelin *et al.* 1998). I combine my interest in language as a *medium* through which power relations are played out and often reproduced (CDA's major concern), with my interest in language as a *topic* in itself, something people talk and argue about, and as a *stake*, in the sense that definitions of the nature, value and function of a language variety have consequences for its speakers (see also Davies, Chapter 8; Androutsopoulos, Chapter 9, this volume).

The analysis in this chapter then, builds on discourse analytical work both within a language-ideological framework and on the work of

CDA scholars such as Norman Fairclough and Ruth Wodak (Fairclough 2001, 1995a, 1995b, 2003; Wodak *et al.* 1999). More specifically, from LA I adopt key concepts such as indexicality and authoritative entextualization, and from CDA the focus on three particular issues: (i) discourse related to the series' production and interpretation by audience members; (ii) the pressures exerted by economic and other factors and awareness of these; and (iii) the discursive argumentation strategies and topoi the interview participants use to justify their decisions, evaluations and/or ideas whereby Wodak *et al.* (1999: 34) define topoi as the 'conventionalized parts of argumentation which take the form of either explicit or inferable premises' that then connect an argument with a conclusion or claim.

The data for this chapter consist mainly of five loosely-structured group interviews (three to seven participants) with 'ordinary' people, a semi-structured interview with the managing director of a TV channel, and those channels' websites that were available (for summary of data sources, see Appendix). The interviews have been conducted by myself in the context of a broader doctoral research project investigating language ideologies and identity in Cyprus. The questions for the group interviews were designed as guides and springboards for further discussion and the latter revolved mainly around the content and language of the Cypriot TV series, use of CG on television/media in general, and the function and value of CG. The individual interview, given the time constraints, was more focused. The questions dealt mainly with the policy decisions of the TV channel regarding programme production. However, the director expanded on these by commenting on the sociolinguistic reality of Cyprus as well as on other more general language issues (e.g. language mixing).

In what follows, my analysis of the interviews in question is complemented by reference to the TV series themselves, selected newspaper articles on cultural events, and existing literature on the sociolinguistics of Cyprus. I aim to make three main points: (i) language use in these series is one of the key factors in the construction of fictional characters, (ii) such usage both reflects and reinforces existing sociolinguistic practices and attitudes, and (iii) the TV director and the lay participants in the interviews conducted tend to focus on the issue of reflection and influence, respectively.

6.3 TV series: mirror or model?

Representations of linguistic varieties draw on linguistic practices and build on indexical links between those varieties and values, attitudes, behaviour and groups associated with them. In my interview data, the script writers of the television series in question appear to capitalize on these indexicalities, and often hyperbolize particular linguistic features (e.g. accent, pronunciation, vocabulary etc) in order to construct characters from different social and educational backgrounds, as well as different personalitities. As John Edwards argues (1999: 107 cited in Kelly-Holmes and Atkinson 2007: 179) 'people perceive, and react to, sensory input on the basis of various types of social, often stereotypical filters'. So, the use of 'heavy' (βαρετά) Cypriot Greek indexes backwardness, roughness, simplicity or a lack of refinement. The use of 'everyday Cypriot' (καθομιλουμένη), by contrast, indexes familiarity, that is, the 'average Cypriot'. Meanwhile, the use of 'polished' Cypriot (εξευγενισμένα) indexes refinement, social mobility, or professional achievement. These terms for CG are labels that participants themselves assign to particular linguistic varieties but which also enjoy wider currency within Cyprus more generally.

The indexical links on which the TV series draw on can function both as resources and constraints in the creation of characters and stories. On the one hand, their exploitation helps in the creation of characters which are easily identifiable by people and to which audiences can easily relate. On the other hand, they limit what can be said and done by whom, thus contributing to the perpetuation of such indexicalities. I should note here, however, that the construction of characters in these television series is based only *partly* on language. Unlike radio, where the construction of characters is based entirely on aural perception (see e.g. Kelly-Holmes and Atkinson 2007: 180), on television, this is also achieved through visual means such as dress or gesture. So for example, the character who speaks a heavier form of CG will usually dress (often in an exaggerated way) according to those indexicalities, e.g. for a male character: gold jewellery and/or an open shirt revealing a hairy chest.

The various 'levels' of CG mentioned above are also often juxtaposed with Standard Greek (SG) (or rather, with varieties identified as of mainland origin), which is used in these series in two main ways. On the one hand, it is used by Greek Cypriot characters who want to present themselves as 'cultured'. These, however, are usually treated as misfits (Roussou 2000: 57) since the use of Standard Greek amongst Greek Cypriots in everyday conversations is often considered pretentious, unnatural or even ridiculous, a view that is also recurrent in the group interviews conducted here. (SG is also used in these series by native-speaker actors originating from Greece.) Such juxtaposition of SG and CG in TV series or the theatre is not, however, new. Although currently accentuated by the participation of more Greek actors, it is an element that has always added to the entertainment. As the interviewed TV director argues: 'The Cypriot who tries to speak like a Greek and the Greek who tries to speak like a Cypriot have always brought about laughter. It sells, it sold, and will always sell, in small doses'.

Of course, while it may well be the case that the content and language use in these TV series *reflect* social and linguistic practices, they also *impact* on language both in linguistic terms (the effect on the language itself) and sociolinguistic terms (the effect on language attitudes and practices) (Jaffe 2007: 150). However, in the group interviews overall the participants exhibited a higher degree of awareness of the former rather than the latter. Linguistically this impact is observed mainly at the level of words and expressions that find their way into everyday interaction (see also Tsiplakou 2004 on young speakers' use of old Cypriot dialectal words or expressions). In sociolinguistic terms, I argue that one of the outcomes of language use in these series is in fact a reinforcement of the perception that CG is a linguistic variety of limited scope and more suited to create humour. (I will return to this point in section 6.5.1 where I discuss in more detail the perception of Cypriot Greek as a 'non-serious' linguistic variety.) Furthermore, while TV series are both a mirror *and* a model for society in general and language use in particular, in the interviews I conducted, many participants placed a different emphasis on this issue. I thus approach their arguments as bids for what Michael Silverstein and Greg Urban (1996: 11) have called 'authoritative entextualization': attempts to indicate that there is one right way of reading a phenomenon – here, the boom of Cypriot series and how they relate to language practices and attitudes. I will begin with an analysis of the way the TV director talks about the use of CG on television.

The TV director uses the 'mirror metaphor'. He employs two key argumentation strategies with which he rationalizes and justifies his own channel's policies with regard to programme production. The first consists of the argument that television series are a mirror of society, which involves a constant emphasis on *reflection,* and the second that the channel provides what the people want. These two strategies have two main functions: (i) to justify the channel's decision-making process and (ii) to guard the channel's productions against accusations often directed toward television in general and these television series in particular. More specifically and with regard to the first argumentation strategy: if the series *merely reflect* practices, they cannot easily be accused of constituting a bad linguistic model, especially for younger generations, or contributing to the deterioration of language standards, television quality, declining morals or otherwise. Similarly, by claiming that the channel merely provides what the people want, the director can again deflect accusations by denying himself (or other executives) agency.

The public is then consistently portrayed as the 'producer' or 'origin' of the series, that is, a source of authority. However, the fact that the public is itself very much 'produced' by these series (see Gal and Woolard 2001) is back-grounded. At the same time there is the question of who this 'public' is, that is, the public that TV producers imagine, represent and in turn *target* as their potential audience.

Below I cite a small extract from the interview with the TV director in order to illustrate some of the points so far. Here the director (D) responds to my probing that – as some people argue – the language and content of these series are in fact a bad model, including linguistically, not least for young people due to the 'heavy' and exaggerated use of dialect. Instead of confirming this argument, D picks up and elaborates on the idea that Greek Cypriots have difficulty speaking Standard Greek, attributing responsibilities to the educational system (see Transcript 6 below). He then turns his attention to dialect use. It is likely that his answer is responding to two different parts of the question: (i) 'a bad linguistic model' is interpreted as a lack of fluency amongst Greek Cypriots in SG to which these series are accused of contributing, and (ii) 'exaggerated and heavy' dialect use interpreted as accusations for the degradation of the dialect. In the following extract he addresses the second:

Transcript 1: Mirroring language use[3]

1	D	So: it's *not* the television's fault fo:r– I don't know if some
2		intellectual or wannabe intellectual accused television fo:r
3		I don't know degradation of the Cypriot dialect o:r?
4	IV	for for imitation anyway perha:ps that a dialect is used that
5		does not re- reflect even the dialect that is spoken bu::t=
6	D	=I think that it reflects it PRECISELY I mean . go to a tavern
7		[. . .] to a park to a stadium and sit and listen to the people
8		talk . I can say that the way it is represented on television is
9		even more polished . of course there is the character who
10		will speak the heavy – *but* I think it is – it mi:rrors *correctly*
11		the way the average Cypriot speaks

The use of the logical connector *So* signals that what follows is to be read as the conclusion originating from the previous part of his argument: television is not to blame for the 'fluency problems' of Greek Cypriots in SG. After the preposition *for*, he changes the sentence and interposes '*I don't know if some intellectual or wannabe intellectual accused television'*. Had the utterance been 'So: it's *not* the television's fault fo:r– fo:r i don't know (the) degradation of the Cypriot dialect o:r', the presupposition would be that the dialect is indeed degraded in these series. By interposing the utterance, the director achieves a number of effects. Following Martin Reisigl and Ruth Wodak's (2001) framework these could be seen as the effects of certain discursive strategies. In this case the director uses a predicational, a mitigating and a framing strategy that – respectively – provide a negative attribute to the 'accusers' (*wannabe* intellectuals), questions the truth of this presupposition (by placing it as the subordinate prepositional phrase of the verb *accuse*) and distances himself from this presupposition at the same time. Moreover, his reference to the intellectuals (I had not introduced this in the discussion) shows an awareness of existing accusations, but rebuffs them as merely being put forward by a limited group. In fact in lines 6–11 he makes clear that the source of the linguistic representations on the TV series is not the language of this group, but the language of the 'average' Cypriot who speaks rather 'heavy' Cypriot Greek and frequents parks, stadiums and taverns. This Cypriot is also the target public of these series.

However, in the group discussions, by contrast, participants challenged both the idea that television reflects practices and that it provides audiences with what they want (especially Groups 1–3). Some argued that the dialect is commodified and ridiculed in these series, being used merely as a means to make people laugh. Others argued that watching these series in general, or a specific series, is not always a choice based on quality, but is often a matter of choosing the best (or often the least bad) from what is on offer. What all participants seem to agree on however, is that television is also an institution with the power to both promote and impose certain ideologies about languages, thereby contributing to long-term language change (see explicit statement in bold in Transcript 2 below) – an assertion that is missing from the interview with the director. This example comes from Group 2 when discussing the use of CG on television, especially by public figures, usage which the participants claim immediately grabs their attention, sounds odd and which they usually laugh at.

Transcript 2: The power of the media and other institutions

```
1 M   subconsciously that he [sp–. he speaks correctly=
2 EL                        [it's how we speak] = of course
3 L   yes but official [lly he has to speak–
4 E                     [but it draws at– it draws attention=
```

5 EL =yes **but it's what we said (x) imposed on us by the
      media** so
6   besides education also the media . education
7 M   [in general the schools, the governments the . magazines]

6.4 TV politics and Cypriot series

According to Fairclough (1995b), the economics of an institution determines to a large extent its practices and its texts. For my purposes,
this means that the relationship between language practices and their
televisual representations cannot be understood without taking into
consideration the politics of television, that is, the pressures that the
market, available resources and/or developments in the media outside
Cyprus exert on the processes of programme production. The interview
with the TV director provides here an insider's, institutional perspective on the factors that motivate policies with regard to the nature,
content and language of these TV series. This is then set against the
reception of these series, i.e. the evaluative perspective of the viewers
and their awareness of television politics.

It is important to note here that the director repeatedly constructs
himself as an 'expert'. He does this, first of all, and not surprisingly, as
a competent businessman, but also as someone interested in language
and knowledgeable about the wider sociolinguistic situation of Cyprus.
He achieves the first through the use of two topoi: (i) a topos of finance,
that is, business rationale for decision-making, and (ii) a topos of comparison, that is, reference to international products, policies and markets (mainly American and British). I cite here two examples:

(T3) the comedy sells more it sells more years so Fawlty Towers
      let's say Mr. Bean eh it remained in history and it sells on
      DVDs and so on they are comedies I mean I can't imag – there
      is no drama in the international market either which sells and
      sells and sells

(T4) the Cypriot programme is by far the most popular programme
      so e:h like in England the English (programme) is more popu-
      lar than the American and that's why English chan – even if
      the language is the sa–me it's not the same . so we have roughly
      the exact same relation if it helps you understand it better

At the same time, the director has an active interest in language(s)
and speaks very confidently about various aspects of the sociolinguistic
situation in Cyprus with regard to, for example, the existence of two

different codes for writing and speaking, the status difference between SG and CG, the wider responsibility of the educational system, and Greek Cypriots' purported lack of fluency in SG:

> (T5) In a *normal* conversation of an hour two persons will use between 800 and 1200 (words) in a *normal* conversation – you are the expert you can confirm this for me but this is how it is because I have been interested in this for several years

> (T6) Our whole system (education) does not encourage reading . one . does not encourage the enrichment of vocabulary two – a:nd does not encourage and creates – and has the extra problem of diglossia[4], that is we read and learn one language while we speak another . this is a problem

Both the TV director and the group interview participants use a topos of 'constraints' to justify the make-up of the television series. The first, however, focuses on the series' positive effect, that is, 'shaking-off' the feeling of guilt traditionally associated with using CG in the public sphere, while the second focus on their low quality. The topos of constraints can be broken down into several *forms* of constraint that influence programme production. I will firstly focus on those the TV director highlights as relevant and then turn to those emerging from the group interviews.

The director points out five constraints as important[5]. These are (i) international media developments and (ii) the need for a unique selling point (USP), iii) audience maximisation, (iv) comedies as business products, and (v) the need to mirror society. More specifically, the director explains that when the TV channel started broadcasting in the mid-1990s, international developments in media technology already pointed to the possibility that Cypriots would also soon be able to have access at very low cost to (inter)national channels via satellite. Given that small local players cannot compete with big international media players in the purchase and production of programmes, the administrative council of the channel the need for its own USP. This selling point then became local series that drew on Cypriot society for their stories, characters and language. As the director notes, a TV series in the dialect is something that can be uniquely Cypriot and it cannot be copied, even in Greece.

Moreover, television channels – especially private ones – as profit-making organizations depend substantially on their capacity to attract large audiences. One way to maximize audience share, the director argues, is by designing the series in such a way that the stories, characters and language can appeal to different groups and interests; that is, children, teenagers, women, men and so on. Another reason for this is that these series are broadcast during prime-time (7–10pm), the time of day when the whole family typically sits in front of the television and offering hence the highest potential number of viewers. This is also the peak time for attracting potential revenue from advertising, another reason why the programmes broadcast during this time must attempt to increase their audience appeal.

Finally, the director argues that early evening audiences need light family entertainment, hence the suitability of comedy series for this time slot. Comedies are also argued to be better business products because their cost can be recouped via repeat fees, unlike dramas which are not so easily repeatable without losing some of their value (see Transcript 3 above). Satire is similarly avoided because, as he explains, its humour is too dependent on current affairs to withstand repeat broadcastings. Last but not least, another form of constraint stems from the perception that audiences in general are interested, above all else, in their immediate environment. In the case of Greek Cypriots, the director argues that people are first interested in Cyprus, then the broader region, mainly Greece, then Europe, and then the rest of the world. This would appear to explain the dramatic increase in Greek-language productions over the last ten years against the backdrop of channel proliferation in Cyprus and the close collaboration between Greek and Cypriot channels.

All of the above provide interesting insights into policy-making. However, participants in group interviews highlighted a number of other constraints which are missing from the director's interview. These relate to the *quality* of the television series in question. Here a key factor is channel competition, a new element on the Cypriot media landscape that came with the proliferation of television channels in the mid-1990s and has gradually led to the production of many similar series that are broadcast simultaneously. In some group discussions, participants argued that the boom of Cypriot productions is due to the channels' interest in having comparable competitive products, without due concern for the quality of what they are broadcasting (Groups 1 and 3). Low quality is also attributed to limited human resources (Group 1). The large increase of Cypriot series has, in turn, created a large demand for actors, script writers etc. Since there are not enough qualified actors, it is not uncommon for ordinary people with no training or experience to be employed as actors in these series. Comedies are also thought to be easier to write and perform, because they do not require a well-drawn plot or very good acting skills (Groups 1 and 2). Finally, some participants attribute the fact that there are more comedies than other types of programmes on television to their lower cost of production (Groups 1 and 5). Interestingly, these same three constraints regarding the quality of programmes, that is, competition, production cost and lack of suitably trained actors, have also been noted by Andreas Sophocleous (1995: 220). Interview participants defined low quality as the lack of a good plot, the lack of good memorable humour, stories or dialogues that become predictable and repetitive, poor quality actors, and exaggerated use of 'heavy' CG which 'sometimes becomes ridiculous'.

I conclude this section by highlighting an argumentation strategy used both by the director and by some group interview participants to explain not only the production, but also the make-up and language, of these television series: that of the small size of Cyprus. Being a small country is part of the Greek Cypriot identity narrative (see Wodak *et al.* 1999 for a similar discussion of Austria). This kind of narrative is frequently used in the public (and private) sphere to explain current affairs (i.e. Cyprus has limited power to determine its own destiny) and is similarly linked to TV programme production where a range of constraints are linked to Cyprus' small size. Without wanting to deny the validity of these constraints, the use of this argumentation strategy nonetheless reinforces the idea of the inevitability of this cyclical process, thus removing agency from individuals and naturalizing the current situation whereby only certain types of TV series are produced and CG is used only for certain functions, not least as a 'non-serious' linguistic variety. In the next section, I will elaborate on what I mean by 'non-serious'.

6.5 CG as a 'non-serious' language variety

There is general agreement amongst group interview participants that Cypriot Greek is more suitable for television series than any other type of programme. In fact, the idea of its use in other programmes, especially those with serious political content, is strongly resisted. Sometimes my question as to whether the use of CG in other types of programmes sounds strange, led to a negotiation over several turns, as to the meaning of this question as illustrated in lines 1 to 15 of Transcript 7 below. This might be because CG is not in fact normally used in other types of programmes, and such use might have not occurred to the participants prior to my question. I cite here an example of one such exchange from Group 1:

Transcript 7: Language use in TV programmes

```
1 IV   if we move away from series let's say and move on to other
2      types of programmes does (the use of) Cypriot Greek
3      seem strange?=
```

```
 4  Λ   =what programmes?
 5  IV  information, specialised programmes anything except comic
 6      series let's say
 7  E   ye:s (rising intonation – urging me to continue/clarify)
 8  IV  does the use of Cypriot seem strange?
 9  Λ   language?
10  E   you mean taking elements fr– from outside (Cyprus)? (not
        very clear what she means, it's likely that she took the Greek
        word xenizei to mean 'copying foreigners'/ 'looking foreign',
        as xenos means foreigner)
11  IV  no I mean the use of Cypriot . in other types of series not
12      only comedies . not only series
13  T   there are no other series
14  IV  in other types of programmes
15  Λ   there are no [other types of programmes
16  E              [in information programmes they don't use
17      Cypriot=
18  T   =they speak 'καθαρα'' Greek= (kathara is used with several
        meanings in CG–could mean only, pure, more or clearly.
        Here it is taken to mean 'not Cypriot')
19  E   =yes
20  IV  where?
21  Λ   in other [programmes
22  E            [in information programmes
23  T   in sports programmes they sp[eak mo::re–
24  E                                [in soci–
25  T   clearer (πιο καθαρα') let's say they don't use the Cypriot
26      dialect [(X)
27  E           [ye:s . only in Cypriot series they use Cypriot
```

Even after twenty-one turns my initial question (lines 1–3) remains
unanswered. The participants work through the meaning of my question, then instead of responding, reject the question's relevance, by
describing the actual use of CG on television (lines 16–27). I have to
acknowledge here that this exchange might have been triggered by the
grammatical form of the question, that is, the question '. . . **does** the
use of CG seem strange?' presupposes that CG is indeed used in other
types of television programmes. It is this underlying presupposition
that the participants seem to respond to, and challenge, in this extract.
However, I think this extract is still illustrative of the limited range of
uses of CG on television (and of viewers' awareness of this), and of the
difficulty speakers find in imagining its use in a greater variety of
programmes.

Another indication that CG is perceived as unsuitable for 'serious' discussion is also the fact that most (though not all) of the group interview participants accept the use of a small number of words or expressions by public figures on TV but criticize the use of CG throughout. This is especially true for politicians, the public figures most referred to in the examples the participants give and discuss. This is due to an indexical link between use of CG (especially on what are considered 'formal' or public occasions) and a lack of refinement, an indexical link mentioned in section 6.3. Few public figures go beyond the occasional use of CG words or expressions on television, and sometimes even these are caricatured. A prominent example of such caricaturing is that of a well-known Greek Cypriot psychologist. This may also be partly due to his general gesturing and forthrightness, but his persistent use of CG on television plays a considerable part here (he is the referent of the pronoun *he* in line 1 of Transcript 2).

The fact that this caricaturing occurs and is, when recounted in the interviews often accompanied by loud laughs, shows that the use of CG on television (besides its use for humour) is still to a large extent a stigmatized practice. The way in which its usage by a public figure on television also attracts attention similarly confirms that this is not a common practice. In the group interviews participants repeatedly describe the effect of listening to public figures using CG on television with expressions as in (selected from Groups 1, 2 and 5): 'it strikes one as odd', 'maybe you'll laugh', 'it doesn't sound right', 'it grabs one's attention', 'our ear picks it up', 'we immediately realize' or 'it's not nice . . . I don't like it'. These reactions remind us that linguistic varieties come with tacit guidelines for appropriate use and these sociolinguistic norms – and their violations – are what the TV series draw upon to produce a humorous effect.

In sum, language in these TV series, just as in the case of Irish on a radio programme discussed by Helen Kelly-Holmes and David Atkinson (2007), is used to create characters via the exploitation of accent, pronunciation, choice of linguistic variety, slang and so on. In both cases laughter is the result of (i) incomprehension arising in interaction with non-CG (or Irish) speakers, (ii) the use of a linguistic variety in an 'inappropriate' environment, and (iii) the hyperbolizing of particular linguistic features. However, the effects of such usage are somewhat different. In the case of CG, the way language(s) is used for humour is part of a process that reinforces the stigmatization of CG as a 'non-serious' variety, while in the case of Irish it seems to be part of a process that to some extent helps legitimize language mixing and code-switching via its use in a public forum such as the media. What these two cases do have in common, however, is the integrating function of CG and Irish as a means of creating an in-group identity (of those who understand and/or speak the variety in question). This integrating function is especially evident in the interactions of speakers with non-speakers of that variety where laughter relies on the viewers' ability to grasp the ludic dimension precisely because they speak (or at least *understand*) both language varieties. Thus, some Cypriot TV series have been hugely successful in spite of their negative evaluations and/or calls for improved quality by both lay people and scholars. Drawing on Kelly-Holmes and Atkinson's (2007) concept of a 'status continuum', perceptions of CG similarly range from being 'at the heart of Cypriot identity' to being incongruous with modernity (where urban forms of CG are typically reduced to a mere accent, or a strange mixture of CG dialect, SG and English). It is here that I find Kelly-Holmes and Atkinson's final comment especially relevant: the very success of the series under discussion appears to lie 'in the exploitation of complex and often ambivalent attitudes, not only in the Irish context, but in all bilingual and diglossic situations' (ibid: 186).

6.6 Discussion and conclusions

The current uses of Cypriot Greek in the media – explored here in the context of television series – do not only reflect dominant ideas about its nature, function and appropriate use (e.g. suitable for humorous effect, 'heavier forms' indexical of lack of refinement, greater appropriacy for informal/private interactions), but also contribute to their reproduction. That said, it is also possible to find examples which put forward alternative theses in an attempt to explain the implications of the co-existence of two main linguistic varieties in the media. So, for example, Alexandra Jaffe argues that the mixing of Corsican and French that occurs in the Corsican media (especially on the radio) 'reflects and implicitly validates the abundant language mixing (and the plural cultural identity it indexes) that characterizes Corsican communicative practice' (Jaffe 1999: 247). It also 'allows for linguistic play and creativity that blurs, rather than emphasizes linguistic boundaries' (ibid). Similar observations have been put forward by Kathryn Woolard (1989) in Catalonia and Monica Heller in Toronto (1994).

As in the case of Corsican, the juxtaposition of CG and SG in the TV series discussed in this chapter is certainly employed creatively to humorous effect. But such humour is by no means the central focus or indeed the only element in these series that marks Cypriot identity; instead it forms part of the whole 'package'. However, what I suggest is that this kind of language use and language juxtaposition does not so much *blur* as *emphasize* difference. The difference lies in the fact that

115

language choice or language alternations in Corsican radio practice, as analysed by Jaffe, are seldom commented upon explicitly, rendering such practices as seemingly natural (Jaffe 1999: 255–56). Conversely, in Cypriot TV series language practices build on and ultimately perpetuate indexical links between linguistic varieties and certain attitudes, behaviour and values.

What is more important, however, is that in the three cases analysed by Heller, Woolard and Jaffe (i.e. Canada, Catalonia and Corsica) these 'creative' linguistic practices occur within a broader context whereby the linguistic varieties involved (French, Catalan, and Corsican, respectively) are also at the centre of organized and institutional efforts at officialization and standardization. In other words, they co-occur with top-down and/or bottom-up policies that also have effects on the valorization of the respective minority linguistic variety. In Cyprus, by contrast, such large-scale initiatives are largely absent. CG is neither codified nor officially recognized and promoted. It is not taught in schools (except through some Cypriot poetry), and although it 'is not absent from the classroom it is confined to very specific functions and domains which do not relate to either the subject taught or the teaching procedure' (e.g. joking, complaining, having a break/casual chat, Pavlou and Papapavlou 2004).

That said, there has recently been an increase of literary publications in the Cypriot Greek dialect (especially poetry), as well as theatrical productions of plays written in or translated/adapted into Cypriot Greek (e.g. Aristophanes' 'Λυσιστράτη' (Lysistrata) adapted in CG by K.Montis; Nicolai Gogol's 'Diary of a Madman' (Ημερολόγιο ενός τρελ– λού) translated by M.Ioannou and S.Charalampous; 'Η Αγάπη της Μαρικκούς' (The love of Marikkou) by K.Akanthiotis reproduced in 2005 by the Cyprus Theatre Organization-ΘΟΚ). There also seems to be a growing number of cinema films, which are presented and receiving prizes at international festivals (e.g. 'Η σφαγή του κόκορα' (Slaughter of the Cock) by A.Pantzis received the prize for best film in the festival of Barcelona 1996; 'Ακάμας' (Akamas) by P. Chrysanthou was shown in the Venice Film festival in 2006). Moreover, the Ministry of Education and Culture established the Festival of Cypriot films in 2000.

However, films (and literary work) are not as immediately accessible to the wider public as television series. The latter, unlike films which are screened in a small number of cinemas for a few days only, address and reach a wide range and number of people in their homes and manage to become, to an extent, part of their everyday lives. As Jaffe notes when discussing the significance of the media in Corsican language activism: 'middle-aged Corsican speakers were also far less likely to read a Corsican novel than to watch or listen to Corsican language broadcasts' (Jaffe 2007: 151). Consequently television has more power in influencing the attitudes and practices of the general public regarding language (and much more besides).

Concluding then, let me summarize the key points of this chapter. Representations of linguistic varieties on Cypriot television series function both as a mirror and a model for language practices and attitudes, although different individuals and (interest) groups may choose to stress one or the other. The interrelationship between such practices and attitudes, framed by television politics, *contributes* to the reproduction of popular perceptions of CG as non-serious. I say 'contribute', because I do not suggest that this is a straightforward, causal relationship. These television series are not the 'root of all evil'. The language-ideological effects stemming from their content and concomitant representations of language need to be seen in the wider socio-political context of Cyprus and the long history of near 'invisibility' of CG within the public sphere and in official policy-making. In conjunction with the lack of alternative discourses (at least voiced publicly or strongly), and the use of CG for a wider range of functions, these television series help to perpetuate ideas that hold CG to be better suited for entertainment purposes. This reproduction of CG as non-serious variety is almost certainly not *intentional* on the part of the writers or producers of the programmes; it is unlikely that the latter set out to intentionally reproduce a hegemonic ideology (Blackledge 2005: 148), but it is the *effects* of their discourse and practices that are most important in the reproduction of language ideologies or practices.

Finally, the kind of relationship I have discussed between language practices and attitudes, television politics, television representations, and language ideology is part of a *cyclical* process. It is cyclical in the sense that popular perceptions of CG influence sociolinguistic practices in the public sphere on which television representations are based. These then have consequences for the production of publics and the reproduction of language ideologies, which in turn further legitimate representations of publics in the sense described by Gal and Woolard (2001). Thus the sociolinguistic plurality in these television series, that is, the use of Cypriot Greek varieties as well as those of Standard Greek, reproduces dominant language hierarchies and ideologies by building on stereotypical indexical relationships between language varieties and 'types' of people.

Notes

1 I am grateful to the UK Arts and Humanities Research Council for funding my doctoral research of which this study is a part. Many thanks to Patrick

Stevenson, Ivan Petrella, Darren Paffey and the editors of this volume for their invaluable comments on previous drafts of this chapter.

2 This chapter focuses on the television scene/practices in the area of Cyprus controlled by the Republic of Cyprus. Any use of 'Cypriot' here (e.g. series, society, dialect) is in relation to the *Greek* Cypriot community.

3 Transcription has been limited to a minimum for the purposes of this chapter.

'IV' indicates the researcher (interviewer). All translations are my own.

Transcription conventions:

=	latching	:	prolonged vowel
–	interruption (self- or other-interruption)	(1.5)	more than 1" pause
(X)	inaudible word	.	pause less than 1"
(comments)	my notes	?	question
[	start of overlap	LOUD	louder voice

4 It is unclear whether he is familiar with academic literature on diglossia. It is likely that he uses it here in its literal etymological sense that means 'two languages'.

5 These emerge from the interview as a whole rather than occurring in the form of a list as presented here.

References

Blackledge, A. (2005), *Discourse and Power in a Multilingual World*. Amsterdam: John Benjamins.

Blommaert, J. (ed.) (1999), *Language Ideological Debates*. Berlin; New York: Mouton de Gruyter.

Blommaert, J. (2005), *Discourse*. Cambridge: Cambridge University Press.

Blommaert, J., Collins, J., Heller, M., Rampton, B., Slembrouck, S., Verschueren, J. (2001), 'Discourse and critique: part one, introduction'. *Critique of Anthropology,* 21(1), 5–12.

Fairclough, N. (2001 [1989]), *Language and Power*. Second edition. London: Longman.

Fairclough, N. (1995a), *Critical Discourse Analysis: The Critical Study of Language*. Harlow: Pearson Education.

Fairclough, N. (1995b), *Media Discourse*. London: Edward Arnold.

Fairclough, N. (2003), *Analysing Discourse: Textual Analysis for Social Research*. London: Routledge.

Gal, S. and Woolard, K. A. (eds) (2001), *Languages and Publics: The Making of Authority*. Manchester: St. Jerome Publishing.

Heller, M. (1994), *Crosswords: Language, Education and Ethnicity in French Ontario*. Berlin: Mouton de Gruyter.

Jaffe, A. (1999), *Ideologies in Action: Language Politics in Corsica*. Berlin: Mouton de Gruyter.

Jaffe, A. (2007), 'Corsican on the airwaves: Media discourse in a context of minority language shift', in S. Johnson and A. Ensslin (eds), *Language in the Media: Representations, Identities, Ideologies.* London: Continuum, pp. 149–72.

Kelly-Holmes, H. and Atkinson, D. (2007), '"When Hector met Tom Cruise": attitudes to Irish in a radio satire', in S. Johnson and A. Ensslin (eds), *Language in the Media: Representations, Identities, Ideologies.* London: Continuum, pp. 173–87.

Kroskrity, P. V. (ed.) (2000), *Regimes of Language: Ideologies, Polities and Identities.* New Mexico: School of American Research.

Meinhof, U. H. and Galasiński, D. (2005), *The Language of Belonging.* Hampshire, New York: Palgrave Macmillan.

Milani, T. M. (2008), 'Language testing and citizenship: a language ideological debate in Sweden'. *Language in Society*, 37(1), 27–59.

Milani, T. M. and Johnson, S. (2008a), 'CDA and language ideology: towards a reflexive approach to discourse data', in I. H. Warnke and J. Spitzmüller (eds), *Methoden der Diskurslinguistik: sprachwissenschaftliche Zugänge zur transtextuellen Ebene.* Berlin: Mouton de Gruyter, pp. 365–88.

Pavlou, P. and Papapavlou, A. (2004), 'Greek Cypriot dialect use in education'. *International Journal of Applied Linguistics,* 14(2), 243–58.

Rampton, B., Maybin, J. and Tusting, K. (eds) (2007), 'Linguistic ethnography: links, problems and possibilities'. Special theme issue, *Journal of Sociolinguistics*, 11(5), 575–716.

Reisigl, M. and Wodak, R. (2001), *Discourse and Discrimination.* London: Routledge.

Roussou, N. (2000), 'The language of television and national identity in Cyprus'. *Cyprus Review*, 12(2), 45–65.

Roussou, N. (2006), 'Research note: Cypriot television, dialect productions and demotic culture: Urbanization, westernization or new resistance identities?', *European Journal of Communication*, 21(1), 89–99.

Schieffelin, B. B., Woolard, K. A. and Kroskrity, P. V. (eds) (1998), *Language Ideologies: Practice and Theory.* New York: Oxford University Press.

Silverstein, M. and Urban, G. (1996), 'The natural history of discourse' in M. Silverstein and G. Urban (eds) *Natural Histories of Discourse.* Chicago: The University of Chicago Press, pp. 1–20.

Sophocleous, A. Σοφοκλέους, A. (1995), 'Η ανάπτυξη των μέσων μαζικής ενημέρωσης στην Κύπρο την περίοδο 1975–1994', στο Ν. Περιστιάνης και Γ. Τσαγγαράς (επιμ.), *Ανατομία μιας Μεταμόρφωσης.* Λευκωσία: Intercollege Press, σελ. 213–27.

Tsiplakou, S. (2004), 'Linguistic attitudes and emerging hyperdialectism in a diglossic setting: young Cypriot Greeks on their language'. *Proceedings of Berkeley Linguistic Society,* 29. California: University of California at Berkeley.

Wodak, R., De Cillia, R., Reisigl, M. and Liebhart, K. (1999), *The Discursive Construction of National Identity.* Edinburgh: Edinburgh University Press.

Woolard, K. A. (1989), *Double Talk: Bilingualism and the Politics of Ethnicity in Catalonia.* Stanford, CA: Stanford University Press.

Appendix: Main data sources

Interviews	Websites
Individual interview with TV director	*www.cybc.com.cy* (RIK 1&2)
Group interview with three participants, two male and one female, in their early twenties. (Group 1)	*www.lumiere.com.cy* (LTV)
Group interview with five participants, all female, between 30 and 55. (Group 2)	*www.sigmatv.com* (SIGMA)
Group interview with seven participants, four female and three male, aged between 16 and 60. (Group 3)	*www.thoc.org.cy/gr/archive* (Cyprus Theatre Organization – ΘΟΚ)
Group interview with six participants, three female and three male, aged between 40 and 65. (Group 4)	Watchmovies Portal to the history of World cinema-Cyprus history of the film industry *http://80.57.161.240/newsite/cyprus.cfm*
Group Interview with three participants, two female and one male, aged between 26 and 40. (Group 5)	

7 Language ideologies and state imperatives: the strategic use of Singlish in public media discourse

Michelle M. Lazar

7.1 Introduction

In 2003, at the height of the SARS (Severe Acute Respiratory Syndrome) pandemic that directly affected Singapore, Singlish – a colloquial variety of Singapore English – was featured prominently in the media, as part of the government's campaign to tackle the deadly disease. Given the long-standing official antipathy to Singlish in the government's efforts to promote Standard Singapore English (SSE) in the linguistic history of the country, the government's endorsement of Singlish for use on national television at this time was unprecedented. From the point of view of language ideological debates (Blommaert 1999), this raises an interesting issue of 'what was going on here?', which this chapter seeks to investigate. Specifically, the chapter addresses two questions: (i) Did this signal a shift, or at least a 'softening', in the government's ideological position concerning Singlish? and (ii) How was it possible to publicly endorse the use of Singlish, and yet sustain the government's unequivocal position of promoting SSE?

'Language ideologies' are understood as ideological appraisals of language and forms of usages based upon such notions, as identified by Jan Blommaert (2006), as 'quality', value, status, norms, functions and ownership. Blommaert (2006) notes that, as ideological constructs, these are invested in relations of power and authority, and may involve the stratification and regimentation of language usage, distinguished on the basis of 'best' versus 'less adequate' language varieties. In the present chapter, the focus is on the Singapore government's language ideologies concerning English, which have had implications for the stratification and regimentation of varieties of Singapore English (SSE and Singlish). The long-standing relation of Singlish to SSE has been mainly one of 'displacement', where the co-presence of the two varieties have been constructed by the state as incompatible and, therefore, requiring the eradication of Singlish. However, also of relevance to this chapter is the surprising presence of another kind of relation based on 'complementarity', which accommodates the functional co-existence of the two varieties (for a discussion of the terms 'displacement' and 'complementarity', see Rappa and Wee 2006). That is, Singlish, which is ordinarily displaced by discourses and practices of the state, was included in the official linguistic repertoire to function in a complementary capacity to SSE during the SARS period. The strategic exclusion and inclusion of Singlish are both ideologically salient. Joshua Fishman's comment generally on the strategic divisiveness and unification of language and other social categories is instructive in this case also:

> differences do *not* need to be divisive. *Divisiveness is an ideologized position* and it can magnify minor differences; indeed, it can manufacture differences in languages as in other matters as easily as it can capitalize on more obvious differences. Similarly, *unification is also an ideologized position* and it can minimize seemingly major differences or ignore them entirely, whether these be in the realm of language, religion, culture, race or any other basis of differentiation. (Fishman 1968: 44–45 – emphasis as in original)

Framed in the terms above, this chapter sets out to address the two questions about the official endorsement of Singlish for use in public media discourse in 2003. In addressing these questions, the chapter adopts a critical perspective on language and discourse, combining the study of language ideologies with analytical resources from critical discourse analysis (see also Paffey, Chapter 3; Georgiou, Chapter 6; and Blackledge, Chapter 8, this volume). Before dealing with the questions, however, it is necessary to sketch out in greater detail the language ideological situation with regards to English usage in Singapore, and the usage of Singlish particularly in the entertainment media sector.

7.2 Language ideologies and English in Singapore

Since Singapore's independence in 1965, under the current leadership of the People's Action Party (PAP), English has been primarily viewed in instrumental terms to achieve socio-economic development. Lee Kuan Yew, Singapore's first prime minister, explained:

> we moved over to English as the working language. It was the first move, one of the first fundamental decisions we made within a few weeks of separation [from Malaysia] because we've got to have a working language. Before that, we were working on Malay as the national language. After that, we had to link up with the outside world and we decided on English. (Han *et al.* 1998: 83)

English thus became the language of government and administration, and was designated the lingua franca amongst Singaporeans of diverse ethnic and language backgrounds. Even more importantly, English served as the gateway to international communication and the modernization of Singapore. English was the language of science and technology, and provided the ticket into the global economy, which would enable Singaporeans to be economically competitive and to generate wealth for the country. The language-economy relation is especially imperative for a country without any natural resources, except its people.

The acquisition of English, therefore, became enshrined in Singapore's official bilingual language policy, which has been aptly described as 'English-knowing bilingualism' (Pakir 1992). Since the 1970s, all Singaporeans have been required to learn English (to this end, by 1987, English became the medium of instruction in all schools) and a 'mother tongue' language associated with their ethnicity. Underlying the bilingual policy was functional polarization that underscored the utilitarian value of English versus the cultural, symbolic value of the 'mother tongue' in providing Singaporeans rootedness in their Asian identity.

Owing to the instrumental value of English, especially as a global language with immense economic capital, it became vital that Singaporeans achieved international intelligibility in their usage of English. The issue, therefore, was not merely about knowing English, as it was about standards and proficiencies, as evident in the official discourse over the last thirty years:

> Whichever way English evolves, we have to ensure that the English spoken is internationally intelligible. (Comment by a cabinet minister, reported in *The Straits Times* 18 August 1977, cited in Low and Brown 2003).

> The ability to speak good English is a distinct advantage in terms of doing business and communicating with the world. This is especially important for a hub city and an open economy like ours. (Prime Minister Goh Chok Tong, 2000b)

> Proficiency in English widens our opportunities, enables us to function effectively in more areas, and of course, increases our competitive edge in many diverse areas. (Koh Tai Ann, former Chair of the *Speak Good English Movement*, 2006)

Given that the priority was proficiency in the English language, the government has been keen to promote Standard English, arrest signs of declining standards[1], and has had little tolerance for the use of Singlish, a local colloquial variety of English, which is hybridized with elements from Singapore's indigenous languages (Malay, Tamil, and Chinese – particularly Hokkien and Cantonese). Singlish is estimated

123

to have emerged in the late 1970s, and is linked to second generation Singaporean speakers of English, born in the post-independence years (Low and Brown 2003). As a variety of Singapore English, it is characterized by a number of distinctive features, some of which are listed below (for a comprehensive list, see Gupta 1998; for the largest Singlish lexicon, refer to Talkingcock.com 2002):

- local address terms, for example, 'Uncle' and 'Aunty' as polite generic terms to refer to older men and women, respectively, even though those persons are not kindred.
- code-mixing involving lexis and phrases from indigenous languages, for example, 'She *kenna* (Malay) scolded' ('She was subjected to a scolding').
- syntax and transliterations of phrases, for example, 'This is my one' patterned after Chinese syntax (*zhe shi wo de*); and reduplications, for example, 'Don't play, play'.
- discourse particles, for example, 'Hurry up *lah*!'
- pronunciation, for example, 'pray' for 'p*l*ay'.

Proponents of Singlish regard the language as unifying speakers of different ethnic groups, and as a cultural marker of Singaporean identity. According to a poll undertaken of 750 undergraduates by the National University of Singapore Students' Political Association, Singlish with 75.3 per cent of the votes was considered 'most Singaporean' (*The Straits Times* 18 November 2004). Offering another angle (from that of the government's) to the language-and-globalization argument, some have argued for the need to preserve Singlish in the onslaught of global western influences:

> When the world is increasingly dominated by the western media, we have to work harder to preserve things that are uniquely our own. And we should not feel embarrassed in doing so. After all, if Londoners can speak Cockney and Liverpudlians Scouse, why shouldn't we be able to speak Singlish? (Talkingcock.com 2002: ix)

Those who support the use of Singlish generally favour a wider, 'inclusive' linguistic repertoire of Singapore English, based upon a diglossic model. Singlish ought to be permitted for use in informal settings, while SSE is used for formal communication:

> those who contend that improper Singlish in the arts will encourage lower standards should be chided for their patronizing view of Singaporeans. [. . .] we're not so stupid that we cannot tell the difference between the kind of language acceptable in casual

settings and the kind expected in business or official correspondence. (Talkingcock.com 2002: ix)

Singlish as a language is not wrong in itself, and Singaporeans should not feel uncomfortable if they use it. After all, in a sense it is the backbone of our cultural identity as Singaporeans. However, it is not the standard form of English to be used in the workplace or in written schoolwork. (a reader of *The Straits Times*, 25 April 2005)

the basilect (or most informal variety of English spoken in Singapore) is distinctively and delightfully Singaporean. We don't have to apologize for it and we should be free to use it. [. . .] let the basilect stay, but let's also have a wide enough repertoire to 'switch' to a higher 'lect' if need be. (a reader writing to *The Straits Times* in 1983, cited in Low and Brown 2003: 17)

Whereas advocates of Singlish view the relation between the Singapore English varieties as one of complementarity, the government's position has been that of displacement of Singlish, in favour of a single standard variety. Former Prime Minister Lee Kuan Yew, who has been among the most vociferous opponents of Singlish, in fact, referred to Singlish as a 'handicap we would not want to wish on Singaporeans' (cited in Low and Brown 2003: 18). Two reasons can be advanced for the official stance of Singlish as a handicap. Firstly, Singlish, comprehensible only to the local speech community, has no communicative value internationally and, therefore, has zero economic utility in the global marketplace (cf. Georgiou on Cypriot Greek, Chapter 6, this volume). Indeed, the usage of Singlish is construed as directly having dire economic consequences on Singapore. In Lee Kuan Yew's words, 'Singlish is a handicap that is stifling the country's economic development' (Rubdy 2001: 345). His successor, Goh Chok Tong (2000b), spells this out in finer detail:

If we speak a corrupted form of English that is not understood by others, we will lose a key competitive edge. My concern is that if we continue to speak Singlish, it will over time become Singapore's common language. Poor English reflects badly on us and makes us seem less intelligent or competent. Investors will hesitate to come over if their managers or supervisors can only guess what our workers are saying. We will find it difficult to be an education and financial centre. Our TV programmes and films will find it hard to succeed in overseas markets because viewers do not understand Singlish. All this will affect our aim to be a first-world economy. (Goh Chok Tong, 2000b)

125

Secondly, Singlish is a hindrance to the mastery of Standard English. Underlying this rationalization is the assumption that people have finite capacities to learn and use a language proficiently. This is compounded by the fact that English is not the home language for some, so that exposure to Singlish may pose challenges in their ability to 'switch' between Singlish and SSE:

> Most of our pupils still come from non-English speaking homes. [. . .] For them to master just one version of English is already quite a challenge. If they get into the habit of speaking Singlish, then later they will either have to unlearn these habits, or learn proper English on top of Singlish. Many pupils will find this too difficult. They may end up unable to speak any language properly, which would be a tragedy. (Goh Chok Tong, 1999)

Even those who are proficient in SSE and can effectively negotiate between the two varieties have been discouraged from using Singlish, for the benefit of other Singaporeans. The official discourse has framed the elimination of Singlish from one's linguistic repertoire as a moral responsibility of every 'good' citizen to speak 'good' English:

> we should nurture the next generation to have higher standards of English than ourselves. We can help them by discouraging the use of Singlish, or at least not encouraging it. (Goh Chok Tong, 1999)

> [Younger proficient speakers] should not take the attitude that Singlish is cool or feel that speaking Singlish makes them more 'Singaporean'. They have a responsibility to create a conducive environment for the speaking of good English. If they speak good English, others will follow suit. If they speak Singlish when they can speak good English, they are doing a disservice to Singapore. (Goh Chok Tong, 2000b)

In order to simultaneously promote the use of 'proper' English *and* eradicate the 'corrupted' form from the public and eventually private domains of life, in April 2000, the government launched the 'Speak Good English Movement' (SGEM)[2], using the slogan 'Speak Well. Be Understood'. Run annually with a special theme each year, the SGEM operates like any other national campaign, for which Singapore is famous (for other campaigns, see for example Lazar 1999, 2003, 2004). The SGEM has a dedicated website, and organizes a range of activities in collaboration with the public and private sectors. In 2006, it published two books titled *English as it is Broken*, a compilation of weekly newspaper columns devoted to educating Singaporeans on the 'correct' usage of English, and *Speak Well, Sell Well*, a retailer's guide to 'good' English.

7.3 The entertainment media and the usage of Singlish

Although Standard English[3] has been traditionally used in institutional local media discourse, the usage of Singlish in the entertainment media sector (including advertizing) has not been uncommon, notably since early 1990s. During that time, the local television network began to produce English-medium entertainment programmes for local consumption, whereas previously most entertainment programmes had been imported from the US and UK. In order to woo audiences and boost ratings, a number of these shows, such as the popular comedy programme *The Ra Ra Show* and the cookery series *Mum's Not Cooking*, featured hosts and characters using Singlish. For example, the catch-phrase of *Mum's Not Cooking's* host, Jacintha Abisheganaden, was 'Join me, don't shy!' (Brown 1999: vi). Although the then broadcasting corporation subsequently proscribed the liberal use of Singlish on television (following complaints from some sectors of the public about the perceived negative influence of the media's use of Singlish on English language learning in schools), the presence of Singlish in the entertainment media was not completely quashed.

In the late 1990s, the issue of Singlish usage in the media re-surfaced robustly with the production of one of the highest-rated shows in Singapore's television history. Titled *Phua Chu Kang Pte. Ltd.*, this was a situation comedy named after the lead character 'Phua Chu Kang', a renovations contractor who, with his trademark yellow wellington boots, big curly hair, and distinctive facial mole, rose to fame speaking Singlish. 'PCK', as he became affectionately known, was a funny and likeable character, as a common man, exhibiting common Singaporean foibles, and speaking a common language. Owing to his huge popular appeal, fans began to imitate his manner of speaking, much to the consternation of the government[4].

In his 1999 National Day address to Singaporeans, then Prime Minister Goh Chok Tong raised the issue of Singlish at some length, and singled out PCK for comment. He said:

> One of the problems MOE [the Ministry of Education] has getting students to speak standard English is that the students often hear Singlish being spoken around them, including on TV. So they learn wrong ways of speaking. Teachers complain that their students are picking up catchphrases like: 'Don't pray, pray.' and using them even in the classroom. The students may think that it is acceptable and even fashionable to speak like Phua Chu Kang. He is on national TV and a likeable, ordinary person. The only character who tries to

> speak proper English is Phua Chu Kang's sister-in-law Margaret, and she is a snob. Nobody wants to be a snob. So in trying to imitate life, Phua Chu Kang has made the teaching of proper English more difficult. (Goh Chok Tong, 1999)

In the speech, the Prime Minister used PCK to also drive home an instructional point and warning:

> Gurmit Singh [the actor who plays PCK] can speak many languages. But Phua Chu Kang speaks only Singlish. If our children learn Singlish from Phua Chu Kang, they will not become as talented as Gurmit Singh. (Goh Chok Tong, 1999)

In a somewhat unprecedented move, the Prime Minister went on to speak to and about PCK as though he were a real person with an actual linguistic trajectory and personal volition.

> I asked TCS [Television Corporation of Singapore] why Phua Chu Kang's English is so poor. They told me that Phua Chu Kang started off speaking quite good English, but as time passed he forgot what he learnt in school, and his English went from bad to worse. I therefore asked TCS to try persuading Phua Chu Kang to attend NTUC's BEST classes[5], to improve his English. TCS replied that they have spoken to Phua Chu Kang, and he has agreed to enroll himself for the next BEST programme, starting in a month's time. If Phua Chu Kang can improve himself, surely so can the rest of us. (Goh Chok Tong, 1999)

Months after the National Day address, the government launched the Speak Good English Movement in 2000, in an effort to bolster standard English and displace Singlish.

7.4 The use of Singlish in the government's national campaign against SARS

In 2003, at the peak of the international SARS outbreak, which directly impacted upon Singapore in terms of the economy and actual lives affected, the Ministry of Health and the Health Promotion Board collaborated with Channel 5, the local English-medium television channel, to co-produce what was called the 'SAR-Vivor Rap', as part of the government's vigorous public education programme. This was an MTV-style rap music video, reminding Singaporeans to observe precautionary measures against the disease. The full version of the video, which was four minutes long, was first screened on Channel 5 and TV Mobile (television on public buses) on 12 June 2003, which was followed by shorter versions in the subsequent weeks. A music CD was later released on 1 July 2003, which was available at music stores island-wide. What was interesting about the 'SAR-Vivor Rap' (the lyrics reproduced below), from the point of view of this chapter, is that it was performed in the usual humorous fashion by television character, Phua Chu Kang, in Singlish.

Verse 1:

Some say 'leh', some say 'lah'
Uncle Phua says time to fight SARS
Everybody, we have a part to play
To help fight SARS at the end of the day.

Wash your hands whenever you can
Wash with soap, then at least got hope
When you get home, take a bath quickly
'Kiasu' a bit – be safe, not 'SAR-ry'.

Try not to travel to SARS countries
Wait a few months lah, wait and see
Eh why you rush to catch that plane?
Use internet lah, use your brain!

Getting protection from this virus
Means getting healthy – inside us
Don't work too much until you're sick
Get exercise and get yourself fit.

Good nutrition and vitamins
Help you to pass the immunity challenge
Eat your proteins, carbo and fibre
Then you can be a . . . 'SAR-vivor'.

PCK say don't play play
Or this stupid SARS is here to stay
But we can fight this, you and me
Help fight SARS in our country.

SARS is the virus that I just want to minus
No more surprises if you use your brain, use your brain, use your braaainnn,
Can't SARS me baby, and I don't mean maybe
You must be steady, just use your brain, use your brain, use your braaainnn.

Verse 2:

Some say 'leh', some say 'lah'
Uncle Phua says time to fight SARS
Everybody, we have a part to play
To help fight SARS at the end of the day.

129

If you're sick, don't go to work
Even if your boss is a jerk
Don't be hero and continue working
Wait the whole company 'kenna' quarantine.

Wear a mask when you see a doctor
See the same one, don't be a doc hopper
Wait at the clinic, stay in one spot
Don't spread your germs at the coffee shop.

Think you got SARS? Call 993
Ambulance will come for free
They'll check you up at Tan Tock Seng
Where they know about SARS like I know about 'Ah Bengs'.

Hey, if you 'kenna' Home Quarantine
Don't you go out except in your dreams
'Tahan' a while and cooperate
Don't give everybody a big headache.

PCK say don't play play
Or this stupid SARS is here to stay
But we can fight this, you and me
Help fight SARS in our country.

SARS is the virus that I just want to minus
No more surprises if you use your brain, use your brain, use your braaainnn,
Can't SARS me baby, and I don't mean maybe
You must be steady, just use your brain, use your brain, use your braaainnn.

Verse 3:

Some say 'leh', some say 'lah'
Uncle Phua says time to fight SARS
Everybody, we have a part to play
To help fight SARS at the end of the day.

Don't throw your tissues all over the shop
Think no one can see you so you don't stop
Make me sick when people don't care
Make you sick when you breathe the air

Even when things are getting better
Don't do things and become a 'regret-ter'
Think SARS is gone? Your head ah.
But listen to me and we'll be ok lah.

PCK say don't play play
Or this stupid SARS is here to stay
But we can fight this, you and me
Help fight SARS in our country.

Keep our country clean and green
Because nowadays, the germs are mean
Don't leave food for stray dogs or cats
Unless you want to keep their germs as pets.

Cover your mouth if you cough or sneeze
You think everyone want to catch your disease?
Don't 'kak-pui'! all over the place
You might as well 'kak-pui' on my face.

SARS is the virus that I just want to minus
No more surprises if you use your brain, use your brain, use your braaainnn,
Can't SARS me baby, and I don't mean maybe
You must be steady, just use your brain, use your brain, use your braaainnn

(Lyrics reproduced with permission from MediaCorp TV Pte. Ltd.)

The video not only was featured regularly on prime-time television, viewers were encouraged to rap along with PCK, as the lyrics were shown at the bottom of the screen in karaoke-fashion. Gurmit Singh, as Phua Chu Kang, also visited workplaces, residential community centers, and schools to perform the rap, and received a popular response. In the actor's own words at the time:

> The feedback I had was very good. Everywhere I go, people start shouting at me 'some say *leh*, some *lah* . . .', and kids keep chanting 'SARS is the virus that I just want to minus . . . '. [. . .] My friend told me that he's been to the CCs [Community Centers] and groups of children even chanted the SARS rap. People have also requested this song on the airways on Perfect Ten 98.7 FM! [. . .] So far it seems to have left an impression on people's minds, especially the young ones. It's quite impactful, I must say. (*MediaCorp* 27 June 2003)

Evidently, in the wake of the SARS pandemic, Singlish vis-à-vis SSE got elevated from a status of displacement to complementarity. It is appropriate, therefore, at this juncture to consider the two questions raised at the start of the chapter. The first of which was whether this reflected a shift or re-negotiation of the government's ideologies pertaining to English, generally, and Singlish, particularly. The answer is both yes and no. Yes, to the extent that allowing the use of Singlish, especially for national public communication, revealed the government's grudging acknowledgement of the social value of Singlish as a community language – the language of the people. The situation offered an ironic spin to the Speak Good English slogan 'Speak Well. Be Understood'. Whereas by the slogan the Movement was referring to the necessity of global intelligibility, at a time of national urgency, it became vital to 'be understood' locally, for which Singlish was expedient.

The use of Singlish, however, cannot be said to indicate a radical departure in the government's language ideologies. For one thing, the SAR-Vivor Rap comprised one aspect only of a very extensive public information campaign, launched by the government during the SARS outbreak. Precautionary measures like washing hands thoroughly with soap, not traveling to SARS-affected countries, and practising general social responsibility were conveyed via numerous conventional public information avenues such as posters, booklets, company bulletins, websites and television. In fact, a special SARS television channel was launched, dedicated to providing up-to-the-minute information on the subject. In all this communication, Standard English was the normative language choice. The function of the SARS music video, through its humorous lyrics in Singlish and catchy rhythm, was to remind and reinforce already known information.

It is important also to bear in mind that this public usage of Singlish occurred in a time of crisis, where the survival of the nation, quite literally, was at stake. Exceptional circumstances, therefore, warranted exceptional measures. Compared to the danger posed by SARS, Singlish appeared a lesser threat, and could in fact be strategically co-opted as an ally to combat the larger, more immediate threat – 'a new and unseen enemy' (Lee Boon Yang, MITA [Ministry of Information and the Arts], 2004), as it was called. Indeed, the use of Singlish in this instance could be accounted for by the government's comprehensive communication strategy, which was described as 'finely calibrated to reach out to the maximum number of people' (Menon 2006), for which the government subsequently earned international commendation. In recognition of Singapore's successful crisis communication strategy, the World Health Organization (WHO) sought Singapore's support in September 2004 to host the first WHO Expert Consultation on Outbreak Communication, and in his welcome speech, the Director-General of WHO had this to say:

> There are few places that have demonstrated so clearly that the principles of outbreak communication work just as well in Asia as anywhere else, perhaps even better. The risk communications Singapore used during the SARS outbreak won praise worldwide . . . (reported in Menon 2006)

Once the SARS crisis had passed, and it was business as usual, Singlish no longer served a national purpose, and was relegated back to the linguistic margins.

Turning to the second question, how did the government manage to endorse the usage of Singlish in the national public space and benefit from it, without undermining its long standing official position regarding SSE and Singlish? The answer, I argue, lies in the exploitation of the resources of 'interdiscursivity' or 'interdiscursive hybridity' (Fairclough 1992, 2006), which refers to the mix of different discourse types that index the networking of different social practices. The SARS video was an instance of 'edutainment', an official public education discourse presented in an entertainment format through the music genre of rap and performed by media icon Phua Chu Kang (for a less official form of linguistic 'edutainment', see Park, Chapter 4, this volume). As a result of the interdiscursivity, the government was able to utilize communicative resources of the entertainment media sector that were otherwise unavailable to the domain of official public discourse. Here, I shall refer to two such communicative resources, and explain how these fit with the government's strategic endorsement of Singlish: (i) the crossing of interactional layers and changes in footing, and (ii) the use of a humorous, entertaining approach.

7.4.1 Crossing of interactional layers and changes in footing

Arising from Erving Goffman's (1981) and related other works (Levinson 1988; Bell 1991) on the complexity of media communication are the concepts of footing and interactional layers, which are useful for explaining the present case. 'Layers of interaction' refer to a communicative situation involving layers of interaction beyond an immediate interactional setting. For example, the immediate setting may be a television studio interview, embedded in another layer of interaction involving live and/or mass audiences. Goffman (1981) noted that communicators change 'footing' (as kinds of speakers and hearers), as they traverse between the layers of interaction.

In the case of the hybridized mediated communication of the SARS video, Phua Chu Kang, as the Singlish-speaking contractor, moves from one domain (sitcom) to another (musical performance-cum-public education). In the shift, the character breaks away from interacting (with other characters) within the fictional world of the sitcom, to directly interacting with the mass home audience. Concomitantly, the discourse roles of the audience changes, from that of 'overhearers' (third person, not ratified but expected to be listening in) to 'addressees' (second person, target audience who is directly addressed).

In terms of communicator roles in the SARS video, PCK is performing as himself (the character) as well as a spokesman for the government. Goffman's categories of 'principal' (originator of the message, whose position is expressed) and 'animator' (a physical sounding box relaying

133

a message verbatim) to refer to the government and PCK, respectively, are therefore not clear-cut. Although PCK is speaking on behalf of the government, he is not strictly an animator, as there is a shift away from an institutional voice to that of the life-world, in which 'Singlishization' is possible. At times, PCK also assumes a pseudo-principal role in the communication. As evident from the lyrics, sometimes directives are personally issued by him: 'PCK say don't play, play . . . But we can fight this, you and me. Help fight SARS in our country'; 'But listen to me and we'll be OK *lah*'; and 'Uncle Phua says time to fight SARS. Everybody, we have a part to play'. Reference to himself as 'Uncle Phua' is noteworthy as he derives authority from the life-world (as someone older, wiser and to be respected) for the communication of the message. It also explains how the generally brusque and bossy tone of the lyrics is made contextually acceptable.

In this way, the public education message is mediated by the ambivalent communicator role of PCK, who directly addresses the public. The communicative resource of Singlish, therefore, is clearly associated with PCK, and not with the government. At the same time that the government is able to get the SARS message across, it manages to keep a distance from being directly associated with the usage of Singlish.

While the interdiscursive space allows the government distance from Singlish, the intertextual history shared between the government and PCK actually helps maintain the government's official stance towards SSE and Singlish. As mentioned earlier, the Prime Minister, in his 1999 National Day Rally Speech, had publicly intervened to ask that PCK attend English classes to improve his language standard. In the National Day Rally address of the following year, the Prime Minister made this comment, while speaking on the topic of the importance of lifelong learning:

> You are never too old to learn. Even if you speak Singlish, you can learn to improve your English. Look at Phua Chu Kang. He attended BEST classes. He is speaking better English already, although still not good as Gurmit Singh. Whether Phua Chu Kang wishes to improve his English further is up to him. But if he is wise, he should keep on learning, for example, how to use the computer and e-commerce to expand his business. (Goh Chok Tong, 2000a)

The choice of PCK to front the SARS public education video, therefore, was an astute one. Not only was he a household name, PCK was a good role model of a Singlish speaker who availed himself of government-initiated programmes to improve his English. Indeed, compared to his original sitcom appearances, the later episodes, as in the case of the 2003 SARS rap, revealed some improvement in his English. No longer did he pronounce 'play' as 'pray', so that his original infamous catch-phrase 'Don't pray, pray' was replaced with the more intelligible 'Don't play, play' (i.e. 'Stop fooling around, this is serious'). In fact, the lyrics are not even wholly in Singlish; a good proportion of the lyrics is recognizably in SSE. Note for example, the whole stanza:

> Good nutrition and vitamins
> Help you to pass the immunity challenge
> Eat your proteins, carbo and fibre
> Then you can be a 'SAR-vivor'.

7.4.2 A humorous and entertaining approach

Given the generally somber mood in Singapore, and what some described was an 'overkill' (Menon 2006) of official government information and directives during the SARS period, the last thing the public would have wanted to hear was another top-down, authoritative public education message. The light, 'edutaining' approach in using PCK, a life-world character and a national media icon, was a shrewd choice, aimed to make the reception of the message more palatable, particularly as it was to be repeatedly aired. PCK, of course, could not be separated from Singlish, as that was an integral part of his fictional identity and the root of his popular appeal. Besides, local humour has been almost synonymous with Singlish, so that in order to be effectively humorous, some usage of Singlish was unavoidable. Talkingcock.com, a humourous website set up by advocates of Singlish in August 2000, in fact, celebrates Singlish as a medium of skilled humour:

> Singlish is unique to Singapore, and listening to its mish-mash of various languages and dialects, often involving bad transliterations, is also very, very funny. Contrary to popular belief, it is not merely badly spoken English, akin to pidgin. There is a conscious art in Singlish – a level of ingenious and humorous wordplay. (Talking-cock.com, 2002)

The lyrics of the SAR-vivor Rap attest to the richness of Singlish as a resource for humour, much of which also depends on shared cultural knowledge. For example, evident in the lyrics are the following:

- new coinages ('Don't be a regret-ter');
- witty wordplay ('be safe, not SAR-ry');
- colourful code-mixing of indigenous languages ('*Kiasu* a bit' ['Be a bit overly cautious'] from Chinese, and '*Tahan* a while and cooperate' ['Wait a while . . .'] from Malay);
- sound words ('Don't '*kak-pui*!' all over the place' ['*kak-pui*' resembles the sound of someone spitting]);

135

- cultural referents ('like I know Ah Bengs' [the latter a generic term for unsophisticated Chinese males]); and
- from PCK's own repertoire made famous ('Use your braaaaainnn' [said in exasperation at someone's stupidity]).

The lyrics' informality and lightness of tone make it possible to remind, instruct and chide without sounding unduly overbearing. For example, the lines 'Wait at a clinic, stay in one spot. Don't spread your germs at the coffee shop' was a direct reference to a well-publicized case of a man and his family, who disregarded the doctor's orders to wait at the clinic for an ambulance, and had instead wandered off to a nearby coffee shop, thus placing other Singaporeans at risk. In the public education message, PCK chides such socially irresponsible behaviour, while at the same time reminding Singaporeans of the correct thing to do.

Finally, the choice of the music genre as the medium of the message was also appropriately of the life-world, informal, and funky, and lent a MTV-style appeal to reach out to the younger public. The blend of rap *in* Singlish connected two quite different worlds and cultures, jointly contributing to the lively, popular, and humorous effect of the communication, which served to heighten memorability, and appeal more generally to campaign-fatigued Singaporeans.

7.5 Conclusion

What the anomalous case concerning the public national usage of Singlish has shown is that underlying the government's language ideologies generally and language choices in particular situations is a broader ideology of pragmatism (Chua 1995). Driven by instrumental rationality, the pragmatism of the government privileges economic development as key to national stability and survival. Although in practice, policies that are rationalized on pragmatic grounds often turn out to be undemocratic, the means are said to justify the ends i.e. for 'the good of the nation' (Chua 1995; Lazar 2001). As a naturalized *modus operandi* that governs most aspects of life in Singapore, language policies and matters of language choice are not exempt from the ideology of pragmatism. This accounts for the government's keen support of Standard English on the one hand, and the displacement of Singlish, on the other, which can have no place in Singapore's linguistic landscape because it is perceived as an obstacle to economic development (Rappa and Wee 2006). The pragmatic ideology also explains the government's flexibility to strategically accommodate the usage of Singlish at a time of national crisis, which adversely affected the economy and the lives of Singaporeans. Singlish had a utility value that could be harnessed for particular purposes and circumstances, without a commitment made to it beyond those purposes and circumstances. As Chua (1995: 58) explains, more generally, 'pragmatism is governed by ad hoc contextual rationality that seeks to achieve specific gains at particular points in time'.

Once the threat of SARS had subsided, there was no longer an instrumental purpose for Singlish, and so it could be 'taken off the airwaves', quite literally. Post-SARS, in fact, the Programmes Advisory Committee for English television and radio stipulated that 'Singlish should be avoided' in programmes (Leo 2005). The SGEM, also, has intensified its efforts to advocate the use of SSE and eradicate Singlish. In 2006, SGEM cleverly re-contextualized one of Phua Chu Kang's trademark expressions to promote 'good' English. PCK's usual boast in his sitcom that his contractor business was the best 'in Singapore, Malaysia, and some say Batam'[6] was appropriated with a twist, for SGEM's tagline 'Be Understood. Not just in Singapore, Malaysia, and Batam' to underscore the importance of Standard English for business and international communication.

Standard English, however, is not only associated with global communication and intelligibility. It is being actively encouraged for use in informal situations among Singaporeans as well, thus directly competing with Singlish as a community language. In the words of the former SGEM's Chair, Professor Koh Tai Ann (2006):

> Each of us has a role. We can take it upon ourselves to speak Standard English with our family members, friends and acquaintances whenever we use the language [. . .]. We hope that in time it will be the norm to speak standard or good English, whether on the playground, at the marketplace or at work.

The Minister of State for Education, who was present at the 2006 SGEM launch, also pointed to the expanded role of Standard English in the future.

> We need emotional literacy to create the social glue that holds us together as a people and as a nation. The language of the heart, of feelings and emotions is the key to connecting with our parents, children, colleagues, our neighbours and especially our loved ones. I [. . .] urge all of you who are present here today to be ambassadors of good English. (Koh 2006)

This current encroachment of Standard English on to the functional turf of Singlish – as well as the strategic public use of Singlish in 2003 – indicate that, when dealing with language ideologies from the perspective of state imperatives, the compartmentalization of the functions of language varieties as 'instrumental versus integrative' (Tollefson 1991) becomes hard to sustain. Where, as in the Singapore case, instrumental

137

rationality is the naturalized, overarching state ideology, the 'instrumental' may be extended to include the 'symbolic/integrative', just as
the 'symbolic/integrative' can also be strategically 'instrumental'.

Notes

1 Over the years, steps were taken to arrest falling language standards and to
promote 'proper' English. For example, in 1977, the British Council and the
Regional English Language Centre were co-appointed to study and make
recommendations on improving the teaching and learning of English in
schools (Low and Brown 2003: 16); and in 1999, the Ministry of Education
worked to 'upgrade standards of English in schools' by revising the English
Language syllabuses, and conducting extensive courses for primary and secondary school English Language teachers (Goh Chok Tong 1999).
2 The SGEM is not the only language campaign in Singapore. Launched in
1979, the 'Speak Mandarin Campaign' has been one of the longest running
national campaigns in the country. Similar to SGEM, this campagin has
aimed to simultaneously promote Mandarin and eradicate the use of other
Chinese dialects from the linguistic repertoire of Chinese Singaporeans. (See
Borkhorst-Heng 1999, for discussion and analysis.)
3 The accent used with standard English has been variable, as evident from the
speech of media personalities over the years. In the 1970s and 80s, television
news presenters spoke with a noticeably British accent, whereas in the 1990s,
news presenters and DJs sported an American accent. Although in the 2000s,
American (and Australian) accents are still popular in the broadcast media,
it is becoming more common to hear Standard English spoken with an educated Singaporean accent.
4 A comparison can be drawn here between PCK and the Irish TV presenter,
Hector Ó hEochagáin, discussed in Kelly-Holmes and Atkinson's (2007)
study. Although PCK is a fictional character, who uses Singlish (in Singapore),
and Hector is a real person, who speaks a non-native variety of Irish (in
Ireland), both are media personalities who have engaged the popular imagination of their respective audiences in regard to marginalized or stigmatized
language varieties. Kelly-Holmes and Atkinson (2007: 175) observe that
'Hector's irreverent brand of code-switching, his highly accented Irish-
English slang and his own brand of particular idiom are very successful'.
The same can be said of PCK in regard to Singlish. Like Hector, too, who the
authors note has become not only a media celebrity but also a powerful
media brand in his own right, PCK has become a national icon, who has
endorsed advertisements and represented Singapore in the reality show *The
Amazing Race*.
5 This refers to a basic literacy programme for adults, organized by Singapore's
National Trade Union Congress.
6 Batam is an island of Indonesia. Located 20km off Singapore's south coast, it
is only 40 minutes away by boat.

References

Bell, A. (1991), *The Language of News Media*. Oxford: Blackwell.

Blommaert, J. (ed.) (1999), *Language Ideological Debates*. Berlin: Mouton de Gruyter.

Blommaert, J. (2006), 'Language policy and national identity', in T. Ricento (ed.), *An Introduction to Language Policy: Theory and Method*. Oxford: Blackwell, pp. 238–54.

Borkhorst-Heng, W. (1999), 'Singapore's Speak Mandarin Campaign: language ideological debates and the imagining of the nation', in J. Blommaert (ed.), *Language Ideological Debates*. Berlin: Mouton de Gruyter, pp. 235–65.

Brown, A. (1999), *Singapore English in a Nutshell: An Alphabetical Description of its Features*. Singapore: Federal Publications.

Chua, B. H. (1995), *Communitarian Ideology and Democracy in Singapore*. London: Routledge.

Fairclough, N. (1992), *Discourse and Social Change*. Cambridge: Polity Press.

Fairclough, N. (2006), *Language and Globalization*. London: Routledge.

Fishman, J. A. (1968), *Readings in the Sociology of Language*. Hague: Mouton.

Goffman, E. (1981), *Forms of Talk*. Philadelphia: University of Pennsylvania Press.

Goh, C. T. (1999), *Prime Minister's National Day Rally Speech*.

Goh, C.T. (2000a), *Prime Minister's National Day Rally Speech*.

Goh, C. T. (2000b), *Speech by Prime Minister Goh Chok Tong at the Launch of the Speak Good English Movement*.

Gupta, A. F. (1998), 'The situation of English in Singapore', in J. A. Foley, T. Kandiah, Bao Zhiming, A. F. Gupta, L. Alsagoff, Ho Chee Lick, L. Wee, I. S. Talib and W. Bokhorst-Heng (eds), *English in New Cultural Contexts: Reflections from Singapore*. Singapore: Singapore Institute of Management and Oxford University Press, pp. 106–26.

Han, F. K., Fernandez, W. and Tan, S. (1998), *Lee Kuan Yew: The Man and His Ideas*. Singapore: Times.

Kelly-Holmes, H. and Atkinson, D. (2007), '"When Hector met Tom Cruise": attitudes to Irish in a radio satire', in S. Johnson and A. Ensslin (eds), *Language in the Media: Representations, Identities, Ideologies*. London: Continuum, pp. 173–87.

Koh, T. A. (2006), *Speech by Chairman, Speak Good English Movement Committee at the Launch of the 2006 Speak Good English Movement*.

Lazar, M. M. (1999), 'Family life advertisements and the narrative of heterosexual sociality', in P. G. L. Chew and A. Kramer-Dahl (eds), *Reading Culture: Textual Practices in Singapore*. Singapore: Times Academic Press, pp. 15–62.

Lazar, M. M. (2001), 'For the good of the nation: "strategic egalitarianism" in the Singapore context'. *Nations and Nationalism*, 7(1), 59–74.

Lazar, M. M. (2003), 'Semiosis, social change, and governance: a critical semiotic analysis of a national campaign'. *Social Semiotics*, 13(3), 201–21.

Lazar, M. M. (2004), 'The Speak Mandarin Campaign'. *News Radio 93.8 Interview*. Singapore: Mediacorp.

Lee, B. Y. (2004), *Speech by Minister for Information, Communications and the Arts at the National Observance Ceremony.*

Leo, D. (2005), *Life's So Like Dat.* Singapore: Pagesetters Services Pte. (Ltd.).

Levinson, S. (1988), 'Putting linguistics on a proper footing: explorations in Goffman's concepts of participation', in P. Drew and A. Wootton (eds), *Erving Goffman: Exploring the Interaction Order.* Cambridge: Polity Press, pp. 161–227.

Low, E. L. and Brown, A. (2003), *An Introduction to Singapore English.* Singapore: McGraw-Hill.

Menon, K. U. (2006), 'SARS revisited: managing "outbreaks" with "communications"'. *Annals Academy of Medicine*, 35(5), 361–67.

Pakir, A. (1992), 'English-knowing bilingualism in Singapore', in K. C. Ban, A. Pakir and C. K. Tong (eds), *Imagining Singapore.* Singapore: Times Academic Press, pp. 234–62.

Rappa, A. L. and Wee, L. (2006), *Language Policy and Modernity in Southeast Asia: Malaysia, the Philippines, Singapore, and Thailand.* New York: Kluwer.

Rubdy, R. (2001), 'Creative destruction: Singapore's Speak English Movement', *World Englishes*, 20(3), 341–55.

Talkingcock.com (2002), *The Oxford Singlish Dictionary.* Singapore: Angsana Books.

Tollefson, J. W. (1991), *Planning Language, Planning Inequality: Language Policy in the Community.* London: Longman.

PART III

MEDIA, ETHNICITY AND THE RACIALIZATION OF LANGUAGE

8 Lost in translation? Racialization of a debate about language in a BBC news item

Adrian Blackledge

8.1 Introduction

Political discourse, its representation in the media, and language ideologies are inextricably linked. We may not be able to measure exactly the extent to which our attitudes to, beliefs about, and values relating to language and languages are influenced by reference to them in print and audio-visual media. However, there is little doubt that such reference has an effect. Whilst debates about the role and value of languages other than English have traditionally been notable only by their absence from the main political agenda in Britain, in recent times senior politicians and influential television news commentators have raised questions about the relationship between use of some minority languages, some people's ability (or inability) to speak English, and problems in society. The terrorist attacks on New York in 2001, and on London in 2005, have generated questions about multiculturalism in Britain and other immigration states. Debates about immigration, 'race', integration, diversity, and social cohesion have begun to incorporate, and to be symbolized by, discourse about minority languages in Britain. Such discourse constitutes a 'common-sense', universal point-of-view, which presupposes that the use of some minority languages is associated with social problems, as is a failure or refusal to learn English. The universal point-of-view is established in constant *méconnaissances* or misrecognitions (Bourdieu 2000), which produce the view that minority languages other than English are harmful to a cohesive society. In this chapter the particular focus of debate is on the public cost of translation and interpreting services for immigrants. The analysis looks at a short BBC Television news item, and situates this in the context of other political texts which emerged in the period December 2006 – June 2007, which involved senior political figures engaging in discussions about public spending on translation services for linguistic minorities. The analysis argues that the introduction of images of Muslim women serves to racialize and Islamicize the debate about language, transforming it into one about immigration and social segregation.

8.2 Language and symbolic racism

Racism does not only consist of white supremacist ideologies of race, or only of aggressive, overt or blatant discriminatory acts. Racism also involves 'the everyday, mundane, negative opinions, attitudes and ideologies and the seemingly subtle acts and conditions of discrimination against minorities' (van Dijk 1993: 5). Racist discourse is not the preserve of extremist groups. Rather, argues van Dijk, it is produced and reproduced in political, educational and media discourses. Ronald Schmidt Sr (2000, 2002) argues that racial categories are social constructs imposed upon biological patterns by the human imagination and through human discourse. Racial groups are socially constructed categories whose boundaries and meaning are subject to on-going change and re-definition. John Richardson (2004) argues that the reproduction of racism in discourse is pervasive:

> if racism is reproduced through discourse, then racism will be in evidence at all three 'levels' of discursive communication – social practices, discursive practices, and the texts themselves – in ways which are integrated and mutually self-supporting. (Richardson 2004: 33)

T. A. van Dijk (2000a: 87) defines racism as 'a system of social inequality in which ethnic minority groups are dominated by a white (European) majority on the basis of origin, ethnicity, or attributed "racial" characteristics'. Philomena Essed (2000: 44) suggests that racism is a process fluently integrated in everyday life, and 'everyday racism adapts to cultural arrangements, norms and values while operating through the structures of power in society'. Schmidt argues that a process of *racialization* occurs in discourse which ascribes to groups certain characteristics which render them so foreign or 'alien' that it is impossible to conceive of them as equal members of the same community as the dominant group. Schmidt (2002: 158) suggests that 'Racialization is a social process whose point is inequality'. Stephen May (2001) points out that the process of racialization occurs in two ways. First, biologically determined characteristics have been held to distinguish between groups. This process has been associated with the scientific racism of the nineteenth century, but continues in popular 'common-sense' discourse in contemporary societies. Second is a similar process of ascribing cultural practices to groups (see also Androutsopoulos, Chapter 10, and Ensslin, Chapter 11, this volume). This has led to what May (2001: 33) calls 'new racisms', which often describe groups in cultural terms without specifically mentioning 'race' or overtly racial criteria. Schmidt (2002: 154) put this point clearly: 'A *new racism* has developed in recent decades in which specific cultural forms have come to signify racialized identities'.

When discussions of 'race' as the basis of group difference are no longer politically acceptable, metaphors are sought. Common-sense public discourse identifies cultural practices which are different from those of the dominant group, and they become symbols of the 'Otherness' of the minority. That is, cultural practices become racialized, and come to represent a group (see also Davies, Chapter 9, and Androutsopoulos, Chapter 10, this volume). Schmidt (2002) argues that in the US a conjunction of the hegemonic position of the dominant English language and the socially constructed normalization of 'Whiteness' creates an ideological context within which Americans speaking languages other than English are racialized as outsiders, as 'Others'. T. A. van Dijk argues that television news has a key role in shaping the way we think about minority groups: 'not only for ordinary citizens but also for the elites themselves, the mass media are today the primary source of "ethnic" knowledge and opinion in society' (2002: 152).

8.3 Islamophobia

In Britain during the last ten years or so, the focus of racist discourse has at least partly shifted from people of Black Caribbean heritage to Muslim peoples whose heritage is often in Pakistan and Bangladesh (although Indian and other Asian-heritage groups are often conflated with these). In Britain (as elsewhere since the attack on the World Trade Centre in New York in 2001), there has recently been a consistent discourse which has characterized Muslim people as alien and 'Other'. Even before that, the *Commission on British Muslims and Islamophobia* (The Runnymede Trust 1997) reported that anti-Muslim prejudice has grown rapidly and considerably in recent years, and is manifested in the media, public policy, education and law. In this climate, a number of cultural practices have come to represent Muslim Pakistani and Bangladeshi groups as different from the majority, including, *inter alia*, speaking and making visible minority languages, wearing ethnic dress, especially the *hijab* or *niqab*, participating in arranged marriages, building and attending mosques, fasting during religious periods, eating Halal meat, engaging in regular prayer, especially on Fridays, and setting up and attending Islamic schools (Bikhu Parekh 2000; The Runnymede Trust 1997). All of these practices have been reported in the media in ways which emphasize the difference between Muslims

145

and the majority 'British' group. Richardson points out that in public reports, 'Islam' and 'the West' are often contrasted in oppositional discourse:

> Muslims are identified as 'Other' by virtue of characteristics which they are presumed or perceived to lack: in other words, their 'lack' of 'Britishness' divides 'Them' from 'Us'. The second method of division is an explicit split, where Islam and/or Muslims are identified as the 'Other' by virtue of values or characteristics which they are perceived to have: in short, their 'Islamic-ness' is used to divide 'Them' from 'Us'. (Richardson 2004: 113)

At the same time, such reporting has often characterized 'Muslims' as a homogeneous group, when there is in fact great diversity among British Muslims. These practices, as reported in political and media discourse, become symbols of difference between the 'White' majority and British Muslim groups (see Blackledge 2002, 2003, 2004, 2005 for examples of media, political and educational discourses which locate some of these practices as markers of difference). As such, they are racialized cultural practices, which become metaphors for 'racial' differences which cannot now be spoken. In this chapter I suggest that language practices of Muslim Asian groups which include speaking languages other than English are racialized in the same way as other cultural practices.

8.4 Re-contextualization of language in political discourse

In order to understand how a discourse contributes to creating the conditions for discrimination, it is necessary to identify how it connects to other discourses. A text is rarely the work of any one individual, but often shows traces of different discourses contending and struggling for dominance (Weiss and Wodak 2003: 15). That is, texts relate to other texts, and relate to the social and historical conditions of their production. This notion of 'context' is crucial in understanding the power of language, and plays a vital role in the analysis of media discourse in this chapter.

No text stands alone and outside of its context. Rather, 'all texts are constituted of transformed elements of other, prior texts' (Kress 2000). Not only are texts constituted of other texts, but they are inevitably transformations of those other texts. Here the concept of 're-contextualization' is useful, as it can be used 'to chart shifts of meanings either within one genre – as in different versions of a specific written text – or across semiotic dimensions' (Wodak 2000: 192). When a social event is *re*-presented, it is incorporated within the context of another social event, and re-contextualized (Fairclough 2003). In this process of re-contextualisation, social events are not merely repeated. Rather, they are transformed in their new setting, perhaps through the addition of new elements, or through the deletion of others. The arrangement of events may change in the new context, or some elements may be substituted for others. The argumentation strategies identified in media and political discourse may recur in a new setting, incorporating new 'voices' as they go. Such arguments may be transformed across genres, and yet remain identifiable as links in the chain of discourse. In the exploration of political discourses, the re-contextualisation of arguments is pursued from one genre to the next, and from one public domain to the next. This 'life of arguments' illustrates the power struggle about specific opinions, beliefs or ideologies (Titscher *et al.* 2000: 156).

While re-contextualisation often involves the suppression and filtering of some meaning potentials of a discourse (Chouliaraki and Fairclough 1999), it is also a process which may expand meaning potential, through additions to, and elaborations upon, the previous text. Re-contextualisation always involves transformation, and that transformation is dependent on the goals, values and interests of the context into which the discursive practice is being re-contextualized (van Leeuwen and Wodak 1999: 96). Discourses may be further linked across a range of genres. However, the re-contextualisation of discourse does not end with the explicit links between, and commentary upon, other discourses. For example, when a Government policy statement is published, it appears in a particular genre, but its arguments and presuppositions are recognizable from discourses which have gone before. That is, the re-contextualisation of arguments across genres invariably includes allusions to, and implicatures of, the many voices influencing the debate, both liberal and illiberal (see also Lazar, Chapter 7, this volume, on the re-contextualization of Singlish).

8.5 The context of debate

In December 2006 the (then) Prime Minister Tony Blair gave a speech in Downing Street which engaged with the notion of 'multicultural Britain' and the integration of immigrant groups. The speech argued that integration was about 'shared, common, unifying British values', and that 'we need to re-assert the duty to integrate'. The Prime Minister set out six 'elements in policy', which underscored what the 'duty to integrate' entailed. These policy elements included a new requirement for

'visiting preachers to have a proper command of English', and a requirement to pass an English language test before permanent residency
would be granted to those seeking leave to remain in the UK.

8.5.1 'Our shared national language'

Several weeks after Prime Minister Blair's Downing Street speech,
David Cameron MP, the Leader of the Conservative Party, and of Her
Majesty's Opposition, gave a speech in Birmingham in which he listed
'five barriers, five Berlin walls of division that we must tear down
together': 'extremism', 'multiculturalism', 'uncontrolled immigration',
'poverty' and 'educational apartheid'. I will consider briefly David
Cameron's remarks about 'multiculturalism':

> For many years, the ruling class in this country believed in some-
> thing called multiculturalism. Multiculturalism sounds like a good
> thing: people of different cultures living together. But . . . it lies
> behind the growth in the translation of public documents and signs
> into other languages. What ought to be about helping people to
> access essential public services has in some cases become an end in
> itself, making it less of an incentive for people to learn English and
> participate fully in our national life. All of these things just create
> resentment and suspicion. And they undermine the very thing
> that should have served as a focus for national unity – our sense of
> British identity. (Cameron 2007)

Here the argument is that the provision of translation services for speakers of languages other than English also creates division by making it
'less of an incentive for people to learn English and participate fully in
our national life'.

In David Cameron's speech there is a presupposition that the provision of translation services prevents some people from learning English,
and creates resentment and suspicion. The Leader of the Opposition
does not question the validity of such resentment and suspicion, rather
taking it as an inevitable response to the visible presence in society of
languages other than English. The further threat here, that the translation of public documents and signs into other languages undermines
'our sense of British identity', proposes firstly that there is a consensus
about what constitutes British identity, and secondly that it does not
include the multicultural and multilingual nature of that society.
Indeed, languages other than English appear to be contrary to national
unity and British identity.

David Cameron then goes on to argue for a policy change:

> I believe that the Government should redirect some of the money it
> currently spends on translation into additional English classes.

Figure 4.1 The set of *Sangsang Plus*

Figure 5.1 Introductory image from *Planeta Brasil*

Figure 5.2 Screenshot from *América Legal*

Figure 11.1 Trader and young hero in *Fable: The Lost Chapters* (Lionhead Studios 2005)

Figure 11.2 Introductory cut-scene, *Black and White 2* (Lionhead Studios 2005)

UNIVERSITY OF LEEDS

✍Tel: 0113 592 0000

Mockba

©

Figure 12.1 Examples of ITEMS

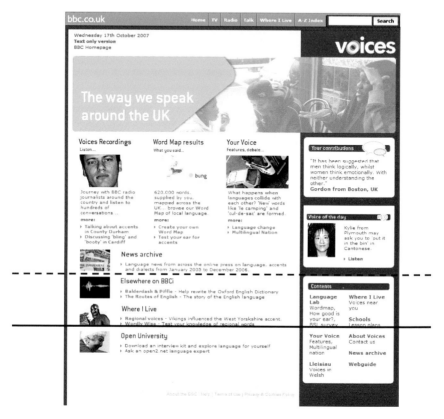

Figure 12.2 Screen shot of the BBC Voices home page frozen on 17 October 2007. The solid black line indicates the fold on a regular 17" monitor with a screen resolution of 1152 x 864 pixels, whilst the dashed black line shows the fold on a laptop with 15" widescreen display with a screen resolution of 1280 x 800 pixels.

Figure 12.3 The heading

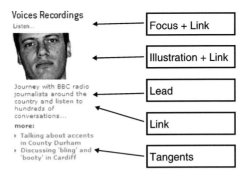

Figure 12.4 An example of a 'newsbite'

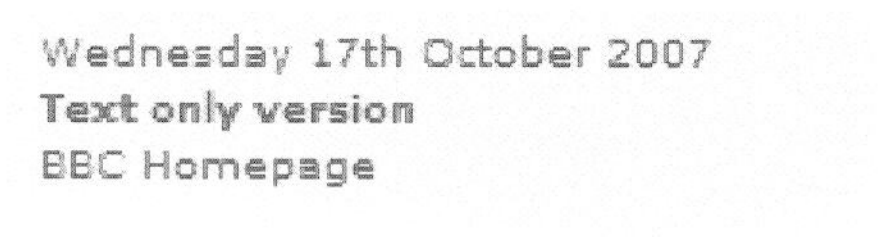

Wednesday 17th October 2007
Text only version
BBC Homepage

Figure 12.5 'Text-only'

Figure 12.6 Section of the Macro-Theme

Figure 12.7 Complete sequence of banner changes (approx. 4.5 seconds intervals) (retrieved on 19 October 2007)

Word Map results

What you said...

bung

620,000 words,
supplied by you,
mapped across the
UK... browse our Word
Map of local language.

more:

▸ Create your own
  Word Map
▸ Test your ear for
  accents

Figure 12.8 Newsbite on the Word Map

> This would help people integrate into society and broaden their
> opportunities . . . We must make sure that all our citizens can speak
> to each other in our shared national language. (Cameron 2007)

Oppositional discourse in the first sentence proposes a choice for
Government between paying for translation services or funding English
classes. David Cameron argues for the latter, insisting that learning to
speak English, rather than having public services provided in their own
language, will 'help people integrate into society'. The prioritization of
English classes over translation services, shared by government and
opposition politicians alike, has none the less gone hand in hand with
a cut in English-language provision in recent years.

Having argued plainly that the presence and visibility of languages
other than English creates social division, brings about resentment and
suspicion, and undermines national unity and British identity, David
Cameron concluded his speech in an egalitarian vein:

> We must bring down the barriers in our country. We must push
> forward the frontiers of fairness. We must create equal opportunity,
> so everyone has the chance to get on in life, to fulfil their dreams,
> and to feel that their contribution is part of a shared national effort.
> (Cameron 2007)

Implicitly at least, the provision of translation services for immigrants is seen as a barrier to equal opportunity, the fulfilment of dreams,
and the shared national effort.

8.5.2 Breaking down the language barrier

On 22 February 2007 the Commission on Integration and Cohesion
(CIC), established by the UK Government, published its Interim Report.
This report engages directly with the question of translation services:

> Clearly there will be times when translation is necessary – to help
> new arrivals in particular, and to ensure that vulnerable groups are
> protected. However, it is also apparent that translation of public
> materials can also prevent interaction between groups, prevent lan-
> guage skills being developed, and in extreme cases even cause sus-
> picion across groups. (CIC Interim Report, paragraph 41)

A 'show concession' (Antaki and Wetherell 1999), or 'apparent concession' (van Dijk 2000b: 40) here appears to acknowledge that translation
services may at times be necessary, but this turns out to be no more
than a preface to the debunking of the same argument, as translation
can 'prevent interaction', 'prevent language skills being developed',
and 'cause suspicion across groups'. This is a re-contextualization of
David Cameron's earlier point about 'failed multiculturalism', in which

149

the funding of translation services exemplified activities which 'just create resentment and suspicion'. A similar point was made in the press briefing which accompanied the launch of the Interim report:

> translation services should be there to help people adapt, not replace learning the language. If they are provided for too long, they can become a crutch for people to get by without learning the English they need to integrate successfully. (http://www.integratio-nandcohesion.org/news)

Once again here the provision of Government-funded translation services is represented as oppositional to learning English, and successful integration, this time invoking the metaphor of the 'crutch' to add persuasive emphasis. The Final Report of CIC was published in June 2007. It found that the English language 'binds us together as a single group in a way that a multiplicity of community languages cannot', and 'translation into community language should not always be the first approach'. In these official discourses it appears that the provision of translations services to migrants is viewed as problematic for social cohesion.

8.5.3 'A lot of money in anyone's language'

In mid-December 2006 and mid-February 2007, the debate about translation services was picked up in a news item, presented on the Ten O'clock News programme on BBC1 on 12 December 2006. The item, titled 'Cost in Translation', begins with a multi-ethnic crowd scene, and the voice-over of BBC journalist Mark Easton:

> it's a lot of money in anyone's language. No one in Government knows quite how much taxpayers now spend translating for UK residents who don't speak English, but new BBC research has come up with the first-ever figure.

The conversationalized beginning here appeals to the assumed audience of the news item, both informal ('it's a lot of money') and cleverly idiomatic ('in anyone's language'). In the second sentence the item appeals to the viewer on a more concerned basis, as the audience may be supposed to be 'taxpayers' who, the item implies, may be paying an almost infinite, or at least unknown, amount of tax 'translating for UK residents who don't speak English'. The final clause here asserts the authority and legitimacy of the item, nominating the report as 'research', which provides the 'first-ever figure' relating to the cost of translation services. The phrase 'come up with' maintains the informality of the item, appealing again to consensus. Here the news item adopts a 'familiar, matter-of-fact rhetoric' (Fowler 1991: 217), which is plain-speaking, sensible, and authoritative.

150

In the next scene of the item Mark Easton speaks to camera as follows:

> we've identified more than one hundred million pounds now spent
> on translation each year and the true figure is probably much much
> higher. The cost to the public purse is soaring.

The informal yet authoritative tone continues here, with 'we've identi-fied'. The intensifier 'more than' combines with 'the true figure is prob-ably much much higher' to create the sense that the cost is out of control. The deictic 'now' proposes that the spending is an ongoing and worsen-ing process. The repetition of 'much' adds emphasis, and the final sen-tence here continues the informal tone ('public purse'), while implying serious concern that spending is out of control. The hyperbolic 'soar-ing' leaves no doubt about the critical perspective of the item.

In the next scene Mark Easton's voiceover accompanies still images and moving pictures which fade in and out to depict the services referred to:

> some is vital, but is money being lost in translation? Local councils
> spend, we calculate, at least twenty-five million pounds a year,
> the police twenty-one million, the courts ten million and more, the
> NHS [National Health Service], a conservative estimate is fifty-five
> million pounds.

The first phrase here appears to concede the argument, but only in the interests of balance. The rhetorical question that follows further engages the audience, speaking not only for the voice of the news item, but also for the assumed viewer. Consensus is assumed, and the dis-courses of the news item and viewer appear to be travelling in the same direction (Voloshinov 1973: 138). The rhetorical question presupposes the response of the audience: yes, money is being lost to the taxpayer through funding these services. Rhetorical questions allow 'argumenta-tive engagement with the imagined points of view of those referred to' (Fowler 1991: 218). Voloshinov suggests that rhetorical questions in text are 'situated on the very boundary between authorial and reported speech' (1973: 137). In this instance, the rhetorical question has the effect of seeking and implying the complicity of the assumed viewer, speaking both for the BBC and for the audience. The clever use of pun adds to the apparent sophistication of the piece. 'Lost in translation' usually collocates in the axiom: 'poetry is that which is lost in transla-tion', although the audience's familiarity with the pun may be more likely to stem from knowledge of the popular film of the same name. The topos of finance (van Dijk 2000a: 97; Wodak *et al.* 1999) then serves to argue that far too much money, and probably more than is known ('at least', 'a conservative estimate') is being 'lost in translation'.

151

The next scene is set in an office in Peterborough. The voiceover continues, overlapping with a recorded telephone message:

> from leaflets and signs to one-on-one interpretation
> [recorded telephone message: *please hold, you will be connected to an interpreter*].
> Here in Peterborough, for instance, Council Tax payers spend more than a million a year translating into seventy-six languages for a growing immigrant population.

The first sentence here is constructed to emphasize both the range and the extent of the translation and interpretation services provided by the local council. Again the intensifiers 'more than' and 'growing' suggest a worsening problem, while the earlier 'taxpayers' is now re-contextualized as the more specific 'Council Tax payers'. In a topos of threat, and a topos of number ('seventy-six languages'), the news item suggests that Council Tax payers are being taxed too heavily to support an ever-demanding immigrant group. In the office scene a woman, Anyeshka, speaks Polish to an interpreter. The voiceover continues:

> This Polish woman has lived in the area for three years but now pregnant and unemployed is given an interpreter to help her apply for Job Seekers' Allowance.

Here the item argues that those who have already had sufficient should be given no more (Reisigl and Wodak 2001; Wodak *et al.* 1999), as there is a suggestion that Anyeshka is receiving support to which she is hardly entitled. The phrase 'three years', allied to 'now pregnant and unemployed' implies that she would have been better served learning English and getting a job, rather than becoming pregnant. Despite this apparent criticism of Anyeshka, she is produced as a witness for the argument that too much money is spent on translation and interpretation. Rather than being given the opportunity to answer the implicit charges about failing to learn English and burdening the state, Anyeshka is asked the following question through the interpreter:

> [*ME to interpreter*] does Anyeshka think that if there wasn't all this help, people like you and all the leaflets, perhaps she would have been more encouraged to learn English?
> [interpreter asks the question and Anyeshka replies]
> [*interpreter*]: yes, absolutely.

Anyeshka, a Polish immigrant who has not yet learned English, becomes an expert, legitimate witness. The fact that she is one of those in receipt of the expensive services lends her view an authenticity and reliability. At the same time, she is heard to speak only one word, and a word in agreement with the BBC journalist.

152

8.5.4 'Doing more harm than good'

The next two scenes show local police and council workers handing out information in "fifteen languages", and in the following scene, filmed in Peterborough 'New Link Centre', a worker there (Leonie McCarthy) speaks to camera: "what we say to people is if they need it in their language we will make sure they have it because we believe that everybody should have equal access". This may be a further "show concession", accepting a point of view before debunking it. In the following scene we shift from Peterborough to the East End of London, with a shot of a road sign on Brick Lane in English and Bengali. The voiceover indeed appears to debunk the apparent concession in Leonie McCarthy's point:

In the following scene we shift from Peterborough to the East End of London, with a shot of a road sign on Brick Lane in English and Bengali. The voiceover indeed appears to debunk the apparent concession in the following comment by Leonie McCarthy:

> The Race Relations Act says that all parts of the community should have access to services, which many public bodies take to mean they must translate.

Both the Race Relations Act and Leonie McCarthy's point are immediately called into question in the phrase 'take to mean'. Having questioned the validity of the witnesses in favour of translation and interpretation services, the news item produces its trump card, calling to the stand its most authoritative witness:

> but in London's East End a Bangladeshi human rights lawyer told me that translation services were doing more harm than good.

This witness carries authority because, first, he is Bangladeshi, second, he represents the unimpeachable status of 'human rights', and third, he is a lawyer. In addition, he is speaking in the East End of London, richly populated with Bangladeshi-heritage people, and he speaks with an accent more reminiscent of the English upper-class than of London East-End Bengalis. The scene moves to an East-End restaurant, where we see the lawyer, Zia Haider Rahman, and the presenter sharing a meal together. The shot cuts to the lawyer, who says:

> They are de-incentivising the Bangladeshis in this area from, they are discouraging them from learning English.

This point is the same as that made by David Cameron in his 29 January speech, and indeed it may have been the source used by Cameron's speech writer. Authoritative and apparently legitimate, the lawyer's point appears to be running in the same direction as the news item.

153

In the next shot another expert witness speaks against translation and interpretation services. The restaurant scene fades to a shot of the back of the head of a woman in a headscarf. Both Mark Easton and the human rights lawyer face the camera, but the woman's face is entirely hidden. The voiceover continues:

> He introduced us to a woman in her forties who's lived in Britain for twenty-two years but speaks not a word of English. She was too frightened to speak openly.

This Bangladeshi woman is a legitimate witness because she appears to be one of those who has suffered segregation and separation caused by the provision of translation and interpretation services. The phrase 'not a word' is emphatic and even critical. Like the Polish woman earlier, this woman is presented as an expert witness because she is unable to speak English. There is a striking example of interdiscursivity here: the statement in the voiceover that 'She was too frightened to speak openly' prompts questions about what it is she fears. It is not uncommon for witnesses/interviewees on television news items to have their faces blacked out, or otherwise hidden, and for something like 'He/she was too frightened to speak openly' to be offered as explanation. However, this almost always occurs when the story concerns violence and danger. In BBC news bulletins in the same week as the 'Cost in Translation' story was broadcast, this occurred twice – the first was a report on arrests for terrorism charges, the second about the murder of a London teenager. The introduction of this method in the item discussed here seems to represent the debate about translation services as somehow linked to violence and/or danger.

In the same scene, we hear the voice of the woman, which fades as the voice of an interpreter takes over in English:

> [woman speaks in Sylheti]
> [voice of interpreter]: when you are trying to help us you are actually harming us. Even before we ask all we have to do is say hello and they're here with their interpreters. We just sit here doing nothing and we don't need to speak in English at all.

As the woman speaks the scene cuts to an image of a grim, high-rise block of flats, behind a blurred shot of a corroded railing which comes into focus in the foreground. This image, a visual echo of the recurrent image of 'barriers' to social cohesion, is juxtaposed with the woman saying 'they're here with their interpreters'. The image cuts to a Muslim woman in a long coat and headscarf on the street. She pulls the scarf across her face as the woman speaking is heard to say 'we don't need to speak in English at all'. Here the image of the headscarf is juxtaposed with the notion of not needing to speak English, and emphatically confirms that the interpretation service is responsible for social segregation and division.

In the next sequence a multilingual sign from St Bartholomew's Hospital in London appears, with the voiceover 'In the NHS Bart's Hospital now spends a million pounds a year translating'. This image cuts to a scene in a health clinic in Islington (also in London), with Mark Easton, a patient, and a bilingual health worker. The voiceover continues:

> Islington Primary Care Trust offers one-to-one stop smoking advice in Turkish. Is that money well-spent, we asked.

The phrase 'one-to-one' is re-iterated here (previously heard as 'one-on-one interpretation'), emphasizing the intensive and expensive nature of the language support offered. It is not clear whether the question is rhetorical, or was asked of the Turkish patient. In the next shot Mark Easton is seen leaning towards her, listening. The Turkish woman has a brief exchange with the Turkish-speaking health worker, and turns back to Mark Easton, saying 'my rights, my rights'. The production of a service-user witness appears to be in the interests of balance. However, compared with the Polish woman, the Bangladeshi human rights lawyer, and the Bangladeshi woman interviewed with her back to the camera, the Turkish woman appears less articulate, and unable to express coherently her defence of the interpreting service. In comparison with the witnesses who took the stand to criticize the translation and interpretation service, the Turkish witness for the defence is less than convincing. This may of course be a result of editing on the part of programme-makers. Indeed in another BBC News item of 21 February 2007, an extended excerpt from the same interview revealed that the Turkish woman offered a much longer response.

The scene now cuts to an interview with a Government minister, Phil Woolas, who says:

> We need to put more emphasis on teaching English, that's what we are doing and we are going to examine, and are examining, whether we need to do more in that respect.

It is notable that the minister does not defend the Government's spending on translation and interpretation services, but rather emphasizes 'teaching English' as a response. This is consistent with the other voices we have heard in this debate, and in particular with the voice of the Leader of the Opposition, David Cameron.

The scene now cuts to the final sequence. The voiceover continues as follows:

> Following our investigation a review is under way as to whether Britain's translation industry helps or hinders integration. Mark Easton, BBC News.

The construction 'a review is under way as to whether Britain's translation industry helps or hinders integration' has the same effect as a rhetorical question, assuming consensus, as the voice of the news item and the assumed audience are running in the same direction. Implicit here is the notion that the review can only find that the 'translation industry' hinders integration. The term 'industry' assumes that the service is too large, and has become a self-serving business. The words would be enough here to convince that the direction of the item is in favour of reducing considerably the translation service. However, in the ten seconds it takes Mark Easton to utter this single sentence the voiceover is accompanied by four images – of Muslim Asian women and children walking in the street. The first image is of a woman in full veil. This image, apparently unconnected to the language debate in the news item, links intertextually with recent debates about Muslim women wearing full veil, or *niqab*, in public. The second shot is of two Muslim women in headscarves (*hijab*) and long coats, filmed from behind. The viewer cannot see whether they have face veils. They are seen walking away from the camera, one of them holding a child by the hand. In the third shot we see a Muslim woman in a scarf which covers her head and shoulders. She is also filmed from behind, under an umbrella, in what is a rather blurred shot. In the final one of the four images, just as the voiceover gives its signature 'Mark Easton, BBC News', the shot is of another Muslim woman in a scarf which covers her head and shoulders, holding a child by the hand. She too is walking away from the camera. In none of the images are we able to see the faces of the women.

The first image in the sequence represents a woman wearing the *niqab* face veil, along with a headscarf and long coat. Almost universally represented in public discourses as an image of separation and division in British society, this is a powerful image to accompany Mark Easton's rhetorical question. The image is a 'visual re-contextualization' of similar images which had proliferated in the British media two months earlier after a senior Government politician, Jack Straw, had argued that he wished women to remove their *niqab* when visiting his surgery for advice and support. The politician's statements provoked considerable debate in the media and elsewhere about the wearing of the *niqab* by British Muslims (a typical example from the BBC, 'Straw's

veil comments spark anger' is available at: http://news.bbc.co.uk/1/hi/
uk_politics/5410472.stm). Although in Mark Easton's BBC News item
there is explicit reference neither to Muslims or to the way they dress,
the 'visual re-contextualization' finds its audience in the 'common
ground' (Bourdieu 1998: 121; van Dijk 2000c: 95, 2005: 80) of recent
discursive history. Both wearing the *niqab* and speaking languages other
than English are frequently 'misrecognized' in discursive 'common
miscognitions' (Bourdieu 2000: 192) as contributors to (and symbols of)
social segregation. It is these 'common miscognitions', these reiterations
of the *niqab* as emblematic of Islam, and of Islam as iconic of social segregation, that provide the 'social memory' on which understanding of
the images is based. The image of the woman in the *niqab* in the first
of the four closing images can therefore be explained. Despite the fact
that the 'text' of the news item is 'about' the relative value-for-money of
translation services, the 'image' provides a new sense, and the item
now concerns certain cultural practices and their relation to social
segregation.

In the second of the images presented during the final ten seconds of
the news item, there are three figures walking down the street, away
from the camera. Two of the figures appear to be women, and one a
child. Each of them is hooded in one way or another: one of the women
in a headscarf, the child in the hood of his or her anorak, and the third
woman in a covering which appears to be similar to that of the woman
in the first of the four images. The viewers 'keep their distance' from
the figures, whose head coverings mark them as 'culturally different'
(van Leeuwen 2000: 336). The three figures are heading, and looking,
away from the camera, but are 'as it were offered to our gaze as a spec-
tacle for our dispassionate scrutiny' (van Leeuwen 2000: 339). The figures are represented not as individuals, but as generic categories, either
as 'victims of social segregation' (in this context social segregation
caused by the 'translation industry'), or as 'causes of social segregation'.
The figures have no voice, and no agency, but are passive representatives of the cultural 'Other'. The head covering is commonly understood to be emblematic of cultural difference and to threaten social
cohesion, and here acts to homogenize the Muslim group. The third of
the four images represents another figure viewed from behind, walking
away from the camera. This also appears to be a woman with a headscarf. She carries an umbrella, and the shot is out of focus. We can only
speculate on the reasons to select such an out-of-focus shot in the editing process. This figure too lacks agency. Her face is not visible, and she
is walking away from the camera. In the final of the four images another
woman is viewed from behind, also walking away from the camera. She
is also wearing a long headscarf. Her face is not visible. She holds the

hand of a child who wears the hood of an anorak. In each of the four scenes we see 'represented participants' (Kress and van Leeuwen 1996: 119). No contact is made between viewer and participants, but the participants are offered as representatives of their group. The non-agentic, distanced, symbolically disempowered figures in the four final scenes are all of women and children, whereas the most articulate actors in the news item (the BBC journalist Mark Easton, the human rights lawyer Zia Haider Rahman, and the Government minister Phil Woolas) were men. Moreover, the women portrayed in the final ten seconds of the item come to represent the 'Muslim' group. This is despite the fact that the content of the news item dealt with the issue of the public cost of translation services. The images accrue meaning through the common knowledge which occurs 'when one can say that everyone knows that everyone knows that everyone possesses certain information or, as is often said, when it is an open secret' (Bourdieu 1998: 97). The open secret which is brought to bear in creating meaning from these images is one which states that wearing certain garments in certain ways, like speaking certain languages in certain places, is a threat to social cohesion and national unity. The debate about language comes to be racialized. Implicit in the collective memory which responds to these images is the popular presupposition that Muslim Asian women are at least partly to blame for social segregation, because they are either unwilling or unable to speak English. It is the juxtaposition of images of representative, non-agentic Muslim Asian women with textual discourse about translation services 'doing more harm than good' that then racializes and Islamicizes a debate which had initially appeared to be about language rather than race or immigration.

8.6 Conclusion

We can say little about the actual effects of such a television news item without engaging with viewers about their responses. However, we are able to identify some features of what Roland Barthes (1977: 46) called the 'rhetoric of the image', or the 'signifiers of connotation' which enable the viewer to understand the message symbolically. The headscarves of the women signify worlds of 'common ground' (Bourdieu 1998: 121), or 'common knowledge' (van Dijk 2005: 80) about the role of Muslim immigrants, and of Muslim women, in British society. These signifiers are commonly understood because they transport meanings from other domains (Machin 2007). That is, meanings articulated or represented in one context are now re-contextualized in another, and are transformed in their re-contextualization (see Androutsopoulos,

Chapter 10 and Ensslin, Chapter 11, this volume for further examples of such cultural re-contextualization in relation to ethnic groups). Not all previous references in public discourse to Muslim women in head-scarves can be identified, but there is a strong sense that the BBC News viewer holds a 'mental model' constructed in the historical dimension of discourse, through what has been said before about the same subject (van Dijk 2006: 367), and according to which such images are viewed symbolically. Of course different viewers will hold different mental models which create different meanings from images. At the same time, much is shared in the common ground of meaning-making. In the BBC News item of 12 December 2006, discussion of the public cost of trans-lation services becomes a symbolic battleground on which to debate wider issues about the kind of society envisaged for the future: one which is plural, heterogeneous, and willing to resource its diversity, or one which is unitary, homogeneous, and insistent on rapid assimilation. The news item raises these issues through argumentation strategies about finance, burden on the state, and the benefit to immigrants them-selves, which are typical of anti-immigrant arguments (van Dijk 2000a; Wodak *et al.* 1999). The main thrust of the news argument is that when the State pays for translation services, some immigrants are less likely to assimilate, and that this constitutes a threat to social cohesion. However, the item powerfully raises the stakes through representative images of Muslim women. The item visually re-contextualizes other images of Muslim women from other semiotic domains, and plays into mental models constructed through other recent and historical debates about Muslims in British society, including debates about terrorism, and debates about language(s) and social segregation. In this way, a debate about *language* is racialized and Islamicized, and is transformed into a debate about immigration and social segregation. In so doing it contributes to the way we think about language(s), race, and migration in contemporary society.

References

Antaki, C. and Wetherell, M. (1999), 'Show concessions'. *Discourse Studies*, 1(1), 7–27.
Barthes, R. (1977), *Image, Music, Text.* Glasgow: Fontana.
Blackledge, A. (2002), 'The discursive construction of national identity in multilingual Britain'. *Journal of Language, Identity and Education*, 1(1), 67–87.
Blackledge, A. (2003), 'Imagining a monocultural community: the racialization of cultural practice in educational discourse'. *Journal of Language, Identity and Education*, 2(4), 331–48.

Blackledge, A. (2004), 'Constructions of identity in political discourse in multilingual Britain', in A. Pavlenko and A. Blackledge (eds), *Negotiation of Identities in Multilingual Contexts.* Clevedon: Multilingual Matters, pp. 68–92.

Blackledge, A. (2005), *Discourse and Power in a Multilingual World.* Amsterdam: John Benjamins.

Blair, T. (2006), *The Duty to Integrate: Shared British Values.* Downing Street speech, December 2006.

Bourdieu, P. (1998), *Practical Reason.* London: Polity Press.

Bourdieu, P. (2000), *Pascalian Meditations.* Cambridge: Polity Press.

Cameron, D. (2007), 'Bringing down the barriers to cohesion'. Speech, Lozells, Birmingham. 29 January 2007.

Chouliaraki, L. and Fairclough, N. (1999), *Discourse in Late Modernity: Rethinking Critical Discourse Analysis.* Edinburgh: Edinburgh University Press.

Essed, P. (2000), 'Beyond antiracism: diversity, multi-identifications and sketchy images of new societies' in M. Reisigl. and R. Wodak (eds), *The Semiotics of Racism.* Vienna: Passagen Verlag, pp. 41–62.

Fairclough, N. (2003), *Analysing Discourse: Textual Analysis for Social Research.* London: Routledge.

Fowler, R. (1991), *Language in the News: Discourse and Ideology in the Press.* London: Routledge.

Kress, G. (2000), 'Text as the punctuation of semiosis: pulling at some of the threads' in U. Meinhof and J. Smith (eds), *Intertextuality and the Media: From Genre to Everyday Life.* Manchester: Manchester University Press, pp. 132–54.

Kress, G. and van Leeuwen, T. (1996), *Reading Images: The Grammar of Visual Design.* London: Routledge.

Machin, D. (2007), *Introduction to Multimodal Analysis.* London: Hodder Arnold.

May, S. (2001), *Language and Minority Rights: Ethnicity, Nationalism, and the Politics of Language.* London: Longman.

Parekh, B. (2000), *Rethinking Multiculturalism: Cultural Diversity and Political Theory.* London: Macmillan.

Runnymede Trust, The (1997), *Islamophobia – A Challenge For Us All.* London: The Runnymede Trust.

Reisigl, M. and Wodak, R. (eds) (2001), *Discourse and Discrimination: Rhetorics of Racism and Antisemitism.* London: Routledge.

Richardson, J. (2004), *(Mis)Representing Islam: The Racism and Rhetoric of British Broadsheet Newspapers.* Amsterdam: John Benjamins.

Schmidt, R. Sr (2000), *Language Policy and Identity Politics in the United States.* Philadelphia, PA: Temple University Press.

Schmidt, R. Sr (2002), 'Racialization and language policy: the case of the U.S.A.'. *Multilingua*, 21(2-3), 141–62.

Titscher, S., Meyer, M., Wodak, R. and Vetter, E. (2000), *Methods of Text and Discourse Analysis.* London: Sage.

van Dijk, T. A. (1993), *Elite Discourse and Racism.* London: Sage.

van Dijk, T. A. (2000a), 'On the analysis of parliamentary debates on immigration', in M. Reisigl and R. Wodak (eds), *The Semiotics of Racism: Approaches in Critical Discourse Analysis.* Vienna: Passagen Verlag, pp. 65–84.

van Dijk, T. A. (2000b), 'New(s) racism: a discourse analytical approach', in S. Cottle (ed.), *Ethnic Minorities and the Media.* Milton Keynes: Open University Press, pp. 33–49.

van Dijk, T. A. (2000c), 'Ideologies, racism, discourse: debates on immigration and ethnic issues', in J. ter Wal and M. Verkuyten (eds), *Comparative Perspectives on Racism.* Aldershot: Ashgate, pp. 91–116.

van Dijk, T. A. (2002), 'Discourse and racism', in D. Goldberg and J. Solomos (eds), *The Blackwell Companion to Racial and Ethnic Studies.* Oxford: Blackwell, pp. 145–59.

van Dijk, T. A. (2005), 'Contextual knowledge management in discourse production: a CDA perspective' in R. Wodak and P. Chilton (eds), *A New Agenda for (Critical) Discourse Analysis.* Amsterdam: John Benjamins, pp. 71–100.

van Dijk, T. A. (2006), 'Discourse and manipulation' *Discourse & Society,* 17(2), 359–83.

van Leeuwen, T. and Wodak, R. (1999), 'Legitimizing immigration control: a discourse-historical analysis'. *Discourse Studies,* 1(1), 83–118.

van Leeuwen, T. (2000), 'Visual racism', in M. Reisigl and R. Wodak (eds), *The Semiotics of Racism: Approaches in Critical Discourse Analysis.* Vienna: Passagen Verlag, pp. 65–84.

Voloshinov, V. N. (1973 [1929]), *Marxism and the Philosophy of Language.* L. Matejka and I. R. Titunik (trans). London/New York: Seminar Press.

Weiss, G. and Wodak, R. (2003), 'Introduction', in G. Weiss and R. Wodak (eds), *Theory, Interdisciplinarity and Critical Discourse Analysis.* London: Palgrave, pp. 1–34.

Wodak, R. (2000), 'Re-contextualization and the transformation of meanings: a critical discourse analysis of decision making in EU meetings about employment policies', in S. Sarangi and M. Coulthard (eds), *Discourse and Social Life.* London: Longman, pp. 185–206.

Wodak, R., de Cillia, R., Reisigl, M. and Liebhart, K. (1999). *The Discursive Construction of National Identity.* Edinburgh: Edinburgh University Press.

9 Metadiscourses of race in the news: the Celebrity Big Brother row

Bethan L. Davies

9.1 Metadiscourse, race and language ideology

In 2007, a major media firestorm (Hill 2007) erupted in the UK after alleged racist language and behaviour occurred on the 'reality' TV show Celebrity Big Brother (CBB). This chapter looks in detail at this mediatized debate and, in particular, the metamediality (Johnson and Ensslin 2007) involved as commentators in British newspapers classified the events as either 'racist' or 'non-racist'. Focus on the meta-level should enable a deconstruction of the justification process used, thus allowing access to some of the underlying ideologies about race current in the UK.

Adam Jaworski *et al.* (2004) outline the complexity of what they term the 'meta-zone', embracing semiotic reflexivity from images and sounds to instances of language about language (equivalent to Dennis Preston's (2004) concept of Metalanguage 1) and to ideologies about language revealed by those metalinguistic realizations. Various terms are used to represent this latter area, including Preston's Metalanguage 3 and also metapragmatics (e.g. Mey 2001). However, while Preston (2004: 87) says Metalanguage 3 represents the 'presuppositions which lie behind much Metalanguage 1 use', he ties this to a concept of 'shared folk knowledge' rather than highlighting its ideological significance; he also disassociates himself from the critical paradigm (Niedzielski and Preston 1999: 315–16), which would be in opposition to the theoretical stance taken here. Metapragmatics can be used to analogize the distinction between linguistics and metalinguistics, but I would argue for the term metadiscourse as a more appropriate analogy. Using metalanguage for realizations of language about language, and metadiscourse for the ideological positions that underlie these realizations works on two levels: it nicely captures the distinction between the (relatively) concrete and

162

the abstract, and it also employs metadiscourse(s) as a parallel term to discourse(s), thus distinguishing a term already used within critical paradigms to indicate hidden ideologies, from a term specifically to be used for hidden *language* ideologies.

This research is at the intersection of language ideology (e.g. Schieffelin *et al.* 1998; Blommaert 1999) and work on language and race (e.g. Blackledge 2005; van Dijk 1992). As Elizabeth Stokoe and Derek Edwards (2007: 341) note, there are two main threads of research in this latter area. Firstly, how minorities are represented and/or constructed in public texts (media discourse, political speeches, government policy documents), and secondly how interviewees construct ethnic groups, asylum seekers or immigration through talk (see also Blackledge, Chapter 8, and Androutsopoulos, Chapter 10, this volume). However, work on 'mock Spanish' by Jane Hill and others addresses issues that are of interest here (e.g. Hill 1998, 2001; Barrett 2006; Schwartz 2006). Hill's other work on metadiscourses of political promising (Hill 2000) and allegations of racism (Hill 2007) is also particularly relevant – a similar use of a personalist ideology (see section 9.4) to justify particular rhetorical moves is found in the CBB data too. There is also the ongoing debate in critical paradigms around the nature of linguistic meaning: is it intrinsic, or is it context-bound? Words like the N-word are perceived by some to always be offensive, regardless of context (an intrinsic reading). Whereas Cameron (1995: 157) reports a dispute over whether saying a group of black students were behaving like a 'herd of water buffalo' constituted racist language or not. The general consensus seems to be that there can be no list of proscribed terms and expressions, because linguistic meaning is not that stable. Judith Butler (1997) argues that this instability is due both to the lack of intrinsic link between the referent and the sign, and the speaker's lack of absolute sovereignty over what they say. Deborah Cameron takes a rather less post-structuralist approach, and appeals to the complexity of context: who says what to whom can be as important as the words said. In terms of meaning then, according to Cameron:

> [. . .] we are back in the looking-glass world of Humpty Dumpty – the only question becomes 'who's to be master': the complainant who says something was racist, the defendant who swears it was not, or the administrator who has to adjudicate the case? (Cameron 1995: 159)

In a sense, the debate we will be looking at in this chapter is an attempt to perform this role of adjudication, albeit without the presence of the complainant or defendant.

163

9.2 (Celebrity) Big Brother and the media

In order to set the context for the debate, some discussion of the Big Brother franchise is required, both in terms of its format and the expectations that it sets up in viewers and (parts of) the media. Big Brother (BB) is one of a number of 'reality' TV shows where a group of people are confined in a particular space together (typically a 'house'). Members are 'evicted' at regular intervals on the basis of a public vote, and the winner is (or should be) the person most popular with the viewing public. The BB concept is one of the most extreme of these as there is virtually no privacy: housemates are recorded perpetually in the (communal) bedroom, living space, outdoors area, and even the bathroom. In terms of its exposure, there is a daily highlights programme, a dedicated website (run by its home channel, Channel 4 (C4)) and also live footage running for large portions of the day and through the night. Celebrity Big Brother uses the same format, although the period in the house is shorter (5 weeks), and the participants are 'celebrities' rather than members of the public. In CBB 2007, there was a media furore over alleged racism inflicted on Shilpa Shetty (an extremely wealthy and middle-class Indian Bollywood star) by several British housemates, in particular Jade Goody, Danielle Lloyd and Jo O'Meara.

'Reality' TV has become a staple of British TV schedules over the last 10 years. Helen Wood and Beverley Skeggs (2004) distinguish two broad types of these shows – the 'makeover' show (which is essentially transformative), or a more voyeuristic show which makes no attempt to change individuals, but rather invites you to take pleasure in 'excessive behaviour and ways of telling and displaying oneself inappropriately' (Wood and Skeggs 2004: 207). While their main focus in this latter category is programmes like *Ibiza Uncovered* (which follows the (s)exploits of the young working-classes in clubbing resorts), their comments apply equally to programmes like BB – especially to housemates like Goody, Lloyd and O'Meara (and many others like them) who are part of the demographic displayed in *Ibiza Uncovered*. Wood and Skeggs (2004: 207) argue that these programmes are 'an ethnographic display of unmediated, unknowing, bad choice culture [. . .] displayed to demonstrate working-class limits to propriety'. Essentially, certain participants in these programmes are set up to fail in their presentation of self, and it is precisely this 'bad choice' culture which is the attraction for a voyeuristic audience.

It is also this desire for sensationalism that gives the whole BB franchise its newsworthiness. Whilst the quality dailies may have limited reports of (C)BB hidden away in review sections, for the red tops[1] such programmes will constitute a major source of stories both in the body of the paper and on the front page – many of them having daily diaries reporting events and gossip about the (C)BB house. If one combines this base level of newsworthiness with the extensive media coverage guaranteed by any story which concerns race issues, then the outcome in this particular case was not surprising: a media firestorm which crossed the boundary into the front pages of the quality papers as well as gaining coverage on TV news.

This level of exposure gained by BB – both through TV transmissions and media attention – also makes it interesting in terms of the dichotomy of private and public space. Hill (2001) discusses the leaky boundary between these, and suggests that the claim of private space (through joking or otherwise informal language) can make racist language allowable. She also suggests that the division between the two is not as clear at it once was – particularly for public figures; one only has to think of the media attention paid to George W. Bush greeting Tony Blair by saying 'Yo, Blair' when he thought the microphone was switched off at the G8 summit in 2006. In the (C)BB house virtually everything is available for the public stage, yet the context is that of a living space, something which we associate with the private realm. This is reinforced by the activities and conversational genres which take place: it is very much of the domestic sphere, with all the informal chat and petty arguments that that entails.[2] In many respects, viewers are 'overhearers' of private conversations, yet these are evaluated on a public stage.

9.3 Data and methodology

The analysis of the media firestorm to be discussed in this chapter is based on a corpus of newspaper articles (op-ed, reportage) from UK national newspapers generated by the NexisUK database. The data was collected in the period 16–21 January 2007, using the search terms *Shilpa*, *Shetty* and *Goody*, although only articles which explicitly classified or commented upon the exchanges in terms of *race* were ultimately used (i.e. 60 out of 350 initial hits). The data collection window represents the period between the story initially breaking and Goody being evicted from the House. This was a deliberate choice, as my primary interest here is to see how the media constructed events *without* access to the participants. One key feature of (C)BB is that the participants are in their own little bubble: they have no access to the outside world (either by contact with friends/family, or access to TV/newpapers), and conversely, the outside world has no access to them.

9.3.1 The participants and what was said

In this section, I shall focus on what was allegedly said to, or about, Shilpa Shetty by four of the other contestants who were in the CBB house as follows:

1. Jade Goody, who built a career on previously being a contestant on BB, and was (in)famous for her seeming lack of education;[3]
2. Danielle Lloyd, a former beauty queen, a model and, at the time, the girlfriend of a well-known UK Premiership footballer;
3. Jo O'Meara, famous for previously being a member of a successful teen pop band, and was allegedly trying to re-launch her solo career through appearing on CBB;
4. Jackiey Budden, Jade Goody's mother, with no other 'celebrity' status.

All four are apparently white,[4] and come from a working-class background.

The following examples were sourced from the corpus of newspaper articles rather than directly from CBB itself. While this means the wider context of the language is not available, it could be argued that this is part of the mediatization process: what is selected for transformation into another genre (Fairclough 2003), and thus transmitted to a wider audience. It is also a re-entextualization undertaken by largely middle-class media organizations (Conboy 2007) of language produced by people from a working class background, marking the beginning of a text trajectory (Blommaert 2005) from transitory spoken language to the relative permanence of the written word. The loss of context is part of the text trajectory, and it is these transformed texts which become the subject of the media firestorm as the transitory spoken texts were not re-shown.

Jade Goody:

- Called Shetty 'Shilpa Poppadum' and 'Shilpa Fuckawallah'[5]
- 'Does that mean I need elocution lessons because she can't understand what I f***king say? She can't even speak English properly.'
- 'You need a day in the slums. Go to those people who look up to you and be real. You fucking fake.'
- 'She makes me feel sick. She makes my skin crawl.'

Danielle Lloyd:

- 'She wants to be white' (Goody, Lloyd and O'Meara were mocking Shetty for using facial hair bleach)

- 'You don't know where those hands have been' (in the context of not wanting to eat food Shetty had touched)
- refused to eat 'spicy food' cooked by Shetty
- 'I think she should fuck off home'
- 'She's a dog'

Jo O'Meara

- Mimicked Shetty's Indian accent
- Said Indians were thin because they were always ill as a result of undercooking their food

Jackiey Budden:

- Asked Shetty 'Do you live in a house or a shack'
- After she was evicted (and on C4) Budden said 'the Indian was jarring me big time . . . Sherpelle, Sherpa, whatever her name is'

While all of the above behaviour is clearly offensive, the reportage and op-ed articles selected do not agree on whether or not it should be classified as racist. Indeed, there is no explicit name-calling (though Lloyd does elevate 'whiteness'), and some of the examples would seem to have been subject to over-interpretation, perhaps due to the nature of the text-trajectory.[6] However, there are a number of racist discourses drawn upon here. Firstly, we see the discourse of the 'other' race being less civilized: inability to cook food properly, questionable hygiene, the implication of poor housing and the use of an animal metaphor. Secondly, there is a discourse surrounding the language which Shetty uses. Shetty doesn't speak 'proper English', her accent is imitated, and little respect is shown for her native language (see also Blackledge, Chapter 8, and Androutsopoulos, Chapter 10, this volume). The apparent inability of Budden to pronounce her name properly, and the use of 'fuckawallah' and 'poppadum' as her surname by Goody shows the same disregard for the integrity of Shetty's native tongue that Hill (2001) comments on in her discussion of mock Spanish in the USA. Cultural items such as food are also used to classify the 'otherness' of Shetty – spicy food and poppadoms. And by calling Shetty 'the Indian', that othering becomes a depersonalization. The use of 'fuck off home', whilst perhaps not evidently racist in itself – after all, Shetty is not British and lives in India – indexes a very common racist discourse from Britain where 'Xs go home' was a frequent racist formula found in graffiti as well as in spoken language; it presupposes that the subject has no right to be in the country. This discourse is still found in alternative, often more complex, forms in the language of the anti-immigration lobby. All of these discourses can be seen to be examples of 'new racisms' (May 2001; Schmidt 2002; Blackledge 2005): where explicit colour terms are now seen as unacceptable by society at large, racism is deflected onto perceived cultural differences (see also especially Blackledge, Chapter 8, this volume).

Given that the discourses drawn on are so easily identified, the interesting aspect here is not so much the language itself. Rather, the significance is in the *ideologies* of language which are drawn on in order to justify the viewpoint of individual articles, and the rhetorical moves used to support them.

9.4 The metadiscourses of racism

One of the key points in the articles is whether intent to be racist is necessary to the ascription of racism. Those that defend Goody *et al.* appear to be drawing on a personalist ideology (Hill 2007) where it is assumed that there is a consistent inner self, and that the intentions of that self are the originator of linguistic meaning. Using Hill's argument, a speaker can disavow a particular linguistic meaning on the basis that they have authoritative knowledge of their own intentions, which cannot be challenged by others. In the absence of the protagonists, the commentators in these data feel able to claim access to the speaker's intentions and offer (authoritative) evidence for doing so (in an apparent extension of personalist ideology). It is these articles that attempt to categorize the event as non-racist that are discussed first, as they set out the arguments which are then challenged by those who take the opposing view.

9.4.1 Categorizations as 'non-racist'

Extracts 1–4

> From what I read, racism has little to do with this. Others have said the problem is pig ignorance, and to an extent this is true. What interests me, though, is what motivates the expression of so many ignorant remarks, and the manifestation of such ignorant behaviour, towards Miss Shetty: and that seems, quite clearly, to be class hatred [. . .] People like Miss Goody, now forbidden by law from making racist remarks, instead indulge in the only form of bigotry the law now permits to go unpunished: that of hating your social superiors. (Heffer, *Daily Telegraph*, 20.01.2007)

> Racism is defined as discrimination based on race, fuelled by the belief that one race is inherently superior to another. There are

20 words in that sentence, thus putting considered racism well beyond the intellectual reach of the alleged perpetrators [. . .] The roots of the Shetty-sniping saga lie in stupidity and a lack of class. (Ahuja, *Times2*, 17.01.2007)

I don't think they're racist, just unbelievably dumb. They're motivated by an intense, aching jealousy they're simply too stupid to process. After all, Shilpa is 20 times more successful than any of them, not to mention 400 times more beautiful. When you're a go-nowhere titflasher, a washed-up singer or a famous dunce, that's bound to rankle, especially since Shetty's also more intelligent, dignified, patient and likable than you could ever, ever be. (Brooker, *Guardian*, 20.01.2007)

[. . .] what has taken place in the [Big Brother] House over the past ten days is not primarily about racism. Yes, the Gang of Three – Jo O'Meara, Danielle Lloyd and their leader, Jade Goody – are using Shilpa's race to abuse her, but their cruel bullying is actually about class. (Seymour, *Daily Mail*, 18.01.2007)

All four extracts above contend that race is not the *reason* for Goody *et al.*'s behaviour. The motivating factor, and thus the *intention*, is variously ascribed to class and/or jealousy. It is particularly interesting to note the rhetorical move made in Extract 4, where it is recognized that the 'Gang of Three' are *using* race in their abuse – and thus there is some degree of admission that race is an issue here – yet the commentator carefully decouples the language use from any implied racist intent. A common factor is also the perceived ignorance of Goody *et al.*. It is perhaps not a coincidence that all of the newspapers quoted above would see their audience as largely middle-class, and thus they can look down on Goody, Lloyd, O'Meara and their ilk – although this is perhaps less predictable from the reputedly more liberal *Guardian*. The way in which Extracts 1 and 2 talk about class would tend to reinforce this: *Telegraph* readers are Goody *et al.*'s 'social superiors', and the *Times* labels them as having a 'lack of class', which plays on the polysemous meanings of *class* in British English usage. This is very much in keeping with the negative attitude towards the working classes which Martin Conboy (2007, Chapter 7) argues is endemic in the British media.

The importance of intent – and thus the ideology of personalism – is also reiterated through this ascription of ignorance. Racism has to 'considered', calculated, meant, and thus racist language or behaviour which can be imputed to stupidity can be dismissed as unpleasant but not illegal. Another aspect of intention is agency/volition, and an alternative rhetorical move used in the construction of this behaviour as 'not racist' is to deny the free will of the participants in some way.

Extracts 5–6

> Of course racism is deplorable and bullying detestable; I wouldn't seek to query that. What I'm finding enormously difficult, as someone who has met Jade Goody on several occasions and can attest to the fact that she's a decent girl who's had a remarkably difficult life, is the notion that she's a bad person [. . .] What irks me as much as the persecution of the elegant and beautiful Shilpa Shetty is the national wrath directed at these three women who are really expressing views and attitudes endemic in the culture from which they came. (Brand, *Guardian*, 20.01.2007)

> What we've witnessed is a class of hybrid individuals who are neither malicious nor wicked, but some of whom are so utterly stupid that they cannot respect or even recognize social parameters [. . .] [Jade] may own a beauty salon, but she still can't speak the Queen's English. Her language is peppered with profanities, among which racist expression are a natural style extension. (Perera, *Daily Telegraph*, 18.01.2007)

The agency for the choices made by Goody *et al.* is here attributed to white working-class culture, of which they are assumed to be a part. This is indubitably linked with the rhetorical move of blaming ignorance, as we are effectively told that they 'don't know any better'. There is also the suggestion that the type of language and behaviour used would not be evaluated as negatively in their 'home' culture as in the alternative [oppositional] middle-class culture constructed by these two commentators. This is reminiscent of Jan Blommaert's orders of indexicality (2005, 2007), where he argues that no variety of language has an intrinsic value – rather that the value of a variety is determined by the cultural capital assigned it by the local/global social order. What a variety indexes (in terms of social position, education, etc.) will depend on the cultural context in which it is produced. Presumably, this concept can be analogized to general cultural values and how these are expressed through language and behaviour, rather than being limited to language varieties *per se*. Both authors re-value Goody *et al.*'s behaviour as 'normal' in the other culture, thus implying that it should not be re-evaluated by the dominant social order, of which these authors are part. We see an explicit expression of this re-valuing in action by a member of the working-class community in which Jade grew up.

Extract 7

> Hairdresser Joanne Wingrove, 35, said Jade has showed she is a typical Bermondsey girl. She blasted: 'I wanted to turn the TV off because it was such disgusting behaviour and definitely wrong.

I think it was bullying not racist. But I don't think it's a bad thing for Bermondsey because people from here are rough and ready anyway.' (*vox pop* from Bermondsey, Partasides, *Daily Star*, 19.01.2007)

While Joanne Wingrove initially values the behaviour negatively, she does not categorize it as racist. She then goes on to re-position the behaviour in the local order of indexicality: Jade *et al.*'s behaviour is seen as indexing positive features of the Bermondsey culture, being 'rough and ready' – it may not 'travel well' (Bloommaert 2005), but locally it is favourably categorized as straightforward, direct and honest behaviour.

There is also appeal to another aspect of personalism in Extract 5. According to Hill (2007), the personalist ideology links behaviour in the world to an enduring inner self. To put this simplistically, if you behave well, then you are an intrinsically good person, and conversely, if you behave badly, then you are not. By trying to get the reader to accept that Goody is a 'decent girl' and not a 'bad person' (partly through the authoritative claim of knowing her), the author Russell Brand (himself a well-known media celebrity) reverses this notion – the implication is that a 'decent girl' is not capable of 'deplorable' racist behaviour.

Out of the 'enduring inner self' also comes the idea that behaviour should not be contradictory, otherwise one would not be able to judge the intrinsic value of the self. Thus, if you are friends with black people, then you cannot be racist. Using a black voice here increases the value of this evidence, as it also does in Extract 2 above.

Extracts 8–10

Now I think she's a bitch, a beast and a bully, but I don't think she's an out-and-out racist – after all, she's of mixed race herself, and she recently hired a black personal assistant, hardly the action of someone who's about to sign up to the [British National Party]. Jade's problem is jealousy mixed with insecurity – the envy of the beautiful Shilpa is rooted in class. (Phillips, *Mirror*, 20.01.2007)

'I don't think Jade is racist. She was one of my great champions when I was on Big Brother.' (Black ex-BB contestant, Derek Laud in Baig and Laud, *Sun*, 18.01.2007)

'Jade has never been racist. She is mixed race herself and suffered racist abuse as a youngster.' (Jackiey Budden quoted in Roberts and Fricker, *Mirror*, 19.01.2007)

The discourse of interest is also used (Hill 2001). If you are of mixed race yourself, then you cannot be racist. Both of these also demonstrate a very simplistic understanding of the notion of 'race', firstly, that a biological construct is equivalent to a social one. In terms of your heritage, you may be mixed race, but if you can 'pass' for the dominant cultural group, then you may choose to identify yourself in that way. Secondly, there is the assumption in all of these texts that racists treat 'the other' as a homogeneous group: they do not recognize the possibility that, for a particular individual, racism might be reserved for certain cultural groups (e.g. those of Asian descent) rather than all non-whites, or that racism exists within colour boundaries as well as across them.

One final strategy is used to deny the charge of racism, and this is to downgrade the actions in one of two ways. Firstly, it introduces the idea that there are degrees of racism, and that what is seen on CBB is not 'real' racism.

Extracts 11–12

> Jade is goaded into wild abuse by the unfamiliar appearance and manners of a woman who's [sic] name she cannot get her tongue round, whose value system she cannot comprehend, and who makes her feel cheap. The footballer's bit of fluff – the one who dresses like a toddler and eats with her mouth open – looks blankly into all she doesn't know about the dining customs of people not from Liverpool, and worries where their hands have been. To confuse this vegetative state with full-blown racism is to dignify it [. . .] We are too soft on stupidity. (Jacobson, *Independent*, 20.01.2007)

> Is Jade a real racist? Probably not. Has she in her stupidity made horribly racist remarks? She certainly has. From her arsenal of abuse she has fired some unforgivable shots but as she has been abusing Shilpa for a fortnight she had to use everything she could lay her hands on. (Robson, *Express*, 20.01.2007)

The use of the noun phrases 'full-blown racism' and 'a real racist' presuppose that such concepts exist and thus that their opposites exist too: 'not full-blown racism' and 'not a real racist'.[7] This rhetorical move allows the behaviour to be categorized as race-related, yet absolves the culprits from full censure. In both cases, this strategy is also combined with further rhetorical moves. In the first example it is combined with the removal of agency, via the rhetorical move of 'ignorance/stupidity'. There is also a suggestion that Jade's actions are not reasoned and not therefore 'meant': she is 'goaded' into 'wild abuse'. Thus through both of these moves intention is denied again. In the second example, we see a further appeal to 'ignorance/stupidity' used, but also a distinction is made between Jade and the language which she used. By categorizing the language as racist, the author denies the link between Jade and the language, and thus removes any question of an intent to be racist.

The other strategy to downgrade the effect of the behaviour is to belittle it by analogizing it to a playground dispute.

Extracts 13–14

'Big Brother treats contestants like children, and most respond by behaving like children. If you put children in the playground they can do some very nasty things.' Black ex-BB contestant, Derek Laud in Baig and Laud. (*Sun*, 18.01.2007)

It has been playground bullying at its nastiest, played out on national TV. (Dunbar, *Express*, 18.01.2007)

This effect seems to be reinforced by the lexical choices 'nasty' and 'bullying' (seen in other extracts too), which are both associated with an informal register and fit well into discourses associated with children. The playground can also be seen as a microcosm, a private space (for children) inappropriate to the evaluations of public space (for adults); this invokes the escape clause of private space noted by Hill (2001), discussed in section 9.2 above.

9.4.2 Categorizations as 'racist'

The commentators below deny the integrity of the rhetorical moves made by those who categorize the events as non-racist. In particular, they argue against the criterion of intention and thus the 'escape clause' of personalist ideology.

Extract 15

'Racism always exists cheek by jowl with, inside and alongside culture and class. As a rule it is inseparable from them. That is why, for example, food, language and names assume such importance in racial prejudice. And that has certainly been the case in Big Brother. [examples omitted] Her colour too – the most obvious manifestation of racial difference – was tangentially drawn into the equation through the comment about make-up and the Indian desire to be white. Of course class is central. Race always comes with class. Jade's reaction to Shilpa has been shaped by her own class background, her racism articulated within that context. The fact that Jade is hardly blessed with great intellectual gifts, that her conversation is littered with profanities, that her behaviour rarely rises above the crude [. . .] makes it easy for the middle class to dismiss her racism as that of a crude, ill-educated, white working-class young woman.' (Jacques, *Guardian*, 20.01.2007)

173

Here Martin Jacques denies the validity of shifting the motivation onto class, and the explanation onto ignorance and cultural values. While his argument does not directly refer to intention or agency, the implicit message is clear: it is behaviour rather than intention that is important.

This approach is also used by the following extracts which remove the possibility of decoupling the acts from the person.

Extracts 16–17

> [. . .] ultimately, if you hate someone and use the weapons of racism because you know they will hurt, is that any different from just being racist? You are still doing the impolite, taboo thing in a desire to debase the other person. (Moran, *Times2*, 18.01.2007)

> But when they've criticized every aspect of her and then made unbelievable ignorant comments about her culture, what are you meant to think? Her race HAS been attacked, therefore they ARE racists [. . .] I also agree a lot of it is to do with class [. . .] But that doesn't dismiss the fact that the baiting has had an element of race to it. (Anila Baig in Baig and Laud, *Sun*, 18.01.2007)

There can be no appeal to a personalist ideology when the speakers' authoritative knowledge of self has been denied. Not only is the importance of intention refuted, but also the ability of speakers to know their own intentions: they may not know they are being racist, but that is not relevant. This latter point is picked up by Fergus Shanahan below:

Extract 18

> She's a chav. This is how chavs behave. Stand on any street corner and you will hear yobs like Jade, Jo and Danielle in action. Low-grade racism is all part of it. Ask Jade if she is a racist, and (assuming she knows what it means) she will deny it. She will honestly believe that her hatred for Shilpa Shetty has nothing to do with her colour. [. . .] But it is the fact that she is Indian that Jade cannot accept, and that's why she targets her. Is it racist? Of course it is. (Shanahan, *Sun*, 19.01.2007)

Although the possibility of 'low grade racism' is mentioned, this is not part of a rhetorical move to downgrade the behaviour. According to Shanahan, 'low-grade racism' is still racism (and thus challenges the position taken in Extracts 11 and 12). Instead, he uses this to further evidence Jade's lack of authoritative knowledge of self.

While the articles that ascribe racism are interesting in the respect that they recognize exactly the rhetorical moves which will be taken by their opponents, largely they don't tell us any more about this metadiscourse. However, they do demonstrate that the metadiscourses of race are part of a well-rehearsed debate, with participants quick to draw on well-established ideological resources. One aspect in which the presentation of the different viewpoints does differ, however, is in the extent of argumentation used. No text which took a 'non-racist' stance merely stated this viewpoint – some rhetorical moves were always used in support. While this was also mostly the case for those who took a 'racist' standpoint, there were a few texts which simply stated that opinion.

Extracts 19–20

> In the face of some 20,000 complaints to Ofcom, [Channel 4], who air the show, disputed this last charge. Shamefully, the channel went further and denied that there had been any racism at all. Racism has clearly been on show – in the mocking of Ms Shetty's accent, for example, and in the questioning of her hygiene. It is untenable to suggest otherwise. (Leader, *Guardian*, 19.01.2007)

> To defend their right to broadcast the treatment of Shilpa Shetty, Channel 4 has sought to deny that there is racism. This claim is irresponsible, self-serving and patently untrue. Their failure to taken any action to put a stop to the racism on this show is an evasion of their responsibilities. (Ken Livingstone (Mayor of London), quoted in Roberts and Fricker, *Mirror*, 19.01.2007)

In Extract 19, some evidence is given to support their statement but they do not otherwise attempt to justify their view. The quotation in Extract 20 baldly categorizes the behaviour as racist, and at no point in the full article does the commentator give any further justification. This perhaps tells us something about the state of the ideological struggle here, that those trying to categorize Goody *et al.*'s behaviour as 'non-racist' had to work harder to do so (their texts were generally longer and more complex). This might lead us to believe that theirs is becoming the non-hegemonic view. However, it is far from the case that these authors do not have a platform to express these views: twice as many texts in the data categorized the events as 'non-racist' rather than 'racist'.

9.5 Discussion

One of the aspects of this event which allowed the media firestorm to persist was the denial by the broadcasters, Channel 4, that any racist behaviour had taken place:

Extract 21

> 'To date there has been no overt racial abuse or racist behaviour directed against Shilpa within the house.'

175

'However there has undoubtedly been a cultural and class clash between her and three of the British females. Unambiguous racist behaviour is not tolerated.' (A source, C4, quoted in Methven and MacLean, *Mirror*, 18.01.2007)

If C4 had accepted racism had occurred, then they would have had no choice but to evict all the perpetrators from the House. This would have damped down the media interest in CBB in two ways. Firstly, the ongoing confrontations between Shetty and Goody *et al.* would have immediately stopped – there would be less to discuss. Secondly, the denial of racism is potentially more newsworthy than its admission. While such an admission would prompt press reportage and the odd op-ed article, the interest would rapidly disappear. It is precisely the 'was it/wasn't it' debate that gave the issue its longevity. Thus policy/editorial decisions on the part of C4 play an important role in the mediatization of the debate. All this media attention was also very beneficial to CBB: the ratings for the highlights show jumped from 3.5m to 4.5m on the day the story first broke,[8] so it was not in C4's interest to remove Goody *et al.* from the House. To support this decision, C4 use a number of the rhetorical moves seen in the 'non-racist' articles quoted previously. The reasons for the behaviour are given as class and culture, thus implying both that intent is important and that in this case the intent is not racist. In addition, racism becomes a gradable concept: it has to be overt and non-ambiguous before it becomes 'proper' racism.

C4 are exploiting precisely that grey area discussed by Cameron (1995): when the semantic content does not directly index race – and perhaps, more particularly, does not index *colour* – then there is always a potential escape clause. And in part, it is this that allows the 'new racisms' discussed by Adrian Blackledge (2005; Chapter 8, this volume) to come into existence. Cultural terms rather than overtly race-based ones are now used to index 'racialized identities' (Schmidt 2002: 154). As Blackledge (2005: 49) says, these 'racialized cultural practices [. . .] become metaphors for "racial" differences which can not now be spoken'. But I think that it is exactly this 'unsayability' which allows these new racisms to flourish. The right to be protected from racism is enshrined in British law; in the face that Britain presents to the world, racism is not tolerated and is viewed extremely negatively (as it is elsewhere, Billig 1991; van Dijk 1992). None of the articles in the database questions the taboo status of racism, indeed we see quite the opposite: Brand in Extract 5 says 'Of course racism is detestable'; others argue that what has happened isn't serious enough to deserve that taboo status. Even within the field of linguistics/discourse analysis there is a certain caution surrounding the topic. For example, in an article about racist jokes Billig (2001) takes the time to both justify his decision not to bowdlerize the N-word (because it is key to the data), and to make clear that he does not find these jokes funny, and nor would he expect his readers to do so. Certainly, this level of care is rarely taken for terms considered potentially offensive on the basis of gender, class or disability.

Thus to ascribe racism to someone becomes a very serious charge. As Hill points out:

> Most white people believe that 'racists' are found only among marginalized white supremacist groups who are behind the times, inadequately educated and socialized. Thus to accuse a speaker of racism is a deep insult that evokes a whole range of highly undesirable qualities. (Hill 2001: 86)

To call someone a racist means categorizing them as a social misfit: to protect the integrity of a 'non-racist society', the offender has to be placed outside that society. Elsewhere, in a discussion of personalism in US media discourse, Hill quotes two newspaper articles (from both sides of the political spectrum) which show this reluctance to assign racist behaviour:

> I am extremely reluctant to call anyone a racist, I frankly have no idea what's in Lott's head. (Cohen 2002 cited in Hill 2007:79)

> One should be very hesitant about ascribing bigotry. It is hard to discern what someone feels in his heart of hearts. (Krauthammer 2002 cited in Hill 2007: 70)

While Hill cites these as an examples of personalist ideology showing the importance of intention to the way in which utterances are judged, and, more particularly, how public figures can be 'let off the hook' for problematic talk, I think this can also be turned on its head. The appeal to intention is equally a 'get out' clause for the journalists who are (understandably) wary of the racism issue. Note that neither of them says that they are hesitant to ascribe racism to Lott in particular: their hesitance is expressed in generic terms.

Indeed, in the media firestorm which surrounded the CBB story the issue became as much about the deficits of the British education system and society as about racism. For the 'non-racists', Goody *et al.* are characterized as ignorant with no social skills (thus explaining their behaviour) whereas those who categorize the articles as 'racist' bemoan the failings of the system which allows such asocial behaviour to still exist.

In both cases, this allows the moral panic (Thompson 1998) to be deflected onto 'declining standards':

Extracts 22–24

> She's a chav. This is how chavs behave. Stand on any street corner and you will hear yobs like Jade, Jo and Danielle in action. (Shanahan, *Sun*, 19.01.2007)

> [. . .] we have been outside our own front doors and seen today's Britain. It is not only on Big Brother than the Goodys and Lloyds and O'Mearas of our country are to be heard cackling and spewing and burping and blaspheming [. . .] (Wilson, *Daily Mail*, 20.01.2007)

> [Jade] may own a beauty salon, but she still can't speak the Queen's English (Perera, *Daily Telegraph*, 18.01.2007)

David Barton (2000) argues that moral panics surrounding *literacy* have been continually recycled, and I would suggest that the scope of that statement could be expanded to include education in general. Revisiting this familiar moral panic with its well-rehearsed moves is probably seen as preferable to facing the unpleasant alternative of admitting to a society where racism is still endemic even though it is supposedly illegal. While Claudia Lacour (1992: 139 cited in Hill 2001: 99) sees the current situation as a paradox – that racism's 'pervasive existence depends on its tenacious non-admission and complicitous non-recognition', the key question would seem to be why we see such a reluctance to assign certain behaviours as racist. I would argue that part of the issue here is that the 'unsayability' of racist language also leads to an 'unrecognizability'. In other words, this could be paraphrased as 'if racism is so bad, it can't have been racism'. This, in turn, leads to another type of 'tenacious non-admission' and 'complicitous non-recognition' than the one I think Lacour intends. For me, the other paradox of racism is now that we have largely succeeded in making racism taboo, how do we surmount the final taboo of naming other people as racist?

9.6 Conclusion

The mediatization of the CBB debate played out on a public stage illustrates the importance of personalism in British (media) culture. Whilst the appeal to a personalist ideology wasn't the only strategy used by those who categorized the events on CBB as non-racist, it was the most prevalent. Intention is seen as the key criterion on which we judge people – did they 'mean' that outcome, or was it merely a 'misfire'.

However, unlike in the episodes discussed by Hill (2007), commentators in the metamedial debates analysed here felt able to assign intention – the authoritative knowledge of the speaker was replaced by the authoritative justification of the commentator. Thus the scope of personalist ideology would appear to be potentially wider than suggested by Hill, and therefore a more flexible tool for the (de)construction of language ideologies in the meta-zone.

Notes

1 This distinction is rapidly replacing that of broadsheet versus tabloid, as the size difference has largely disappeared.
2 It is worth noting that one of the first confrontations between Shetty and Goody was about an item of food.
3 In her initial appearance on BB, Goody reportedly said that she thought Cambridge was in London, and when told it was actually in East Anglia, she said that she thought 'East Angular' was in continental Europe. A discussion of this, and Goody's presentation of self in BB, can be found in Wetherell (2007).
4 It later becomes evident that Goody is in fact of mixed heritage, as her father was of West Indian descent (see Extract 10 and following discussion).
5 Words in quotation marks were reported as direct speech in the reportage, and any censoring of the language is retained as in the original.
6 When telling Shetty she should visit her Bollywood fans in the slums, Goody seems to be indexing a class rather than a racial difference between herself and Shetty, by claiming a 'real' working-class persona for herself. However, this was cited as an example of racism in reportage.
7 Technically, only definite referring expressions should trigger presuppositions, but perhaps because these are concepts rather than concrete entities, I believe the categorization holds. In both cases, the presupposition survives negation, and both presuppositions are cancellable.
8 'Storm in a TV show: India's fury over taunting of Shilpa'. Verkaik, R., Russell, B. and Huggler, J. *Independent*, 18.01.2007.

Primary sources

Ahuja, A., *Times2*, 17.01.2007.
Baig, A. and Laud, D., *Sun*, 18.01.2007.
Brand, R., *Guardian* sports pages, 20.01.2007.
Brooker, C., *Guardian*, The Guide, 20.01.2007.
Dunbar, P., *Express*, 18.01.2007.
Heffer, S., *Daily Telegraph*, 20.01.2007.
Jacobson, H., *Independent*, 20.01.2007.
Jacques, M., *Guardian*, 20.01.2007.
Leader, *Guardian*, 19.01.2007.
Methven, N. and MacLean, S., *Mirror*, 18.01.2007.

Moran, C., *Times2*, 18.01.2007.
Perera, S., *Daily Telegraph*, 18.01.2007.
Partasides, M., *Daily Star*, 19.01.2007.
Phillips, F., *Mirror*, 20.01.2007.
Roberts, B. and Fricker, M., *Mirror*, 19.01.2007.
Robson, D., Leader, *Express*, 20.01.2007.
Seymour, D., *Daily Mail*, 18.01.2007.
Shanahan, F., *Sun*, 19.01.2007.
Verkaik, R., Russell, B. and Huggler, J. *Independent*, 18.01.2007.
Wilson, A.N. , *Daily Mail*, 20.01.2007.

References

Barrett, R. (2006), 'Language ideology and racial inequality: competing functions of Spanish in an Anglo-owned Mexican restaurant'. *Language in Society*, 35(2), 163–204.
Barton, D. (2000), 'Moral panics about literacy'. *CLSL Working Papers* No.116. Lancaster University.
Billig, M. (1991), *Ideology and Opinions*. London: Sage.
Billig, M. (2001), 'Humour and hatred: the racist jokes of the Ku Klux Klan'. *Discourse & Society*, 12(3), 267–89.
Blackledge, A. (2005), *Discourse and Power in a Multilingual World*. Amsterdam: John Benjamins.
Blommaert, J. (ed.) (1999), *Language Ideological Debates*. Berlin/New York: Mouton de Gruyter.
Blommaert, J. (2005), *Discourse: A Critical Introduction*. London: Routledge.
Blommaert, J. (2007), 'Sociolinguistics and discourse analysis: orders of indexicality and polycentricity'. *Journal of Multicultural Discourses*, 2(2), 115–30.
Butler, J. (1997), *Excitable Speech: A Politics of the Performative*. New York/ London: Routledge.
Cameron, D. (1995), *Verbal Hygiene*. London: Routledge.
Conboy, M. (2007), *The Language of the News*. London: Routledge.
Fairclough, N. (2003), *Analysing Discourse: Textual Analysis for Social Research*. London: Routledge.
Hill, J. H. (1998), 'Language, race and white public space'. *American Anthropologist*, 100(3), 680–89.
Hill, J. H. (2000), '"Read my article": ideological complexity and the overdetermination of promising in American presidential politics', in P. V. Kroskrity (ed.) *Regimes of Language: Ideologies, Politics and Identities*. Santa Fe, New Mexico: School of America Research Press, pp. 259–91.
Hill, J. H. (2001), 'Mock Spanish, covert racism, and the (leaky) boundary between public and private spheres', in S. Gal and K. A. Woolard (eds), *Languages and Publics: The Making of Authority*. Manchester, UK: St. Jerome's Publishing Ltd., pp. 83–101.

Hill, J. H. (2007), 'Crises of meaning: personalist language ideology in US media discourse', in S. Johnson and A. Ensslin (eds), *Language in the Media: Representations, Identities, Ideologies*. London: Continuum, pp. 70–88.

Jaworski, A., Coupland, N. and Galasiński, D. (2004) (eds), *Metalanguage: Social and Ideological Perspectives*. Berlin/New York: Mouton de Gruyter.

Johnson, S. and Ensslin, A. (2007), 'Language in the media: theory and practice', in S. Johnson and A. Ensslin (eds) *Language in the Media: Representations, Identities, Ideologies*. London: Continuum, pp. 3–22.

Lacour, C. B. (1992), 'Doing things with words: "racism" as a speech act and the undoing of justice', in T. Morrison (ed.), *Race-ing Justice, En-gendering Power*. New York: Pantheon Books, pp.127–58.

May, S. (2001), *Language and Minority Rights: Ethnicity, Nationalism, and the Politics of Language*. Harlow: Longman.

Mey, J. (2001), *Pragmatics*. 2nd edn. Oxford: Blackwell.

Niedzielski, N. and Preston, D. R. (1999), *Folk Linguistics*. Berlin: Mouton de Gruyter.

Preston, D. R. (2004), 'Folk metalanguage', in A. Jaworski, N. Coupland and D. Galasiński (eds), *Metalanguage: Social and Ideological Perspectives*. Berlin/New York: Mouton de Gruyter, pp. 75–101.

Schieffelin, B. B., Woolard, K. A. and Kroskrity, P. V. (eds) (1998), *Language Ideologies: Practice and Theory*. New York/Oxford: Oxford University Press.

Schmidt, R. Sr (2002), 'Racialization and language policy: the case of the USA'. *Multilingua*, 21(2–3), 141–62.

Schwartz, A. (2006), 'The teaching and culture of household Spanish: understanding racist reproduction in "domestic" discourse'. *Critical Discourse Studies*, 3(2), 107–21.

Stokoe, E. and Edwards, D. (2007), '"Black this, black that": racial insults and reported speech in neighbour complaints and police interrogations'. *Discourse & Society*, 18(3), 337–72.

Thompson, K. A. (1998), *Moral Panics*. London: Routledge.

van Dijk, T. A. (1992), 'Discourse and the denial of racism'. *Discourse & Society*, 3(1), 87–118.

Wetherell, M. (2007), 'A step too far: discursive psychology, linguistic ethnography and questions of identity'. *Journal of Sociolinguistics*, 11(5), 661–81.

Wood, H. and Skeggs, B. (2004), 'Notes on ethical scenarios of self on British Reality TV'. *Feminist Media Studies*, 4(2), 205–08.

181

10 Ideologizing ethnolectal German

Jannis Androutsopoulos

10.1 Introduction

Ideologizing refers to the process by which ways of using language become socially recognized, classified, evaluated, debated – in short: invested with language ideologies. Such a process lies at the core of the 'social life of language' (Cameron 2004), and the notion of 'language' encompasses here both micro-level phenomena and macro-units such as language varieties and styles. However, ideologizing processes become particularly salient when their objects are new to the sociolinguistic matrix of a society. In a German context, the focus of this article, such new developments are variably associated with the consequences of globalization (cf. Gardt and Hüppauf 2004) and fall into three broad categories: the use of English in various institutional domains; the visibility of societal multilingualism; and the emergence of migration-related varieties of German, which I shall term ethnolects. Drawing on a recent discussion of Japan, we might say that all three are simultaneous facets of 'the transformation of a society operating largely under monolingual assumptions into one which has come to terms with greater linguistic plurality' (Coulmas and Watanabe 2002: 249). At the same time, all are the object of language-ideological debates in the German-speaking area. Such debates are nowhere carried out with more visibility and impact than in the media. This chapter shares with other recent research (e.g. Stroud 2004; Milani 2008) the key assumption that mainstream media – those designed for, and consumed by large and heterogeneous audiences – are key arenas for the production and reproduction of language ideology. This assumption is, in turn, a meeting point of the disciplines that inform this chapter, that is, sociolinguistics, language ideology research, and media discourse studies. Researchers at the interfaces of these fields (e.g. Blommaert 1999a; Cameron 1995; Johnson 2005; Johnson and Ensslin 2007; Johnstone 2004; Milroy and Milroy 1999; Spitzmüller 2005) all agree on the potential of discourse in mainstream media to shape the language ideologies of their audience, that is, their 'beliefs, or feelings, about languages as used in their social worlds' (Kroskrity 2004: 498; see also Bauman, Chapter 13, this volume). And if the 'languages' in question are emerging varieties, media discourses are in a position to ideologize them from the very start of their social life.

Taking its cues from sociolinguistics, media discourse studies and language ideology research, this chapter examines ways in which ethnolectal German is represented in contemporary media discourse.[1] Its motivation is twofold: as a contribution to language ideology research, it draws on a case not previously studied to examine the mass-mediation of language ideologies and the subtleties of media discourses in doing ideological work. In the context of current ethnolect research, it extends the agenda to language-ideological issues and examines how media discourse articulates and shapes the social meaning of ethnolects in Germany.

A more explicit contextualization of language ideology research seems in order before we proceed. Originating in linguistic anthropology, language ideology research offers sociolinguistics a rich conceptual and methodological toolkit for the study of metalanguage and an alternative to existing methods such as language attitudes and folk linguistics (cf. Coupland and Jaworski 2004). A particular strength of language ideology research lies in the qualitative, critical study of public and institutional discourses on language, and in recent years it has been used by an increasing number of researchers to examine media discourses on language, be it specific language varieties such as Rinkeby Swedish (Stroud 2004) or debates in a specific country such as Luxembourg (Horner 2007). Taking my cue from these studies and a number of seminal texts (e.g. Kroskrity 2004; Blommaert 1999a; Irvine and Gal 2000), I summarize below some assumptions and concepts which inform my analysis.

First, language ideologies are not about linguistic facts alone, but rather constitute 'links between linguistic forms and social phenomena' (Irvine and Gal 2000: 25); put differently, they map understandings of linguistic varieties 'onto people, events, and activities' (ibid.). In linking the linguistic and the social, language ideologies are not 'neutral' or 'objective', but serve individual or group-specific interests, that is, they are always formulated from a particular social perspective and have particular referents and 'targets'. Not all ways of using language are ideologized in the same way or to the same extent, and one effect of language-ideological practices and traditions is that some ways of using language are neutralized, that is, taken as self-evident normality and set as a backdrop against which other varieties of language may be judged as deviant. A case in point is 'standard language ideology' (Milroy and Milroy 1999), which makes an abstract, idealized, homogeneous

183

standard language to a normative point of reference for all other varieties of the same language. As a consequence, engaging in language-ideological work is embedded in relationships of power and constructions of identity. Language ideologies – especially those surrounding dialects, contact varieties or non-standard speech generally – provide social actors with resources for the discursive construction of social and cultural identities, and are important tools in excluding, stigmatizing or 'othering' individuals and groups. A final assumption is that language ideologies are constantly produced, reproduced, circulated in a variety of discursive arenas, including (but not restricted to) mediated public discourses.

My analysis draws on the three semiotic processes of language ideology posited by Judith Irvine and Susan Gal (2000) and subsequently widely used in studies of media discourse (e.g. Horner 2007; Milani 2008). Quoting their definitions, the first process, *iconization,* 'involves a transformation of the sign relationship between linguistic features (or varieties) and the social images with which they are linked. Linguistic features that index social groups or activities appear to be iconic representations of them, as if a linguistic feature somehow depicted or displayed a social group's inherent nature or essence.' The second process, *fractal recursivity* 'involves the projection of an opposition, salient at some level of relationship, onto some other level. For example, intra-group oppositions might be projected outward onto inter-group relations, or vice versa.' Finally, *erasure* 'is the process in which ideology [. . .] renders some persons or activities (or sociolinguistic phenomena) invisible. [. . .] a social group or language may be imagined as homogeneous, its internal variation disregarded.' (Irvine and Gal 2000: 37–8). In examining how ethnolectal German is represented in news discourse in this chapter, I shall be asking what is erased from these representations; what social groups or activities ethnolectal German iconically stands for; and how these ideologies, once semiotically established, are applied to further groups or activities. This analysis is, in turn, grounded in principles and techniques of (critical) media discourse analysis, examining *what* is said in conjunction with *how* it is said, and focusing on patterns and processes such as linguistic variability, metaphor, and their textual and generic contexts.

In the next section I introduce the notion of ethnolects and some characteristics of ethnolects in Germany before examining the presence and representation of ethnolects in media discourse, arguing against a blanket notion of 'media'. Language-ideological work takes place in a wide range of media formats and genres and is therefore contextualized in highly genre-specific ways. I then embark in an analysis of three interrelated cases of media discourse from early 2006. Four research questions shall be asked, the answers summarized in the concluding discussion: *First*, how are iconization, recursivity and erasure operating in these cases? *Second*, what are the key elements of ethnolect ideologies that emerge? *Third*, what are the key linguistic features used to illustrate, exemplify, stereotype ethnolectal German? *Fourth*, how does the ideologization of ethnolectal German differs across and within media genres?

10.2 Ethnolects

A lively debate is currently taking place in European sociolinguistics over the language of migrant youth (e.g. Cornips and Nortier 2008; Jaspers 2007), and while transnational similarities of the processes at stake are widely agreed upon, no equal agreement is achieved over adequate conceptualizations and research frameworks. The term 'ethnolect', widely used in this discussion, was originally coined in reference to varieties of US or Australian English used by ethnically Polish, Italian, Jewish and Greek speakers (Clyne 2000; Wölck 2002). In its original conception, an ethnolect is characteristic of speakers from a migrant background who are born or raised in the host country. It is acquired as second language and used partly alongside, partly in place of, the group's home language. Ethnolects are characterized by co-occurring sets of linguistic features on several structural levels, from prosody to lexicon, and are distinct from both learner varieties and native vernaculars. Michael Clyne further distinguishes between the ethnolect of a specific ethnic minority group (e.g. Greek Australian English) and a 'multi-ethnolect', which is employed by a linguistically diverse group (Clyne 2000; Clyne *et al.* 2002).

In the European context, both terms are being used with reference to the language of (young) speakers of migrant descent across north-western Europe. Talking of ethnolects suggests a system-oriented perspective, which frames the referents as non-standard varieties of the majority language and compares their structural patterns to the respective standard variety (Wiese 2006 is an example of this approach). Meanwhile other researchers tend to focus on ethnic speech styles and the conversational negotiation of their social meaning (e.g. Keim 2007; Kern and Selting 2006). Still others (e.g. Jaspers 2007; Stroud 2004) view the notion of ethnolect as an ideological construct, which prematurely suggests the existence of distinct ethnic varieties, thereby homogenizing a set of highly dynamic and fluid sociolinguistic processes.

Against this backdrop, my own usage is motivated by the need for a cover term: I define ethnolects as ways of speaking that are associated, by speakers themselves or other social groups, with ethnic minority

185

groups (cf. Auer 2003; Dirim and Auer 2004), and do not imply a priority of structural or interactional issues. In addition, ethnolect is useful as an ideological cover term, because it captures the predominant perspective of mainstream media discourse on these issues, which is precisely a homogenizing one. The media may use a variety of labels, but their predominant understanding is, more than anything else, that of a variety of German.

Research on German ethnolects cannot be given extensive coverage here (cf. Kallmeyer and Keim 2004; Keim 2007; Deppermann 2007). The linguistic features discussed as characteristic of German ethnolects cut across all linguistic levels, including phonology (e.g. epenthetic vowels; coronalization of the *ich* sound, /iç/, to *isch*, [iʃ]; reduction of the *st* cluster to *t*, shortening and unrounding of vowels); prosody (syllable-timed instead of stress-timed delivery; 'staccato' speech); syntax (deletion of pronouns and prepositions; lack of word-order inversion); lexicon and discourse (high frequency of certain adjectives and discourse markers; new idioms). But there is less agreement on their social distribution and on whether their speakers switch and shift between ethnolects and other styles of German. In any case such switching practices are erased from the news discourse examined here.

At this point, the importance of extending ethnolect research to media discourse should be clear. Ethnic styles of majority languages are widely performed and reported about in the media, and thereby labelled, evaluated and positioned against other language varieties and styles. Even though this process is unlikely to have any *direct* repercussions on the structure or the everyday conversational use of ethnolects, it might nonetheless impact on their social meaning and evaluation in society at large. Such ongoing ideologizing of ethnolects becomes obvious when we turn to the folk-linguistic labels, which currently circulate in public metalinguistic discourses. As Jan Blommaert (1999b: 431) argues, rather than being purely descriptive and 'neutral', labels for language varieties provide hints to the perceived properties of, and the power relationships projected onto, these varieties. They index social debates, values and evaluations, prestige and stigma. A semantic and intertextual analysis of such labels may offer insights into the language ideologies projected onto ethnolects. These labels are built in German as compounds, and their examination reveals four semantic patterns:

 (a) ethnic German: *Türkendeutsch* ('Turks' German'), *Emigranten-deutsch* ('immigrants' German')
 (b) ethnic speech style: *Kanak Sprak* (see below), *Lan-Sprache* ('Turkish guy speech')[2]

(c) ethnic non-standard speech: *Türkenslang, Migranten-Slang* ('migrants' slang')
(d) language of neighbourhood and 'ghetto': *Stadtteilsprache* ('district language'), *Kiez-Sprache* ('hood language'), *Ghettodeutsch* ('ghetto German')

The three first sets emphasize the ethnic marking of their referents and describe them as (a) a certain kind of German, (b) a distinct language variety, and (c) non-standard speech. The items in the fourth set emphasize the local character of their referent, restricting their prototypical reach to low status contexts. A few labels denote a single ethnic group, while others generalize across immigrant groups. The most long-standing item here is *Kanak Sprak*, a term coined by author Feridun Zaimoglu. His celebrated book of the same title (Zaimoglu 1995) is a documentary-style collection of underdog stories from the second generation of Turkish migrants in Germany. *Kanake* is derogatory term for (southern European) immigrants, and Zaimoglu's use of it reclaims this stigmatized social label as a positive emblem of immigrant identity (cf. Pfaff 2005; Yildiz 2004). Zaimoglu discusses *Kanaken* and their language, *Kanak Sprak*, which he views as an 'underground code' and 'a sort of Creole with secret codes and signs'. He also stresses the analogy between their (alleged) imperfect competence of both German and Turkish and their position between two cultures. In the light of the language ideology framework, this is a classic case of iconization, which establishes the distance of *Kanak Sprak* from 'normal' German as iconic of the distance of *Kanaken* from German society – note that even the form of the term is iconic, its non-normative spelling (*Sprak* instead of *Sprache*) signifying distance from the linguistic norm. However, the language used by the book's voices is a literary construct (cf. Pfaff 2005), and the original conception of *Kanak Sprak* by Zaimoglu is therefore best understood as an imagined variety of German (cf. Yildiz 2004; Stroud 2004: 197). Nevertheless, the label caught on and is widely used as descriptive of the language of migrant-background youth. Thus this early instance of language-ideological work sparked complex chains of follow-up discourses and still operates in contemporary discourse on ethnolects.

10.3 Ethnolects in media discourse

Previous research has discussed ethnolectal German in only a few media genres, in particular comedy (Androutsopoulos 2001; Kotthoff 2004). Comedy has indeed been influential in stereotyping and popularizing ethnic speech styles, but the current spread of ethnolects in the German media is encompassing a much wider range of media genres. My attempt to offer an overview of this field departs from a distinction between two types of genres, that is, show/fiction and news discourse.

The dual category of show/fiction encompasses instances of media discourse in which actors such as scriptwriters, comedians or participants in shows use ethnolects as a resource to cast the speech of the characters or roles they design or enact. 'Fiction' subsumes genres displaying action in a possible world (films, series, soap operas), while 'show' refers to talk, game and reality shows which stage more or less scripted activities by professional and amateur participants (cf. Park, Chapter 4; Georgiou, Chapter 6; Lazar, Chapter 7, Ensslin, Chapter 11, this volume). Both genre types have been prolific propagators of ethnolects in the German mediascape. Ethnic comedy drawing on stylized ethnolectal speech has been popular since the late 1990s, films playing in migrant urban milieus are regularly released and various rap artists of migrant background use more or less marked forms of ethnolectal German (cf. Androutsopoulos 2007). As these genres draw on ethnolects as resources for the performance of characters or roles, processes of styling and stylization, that is, the production and reproduction of sociolinguistic stereotypes, are of central importance. Being part of popular media culture, such texts are heavily recycled, continued, reviewed etc, thereby forming intertextual chains in which bits and pieces of ethnolectal German are constantly de- and recontextualized. As a result, the persona of 'the naïve, uneducated, swanky, macho ghetto youngster' (Kallmeyer and Keim 2004:54 – my translation), complete with their stylized ethnic German, is widely available and immediately recognizable in Germany's entertainment media.

By contrast, the dimension of news discourse encompasses instances of media text and talk in which professional actors of a different kind, that is, journalists, engage in the explicit discussion, definition, evaluation and so on, of ethnolects. An important distinction here is the degree of explicitness and topical centrality of such metalinguistic discourse. Some media features are dedicated to metalanguage, covering issues such as the language of migrant youngsters or the relation of language and integration. Other fragments of metalinguistic discourse are embedded within a different main topic, as when a film review happens to mention in passing the language used in that film. News reports of all things migrant in Germany may be expected to contain sporadic references to 'their' language, but as a whole, such incidental metalinguistic discourse is less predictable and therefore more difficult to trace than dedicated, canonical metalinguistic discourse (see also Moschonas and Spitzmüller, Chapter 2, this volume).

188

Taking both genre types together suggests that the media are a multi-dimensional site of representation and diffusion of ethnolects. Media texts from a broad generic spectrum deliver snapshots of ethnolects in use, accompanied by fragments of metalinguistic knowledge and interpretation, to a mass audience, some sectors of which may have very little personal experience with ethnolects. As a consequence, 'people, who previously would not have had access to [an ethnolect, J.A.] because of its very situated confinement to local neighbourhoods, can now boast a familiarity with trendy turns of phrase and hip styles of speech' (Stroud 2004: 205–6). However, two further points should be borne in mind: first, the general tendency of media discourse to self-organize in intertextual chains means that discourse on ethnolects which is sparked by a specific occasion or event will often be recycled and continued in a variety of forms. Second, the genre distinction introduced here is a purely analytical one, as elements from the two genre types may of course merge in practice, with newspaper reports on ethnolects incorporating elements of fictionalization (cf. also examples by Stroud 2004) and fictional genres featuring bits of academic, apparently factual, metalinguistic talk.

The data to be discussed below are of the second type, that is, news discourse. Its selection was based on recent media coverage of events in which ethnolectal German played a certain role or itself was the main topic. All three cases originated in the spring of 2006; one is 'dedicated' and two 'incidental', and two of them are sequentially related. The first case is *Grup Tekkan*, a young Turkish-German band that enjoyed short popularity (see the relevant article in German-language Wikipedia, http://de.wikipedia.org). Besides a number of news reports that are the focus of my discussion here, I analysed a song by them alongside some of their TV interviews and live appearances. The second case is *Rütli Schule* – a secondary school in a deprived district of Berlin, whose teachers publicly requested its closure because they were no longer able to cope with their immigrant pupils' violent behaviour (cf. relevant entry in German-language Wikipedia). From the media reporting that followed, I only discuss here a lengthy front-page feature from *Spiegel*, an influential weekly news periodical. The *third case* is the wave of news reports on the language of immigrant youth that was prompted by the *Rütli Schule* incident. I examined in detail three lengthy features from prestigious public radio channels (*Deutschlandradio, Deutschlandfunk, Deutsche Welle*) and four newspaper pieces (including national daily *Die Welt*). It is worth noting that most of these feature expert voices, including mine, which are not however discussed in detail. Even though this dataset is obviously limited in terms of quantity, it still offers a variety of cases in different media, prompted by different events, and forming intertextual chains. I therefore argue that its analysis may bring to the fore important insights into the four research questions posited in the introduction.

10.4 Three cases of language-ideological discourse

10.4.1 'Turk-German and Palatine slang': reports on Grup Tekkan

At the centre of the first case is *Sonnenlicht* ('Sunshine'), a pop song published on the Internet by an amateur Turkish-German band called *Grup Tekkan*. The song developed into a sort of 'kitsch cult', its popularity snowballing within a couple of weeks, thereby catapulting the four teenagers to nationwide TV shows, to be just as quickly forgotten again thereafter. Mainstream media reports were generally framed as ironic, leaving the four youngsters, and their language, prey to ridicule. The reports' attention to language originates in the song lyrics themselves, which feature ethnolectal features in phonology, including the *isch* variant of the *ich* sound which also occurs in the song title (i.e. *Sonnenlischt* instead of standard *Sonnenlicht*)[3].

One common feature of many media reports on *Grup Tekkan* is the way in which they construct a link between aesthetic and linguistic devaluation. This is obvious in the two extracts below, which are the longest metalinguistic passages in my data. (Bold type indicates representations of non-standard features in the original; all translations are my own.)

Excerpt 1

*Eine gewisse Attraktivität entfaltet wohl auch die absolut unbekümmerte Naivität dieser Teenager, die sich ihres Dialekts ('**isch** respektier **disch**') nicht schämen und auch vor Zeilen wie 'Isch kann ohne dich nicht sein / wir müssen uns wieder verein' nicht zurückschrecken. (laut.de, 17 March 2006)*

[There is a certain attractiveness in the absolutely happy-go-lucky naivety of those teenagers who are not ashamed of their dialect ('**I** respect **you**') and do not shrink away from lines such as 'I can't be without you / we have to unite again.']

Excerpt 2

*Der Song ist schlecht – unfassbar schlecht sogar. Aber eigentlich sollte er ja auch nie veröffentlicht werden: 'Wo bist du, mein Sonnenlicht?', fragt das Trio die Angebetete. Wobei 'Sonnen**lischt**'* *der phonetischen Wahrheit eigentlich näher kommt – so etwas passiert, wenn Türk-Deutsch und pfälzischer Slang eine unheilige Verbindung miteinander eingehen. Und auch Gesang und Grammatik sind, nennen wir es mal - unkonventionell: 'Ich vermisse **deinem Aten**' lautet eine Zeile. (netzeitung.de, 23 March 2006)*

[This song is bad – unbelievably bad indeed. But it wasn't meant to be released anyway. 'Where are you, my Sonnenlicht?' the trio asks its adored one. However, Sonnen**lischt** is closer to the phonetic truth. That is what happens when Turkish German and Palatinate slang establish an unholy connection. Singing and grammar are, let's put it this way, unconventional. 'I'm missing **your breath**', a line goes.]

On the propositional level, we witness how judgement on music and language is coordinated, as in 'singing and grammar' (Excerpt 1) or 'striking the right tone or correct grammar was of minor importance'.[4] The fact that the song's syntax is not deviant from standard German (see note 3) suggests that 'grammar' is to be read here as a metonym for 'good German', which is implicitly understood as standard German. We also see how the band's low artistic status (their 'absolutely happy-go-lucky naivety') is linked to their language, labelled 'dialect' or 'slang', which, as inferred from Excerpt (1), is nothing to be proud of in the context of pop music. These news reports ethnicize and provincialize the band and their language (they are e.g. 'Turkish guys from the Palatinate province'), ascribing them the double stigma of dialect and ethnolect which are seen to form an 'unholy connection' (Excerpt 1). Note also how both excerpts choose for illustration the same linguistic feature, that is, the coronalization of the *ich* sound, which also occurs in the headlines below.

Excerpt 3

a. *Bizarre Netz-Karriere: Tokio Hotel verblasst im Sonnenlischt* [Bizarre web career: Tokyo Hotel fades in Sonnenlischt] (*Spiegel Online*, 17 March 06)
b. *Konkret kopiert: Die krasse Story vom 'Sonnenlischt'* [Concretely copied: the gross story of 'Sonnenlischt'] (*Spiegel Online*, 21 March 06)
c. *Grup Tekkan: Mit 'Sonnenlischt' bei Stefan Raab* [Grup Tekkan: with 'Sonnenlischt' to Stefan Raab] (*laut.de*, 17 March 06)

The first two headlines are from the online outlet of a mainstream magazine, the third from a special-interest website. All are replete with references to pop culture, with (a) ironically comparing *Grup Tekkan* to a teen idol band, (c) announcing the band's visit to a popular TV show, and (b) evoking the ethnic comedy craze of the late 1990s by means of two lexical items, *konkret* ('concrete') and *krass* ('gross') (cf. Androutsopoulos 2001). Thus ethnic comedy is offered by the media as a frame of interpretation, increasing the ridicule of the band and associating their language to stylized comedy speech. All headlines draw on the *isch* variant as an attention-grabber, with marked and unmarked forms of the noun alternating in the subsequent text. Meanwhile the chronological sequence of the examples suggests that the marked form is repeated as the reports unfold, eventually becoming iconic of the song and the band.

10.4.2 'The way they talk': the Spiegel report on Rütli Schule

Almost simultaneous to *Grup Tekkan*, the *Rütli Schule* incident was quite a different type of event. This unprecedented case of the teachers of a Berlin secondary school publicly requesting the school's temporary closure due to pupil violence was widely regarded as symptomatic of the failure of the German educational system to integrate migrant-background pupils. The *Spiegel* front-page feature, published two weeks after the beginning of the incident, is headlined *Die verlorene Welt* ('The lost world'), and makes the pupils' language a salient issue, featuring six metalinguistic passages of various lengths, with the first and longest one, reproduced below as Extract 4, coming in quite early in the report. This serves as a first take on 'the reality of the *Rütli Schule*' leading the way to an attempt to interpret the meaning of 'respect' in the culture of the Turkish or Arabic-background pupils.

Excerpt 4

Die verlorene Welt ('The lost world'), *Der Spiegel* 14/2006, p. 24.

Und dort scheint sich inzwischen eine verlorene Welt neben der ganz normalen deutschen Wirklichkeit geformt und längst verfestigt zu haben, die mit der anderen Wirklichkeit nichts mehr zu tun hat.

Aufklärung? Bildung? Lernen, für Zensuren, vielleicht sogar fürs Leben?

Was soll der Scheiß?

So reden die Bewohner dieser Welt. *Ey, Mann, ey. Nutte. Killer. Krass.* Es gibt viele 'sch' und 'ch'-Laute in dieser Sprache, kaum noch ganze Sätze. *Dreckische Deutsche*, so reden sie.

[. . .] Respekt bekommt, wer die eigene, also die türkische oder libanesische Schwester vor Sex und Liebe [. . .] schützt und selbst *deutsche Schlampe fickt.*

Ohne Artikel. Wie sie eben reden.

[Meanwhile, a lost world is apparently constituted and consolidated there, alongside normal German reality, a world that has
nothing to do with that reality.

Enlightenment? Education? Learning for exams, maybe for life?
What's that crap?

That's how they talk, the inhabitants of that world. *Ey, Mann, ey.
Nutte. Killer. Krass.* There are many 'sch' and 'ch' sounds in that
language, hardly any full sentences. *Dreckische Deutsche* [dirty
Germans], that's how they talk.

[. . .] Only those gain respect who protect their own Turkish or
Lebanese sister from sex and love [. . .] and *shag German slut*
themselves.

Without an article. That's the way they talk.]

This passage is the first to take up the wording of the title, 'lost world',
which is juxtaposed to 'normal German reality'. Thus an opposition
between a taken-for-granted normalness and the supposedly 'lost world'
of that school ('lost' obviously from the perspective of the majority) is
set up from the outset. This opposition is then developed with Bakhtinian
double voicing, in which the voice of the 'normal reality', cast in rhetorical questions, is juxtaposed to the voice of the 'lost world', which is
typographically and stylistically set apart. Taking front stage again, the
voice of the narrator now introduces language as first characteristic of
'the inhabitants of that world'. Thus language is staged as an icon of the
pupils' 'inherent nature or essence' (Irvine and Gal 2000: 37), and that
essence is already delivered by the title ('the lost world') and amply
displayed throughout the feature. All subsequent discussion of 'that
language' then mirrors the distance of the 'lost world' from 'normal
German reality': these pupils are as deviant from 'normal German reality' as their language is from normal German. At the same time the
portrayal of their language arguably offers local colour in a way that
resembles Stroud's analysis of reports on the Rinkeby district of Stockholm (Stroud 2004: 201).

The report illustrates the pupils' language through a number of linguistic features, and the commentary ('that's the way they talk') suggests a stable, invariant speech style. The features come from phonology
(coronalization), syntax (incomplete sentences, no articles), and lexicon/
set phrases. Compared to actual research findings the list is only partly
accurate, for while coronalization and article deletion may count as
typical ethnolect features, most lexical units quoted here are familiar
from German youth slang generally, and the reported lack of 'full sentences' is reminiscent of the complaint tradition against spoken language.
Thus what is constructed as 'their language' overlaps to a considerable

extent with native youth vernaculars, but this overlap is itself erased. Significantly, the phonological and syntactic features are exemplified through phrases which emphasize the pupils' social deviation: even though the phrases 'dirty Germans' and 'shag German slut' are apparently used to illustrate *how* the pupils talk, i.e. to exemplify features of linguistic form, the wording inevitably draws attention to propositional content, that is, *what* they say about 'us'.

10.4.3 '"Kanaksprak" is on the advance': media reports on ethnolects

This and other features sparked a wave of media interest in the language of migrant youth in the weeks following the *Rütli Schule* incident. Such reports are, on the one hand, part of a specific complaint tradition (Milroy and Milroy 1999), in which youth language is constructed as deviant, incomprehensible and exotic. Additionally, they are motivated by a specific incident in which the language of migrant youth is cast as iconic of social otherness and deviance. This contextualizes from the outset the questions asked and the answers offered in these reports, thereby underscoring the problematic nature of ethnic styles of German. At the peak of their popularity in April 2006, such reports appeared in a range of newspapers and radio stations. Regardless of medium and institution, the dominant perspective in these features positions ethnolects as a deviation from an undifferentiated 'German', and debates their potential influence on the future of German. The essence of this perspective becomes perhaps most obvious in pragmatically prominent chunks such as headlines and leaders, which are conventionally read as summarizing the essence of a news item:

> ### Excerpt 5
>
> Headlines and leaders of media features on ethnolects (April 2006)[5]
> (a) *Sprachexperte: Migranten-Slang breitet sich in Deutschland aus*
>   [Language expert: Migrant slang is spreading across Germany]
> (b) Die *'Kanaksprak' ist auf dem Vormarsch*
>   ['*Kanaksprak*' is on the advance]
> (c) *Der neue Ethnolekt des Deutschen nimmt Einfluß auf die Hochsprache*
>   [New German ethnolect is influencing the standard language]

In a manner strikingly similar to debates on Anglicisms (cf. Spitzmüller 2005), German is constructed here as a unity that is confronted with (and potentially threatened by) new varieties. These reports use the same metaphors as media discourse on the influence of English on German and also on migration (cf. Moschonas and Spitzmüller, Chapter 2, this volume). Ethnolects are metaphorically constructed as a spreading virus or an alien force, while German is placed as a victim in need of protection.[6] In terms of metaphor, then, ethnolects are treated as something as alien and threatening to German (and Germany) as a foreign language or foreign people. These examples also suggest that media reports are themselves multipliers of metalinguistic labels. The three headlines feature three different labels (*Migranten-Slang*, '*Kanaksprak*', *der neue Ethnolekt*) which are used as co-referential, and this proliferation of seemingly interchangeable labels is typical for all reports examined. Motivated as it may be by journalistic imperatives such as variation in expression and transfer of expert knowledge, this practice has the effect of concealing referential differences and neutralizing evaluative connotations. As far as these reports are concerned, academic terms (*Ethnolekt*), literary constructs ('*Kanaksprak*') and colloquial, derogatory labels such as *Migranten-Slang* or *Sprachgemisch* ('language mixture') are all legitimate descriptors of the same phenomena.

The following excerpt illustrates the representation of ethnolect in the introduction of a dedicated radio feature. This is the second of three introductory chunks coming right after the host has greeted the audience and serving as a sort of lead before the main story:

Excerpt 6

Radio feature on '*Kanaksprak*' (*Deutschlandradio Kultur,* 6/4/2006; English translation only)

'*Kanaksprak*' is on the advance. Meanwhile, native German youngsters are themselves talking '*Kanaksprak*', a kind of emigrant's German, consisting of chunks of Turkish or Arabic or Russian. As far as Berlin's *Rütli Schule* is concerned, it was reported that the few native German speakers there adopt the slang of their Turkish or Arabic classmates. How is the German language changing as a result of this migrant slang?

All three introductory chunks begin with the same statement: "Kanaksprak' is on the advance' (*Die 'Kanaksprak' ist auf dem Vormarsch*). This enhances topical cohesion, but also presents itself, by means of topicalization and iteration, as the essence of this report, and at the same time reproduces the metaphor of military advance. As in other reports, the interest in ethnolects is explicitly motivated by the school incident, and the object of attention is multiply paraphrased, thereby indexing emigration (*Emigrantendeutsch*), mixture

195

(*Sprachgemisch* – in the first introduction), fragmentation (*Brocken.* i.e. 'chunks') and non-standardness (slang). Young native speakers are presented as directly affected by this 'advance', and the concluding question stresses, again, the consequences for German. Thus the report reproduces the distinction between 'the German language' and the language of migrant youth. Also noteworthy here is how in the third introductory chunk, which comes right before the expert voice, the host introduces ethnic comedy as a 'prominent example' of 'Turkish-German language mix' and then calls the expert (in this case myself) to discuss its authenticity. This again perpetuates comedy as a frame of interpretation for current metalinguistic discourse (cf. Excerpt 3), and even though the expert challenges the straightforward relationship between comedy and everyday speech, this relationship is nonetheless made relevant by the host in advance (see also Georgiou, Chapter 6, this volume).

In this and other cases in my data, press and radio features construct 'the German language' as a homogeneous whole and set it apart from new migrant varieties. They do so by drawing on metaphors of invasion and infection that are common in discourse on migration and English language influence; and they act as multipliers of linguistic labels, thereby treating popular and technical labels as interchangeable. Erased in this process is the continuity between ethnolects and other German vernaculars as well as the overall diversity of German, which is itself reduced to a normative uniformity.

This account should not of course be taken as indicating a total lack of other voices and perspectives. There is indeed an alternative discourse, which positions *'Kanaksprak'* not as something exotic and deviant but as linguistic normality in urban space, thereby foregrounding its speakers as opposed to an imaginary, uniform version of German (cf. Androutsopoulos 2007: 146). However, this appeared to be a minor voice in the chain of reports examined here.

10.5 Discussion and conclusions

Starting from the assumption that media discourse is a key force in the ideologization of newly emerging varieties of language, this chapter aimed at tracing the mechanisms of language ideology in German news reports on ethnolects. I will now conclude by re-visiting the four questions introduced earlier: (i) How the semiotic processes of language ideology manifest themselves in my data; (ii) what key elements of ethnolect ideologies emerge; (iii) what linguistic features are foregrounded; and (iv) how representations of ethnolects vary across and within media genres.

First, the three semiotic processes of language ideology formation postulated by Irvine and Gal (2000) are useful in illuminating the discursive processes under scrutiny here; however, I also found that they are neither equally ubiquitous nor equally easy to grasp. Most obvious is the process of erasure, that is, the stripping of details from the ideological picture. Erasure affects the linguistic variability of individuals and groups, which are consistently portrayed in my data as lacking competence of other varieties or styles of German – they 'just speak this way'. Processes of multilingualism, code-switching or style-shifting are equally absent from these reports. Erasure also affects the way relationships between different varieties of German are portrayed, for example, similarities between ethnolectal and native colloquial German, the regional and social variability of ethnic styles together with the diversity of German in general. While it might be fair to say that any representation of linguistic diversity will inevitably entail some degree of erasure, its effects accumulate here to form crude images of mono-stylistic speakers and ways of speaking that are alien to 'the German language'.

These ways of speaking are, in turn, presented as a core property of their speakers, and their opposition to (or deviance from) 'normal German', which by means of erasure is assumed to be standard German, is firmly linked to a social opposition between 'us' (natives) and 'them' (migrant-background youth). The process of iconization links linguistic and ethnic otherness based on a similarity (i.e. an iconic relationship) between evaluations of the linguistic and the social. Thus language that is deemed non-standard stands for people depicted as uncultivated, non-integrated, ghettoized or downright criminal. However, using data from an array of synchronic cases allows us to see how the same linguistic features may do quite diverse iconizing work as they are placed in relation to different groups and activities: thus coronalization (the *isch* variant for the *ich* sound) is iconic to the naïve, provincial pop group here, the dangerous ghetto kids there. We might therefore say, in line with Gunter Kress, that coronalization and a few other ethnolect stereotypes are currently '. . . available as a highly charged signifier ready for ideological and political deployment and exploitation' (Kress 1986: 400).

The third process, fractal recursivity, is evident in my data in relation to a double sociolinguistic opposition: that between standard and ethnolect, on the one hand, and native and non-native speakers ('us' and 'them') on the other. Already an outcome of erasure and iconization, this language-ideological mapping charts standardness and nativeness as a 'natural' pair, which is juxtaposed to an equally 'natural' pair consisting

197

of ethnolect and non-nativeness. Significantly, the first pair is not debated here, that is, 'German' and 'nativeness' are a taken-for-granted backdrop to the focus on otherness. This basic opposition is then applied to particular social groups or domains of social activity, depending on the events at stake. So in the first case study, ethnolectal German is 'naturally' associated with amateurish music characteristic of poor taste, whereas standard German is the implied 'normal' backdrop for professional-standard pop music. In the second and third case, ethnolect is the code of 'problem youth' whereas the 'normal German reality' is implicitly associated with 'normal', that is, standard German. In another discourse arena, that is, films portraying urban ethnic milieus (cf. Androutsopoulos 2007), the same sociolinguistic opposition is instantiated within an ethnic milieu, in a manner strikingly reminiscent of Hollywood movies (cf. Lippi-Green 1997). Here ethnic protagonists and successful migrant characters are cast as quasi-nativized speakers of standard German, while villains and/or minor figures are allocated linguistic otherness. Across all such recursive applications of the basic opposition, ethnolects are placed on the negative side, which is itself the marked category, whereas the positive side remains undifferentiated.

Moving now to the second point, my findings suggest three interrelated main elements of German ethnolect ideology: *non-standardness*, *foreignness*, and *negativity*. The first is the outcome of the constant juxtaposition of ethnolects to 'normal' German. Ethnolects are not just another part of the diversity of German, but rather 'naturally' treated as *slang*, a *dialect,* or downright 'bad German'. The second element, *foreignness,* refers to the gap between ethnolectal German and 'the German language'. This is obvious in the constant juxtaposition of the two, and more specifically in the use of the same metaphors as in discourse on Anglicisms and migration. Thus ethnolectal varieties, being cast by means of iconization as the language of 'another world', are seen to invade and threaten German. The third element, *negativity*, is constituted by the allocation of ethnolectal German to individuals and groups who are portrayed as low-status, socially problematic (marginal, ghettoized, criminal, threatening) or lacking cultural skills and taste. The three elements co-occur, mutually reinforcing each other and leaving little space for alternative representations.

With regard to the third point, the various media texts in my data are strikingly similar in their selection of the apparent linguistic features of ethnolects. This includes some well-documented features (phonology: coronalization; syntax: article and preposition deletion; lexicon: certain German or Turkish items, such as terms of address), all of which have featured prominently in the research literature. On top of that, however, comes what we might call a 'double distortion' when compared to research findings. One dimension of this is the absence of several research-documented features, especially in prosody but also syntax (e.g. word order inversion), which only expert voices occasionally bring into the picture. The other aspect is the addition of those features that are presented as typical for ethnolects but are either more widespread features of colloquial German or indeed fictitious creations, as already observed in the case of ethnic comedy (Androutsopoulos 2001; Deppermann 2007). We also noticed the tendency of media reports to repeatedly use a few features in salient textual spots, and it seems legitimate to ask what the impact of such textual practice may be for the consolidation of stereotypes of ethnolectal German.

Finally, it is worth pointing out that representations of German ethnolects vary considerably across and within media genres. This is of course self-evident with regard to my main distinction between fiction/shows and news, as these two types of discourse implicate quite different constraints with respect to styling and stylization, factualness, entertainment and so on. However, it was surprising to be able to observe marked differences amongst various radio features from prestigious public radio channels. While *Deutschlandradio* (cf. Excerpt 6) unquestionably reproduced the dominant ideology of ethnolects, this was challenged by the *Deutschlandfunk* feature which foregrounded the normalness of ethnolects and the views of their speakers. Having personally been implicated as an 'expert voice' in both of these features, I conclude that differences in language-ideological work may be less a matter of audience type than of the sensibility and interest of individual professional protagonists. On the other hand, it is striking just how much ideological work is being done in what I term 'incidental' metalinguistic discourse. It seems that discourse which just touches on language without it being its main topic bears other regularities than 'dedicated' pieces. Mentioning language in passing seems to relieve journalists from the obligation to call upon expert voices, and offers more leeway to play with, allude to, and eventually ratify sociolinguistic stereotypes. Many incidental comments are framed as subjective and jocular, but of course they are doing ideological work all the same. Such incidental discourse would therefore seem worthy of further attention in future research, and new techniques may be needed for tracing it (see e.g. Moschonas and Spitzmüller, Chapter 2, this volume).

To what extent are these findings generalizable? Evoking research on language and national identity in the German-speaking area suggests that at least part of the picture is indebted to a specifically German sensitivity towards the bond between language and nation, which finds its expression in romantic nationalism and the emergence of the German nation-state in the nineteenth century (cf. chapters in Gardt and Hüppauf 2004). One repercussion of this is an understanding of German as the most essential feature of German-ness, and thus an attention to language as a boundary of national belonging. An indication of this in my data is perhaps the fact that the future of German is so widely debated in dedicated media reports. Clearly, such a close relationship between language and national identity cannot necessarily be transferred directly to other (European) societies, and comparative research on ethnolect ideologies is needed to clarify the generalizability of my findings. The same holds true for the main assumption of this chapter, namely that metalinguistic media discourses are key agents in ideologizing emerging ethnic varieties, and the language ideologies they articulate are bound to contribute to the wider social meaning of ethnolects.

Notes

1 This is a considerably revised version of a paper first published in German (Androutsopoulos 2007), which examined a wider range of media genres and is therefore referred to when the discussion turns to film, comedy and music.
2 *Lan* is a Turkish noun meaning 'guy', metonymically extended to an ethnic label.
3 The song lyrics feature no ethnolectal features in morphology and syntax, but the band members' speech in their TV interviews displays an abundance of such features (e.g. absence of articles, errors in gender and congruence), suggesting that the song lyrics were designed as more standard-oriented than the members' spoken language.
4 Report on the public radio website hr-online.de, 24/3/2006.
5 Source of examples (a) and (b) is the radio show *Deutschlandradio Kultur Radiofeuilleton*, 6/4/2006; (a) is from the show's website, (b) from the show's introduction. Item (c) comes from national daily *Die Welt*, 5/4/2006. Cf. full references and weblinks in Androutsopoulos (2007).
6 *Vormarsch* ('military advance') and *Ausbreitung* ('expansion') are well-documented metaphors in discourses of immigration and foreign language influence on German (cf. Spitzmüller 2005: 221, 226); *Schutz* ('protection') was used by a journalist who asked me whether 'the German language' ought to be *protected* from *Kanak Sprak*.

References

Androutsopoulos, J. (2001), 'From the streets to the screens and back again: on the mediated diffusion of variation patterns in contemporary German'. *LAUD Linguistic Agency, A:522*, University of Essen. (www.linse.uni-due. de/linse/laud/, last accessed on 15 April 2008).
Androutsopoulos, J. (2007), 'Ethnolekte in der Mediengesellschaft. Stilisierung und Sprachideologie in Performance, Fiktion und Metasprachdiskurs',

in C. Fandrych and R. Salverda (eds), *Standard, Variation und Sprachwandel in germanischen Sprachen*. Tübingen: Narr, pp. 113–55.

Auer, P. (2003), '"Türkenslang": ein jugendsprachlicher Ethnolekt des Deutschen und seine Transformationen', in A. Häcki-Buhofer (ed.), *Spracherwerb und Lebensalter*. Tübingen: Francke, pp. 255–64.

Blommaert, J. (ed.) (1999a), *Language Ideological Debates*. Berlin, New York: Mouton de Gruyter.

Blommaert, J. (1999b), 'The debate is closed', in J. Blommaert (ed.), *Language Ideological Debates*. Berlin, New York: Mouton de Gruyter, pp. 425–38.

Cameron, D. (1995), *Verbal Hygiene*. London: Routledge.

Cameron, D. (2004), 'Out of the bottle: the social life of metalanguage', in A. Jaworski *et al.* (eds), *Metalanguage: Social and Ideological Perspectives*. Berlin, New York: Mouton de Gruyter, pp. 311–22.

Clyne, M. (2000), 'Lingua franca and ethnolects in Europe and beyond'. *Sociolinguistica*, 14, 83–89.

Clyne, M., Eisikovits, E. and Tollfree, L. (2002), 'Ethnolects as in-group markers', in A. Duszak (ed.), *Us and Others*. Amsterdam: John Benjamins, pp. 133–57.

Cornips, L. and Nortier, J. (eds) (2008), *Ethnolects? The Emergence of New Varieties among Adolescents*. Double special issue of *International Journal of Bilingualism* 12(1-2).

Coulmas, F. and Watanabe, M. (2002), 'Japan's nascent multilingualism', in Li Wei, J-M. Dewaele and A. Housen (eds), *Opportunities and Challenges of Bilingualism*. Berlin, New York: Mouton de Gruyter, pp. 249–71.

Coupland, N. and Jaworski, A. (2004), 'Sociolinguistic perspectives on metalanguage: reflexivity, evaluation and ideology', in A. Jaworski *et al.* (eds), *Metalanguage: Social and Ideological Perspectives*. Berlin, New York: Mouton de Gruyter, pp. 15–52.

Deppermann, A. (2007), 'Playing with the voice of the other: stylized *Kanaksprak* in conversations among German adolescents', in P. Auer (ed.), *Style and Social Identities: Alternative Approaches to Linguistic Heterogeneity*. Berlin, New York: Mouton de Gruyter, pp. 325–60.

Dirim, İ. and Auer, P. (2004), *Türkisch sprechen nicht nur Türken*. Berlin: Mouton de Gruyter.

Gardt, A. and Hüppauf, B. (eds) (2004), *Globalization and the Future of German*. Berlin: Mouton de Gruyter.

Horner, C. (2007), 'Global challenges to nationalist ideologies: language and education in the Luxembourg press', in S. Johnson and A. Ensslin (eds), *Language in the Media: Representations, Identities, Ideologies*. London: Continuum, pp. 130–46.

Irvine, J. T. and Gal, S. (2000), 'Language ideology and linguistic differentiation', in P. V. Kroskrity (ed.), *Regimes of Language: Ideologies, Polities, and Identities*. Santa Fe, NM: School of American Research, pp. 35–84.

Jaspers, J. (2007), 'In the name of science?: On identifying an ethnolect in an Antwerp secondary school', *Working Papers in Urban Language and Literacies*, 42, King's College London. (www.kcl.ac.uk/content/1/c6/01/42/29/paper42.pdf, last accessed on 16 March 2008.)

Jaworski, A., Coupland, N. and Galasiński, D. (eds) (2004), *Metalanguage: Social and Ideological perspectives*. Berlin, New York: Mouton de Gruyter.

Johnson, S. (2005), *Spelling Trouble: Language, Ideology and the Reform of German Orthography*. Clevedon: Multilingual Matters.

Johnson, S. and Ensslin, A. (eds) (2007), *Language in the Media: Representations, Identities, Ideologies*. London: Continuum.

Johnstone, B. (2004), 'Place, globalization, and linguistic variation', in C. Fought (ed.), *Sociolinguistic Variation: Critical Reflections*, Oxford: Oxford University Press, pp. 65–83.

Kallmeyer, W. and Keim, I. (2004), 'Deutsch-türkische Kontaktvarietäten. Am Beispiel der Sprache von deutsch-türkischen Jugendlichen', in S. Moraldo and M. Soffritti (eds), *Deutsch aktuell*. Rom: Carocci, pp. 60–80.

Keim, I. (2007), *Die 'türkischen Powergirls'. Lebenswelt und kommunikativer Stil einer Migrantinnengruppe in Mannheim*. Tübingen: Narr.

Kern, F. and Selting, M. (2006), 'Einheitenkonstruktion im Türkendeutschen: grammatische und prosodische Aspekte'. *Zeitschrift für Sprachwissenschaft*, 25, 239–72.

Kotthoff, H. (2004), 'Overdoing culture. Sketch-Komik, Typenstilisierung und Identitätsbildung bei Kaya Yanar', in K. H. Hörning and J. Reuter (eds), *Doing Culture*. Bielefeld: Transcript, pp. 184–201.

Kress, G. (1986), 'Language in the media: the construction of the domains of public and private'. *Media, Culture and Society*, 8(4), 395–419.

Kroskrity, P. V. (2004), 'Language ideologies', in A. Duranti (ed.) *A Companion to Linguistic Anthropology*. Malden, MA: Blackwell, pp. 496–517.

Lippi-Green, R. (1997), *English with an Accent: Language, Ideology and Discrimination in the United States*. London/New York: Routledge.

Milani, T. M. (2008), 'Language testing and citizenship: a language ideological debate in Sweden'. *Language in Society*, 37(1), 27–59.

Milroy, J. and Milroy, L. (1999), *Authority in Language: Investigating Language Prescription and Standardization*, 3rd ed. London: Routledge.

Pfaff, C. (2005), '"Kanaken im Alemannistan": Feridun Zaimoglu's representation of migrant language', in V. Hinnenkamp and K. Meng (eds), *Sprachgrenzen überspringen*. Tübingen: Narr, pp. 195–225.

Spitzmüller J. (2005), *Metasprachdiskurse: Einstellungen zu Anglizismen und ihre wissenschaftliche Rezeption*. Berlin: Mouton de Gruyter.

Stroud, C. (2004), 'Rinkeby Swedish and semilingualism in language ideological debates: a Bourdieuean perspective'. *Journal of Sociolinguistics*, 8(2), 196–214.

Wiese, H. (2006), '"Ich mach dich Messer": grammatische Produktivität in Kiez-Sprache ("*Kanak Sprak*")'. *Linguistische Berichte*, 207, 245–73.

Wölck, W. (2002), 'Ethnnolects – between bilingualism and urban dialect', in L. Wei, J-M. Dewaele and A. Housen (eds), *Opportunities and Challenges of Bilingualism*. Berlin: Mouton de Gruyter, pp. 157–70.

Yildiz, Y. (2004), 'Critically "Kanak": a reimagination of German culture', in Gardt and Hüppauf (eds), *Globalization and the Future of German*. Berlin: Mouton de Gruyter, pp. 319–40.

Zaimoglu, F. (1995), *Kanak Sprak*. Hamburg: Rowohlt.

PART IV

LANGUAGE IDEOLOGIES AND NEW-MEDIA TECHNOLOGIES

11 'Black and white': language ideologies in computer game discourse

Astrid Ensslin

11.1 Introduction

Recent creative industry sales figures leave little doubt that video games[1] have become one of today's most popular and commercially viable genres of multimodal discourse. According to the Entertainment and Software Publishers' Association (ELSPA), during the first half of 2007 the UK's interactive entertainment software industry saw an increase of 19 per cent compared to the first half of 2006, with a total of over 26.01 million units sold for an overall amount of £519 million.[2] To a significant degree this is due to the success with which video games combine straightforward narrative and ludic elements, immersive, state-of-the-art 3D graphics, physical interaction and a variety of feedback and reward systems. On the other hand, I argue that a significant part of the popularity particularly of mainstream game series such as *The Sims, Tomb Raider, Castle Wolfenstein* and *Halo* derives from the strategic reiteration of stereotypes relating to gender and race, and also language attitudes. This chapter will be dedicated to an analysis of the latter.

Earlier research into the use of non-native and non-standard accents in popular visual narrative has focused primarily on Disney and Hollywood movies (e.g. Lippi-Green 1997) and the use of explicit and implicit metalanguage and metacommunication in American TV series (Richardson 2006). More recently, attempts have begun to be made by social semioticians to characterize the global discursive pattern of war games (Machin and van Leeuwen 2007). That said, comparably few sociolinguistic and social semiotic studies have looked into the spoken, written and multimodal discourse of virtual gaming environments insofar as this reveals underlying, seemingly unreflected and undocumented language ideologies. The present chapter seeks to contribute to filling this gap by providing a methodologically qualitative insight into what appear to be prevailing communicative patterns within such discourse.

This study forms part of a larger research project I am currently undertaking, entitled The Language of Gaming: Discourse and Ideology' (Ensslin, forthcoming). Drawing on the work of Tim Shortis (2001) and Mark Boardman (2005), the project aims to explore issues of games textuality (processurality, multimodality, narrative, ludic agency, interactivity and intermediality – e.g. cinematographic 'cut scenes'); lexis and morphology (e.g. onomastic, neologistic and mythological borrowings); phonology (the use of accent to characterize gendered, regional and ethnic identities in the game world); and pragmatics, which will involve dominant uses of illocutionary types, for example, directives for rules, constatives for text world creation and acknowledgements for feedback, register, as well as conversation analyses of human-avatar and human-machine interaction more generally. An integral yet separately published aspect of the project is dedicated to language ideologies and how they are revealed textually through implicit metapragmatics, that is, 'linguistic signalling that is part of the stream of language use in process and that simultaneously indicates how to interpret that language-in-use' (Woolard 1998: 9; cf. Lucy 1993; Silverstein 1993). Without claiming any quantitative authority, this chapter aims to outline some early general observations via the close-reading of a small number of language-ideologically charged game sequences in the light of multimodal discourse analysis.

I shall begin by flagging up the significance of sociolinguistic research into computer games by outlining recent trends in consumer behaviour, economic imperatives and sales figures in the UK and the US. This will be succeeded by an introduction to the perceptive and phenomenological implications of games consumption and the implications for the reception of individual semiotic modes and their entextualized ideological content. A brief overview of previous research into sexism and racism across various game genres will highlight a number of tenets that parallel and multiply the effect of ideologized language use in associative semiotic processes that may be described in terms of Judith Irvine and Susan Gal's (2000) 'iconicity' and 'fractal recursivity'.[3] By looking at individual examples of the genres 'first person shooter', 'role playing adventure' and 'god game', I will then go on to demonstrate how Received Pronunciation (RP) and Standard North American, on the one hand, and non-standard accents, on the other, are used in combination with other semiotic modes and registers to construct and maintain dominant language attitudes towards varieties of global English. It will become evident that games designers' deliberate functionalization of emotionally and politically charged accents confirms recent accent-attitudinal research (e.g. Lippi-Green 1997; Coupland and Bishop 2007), particularly with respect to the hegemonial phenomenon of 'Pax Americana' (Bayard *et al.* 2001). I will then go on to demonstrate how the integrative use of conventional and unconventional oppositions (Jones 2002; Davies 2007; Jeffries 2009) in computer game discourse takes advantage of the 'economy of Manichean allegory' (JanMohamed 1995: 20), thus perpetuating binary thought and stereotyping (themselves aspects of iconization and fractal recursivity) particularly with respect to morality, erudition, social class, gender and race. At the same time, however, I argue that the characteristically *subversive* context of interactive gaming – as opposed to largely *conformist* consumption of Hollywood cinema – causes a transformation of the established Western-Christian value system. After all, the generic 'semantic prosody'[4] of computer games predominantly entails *ludic teleology* – the inherent need to internalize the aims, rules and moves of individual games so as to arrive at the final level as quickly and efficiently as possible removing all obstacles on the way (mostly by applying violence) – alongside *hacker culture* – the overarching paradigm adhered to by frequent and expert gamers, which involves cheating and modding, that is, subverting the rules or even '*mod*-ifying' (manipulating) the source code.

Against this backdrop, gaming as a complex textual and interactive human activity bears potential for processes of emotional and pragmatic re-evaluation on the part of the gamer as well as for anti-stereotyping in relation to representations of non-standard varieties on the part of the game designer. Indeed, in an ideal scenario, dominant language ideologies could in fact be challenged by careful, sociolinguistically informed game design. I have to concede, however, that – regrettably – this is only realistically conceivable if commercial game designers see an economic benefit in changing their ideological framework.

11.2 Video games as media texts and industry

Over the past 10 years, and triggered partly by Espen Aarseth's ground-breaking monograph *Cybertext: Perspectives on Ergodic Literature* (1997), gameology (the theoretical and critical study of video games across various platforms and genres) has rapidly become established as an academic discipline in literary, media and cultural studies. In this context, one of the major debates amongst gameologists has revolved around the question as to what extent established narratological and critical tools and practices are applicable to what are perceived by many to be largely ludic, rule-based, interactive and hence experiential rather than perception-oriented structures. So-called 'ludologists' (e.g. Espen Aarseth, Stuart Moulthrop, Markku Eskelinen and Jesper Juul) argue against narrativists (e.g. Janet Murray, Lev Manovich, Jay David Bolter, Richard Grusin and Marie-Laure Ryan) that games should be

207

analysed not in terms of their textual, story-related features but rather their underlying rules, interfaces and more general philosophical concepts of play. More recently, video game researchers have come to accept that both aspects have to be taken into account in order to achieve analytical comprehensiveness (Johnson 2007; Ciccoricco 2007). After all, games *are* texts, and whilst their generic characteristics may not be causal or deterministic with regard to human behaviour – as psychological games research has confirmed (see Lee and Peng 2006) – 'they are definitely not neutral' (Everett 2005: 323) in their ideological make-up. After all, it is commonly assumed that the gaming industry is in its essence reliant upon commercial imperatives and hence unable 'to break out of dominant culture's discursive formations' (Everett 2005: 314).

Despite facing a media genre with huge text-critical potential, sociolinguists and discourse analysts have hitherto been reluctant to tackle this highly dynamic and textually complex, if not evasive, media genre. This is particularly surprising given the fact that the typically high degrees of immersion and *flow* experienced during gaming (Dovey and Kennedy 2006: 114–16; cf. Csíkszentmihályi 1996), combined with a sensory focus on the visual and haptic (i.e. touch-related) channels, potentially results in perceptive neglect and thus ideological normalization of individual semiotic modes, for example, phonetic and dialectal details of spoken language. This may easily lead to recurring processes of cognitive association that encourage and facilitate the construction and long-term retention of language attitudes which are, in a simultaneous process of fractal recursivity, transferred to ethnic and gender stereotypes more generally. If, on a broader sociological level, we bear in mind the facts and figures relating to gaming behaviour in the US and UK alone, we simply cannot deny the considerable ideological impact that games can have, especially on younger generations of players.

To give only a few facts recently released by the Entertainment Software Association (ESA):[5]

- sixty-seven percent of American heads of households play computer and video games;
- the average American game player is 33 years old and has been playing games for 13 years;
- in 2007, circa 24 per cent of all games were older than 50 years of age, and circa 48 per cent between 18 and 49 years old;
- the US computer and video game software sales grew by six per cent in 2006 to $7.4 billion, almost tripling industry software sales since 1996 – figures that suggest the gaming industry is now on a par with, if not overtaking, Hollywood.

208

A recent study carried out by the BBC (Pratchett 2005) has shown that 100 per cent (i.e. 3.7m) of all 6 to 10-year-olds in the UK are gamers, as well as 97 per cent of all 11 to 15-year-olds (3.7m), 82 per cent of all 16 to 24-year-olds (5.1m), 65 per cent of all 25 to 35-year-olds (5.5m), 51 per cent of all 36 to 50-year-olds (6.7m) and 18 per cent of all 51 to 65-year-olds (1.7m). Hence a total of 59 per cent of all 6 to 65-year-olds in the UK play computer games on a regular basis, which equals a total of 26.5 million – numbers which continue to rise. I consider these figures reason enough to justify a detailed investigation into the discoursal design of video games more generally, and my focus on computer games could be seen as potentially applicable to other gaming platforms (e.g. Playstation 2 and 3, Nintendo Wii, and Xbox 360).

The dominant critical discourses surrounding the effects and risks but also *potential* of games have been, on the one hand, educational issues including literacy, socio-critical awareness, senso-motoric skills and therapy (e.g. Gee 2003; Griffiths 2005) as opposed to the widely assumed yet only partially confirmed negative effects of physical violence (e.g. Goldstein 2005). Similarly, ever since the 'birth' of Lara Croft as the 'prototype' of the posthuman 'shero' (Richard and Zaremba 2005) in 1996 (Eidos Interactive Ltd.), *gendered* gaming in representation and performance (e.g. 'girl gamers' vs. 'grrl gamers', cf. Bryce and Rutter 2005: 304) has been of major concern amongst cyberfeminists and gender scholars. Meanwhile, an excellent contribution to *racism* in computer games has been delivered by Anne Everett (2005), who, drawing on Aldon Lynn Nielsen (1988: 6), observes that 'representational blackness' is constructed 'within a "white discourse as a set of self-confirming propositions"' (Everett 2005: 315). Moreover, as Nielsen points out, echoing Hans Robert Jauss, only one element of the system of imagined Blackness suffices to evoke the 'entire structure' of the hegemonial concept (1988: 6, cited in Everett 2005: 315 – see also Davies, Chapter 9, and Androutsopoulos, Chapter 10, this volume).

Finally, a recent study by David Machin and Theo van Leeuwen (2007) forms a so far rare example of how games discourse may be analysed within the framework of social semiotics. Here Machin and van Leeuwen (2007) are primarily interested in global media discourse generally and the ideological issues arising from opposing value systems in war games (i.e. technology prioritized by the US as opposed to territory preferred by Hezbollah) and from semiotic processes of collectivizing and demonizing the enemy and individualizing the hero. At the same time, however, the authors draw attention to the way in which the 'quest' format typical of games discourse generally is employed on a global scale, thereby communicating the assumption that military and physical elimination is ultimately more efficient in the solution of bilateral

209

conflict than diplomatic language use. And it is this genre-specific dictate – that verbal behaviour is considered inferior to physical warfare in resolving political and social disagreement – that functions as a useful starting point for any attempt at documenting language ideologies in computer games.

11.3 Language ideologies in games discourse

In this section, I now turn to the main concern of this chapter: the implicit representation of underlying language ideologies, or 'Metalanguage 3' (Preston 2004: 87; cf. Ensslin 2007), in computer game discourse.[6] First and foremost, we are dealing here with a text genre that relies heavily on situated representation. In-game worlds, societies, communities and avatars are constructed three-dimensionally and multimodally within virtual environments representing coherent, self-contained microcosms that are based, phenomenologically, on the teleological concepts of progress and evolution and, simultaneously, the cyclical notion of infinite reincarnation. Avatars are then used as first- or third-person physical and visual representations of the player, thus forming secondary identities (cf. Turkle 1995). This situation has been described in terms of 'corporeal double situatedness' (Dovey and Kennedy 2006; Ensslin 2009), that is, user-readers are 'embodied' as direct receivers, whose bodies interact with the hardware and software of a computer and simultaneously 're-embodied' through feedback which they experience in represented form, for example, through visible or invisible avatars. As already noted, this results in a multi-sensory, immersive experience that potentially obstructs the perception of individual semiotic modes. Furthermore, both discourse and technological settings need to be taken on board, that is, adapted to, for a successful gaming performance, thereby further increasing ideological susceptibility.

At this juncture, it will be useful to outline some significant observations made by recent research into language attitudes towards Global Englishes. As we shall see in the following sections, language ideologies as revealed in computer game discourse seem to reconfirm those findings, a trend that may either be intuitive or based on targeted research undertaken by game designers.

Early research into the attitudinal evaluation of variants of English in the 1970s revealed a significant degree of conservativism, with subjects favouring standard RP whilst denigrating ethnic and urban varieties for both prestige and attractiveness (Giles 1970). Roger Shuy and Frederick Williams (1973) found in a comparison between British RP and Standard North American (SNAm) that RP was considered by subjects to be more complex and active, yet less potent and valuable than SNAm, a trend that seems to have been perpetuated and expanded given the influence of increasingly globalized, Americanized media especially on young people (Bayard *et al.* 2001: 23). In a survey involving US undergraduates, Mark A. Stewart *et al.* (1985) established that RP was attributed a higher social status than subjects' own accents yet was regarded as less intelligible and as arousing more discomfort.

Of particular relevance to the present chapter is Rosina Lippi-Green's (1997) comprehensive survey of accents used in Hollywood and Disney characters, in which she finds that, while standard North American and RP accents are particularly prevalent in lead roles, non-standard, foreign accents are used mostly as negative stereotyping short-cuts for indexing marginal and roguish characters. Following on from Shuy and Williams (1973), research carried out by Donn Bayard in the 1990s has found that RP is rated highly for status and power variables yet is closely followed or even being gradually replaced and supplemented by SNAm. Of further importance is the phenomenon of 'dialect/accent loyalty' (Cargile *et al.* 1994; Giles and Powesland 1975), which refers to subjects' positive attitudes towards their own local and regional accents, mostly for emotive features such as warmth, friendliness and sense of humour. This is confirmed by Bayard *et al.* (2001), who claim that the so-called 'Pax Americana' – the hegemony in the sense of normalized acceptance rather than imperialism of SNAm – is, at least amongst their subjects (students from New Zealand, Australia and the US), gradually replacing accent loyalty, with far-reaching global implications. Finally, and perhaps of most interest for further research into language ideologies in video games, is Nikolas Coupland and Hywel Bishop's (2007) observation that, among British subjects, positive ratings of RP rise proportionally to age, and that both younger and female respondents tend to be more positively inclined towards diversity. Generally low in prestige are (and always have been), according to Coupland and Bishop (2007), urban vernaculars, especially from Birmingham, Glasgow and Liverpool.

11.3.1 Emotive and political uses of standard and variety: power, mystification, naturalization

Turning from sociolinguistic research to computer game discourse, the following trends are noticeable. Firstly, quasi-standard varieties – mostly SNAm, but sporadically also RP – are used for both voice-over narrative and instructions given to the player. While it could be argued that this makes for maximum levels of clarity and efficiency in information transfer, it also raises the question of authenticity and naturalness. From a stylistic point of view, this phonological prevalence causes any deviation to be understood as foregrounding and hence to deserve specific analytical attention.

Looking at so-called 'first person shooters', it becomes clear that, even in British products, SNAm is used functionally to signal – in a process that may well be described in terms of Irvine and Gal's (2000: 37) 'iconization' – military and physical prowess, as well as living up to its image of being the most socially attractive variety of English. Even more interesting perhaps is the phenomenon of mixing standards in processes of 'fractal recursivity' (Irvine and Gal 2000: 38), which appears, for instance, in the introductory cut-scene of *Return to Castle Wolfenstein* (Id Software/Activision 2001). Here *political* and *military* power on the side of the 'goodies' is represented by characters who speak either RP or Queen's English: the central, decision-making character's major characteristics in the scene are positively connoted, in terms of rationality, decision-making ability and sharpness of political reasoning, and he speaks an unmarked RP variety to further signal his moral integrity. Other more marginal, but nonetheless politically powerful characters with less decision-making power, on the other hand, are characterized, in their shallowness of argument and assumed lack of reasoning power, by a potentially unattractive clipped accent, which is further enhanced through paralinguistic features, for example, pitch of voice and body language, thus evoking an image of snobbery and superficiality.[7] The central opposition in this scene, however, is formed by the juxtaposition between RP and SNAm. As opposed to political power attributed to Britishness, cognitive, intellectual, heuristic and hence strategic power is represented by a young researcher speaking with a SNAm accent, whose general attire, relative youth and self-effacing yet confident body language further attract the viewer's sympathy.

The only game I have encountered thus far which clearly functionalizes non-standard varieties of British English as a means of characterization is Guildford-based Lionhead Studio's *Fable: The Lost Chapters* (2004). This deserves close attention not merely because it foregrounds non-standard accents but because it does so in both expected and unexpected ways. In an example from the first level, a Dickensian North-East London (urban, hence socially unattractive) accent, reminiscent of Ron Moody playing rogue Fagin in the film musical *Oliver!*, is used to characterize an uncanny 'trader' set against the idyllic, pastoral village of Oakvale, where the game is set (see Figure 11.1).

The trader is thus rendered morally dubious and potentially dangerous as he offers his goods to the still inexperienced young hero. At the same time, he is juxtaposed phonetically to the hero's father and sister, the two 'commissioners' and undoubtedly most trustworthy roles in

Figure 11.1 Trader and young hero in *Fable: The Lost Chapters* (Lionhead Studios 2005) (see colour plate section)

level one. The trader's ultimate teleological function, on the other hand, is that of the present game level's overriding objective: to sell the hero a present for his young sister, which will earn him the praise of his family and the moral maturity to move on in life. In order to purchase the present, however, the hero first needs to earn the money for it by performing 'good' rather than 'bad' deeds in the traditional Manichean sense. Therefore, whereas the trader's accent is in the first instance used to demonize him and his 'trade' in general – in the Christian sense of 'temptation' – the 'semantic prosody' of the quest genre as such (cf. Jeffries 2009) demystifies and naturalizes his thus portrayed immorality.

The recursive effect on underlying language attitudes seems to confirm Coupland and Bishop's (2007) finding that young people – no doubt the target group of *Fable* – tend to be more open to linguistic diversity than older generations. Against this backdrop, the black female character Whisper, the hero's physically and intellectually equal peer trainee and increasingly potent rival, strikes the linguistically conscious player as a curiously non-stereotypical in-game female. Her African (possibly Namibian) accent together with her ethnically marked, uneroticized body language contradict that of the default sexualized, fetishized or demonized Lara Croftian heroine (Richard and Zaremba 2005). Furthermore, Whisper's ethnically and phonologically identical elder brother Thunder – an imposing character of massive built and splendid attire – is presented to the apprentice as the heroic 'ideal' to strive for, which adds a further positive layer to the textual construct of the non-white, non-RP heroic metric. It has to be said, however, that Thunder never ceases to look down on the hero and later on develops into his main sexual rival in their struggle over the favour of 'Lady Grey'.

213

Despite the tendency to foreground non-standard accents in ways that are either positively or negatively connoted (a 'cuddly' Northumbrian accent is used occasionally to signal the need for sympathy and help in illness in various minor characters), the game's main communicative framework remains firmly anchored in what Nielsen (1988: 3) refers to as 'white [standard RP] discourse as a set of self-confirming propositions' (see above). The all-important Guildmaster, a Dumbledorian, Gandalfian character of infinite wisdom, martial experience, untainted moral integrity and a white Western phenotype, speaks with a standard RP stage accent reminiscent of Shakespearean actor, John Gielgud. Furthermore, the hero himself – also a white male – speaks with an RP accent, thus adding to the standard 'awe-inspiring', 'prestigious' (cf. Coupland and Bishop 2007) RP matrix underlying the macrostructure of the game. The deliberate choice of British English over Standard North American matches the decisively British (albeit fantastical) setting of the game (quasi-medieval 'Albion'), and it may be argued that the contextually coherent, stylized use of less popular British urban vernaculars actually contributed to the fact that overseas sales, especially in the US, rocketed to a record 375,000 sold units in the first week after release (Xbox365.com[8]).

11.3.2 Interaction and choice: simple and complex oppositions

Generally speaking, game designers tend to use conventional and unconventional semantic oppositions (see e.g. Jones 2002; Davies 2007; Jeffries 2009) to construct either simple Manichean binaries of morally good or bad behaviour, or indeed more numerous and therefore complex semantic and pragmatic oppositions resulting from the player's choice between, for instance, a number of illocutionary acts. Importantly, whereas games allow the player to act creatively within the limits of the game world, for example, by hack-cheating their way into otherwise inaccessible locations, natural (rather than programming) language cannot normally be used in a productive-creative way. Players are entirely subjected to the use of language coded into the gaming interface, which results in the inadvertent processing of either simple or – albeit more rarely – complex pragmatic *choices*.

With reference to the title of my chapter, perhaps the most striking example of simple oppositional gaming discourse is Lionhead Studio's *Black and White 2* (2005), a god game in which the player assumes the role of an either good (generous, lenient and protective) or bad (militant, aggressive, tyrannical) divinity. Most interesting from an language-attitudinal point of view is the embedding of the *un*conventional accent opposition in a *conventional* visual, mythopoetic, religious opposition:

Figure 11.2 Introductory cut-scene, *Black and White 2* (Lionhead Studios 2005) (see colour plate section)

in the introductory cut-scene of the game, a white, elderly, angelic character speaking with an over-articulated RP accent mixed in with a formal register is set against a dark-skinned, thick-lipped, demonic character speaking a with a SNAm accent mixed with a non-formal register (see Figure 11.2). What happens here semiotically is precisely what Nielsen (1988: 6) points out: 'only a suggestion of blackness need appear for the entire structure to be articulated'.[9]

It is not surprising that, when I asked my undergraduate media (not linguistics) students, after watching the sequence for the first time, what accents they had heard, at first none of them appeared to remember anything. This observation seems to reconfirm the phenomenon I mentioned earlier: the neglect of individual semiotic modes against the backdrop of full game-world immersion – even in a non-interactive cut-scene. Upon further reasoning, one student in the group said that he thought the dark character had been speaking with a 'Black New York accent'. This seems to confirm, in Nielsen's (1988: 6) words, that merely one aspect of blackness activated the whole cognitive structure in the student's mind, and, in Irvine and Gal's (2000) terminology, that *reverse* fractal recursivity (from the visual to the linguistic level rather than vice versa) with regard to accent attribution took place in the student's reception process, triggered by visual and auditive stimulants.

During the same introductory level of *Black and White 2*, the use of conventional and unconventional oppositions is taken further onto a lexical level. After a general introduction to the aims of the game, provided by the two afore-mentioned characters, players are requested to choose an animal as their avatar 'creature' (as expressed by the 'white' character) or 'beast' (as the 'dark' character puts it), which, depending on the player's actions, will become either a 'loveable, mischievous pet' (white) or 'the ultimate disciplined weapons of destruction and war' (dark).

215

This seemingly clear-cut traditional Manichean allegory, however, undergoes a semantic shift if seen in the context of computer games' generic semantic prosody. As we have seen in the analysis of *Fable* above, semiotically encoded moral degeneracy does not necessarily communicate a social taboo in computer games – on the contrary, seen against the backdrop of ludic teleology, which prioritizes confronting challenges and overcoming impediments, a complete shift in the conventional Western-Christian value system takes place. Thus the defeat of evil by violent means becomes desirable, and in order to achieve this end, players need to adopt a positive, affirmative attitude towards belligerent, aggressive, destructive in-game behaviour, which results in an 'eye-for-an-eye' moral trajectory. This again confirms Machin and van Leeuwen's (2007) observation, that physical and military problem-solving is by default favoured over the diplomatic use of language, a logic which is clearly easier to program into a game engine than complex conversational discourse.

By the same token, a closer multimodal look at the 'dark' character reveals the following de-mystifying processes: his informal register is aligned with the ideal (implied) gamer's colloquial register. Furthermore, the youthful, relaxed, dynamic gestures and prosodic features used by the dark character are designed to appeal to young players in particular. This effect is further reinforced by the visible age difference (marked, for instance by white vs. black hair colour), which places the 'dark' character closer to the ideal player than his 'white' counterpart. His SNAm accent follows, inadvertently or not, the 'Pax Americana' highlighted by Bayard *et al.* (2001). What is more, the 'dark' character's functional role as incorporating and indeed promoting the inner voice of the Freudian 'id' figures prominently in a game whose title symbolically juxtaposes good and bad yet simultaneously puts them on the same level of dialectic importance and prestige. The fast-paced, innocuously trickling musical soundtrack accompanying the sequence further reinforces the overall image of harmony, thus legitimizing emotively both moral extremes for the sake of successful game-play.

11.4 Conclusions and directions for future research

In this chapter I have sought to fill what I see as a gaping *lacuna* in contemporary sociolinguistics by demonstrating the significance of the critical analysis of computer game discourse for research into language ideologies in the (new) media, particularly with respect to the construction of conventional and unconventional oppositions and of accent attitudinal evaluations. The fact that, despite the present economic downturn, the global games industry continues to boom indicates a paradigm shift in the reception of, and need for, new forms of visual and interactive narrative and entertainment. As the younger generations, in particular, are drawn to gaming as a major leisure-time activity, the lasting (language-) ideological impact exerted by commercial[10] video games cannot be underestimated.

Although future research will need to provide quantitative back-up or indeed statistically qualify the findings presented in this chapter, a few preliminary conclusions can be drawn that may serve as hypotheses for further investigation. Firstly, the default use of SNAm in computer games reconfirms the 'attitude hegemony' described by Bayard *et al.* (2001) as 'Pax Americana'. This strategic, profit-driven choice on the part of game designers appears to support the increasing degree of social attractiveness attributed to SNAm by native speakers of English at a global level. Non-standard varieties, on the other hand, are used rarely, and if they are, they tend to be functionalized for character portrayal throughout.

As my analysis of *Fable* has shown, non-standard accents of English are embedded in an overarching 'white' linguistic matrix to functionalize, emotionalize and demonize individual characters and their moral outfits, thus again reconfirming recent research into stereotypical language attitudes (e.g. Coupland and Bishop 2007). On the other hand, this shows a considerable degree of sociolinguistic potential inhibiting computer games as one of today's dominant narrative genres, which could – and should – be used to at least question prevailing language attitudes amongst gamers. This is not least because games are socially embedded in an essentially subversive culture, which encourages cheating and hacking on the one hand whilst, so far, mostly perpetuating dominant racist, sexist and language ideologies by means of their interface discourse.

The fact that computer game discourse tends towards the construction of unconventional opposites and generally seems to take advantage of the ideological benefits arising from their embedding in conventional Manichean oppositions – as the archetypal example of *Black and White 2* has revealed – is one of the most alarming observations of this study, which further confirms Lippi-Green's (1997) findings with regard to Disney characters. The 'economy of the Manichean Allegory' (JanMohamed 1995: 20) is used heavily by game designers, not least because the simplicity of pigeon-holing facilitates players' concentration on motoric interaction with the specific game engine. This results in heightened degrees of susceptibility to underlying ideological content, which tends to go unnoticed yet continues to be 're-implanted' multimodally in players' subconscious minds. On the other hand, it could be argued that the semiotic potential inhabiting the construction of unconventional oppositions could instead be harnessed by video game developers to create more multi-faceted, less stereotypical gaming environments with regard to character portrayal and language use.

As previously mentioned, for a comprehensive survey of language attitudes in games discourse more generally, an in-depth quantitative investigation is needed. Firstly, the research outlined in this chapter focuses solely on English, and it would be most insightful to learn about the language-ideological processes at play where video/computer games are composed in other languages or indeed translated from English. A second idea worth pursuing would be a multimodal corpus of game clips (cf. Gu 2007) involving various levels of representation, that is, streaming video, audio, as well as multimodal and phonetic transcription. Of interest to such a project would be written, spoken and paralinguistic features emerging from dialogues between characters and human-machine verbal interaction. Particularly revealing would be cross-genre comparisons establishing dominant practices particularly in sociologically significant genres such as god, society, and role-playing games.

Notes

1 I shall use the term 'video games' to refer to commercially driven electronic games across various platforms and consoles, whereas 'computer games' will be used to denote PC-based games only.
2 See ELSPA press release of 06 July 2007 at http://www.elspa.com/?i= 6392&s=1111&f=49&archive= (accessed 24/01/2008).
3 Irvine and Gal's (2000) third semiotic process of ideological representation, 'erasure', is deliberately excluded from this study as it would distract from my main focus, the construction and reinforcement of conventional and unconventional oppositions. This is not to say, however, that erasure does not take place. Indeed, those accents that are represented by default (SNAm and, less frequently, RP) clearly reveal an unrealistic image of language variety, as artificial homogeneity rather than real-life variation is projected in English video-game discourse. (For further discussion of iconization, fractal recursivity and erasure, see also Androutsopoulos, Chapter 10, this volume).
4 The term 'semantic prosody' goes back to John Sinclair (1991, cf. Louw 1993, Cotterill 2001, and Carter 2004) and is derived from John Rupert Firth's (1955 [1968]) notion of phonological colouring. The underlying assumption is that habitual collocates of a given word form or lemma 'colour' its connotational meaning(s). Michael Stubbs (2001) has expanded the concept to include the level of discourse in the sense of supra-lexematic semantic relations. In this chapter I refer to 'semantic prosody' at a text- or medium-generic level, which is inextricably interlinked with patterns of user behaviour and expectations.
5 See http://www.theesa.com/archives/files/ESA-EF%202007.pdf (accessed 24/07/2008).

218

6 In his important essay on folk metalanguage, Dennis Preston (2004) distinguishes between three types of metalanguage: 'Metalanguage 1', which is
conscious, 'overt comment about language' (2004: 75); 'Metalanguage 2',
which refers to the mere '*mention* of talk itself' (ibid: 85; emphasis in
original), much like Roman Jakobson's phatic function of language; and
'Metalanguage 3', which Preston understands to be the conceptual and ideological background to Metalanguage 1 in that it designates 'beliefs which
members of speech communities share' (ibid.: 87). Preston himself does not
theorize the ideological implications of Metalanguage 3 as comprehensively
as this has been done by scholars working in the field of language ideology
studies, who have incorporated theoretical insights from ideology studies
more generally with a view to bridging the gap between linguistic and social
theory (e.g. Woolard 1992; cf. Johnson and Ensslin 2007: 7). (For further
discussion of this debate, see Moschonas and Spitzmüller, Chapter 2,
Davies, Chapter 9, and Androutsopoulos, Chapter 10, this volume).
7 For more details on social meanings attributed to salient phonological
features, such as 'posh' or 'super-standard' English (cf. Niedzielski and
Preston 2003), as exemplified here, see Coupland (2007: 93–9).
8 See Xbox360.com at www.xbox365.com/news.cgi?id=EpAypuEyZZhAYiJH
ha1677 (accessed 23/01/2008).
9 One may argue that 'blackness' is indeed very clearly marked in this particular example. Upon close inspection, however, the 'dark' figure is not
strictly speaking 'black', but 'red', and what appears like dark skin is in fact
more likely to be a thin fur coat. In fact, the reading of 'blackness' is evoked
by a distinct combination of individual anthropomorphic features in a
gestalt sense. Furthermore, the SNAm accent used does not specify the
character as belonging to a specific ethnic or social group; it is the opposition to the 'white', RP-speaking character, rather, which triggers the concept
of blackness on a phonological level.
10 For economic reasons, so called 'serious' (i.e. non-entertainment, often non-
profit critical and educational) games are still forced to live a niche existence.
That said, an important move towards public funding of culturally and ped-
agogically valuable video games has recently been made by the German
Government, which announced a national computer game award in spring
2008 (*Computerspielemagazin GEE*, Feb./March 2008). In Britain, the first
separately held BAFTA *Games* Awards took place in 2004, a development
which renders video games a fully-established art form alongside feature
films and other audio-visual media in the UK. Nevertheless, the BAFTAs
mostly cover the commercial sector. The ideological contentiousness inherent in mainstream video games therefore remains largely unchallenged.

Primary sources

Id Software, Inc. (2001), *Return to Castle Wolfenstein*. [DVD-ROM].
Lionhead Studios Limited (2005), *Black and White 2*. [PC DVD-ROM].
Lionhead Studios Limited (2005), *Fable: The Lost Chapters*. [PC DVD-ROM].

References

Aarseth, E. J. (1997), *Cybertext: Perspectives on Ergodic Literature*. Baltimore: The Johns Hopkins University Press.

Bayard, D., Weatherall, A., Gallois, C. and J. Pittam (2001), 'Pax Americana? Accent attitudinal evaluations in New Zealand, Australia and America'. *Journal of Sociolinguistics*, 5(1), 22–49.

Boardman, M. (2005), *The Language of Websites*. London: Routledge.

Bryce, J. and Rutter, J. (2005), 'Gendered gaming in gendered space', in J. Raessens and J. Goldstein (eds), *Handbook of Computer Game Studies*. Cambridge, MA: MIT Press, pp. 301–10.

Cargile, A. C., Giles, H., Ryan, E. B. and J. J. Bradac (1994), 'Language attitudes as a social process: a conceptual model and new directions'. *Language and Communication*, 14(3), 211–26.

Carter, R. (2004), *Trust the Text: Language, Corpus and Discourse*. London: Routledge.

Ciccoricco, D. (2007), 'The literary turn in contemporary video games'. *dichtung-digital*, 37. [online]. www.dichtung-digital.com (24/01/2008).

Cotterill, J. (2001), 'Domestic discord, rocky relationships: semantic prosodies in representations of marital violence in the O. J. Simpson trial'. *Discourse & Society*, 12(3), 291–312.

Coupland, N. (2007), *Style: Language Variation and Identity*. Cambridge: Cambridge University Press.

Coupland, N. and Bishop, H. (2007), 'Ideologized values for British accents'. *Journal of Sociolinguistics*, 11(1), 74–93.

Csíkszentmihályi, M. (1996), *Creativity: Flow and Psychology of Discovery and Invention*. New York: Harper Perennial.

Davies, M. (2007), 'The attraction of opposites: the ideological function of conventional and created oppositions in the construction of in-groups and out-groups in news texts', in L. Jeffries, D. McIntyre and D. Bousfield (eds), *Stylistics and Social Cognition*. Amsterdam: Rodopi, pp. 71–100.

Dovey, J. and Kennedy, H. (2006), *Game Cultures: Computer Games as New Media*. Maidenhead: Open University Press.

Ensslin, A. (2007), 'Of chords, machines and bumble-bees: the metalinguistics of hyperpoetry', in S. Johnson and A. Ensslin (eds), *Language in the Media: Representations, Identities, Ideologies*. London: Continuum, pp. 250–68.

Ensslin, A. (2009), 'From (w)reader to breather: cybertextual de-intentionalization in Kate Pullinger *et al.*'s *Breathing Wall*', in R. Page and B. Thomas (eds), *New Narratives: Theory and Practice*. Lincoln, NE: University of Nebraska Press.

'Ensslin, A. (forthcoming), *The Language of Gaming: Discourse and Ideology*. Houndmills: Palgrave Macmillan.

Everett, A. (2005), 'Serious play: playing with race in contemporary gaming culture', in J. Raessens and J. Goldstein (eds), *Handbook of Computer Game Studies*. Cambridge, MA: MIT Press, pp. 311–25.

Firth, J. R. (1955) [1968], 'Structural linguistics', in F. R. Palmer (ed.), *Selected Papers of J. R. Firth 1952–1959*. London: Longman.

Gee, J. P. (2003), *What Video Games Have to Teach Us about Learning and Literacy*. New York: Palgrave.

Giles, H. (1970), 'Evaluative reactions to accents'. *Educational Review*, 22(3), 211–27.

Giles, H. and Powesland, P. F. (1975), *Speech Style and Social Evaluation*. London: Academic.

Goldstein, J. (2005), 'Violent video games', in J. Raessens and J. Goldstein (eds), *Handbook of Computer Game Studies*. Cambridge, MA: MIT Press, pp. 341–58.

Griffiths, Mark (2005), 'The therapeutic value of video games', in J. Raessens and J. Goldstein (eds), *Handbook of Computer Game Studies*. Cambridge, MA: MIT Press, pp. 161–71.

Gu, Y. (2007), *The Spoken Chinese Corpora of Situated Discourse*. [online]. http://www.multimodal.cn (01/09/2007).

Irvine, J. T. and Gal, S. (2000), 'Language ideology and linguistic differentiation', in P. V. Kroskrity (ed.), *Regimes of Language: Ideologies, Polities and Identities*. Oxford: James Currey, pp. 35–83.

JanMohamed, A. R. (1995), 'The economy of the Manichean allegory', in B. Ashcroft, G. Griffiths and H. Tiffin (eds), *The Post-colonial Studies Reader*. New York: Routledge, pp. 18–23.

Jeffries, L. (2009), *Opposition in Discourse*. London: Continuum.

Johnson, M. S. S. (2007), 'Storytelling to storygaming: playing with narrative in computer games'. *dichtung-digital*, 37. [online]. www.dichtung-digital.com (24/01/2008).

Johnson, S. and Ensslin, A. (2007), 'Language in the media: theory and practice', in S. Johnson and A. Ensslin (eds), *Language in the Media: Representations, Identities, Ideologies*. London: Continuum, pp. 3–22.

Jones, S. (2002), *Antonymy: A Corpus-based Perspective*. London: Routledge.

Juul, J. (2005), *Half-real: Video Games between Real Rules and Fictional Worlds*. Cambridge, MA: MIT Press.

Lee, K. M. and Peng, W. (2006), 'What do we know about social and psychological effects of computer games? A comprehensive review of the current literature', in P. Vorderer and J. Bryant (eds), *Playing Video Games: Motives, Responses, and Consequences*. Mahwah: Lawrence Erlbaum, pp. 325–45.

Lippi-Green, R. (1997), *English with an Accent: Language, Ideology and Discrimination in the United States*. London: Routledge.

Louw, B. (1993), 'Irony in the text or insincerity in the writer? The diagnostic potential of semantic prosodies', in M. Baker, G. Francis and E. Tognini-Bonelli (eds), *Text and Technology*. Amsterdam: John Benjamins, pp. 157–76.

Lucy, J. (1993), 'Reflexive language and the human disciplines', in J. A. Lucy (ed.), *Reflexive Language: Reported Speech and Metapragmatics*. Cambridge: Cambridge University Press, pp. 9–32.

Machin, D. and van Leeuwen, T. (2007), *Global Media Discourse: A Critical Introduction*. London: Routledge.

Niedzielski, N. and Preston, D. (eds) (2003), *Folk Linguistics*, Berlin: Mouton de Gruyter.

221

Nielsen, A. L. (1988), *Reading Race: White American Poets and the Racial Discourse in the Twentieth Century*. Athens: University of Georgia Press.

Pratchett, R. (2005), 'Gamers in the UK: digital play, digital lifestyles' [online]. http://open.bbc.co.uk/newmediaresearch/files/BBC_UK_Games_Research_2005.pdf (22/08/07).

Preston, D. (2004), 'Folk metalanguage', in A. Jaworski, N. Coupland and D. Galasiński (eds), *Metalanguage: Social and Ideological Perspectives*. Berlin: Mouton de Gruyter, pp. 75–101.

Richard, B. and Zaremba, J. (2005), 'Gaming with grrls: looking for sheroes in computer games', in J. Raessens and J. Goldstein (eds), *Handbook of Computer Game Studies*. Cambridge, MA: MIT Press, pp. 283–300.

Richardson, K. (2006), 'The dark arts of good people: how popular culture negotiates "spin" in NBC's *The West Wing*'. *Journal of Sociolinguistics*, 10(1), 52–69.

Shortis, T. (2001), *The Language of ICT: Information and Communication Technology*. London: Routledge.

Shuy, R. and Williams, F. (1973), 'Stereotyped attitudes of selected English dialect communities', in R. W. Shuy and R. W. Fasold (eds), *Language Attitudes: Current Trends and Prospects*. Washington, DC: Georgetown University Press, pp. 85–96.

Silverstein, M. (1993), 'Metapragmatic discourse and metapragmatic function', in J. A. Lucy (ed.), *Reflexive Language: Reported Speech and Metapragmatics*. Cambridge: Cambridge University Press, pp. 33–58.

Sinclair, J. (1991), *Corpus, Concordance, Collocation*. Oxford: Oxford University Press.

Stewart, M. A., Ryan, E. B. and Giles H. (1985), 'Accent and social class effects on status and solidarity evaluations'. *Personality and Social Psychology Bulletin*, 11, 98–105.

Stubbs, M. (2001), *Words and Phrases: Corpus Studies of Lexical Semantics*. London: Blackwell.

Turkle, S. (1995), *Life on Screen: Identity in the Age of the Internet*. New York: Touchstone.

Woolard, K. A. (1992), 'Language ideology: issues and approaches'. *Pragmatics*, 2(3), 235–50.

Woolard, K. A. (1998), 'Introduction: language ideology as a field of inquiry', in B. B. Schieffelin, K. A. Woolard and P. V. Kroskrity (eds), *Language Ideologies: Practice and Theory*. New York: Oxford University Press, pp. 3–47.

12 Language ideological debates on the BBC 'Voices' website: hypermodality in theory and practice

Sally Johnson, Tommaso M. Milani
and Clive Upton

12.1 Introduction

In 2004, Mandy Rose, a broadcast journalist in the New Media Department at BBC Wales in Cardiff, put forward a proposal for a project on language in the UK that aimed to build on previous programming successes such as Robert McCrum's *The Story of English* (McCrum *et al.* 1986) and Melvyn Bragg's *The Routes of English* (Elmes 2000, 2001; Elmes & Bragg 2001):[1]

> 'The UK Speaks' (working title) is a major project led by BBC Nations and Regions which will celebrate and explore the diverse languages, dialects and accents of the UK. [. . .] Working with a range of expert partners the BBC will undertake a unique survey of language in the UK at the start of the 21st century. [. . .] The project will be both entertaining and have a strong social purpose; celebrating the diversity of the UK by affirming the value of regional and ethnic differences as expressed through language. The survey will provide the starting point for an ongoing study of language in the UK. (Rose and Mowbray, no date)

The upshot of this proposal – subsequently re-named the 'Voices' project – can undoubtedly be described as a major success for the BBC. Working in close consultation with one of the authors of this chapter, Clive Upton in the School of English at the University of Leeds, the project began with a survey of English around the UK led by a team of BBC broadcast journalists. This research drew on, and has now become integral to, the *Survey of Regional English* (SuRE) devised by Upton and others in the 1990s, itself building upon the pioneering work of Upton's predecessor at Leeds, Harold Orton, some 50 years earlier (cf. Kerswill *et al.* 1999; Upton *et al.* 1994; Upton and Llamas 1999; Upton and Widdowson 2006). The results of this new survey then provided the basis for a range of media outputs in 2005. These included a dedicated series on BBC Radio 4 entitled *Word4Word*, further programmes across local radio stations (e.g. BBC Nations and Regions/ Asian Network) as well as TV contributions such as BBC 2's *The Way That We Say It*. Finally, the project was documented in book form – Simon Elmes' *Talking for Britain: A Journey through the Nation's Dialects* (2006) – and also led to the production of an interactive website (www.bbc.co.uk/voices) which provides access to more than 300 professional recordings of different varieties of English as well as constituting the medium through which some 50,000 electronic postings on a range of language-related themes have been gathered. By the end of 2005, the Voices website had received over one million hits, by far exceeding original expectations.[2]

Our point of departure in this chapter is that the BBC Voices project constitutes a prime example of what Blommaert (1999a, 1999b) has referred to as a 'language ideological debate'.[3] Or, more specifically, we see the project, and in particular its related website, as consisting of one 'macro' debate on language issues in the UK. This, in turn, is made up of a series of 'micro' debates encompassing a range of linguistic topics from the distribution of dialect features to the value of bilingual education through to the purported differences between men and women's use of language. Here we share Blommaert's (1999b: 1) view that such debates are not ideologically neutral, but constitute the very moments in which views and beliefs *about* languages and their speakers (i.e. language ideologies) are crystallized, enforced and/or challenged (see also Jaffe 2006). However, our focus on an interactive website such as this raises a raft of new theoretical and methodological challenges. This is insofar as we are dealing with forms of 'language representation' (Coupland and Jaworski 2004: 27–33) that find their expression not only through written and/or spoken language but through the co-deployment of the *linguistic* with other semiotic modes such as the *visual* and *phonic*. This, in turn, will require an extension of the analytical repertoires traditionally associated with the study of language ideological debates, for example, ethnographic techniques (see the various contributions to Blommaert 1999a) and/or more textually-oriented approaches that draw on insights from (Critical) Discourse Analysis (e.g. Blackledge 2005; Milani 2008; see also discussion in Milani and Johnson 2008a).[4]

In this chapter, we will be focussing on one specific dimension of the BBC Voices website, namely its home page[5] (see Figure 12.2 below) and will be working towards the development of a *hypermodal* approach that can capture the ways in which linguistic, visual and phonic function together in the representation of language(s) on websites. We will begin by outlining a methodology for the analysis of websites in general and will then move on to a closer analysis of the BBC Voices home page. It goes without saying that this analysis will not be able to do justice to all the details of the structure, layout and contents of the page in question. Rather, our focus on a few specific aspects of the home page will be geared towards an understanding of the *purpose* and the potential ideological *effects* of particular semiotic choices. The chapter will then end with a reflection on processes of mediatization where hypermodal representations of language are concerned (see Johnson and Ensslin 2007: 12–13), together with the wider implications of our analysis for the study of language ideologies and media discourse.

12.2 Website analysis: theory and method

> In this age of the multimedia, there is an increasing awareness that meaning is rarely made with language alone. [. . .] we live in a multimodal society which makes meaning through the co-deployment of a combination of semiotic resources. Visual images, gestures and sounds often accompany the linguistic semiotic resource in semiosis. As such, there is a pressing need to understand the dynamics of meaning-making, or semiosis, in multimodal discourse. Academic disciplines that focus on mono-modality, such as that of linguistics, must come into dialogue with other fields of research, for instance, visual communication studies and media studies, to facilitate the interdisciplinary nature of multimodal research. (Lim 2004: 220)

Over the past few years, the kind of interdisciplinary research advocated here by Lim has gathered considerable momentum. As a result of increasing collaboration between linguists and (critical) discourse analysts, on the one hand, and media/visual communications specialists, on the other, there is now a burgeoning literature that is developing the theories and methods required for the analysis of multimodal discourse (e.g. Baldry 2000; Iedema 2003; Kress 2003; Kress and van Leeuwen 2001, 2006; Levine and Scollon 2004; Machin 2007; Machin and van Leeuwen 2007; Norris 2004; O'Halloran 2004; van Leeuwen 1999, 2004). As Lim (2004: 221) points out, one of the key aims of this research is to explore the ways in which the differing semiotic modes of the *linguistic* (spoken and written language), the *visual* (image, gesture, typography and graphics) and the *phonic* (sound and music) contribute to processes of meaning-making both in their own right, that is to say, *intra*-semiotically, as well as when arranged and co-deployed, that is,

225

inter-semiotically (see Kress and van Leeuwen 2001). Moreover, within this literature, there is now a growing body of work that focuses on the analysis of websites. One of the theoretical/methodological issues at stake here is to fully account for one semiotic peculiarity of websites, namely the interplay between multimodality and the medium of *hypertext* (see Aarseth 1997; Boardman 2005; Ensslin 2007a, 2007b; Knox 2007; Kok 2004; Lemke 1999, 2002; Nielsen and Tahir 2002). This has led Lemke (2002: 301) to propose going beyond the notion of multimodality itself, and to fully engage with what he refers to as *hypermodality*, that is, 'the conflation of multimodality and hypertext'. In what follows, we will begin by providing an overview of the key terms and issues that underpin our attempt to develop a suitable methodology for our analysis of the BBC Voices home page.

12.2.1 Hypertext, ergodicity and rank orders

Following Boardman (2005: 9–10), we define hypertext as a specific type of dynamic and non-linear electronic text that contains one or more *hyperlinks* (see also Ensslin 2007a; Kok 2004). These hyperlinks allow the reader/viewer to branch out to other pages that are either *internal* or *external* to the domain in question (Kok 2004: 131). Because of the manifold trajectories that web users may pursue through hypertext, we agree with Kok (2004), who proposes that traditional theories of reading/viewing are inadequate when attempting to capture the ways in which users navigate their way around websites. By contrast, Kok underscores Aarseth's (1997) notion of *ergodicity*[6] as particularly pertinent here. This is insofar as ergodicity attempts to capture the interplay between the potential pathways laid down by a website creator, on the one hand, and the actual routes followed by the 'choice making' individual user – or *ergodist* – who interfaces with that site, on the other. Finally, Kok (ibid.: 133–37) outlines four 'ranks or levels' relevant to the analysis of hypertext as follows.

An ITEM is a visually-bounded semiotic aggregate in which several signs (e.g. linguistic, visual and phonic) are co-deployed by way of hypertext technology. This could include the kinds of ITEMS illustrated in Figure 12.1 or a sound clip such as the chime that is heard upon the arrival of a new email in one's inbox.

LEXIA meanwhile – a term derived from Barthes (1977) – refers to the 'scrollable webpage' (Kok 2004: 135). LEXIAS typically consist therefore of groups of ITEMS or textual chunks that are arranged in order to form a 'complete' web page (see also Ensslin 2007a: 14). However, on smaller computer screens (such as the 17" display units characteristic of modern laptops) and depending upon one's browser settings, it may not

Figure 12.1 Examples of ITEMS (see colour plate section)

always be possible to view a LEXIA in its entirety. As a result, the issue of 'scrollability' and 'guaranteed viewing area' (Kok 2004: 146) become analytically relevant insofar as one will need to consider which ITEMS of a given LEXIA are visible/accessible at any one time as the ergodist scrolls up or down the screen.

Finally, the concept of CLUSTER refers to the networks of LEXIAS that are 'internal' to a web domain as laid out by its designer. In practice, however, it can become ontologically problematic trying to distinguish between such internal clusters from a broader WEB, which includes networks of LEXIAS that are both internal and *external* to the domain in question. Either way, it is the sum of these internal and external networks that ultimately comprise what is popularly referred to as the 'World Wide Web'.

12.2.2 Representation of social actors, modality markers and the 'Space of Integration'

Much of the literature on multimodality and/or hypermodality has its foundations in Kress and van Leeuwen's seminal work *Reading Images: The Grammar of Visual Design* (2006 [1996]), itself grounded in a Hallidayan functional systemic approach to textual structure. Although the authors do not focus extensively on the analysis of websites here, two particular aspects of their analyses of visual grammar remain key points of departure.

The first is what Kress and van Leeuwen refer to as the 'representation of social actors' (2006: 114–53), that is, the portrayal of real people or fictional characters, photographically or otherwise. The ways in which such actors are visually represented is then closely tied to the relations of social power as indexed by the positioning of the reader/viewer. Such relations may be activated by a range of semiotic means

227

such as size of frame, camera angle (vertical and horizontal), and apparent social distance. Of particular importance is the concept of *gaze*, that is, the imaginary eye contact between represented participant and viewer. Here there are two main possibilities: the *demand*, that is, the kind of direct eye contact that positions the viewer as active participant in the discourse versus an *offer*, whereby the viewer becomes more of an invisible onlooker and, by implication, discursive 'outsider' (ibid.: 118–19; see also Johnson 2007: 97–9).

The second area of interest comprises so-called 'modality markers', that is, the semiotic means by which mood and notions of 'truth value' (as in language) are afforded by compositional choices (Kress and van Leeuwen 2006: 154–74). Here so-called 'high' modality is more often accorded to seemingly naturalistic images whose features most closely correspond to those of a 35mm photograph in terms of the degree of contextualization and background detail as well as depth, illumination and brightness. This compares to images characterized by 'low' modality, which may appear somehow 'less' realistic or life-like. Of key importance is also the use of colour (ibid.: 232–8), the analysis of which can include attention to *value* (from light to dark on a scale of black/grey/white), *saturation* (from intensely saturated colour to tones that are pale or dull), *purity* (from 'pure' to hybrid varieties of a specific colour), *modulation* (from richly textured shades to 'flat', often primary, colours), *differentiation* (from a palette ranging from monotone to varied) and *hue* (the scale of blue to red in relation to temperature). As Kress and van Leeuwen (2002) emphasize, colour is a powerful semiotic mode, possibly with a grammar all of its own, that can activate a range of emotional, aesthetic and/or sensory responses. Moreover, with regard to the sensory aspect of semiosis, we should not overlook the role played by the *phonic*, which, as van Leeuwen (2007: 138) suggests, surrounds us, placing us '[. . .] at the centre of the world, and at the heart of sensation and existence'. Sound, he continues, '[. . .] asks us to surrender ourselves and to immerse ourselves in the sensory world and in participatory experience' (ibid.; see also van Leeuwen 1999).

Finally, in his concept of an 'integrative multi-semiotic model' (IMM), Lim (2004) is particularly concerned to develop a theoretical paradigm that emphasizes the interaction between two aspects of the visual, namely images/graphics, on the one hand, and language/typography, on the other (see also van Leeuwen 2005, 2007 on typographic meaning). This emanates partly from a desire to rehabilitate the visual into a relationship of 'perceptual equity' with the linguistic (Lim 2004: 228–30), according to which images, graphics and typography are theorized as analytically on a par with language. However, it is clear that our need to capture what Lim refers to as the 'Space of Integration' (SoI) between the visual/graphic and linguistic/typographic[7] is also central to our ability to understand practices of viewing where multimodal and, in particular, *hyper*modal texts are concerned. This is insofar as the ergodist is not just engaged in simultaneous acts of 'looking' and 'reading' but is typically involved in a complex process of perceptual *scanning*, to which we will now turn.

12.2.3 Traversals and web composition

In their discussion of written texts, Kress and van Leeuwen (2006: 204) describe how, in Western literacy practice, linear reading paths are generally compulsory such that readers have little choice but to move across the page from left to right and top to bottom. This view has been challenged (amongst others) by Lemke, who argues that 'our eyes wander [. . .] [and] we may look away from nearby words on a page to more distant words' (2002: 300–01), words which are made more salient through typeface or position in the page or paragraph. This observation is particularly significant with regard to the structure of scanning *hypertext*, which combines two kinds of perceptual movements. On the one hand, we are dealing with a so-called 'simultaneous and holistic gestalt-perception' (Stöckl 2004: 17) whereby a webpage is perceived as a structured *whole*. On the other hand, however, the attention of the ergodist is constantly drawn to *particular* sections of a webpage not least as a prerequisite to making decisions about which hyperlinks, and hence which navigational pathways or 'traversals' (Lemke 2002), to follow. Needless to say, the perceptual dynamics of 'part versus whole' can be more or less strategically influenced by the compositional choices made by web designers.

In this regard, Kress and van Leeuwen (2006: 177–201) propose three main dimensions according to which the composition of multimodal texts – and hence acts of viewing – can be analysed. First, in relation to the horizontal axis, we can identify a GIVEN-NEW distinction, where (as with language), old information (or 'theme') is likely to be placed to the left of the text, with new information (or 'rheme') on the right. Second, along a vertical axis, the authors propose an IDEAL-REAL contrast, according to which the upper part of a text is often dedicated to the realm of the 'Ideal' (as in product descriptions in advertizements), as opposed to the lower part, which may be given over to more factual information (such as tables, graphs or 'small print'). Finally, multimodal texts can be viewed in terms of a CENTRE-MARGIN distinction. As Kress and van Leeuwen note (ibid.: 194), 'central' composition has been relatively unusual in Western visual traditions such that information is more likely to be hierarchically structured in relation to the horizontal margins, with the central item acting as a *bridge* between old and new information on the left and right, respectively. To sum up, the authors show how, in conjunction with the representation of social actors and the kinds of modality markers described above, multimodal composition works in ways that help to *frame* particular ITEMS as coherent semiotic units (ibid.: 203–4) as well as assigning to them a greater or lesser *salience* (ibid.: 201–3).

Whilst Kress and van Leeuwen's concepts of the representation of social actors and modality markers translate well from multimodal genres, in general, to hypermodal texts, in particular, it is in the area of information value and reading/viewing paths described above that the analysis of hypertext presents a number of rather different challenges. This is because, as Knox (2007) has demonstrated in his discussion of online newspaper home pages, the materiality of the computer screen is characterized by a number of differing affordances and constraints to that of the printed page (and, we might add, other visual media such as TV and cinema). As already noted in section 12.2.1, since the 'guaranteed viewing area' of the computer screen is unlikely to coincide with the whole of a given LEXIA, the single most important contrast between multimodal texts, in general, and hypermodal texts, in particular, is that the ergodist must scroll the screen *vertically* and/or *laterally* in order to view the text in its entirety. Accordingly, the key distinction becomes that of 'first screen' versus 'remainder' of a webpage, which Knox (drawing on Nielsen and Tahir 2002: 23) refers to as 'above' and 'below the fold' (Knox 2007: 38). Moreover, given that there is not only a *spatial* but also *temporal* dimension to website navigation, Knox (ibid.) shows how the hierarchy of information is typically indexed according to a continuum of 'diminishing salience', that is, the longer it takes to reach the information in question, the lesser its overall importance. Knox therefore proposes (ibid.) a modification of Kress and van Leeuwen's 'Ideal-Real' distinction for the vertical axis in visual media to that of a HEAD-TAIL contrast for online texts.

This re-configuration of the vertical axis in multimodal texts also has implications for any analysis of the 'centre-margin' contrast where hypermedia are concerned, with websites often organized as 'vertical triptych' characterized by a margin-centre-margin structure (Kress and van Leeuwen 2006: 198). Here Knox (2007: 39) demonstrates how, unlike in other visual media, particular significance tends to be accorded to the *central* column (which typically contains the main ITEMS) whilst less important information (such as minor features or further hyperlinks) is generally located in the left- or right-hand columns. For this distinction, Knox (ibid.: 39) therefore replaces the centre-margin distinction with a concept of PRIMARY-SECONDARY information value.

230

Finally, the re-contextualization of both the vertical and centre-margin structure in relation to images versus online texts also has implications for the role of the *horizontal* axis. Here, again, we can observe how the materiality of hypermodal text affords particular significance to the top-left hand corner of the screen immediately below the browser window. This constitutes *the* guaranteed viewing area on any computer screen and is therefore a strategic location which is most often employed for foregrounding of, say, the corporate identity (Kok 2004: 140). Moreover, it is on this part of a web page that we typically find what Knox (2007: 43) refers to as the 'MacroTheme'. This consists of macro-categories (e.g. 'About Us', 'Events', 'Letters', 'Sport', etc.) that *flag up* the main contents of a website, that is, what the ergodist might expect to find elsewhere in that site. Most typically, as part of the MacroTheme, there is a sidebar (see Boardman 2005) or navigator, that is, a menu of LEXIA-internal hyperlinks that highlights the location of the other kinds of information to be found elsewhere across a specific site. For this distinction, Knox (2007: 43) proposes a third category to replace that of 'Given-New', namely MacroTheme-Rheme.

12.3 The BBC 'Voices' home page

Having summarized the main theoretical and methodological issues that are germane to an understanding of the semiosis of websites in general, this section will now describe and analyse the BBC Voices home page in particular. Before delving into the analysis, however, a few caveats need to be made. First, we want to highlight that a linear and unifying narrative afforded by print technology – that is, our words written on this page – is unlikely to be able to account for the complexity of interacting with multi-sequential hypertext (see also Lemke 2002). This becomes even more problematic when one considers that a static reproduction of a web page – see for example, the screen shot in Figure 12.2 – can never convey the visual dynamics afforded by hypertextual features such as hyperlinks, kinetic typography and flashing banners. Second, we want to emphasize that the suggested traversals, that is, reading paths, that we will explore below should *not* be seen as the 'ideal' or even necessarily 'typical' trajectories that would be followed by any ergodist browsing this specific webpage. In this respect, further empirical research is needed to map out how different ergodists perceive and *actually* interact with the home page in question (something which is beyond the scope of this particular chapter). Third, for the purpose of the analysis below, it is crucial to take into account the aims of the BBC Voices website. This is relevant because the home page functions as a gateway to the data generated by the Voices project, and thus

231

Figure 12.2 Screen shot of the BBC Voices home page frozen on 17 October 2007. The solid black line indicates the fold on a regular 17" monitor with a screen resolution of 1152 x 864 pixels, whilst the dashed black line shows the fold on a laptop with 15" widescreen display with a screen resolution of 1280 x 800 pixels. (see colour plate section)

provides us with an entry into a fixed virtual archive about languages and language representations in the UK. However, one should not forget that the website has also been an important *medium* through which such data was gathered, for example, by way of electronic questionnaires on lexical variation or postings on language-related issues (e.g. Americanisms, bilingual education, etc.).

12.3.1 Deconstructing the home page: general composition and individual ITEMS

As Lemke (2002: 310) has proposed, 'It is often useful to begin a multimodal analysis with the visual-organizational composition of the whole page, because, as Arnheim (1956) noted, this is the salient structure which guides the eye in its traversals across the page'. In the specific case of the BBC Voices home page, we believe that *colour* and *framing* (see Sections 12.2.1 and 12.2.3 above) might be seen as the main features through which the overall compositional unity is realized. More specifically, a geometrical pattern of perpendicular lines creates an orderly grid-like structure consisting of interrelated frames of different sizes and colours containing a number of interrelated ITEMS as follows.

The top of the page is occupied by a *masthead* with dark grey background and white non-serif typeface[8]. Here the logo of the BBC web domain is positioned in the 'guaranteed viewing area' in the left-hand corner aligned to the right with a search engine and hyperlinks to other relevant websites within this specific domain (e.g. TV, radio, talk, index). Three elements are of particular relevance here. First, in line with Kok's (2004: 140) observations, a masthead with a corporate logo in the top-most position does not simply follow a well-established convention through which to welcome and introduce the ergodist to a website; it is also the manifestation of a strategic choice to shore up the *institutional identity* of that site. However, the masthead is narrow and the typographical weight of the logo relatively modest when compared to the rest of the page, thus contributing to an overall downplaying of the masthead's visual prominence. Second, it is important to point out that the logo is *not* the same as that of the BBC TV or radio. Rather, it is a verbal/visual string (white letter forms and Arial Narrow typeface) that reproduces the URL of the BBC home page (bbc.co.uk), also functioning as a hyperlink to it. This may seem like a rather commonsensical choice through which the BBC is branding its web services as clearly separated from its other broadcast activities. Nonetheless, it can also be read as a way of making a specific URL 'memorable' (Nielsen and Tahir 2002: 26), such that the ergodist will recall it more easily in future browsing. Third, it is crucial to note that the layout of the masthead is identical for all websites within the BBC domain. In this way, corporate visual uniformity contributes to creating a sense of coherence and cohesion *across* interrelated LEXIAS, at the same time as highlighting which LEXIAS constitute a specific CLUSTER.

Below the masthead, and clearly separated by a border of a darker shade of grey, the remainder of the page is divided vertically into two sections of different size and colour. There is no doubt that the two partly overlapping grey and white frames on the left-hand side occupy more than two thirds of the page. However, despite being narrower, the pink frame on the right-hand side appears no less powerful in attracting the gaze of the ergodist thanks to its unmodulated and highly saturated colour. As Kress and van Leeuwen have pointed out, the key function

Figure 12.3 The heading (see colour plate section)

of colour saturation is to stimulate the viewer in a *sensory-emotional* way on a scale 'that runs from maximum intensity of feelings to maximally subdued, maximally toned-down, indeed neutralized feeling' (2006: 233). To this, they also add that colour modulation has an emotional component. While highly-modulated colours are perceived as more naturalistic and 'real', unmodulated colours may express abstractness, simplicity and *boldness*. These theoretical observations are particularly relevant to the description of the visual impressions produced by the home page under investigation here. Thus the unmodulated and highly-saturated pink makes the right-hand side of the page stand out as bold and sensorily prominent in comparison to the softer tones of the left frame. Finally, the visual salience of the right-hand frame is accrued by the heading of the website – 'voices' – with its large white typographical/visual letter forms (Figure 12.3).

Lim (2004) and van Leeuwen (2005) both argue that typography has yet not been regarded as a semiotic mode in its own right because of its well-established function as the default means through which to represent written language in standardized graphic forms. Or, as van Leeuwen's suggestively puts it, typography has traditionally been viewed as 'the humble craft in the service of the written word' (2005: 142). Crucially, this has led to a downplaying, or overlooking even, of the visual dimension of graphemes in favour of the linguistic. However, as the heading of the Voices home page shows, it is at times difficult, not to say impossible, to separate these two dimensions of meaning-making. In fact, the relevant aspect here is not simply 'the word image' (Bellantoni and Woolman 2000 cited in van Leeuwen 2005), that is, the linguistic concept evoked by a graphic string of letter forms in the 'voices' heading, but also the 'typographic image', that is, the holistic sensory impression generated by the interplay between specific typeface, size, weight (i.e. thickness or thinness), colour contrast, and so on. In this respect, the letter forms in the heading are clearly both *assertive* and *salient* in view of their size, thickness and white colour against the bold pink background. This, together with their regularity and rounded curvature, contributes to making them stand out as *steady* and *smooth* (cf. van Leeuwen 2005: 148–49). That said, the overall uniformity and solidity of the letters are contrasted by a sense of movement, vibration and sound expressed through the blurring of the 'o'. It is at this juncture that it becomes increasingly difficult to separate 'word image' from 'typographic image', thus compelling us to account for the dialectic relationship between the two – what Lim (2004) calls the Space of Integration (see Section 12.2.2 above). This is insofar as we experience here the interplay between the conceptual image evoked by the grapheme 'voices', on the one hand, and the visual means employed to represent the letter form 'o', on the other. This produces a chain of culturally-situated synaesthetic associations (blurred typeface → vibration → sound) whereby we come to *sense* sound through the interaction between visual and conceptual images.

The visual weight of the heading and the pink frame to the right, however, is counterbalanced by the larger size of the grey and white frames on the left-hand side (see e.g. Kress and van Leeuwen 2006; Knox 2007). Moreover, the lower degree (or even lack) of colour saturation in these frames contributes to a toning down of the ergodist's sensory experience in favour of a calmer, more ordered or even rational and objective impression. Such rationality and orderliness are then conveyed further by the geometrical arrangement of the text within the white frame, where seven analogous 'newsbites' (Knox 2007) – three stacked vertically and four horizontally – are consistently separated from each other by white empty space (see Machin 2007: 152).

According to Knox (2007: 26), newsbites are poignant verbal/visual summaries found in the home page of online newspapers that work as gateways to longer written, audio, or video narratives posted elsewhere in that site. In terms of structure, Knox points out how a newsbite typically consists of three elements: *Focus* (i.e. headline), *Event* (i.e. the lead) and *Link* (i.e. hyperlinks). However, Knox also acknowledges that this basic structure can be expanded through *Illustration*, *Issue* and *Tangents*. While *Illustration* indicates a smaller image juxtaposed to the verbal text of a newsbite, *Issue* labels a heading in smaller typeface that is often positioned above the headline with the aim of 'plac[ing] the newsbite in a wider social context' (ibid.: 27). Finally, *Tangents* are 'headline-only hyperlinks' that 'expand the potential for readers to follow one or more links to stories which are related to a given newsbyte' (ibid.: 27). In line with these observations, Figure 12.4 shows that the newsbites in the BBC Voices home page present a similar structure encompassing: (i) a Focus, that is, a brief headline that aims to attract the attention of the ergodist (the three newsbites stacked vertically at the top also present a sub-heading); (ii) an Event, that is, the lead which summarizes the content of the page to which the ergodist might want to navigate; (iii) the Link, that is, the hyperlink(s) which allows access to

235

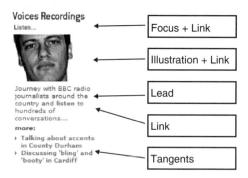

Figure 12.4 An example of a 'newsbite' (see colour plate section)

that page; and (iv) Tangents, that is, further hyperlinks that lead the ergodist to other pages with related contents. Hyperlinks are indexed here by bold typeface that becomes underlined whenever the mouse cursor is moved over them – note however that the headlines, the sub-headings, and the pictures also function as hyperlinks.

Another interesting area for analysis is the left-hand corner of the grey frame where today's date is positioned above hyperlinks to a 'Text only version' (in bold typeface) and the 'BBC homepage' (Figure 12.5). While the latter can be viewed as a hypermodal anaphora of the logo that repeats and reinforces the path via which the BBC home page can be reached, the former can be interpreted as a manifestation of the *ethos* of the BBC as a public service provider (see also Coupland 2007; Jaffe 2006). In fact, a text-only option for a website is not simply a useful alternative for those who might experience difficulties in downloading images because of hardware or bandwidth constraints (Boardman 2005: 13). Such an option is also the realization through the medium of hypertext of a political choice that recognizes and addresses the spe-cific needs of blind or visually-impaired ergodists, who often rely on screen readers and/or screen magnifiers to access electronic informa-tion. Moreover, the position of a hyperlink to a text-only version in the upper-left area is itself meaningful insofar as it shows a consideration for the *practical* experiences of blind and visually-impaired users deal-ing with hypertext who 'will hear this link as [one of] the first option[s] when accessing the page through their screen readers' (Nielsen and Tahir 2002: 85).

Finally, we come to the horizontal frame, or *banner*, which displays an arrow-shaped green figure with the script 'The way we speak around the UK' partly overlapping onto a picture of three black teenagers engaged in a seemingly friendly conversation in a café. Whilst it is

236

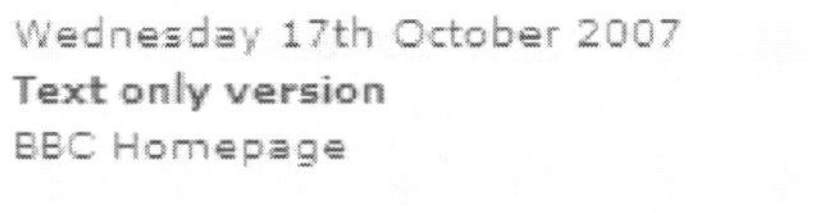

Wednesday 17th October 2007
Text only version
BBC Homepage

Figure 12.5 'Text-only' (see colour plate section)

impossible to replicate this in a static screen shot, it is crucial to note how the banner flashes at intervals of approximately five seconds, thereby displaying four different combinations of verbal/visual text, to which we will return in more detail in the final section. Most importantly in terms of composition, the banner not only functions as an element of *division* that demarcates a boundary between the corporate identity of the home page and its main content below, but also works as a visual link that unifies the left and right frames into a cohesive unit.

In conclusion, we hope to have shown here how the notion of compositional coherence and cohesion can be usefully applied not only to print but also *hypermodal* texts. That said, the latter present us with many more challenges in relation to visual salience. As noted above, whilst it is true that the heading, the unsaturated pink frame and the banner appear more prominent than other elements, it is also important to bear in mind that LEXIAS are not necessarily co-extensive with computer screens. Accordingly, following Knox (2007) and Kok (2004), one needs to distinguish between the *first screen* or *initial window* – that is, the portions of LEXIA visible when opening a webpage – and the remainder of that page. In the case of the BBC Voices home page, the solid black line used in Figure 12.2 indicates that the first screen on a 17-inch standard monitor encompasses almost the whole LEXIA except for (i) the newsbite dedicated to the Open University on the left, and (ii) a lower section of the 'Contents'. However, the dashed black line shows that the initial window on a laptop with a 15-inch widescreen display appears quite different, because it rules out all ITEMS below 'News archive' and 'Voice of the day'. This does not simply mean that the ergodist, depending on the size of their computer monitor (together with screen resolution and the configuration of the desktop and the browser) will be more or less engaged in scrolling down the page in order to access the information excluded from the first screen. It also implies that the visual salience of different ITEMS varies such that in the BBC Voices home page the already prominent banner becomes *even more* salient on a 15-inch widescreen laptop given that it covers almost one third of the first screen viewing area.

12.3.2 Re-constituting the home page: credibility, interactivity and playfulness in the service of the BBC Voices project

Having provided a detailed analysis of the home page layout, our aim in this section is to move towards an understanding of the overall *purpose* of marshalling together certain visual, linguistic and phonic means (and not others) into a coherent unit. In order to do this, it will be relevant to make a few comparisons between the BBC Voices home page and the front pages of three online newspapers analysed by Knox (2007).

Knox points out with regard to his own newspaper sample how 'Visual elements on the pages are all squared – there are no circles or curves, no tangential lines and no oblique angles, presenting a two-dimensional view to the reader' (ibid.: 30). He also notes that the exclusive use of monochrome (i.e. black text on white background) to signify the 'news' at the centre of the page is contrasted only by the colours of hyperlinks and sidebars. Knox therefore concludes that online newspapers make use of a 'modality of factuality' (ibid.), that is, a set of hypermodal strategies through which newspapers 'foreground credibility and background "playfulness"' (Kok 2004: 30), thereby presenting themselves as a trustworthy conduit of factual, objective and rational world-views.

Reasoning along similar lines, we can see how the BBC Voices home page clearly shares some of the compositional features of online newspapers. This is illustrated by the position of a masthead at the top, the choice of frames in order to achieve compositional coherence, and the use of newsbites in black typeface on white background. Accordingly, one might conclude that a fairly prominent corporate identity, coupled with a squared structure and use of monochrome as a visual signifier of the main 'news' of the home page, expresses a Gestalt of stability and *credibility* or, conversely, a general lack of dynamism (see Kok 2004: 145 for a similar line of argument with regard to the home page of Singapore's Ministry of Education). Nevertheless, if we consider the home page in its entirety, our analysis has also suggested that some ITEMS do indeed convey a stronger sense of dynamism. Moreover, the BBC Voices home page appears to be characterized by a rather non-conventional structure in terms of information value. The notions of MacroTheme versus Rheme, and Head versus Tail (see Section 12.2.3 above) will help us to explore this impression more fully.

We have already noted how the material constraints of computer screens afford greater visual salience to those ITEMS that are viewable on the left/central part of the first screen. This is the space where the home pages of online newspapers typically list, within a sidebar, a number of

238

Figure 12.6 Section of the Macro-Theme (see colour plate section)

macro-categories that highlight what the website is about, that is, its MacroTheme (see also Nielsen and Tahir 2002). Although we do not deny the analytical potential of the notions of MacroTheme and Rheme per se, the BBC Voices home page does in fact appear to demonstrate a rather more innovative and unconventional way of structuring these elements visually. This is insofar as the MacroTheme is foregrounded through colour contrast (pink/white), but spatially reversed. Furthermore, unlike in online newspapers, the navigator is positioned at the bottom of the page and thereby infused with secondary information value given that it falls more or less completely within the Tail of both a 15-inch and 17-inch screen monitor. By contrast, the section of the MacroTheme that appears in the Head, and has thus primary information value, encompasses, apart from the heading of the website, two short samples of actual data from the Voices project, framed under the headings 'Your contributions', and 'Voice of the day' (see Figure 12.6). The former consists of a permanent extract from the electronic postings. The latter, on the contrary, varies daily and is a summary of a longer interview.

These frames are complex semiotic aggregates that epitomize the main topic of this website, namely language in terms of: (i) written meta-linguistic commentaries, and (ii) actual recordings of verbal production. In this context it is crucial to explore how these two aspects of language are themselves represented through differing sign modalities (see Agha 2003: 238). In the first example, the speech bubbles – prototypical icons of speech (e.g. in comics) – visually echo an actual instance of direct report, typographically indexed by quotation marks.

239

In the second example, by contrast, the stylized loudspeaker, which stands for acoustic production/reception, clearly indexes the hyperlink 'listen', and thus plays with and enhances the auditory dimension of the frame entitled 'Voice of the day'. In addition, the imperative form of address 'listen' directs the ergodist to an audio file of the interview in question. In conjunction with the use of the imperative in hyperlinks, direct address is then similarly encoded in the possessive adjective 'your' ('Your contribution'), which also occurs elsewhere in the home page (see Section 12.4 below). Taken together, the imperative and the deictic expression 'your' can be interpreted as tokens of *synthetic personalization* (Fairclough 2001: 168), a discursive strategy through which the mass media construct a less anonymous, more personalized relationship with their audiences. In the specific case of hypertext, this further involves encouraging the ergodist to actively interact with the medium itself.

To sum up, we would argue that the BBC Voices home page represents an interesting attempt to *mediate* between credibility, interactivity and playfulness, whilst trying to function simultaneously as a channel of trustworthy information, thereby constituting a good example of 'infotainment' (see e.g. Talbot 2007). This is insofar as the home page is built on two co-existing features: (i) a rather conventional use of masthead, squared structure and newsbites; and (ii) a more innovative visual arrangement of the information value. The latter, together with the discursive strategy of synthetic personalization, enhances a sense of 'playfulness' thereby aiming to stimulate the ergodist's active engagement with the website. This is entirely in line with one of the main aims of the website, which, according to the original Voices Project proposal, would 'be designed and built to maximize user interaction and particularly user contribution' (Rose and Mowbray, no date). In brief, credibility, interactivity and playfulness are consistent with the dual role of the website as a medium through which to gather data for the Voices project, and as an archive of those data, and more broadly with the aim of the BBC to 'enrich people's lives with programmes and services that inform, educate and entertain' (BBC 2008).

12.4 Celebrating diversity? Language ideologies and hypermodal performativity

Mazzarella (2004: 357), commenting on Peters (1997), argues that the 'concept of media as practices and technologies of "social envisioning" [. . .] usefully captures the fact that media [. . .] make society *imaginable* to itself' (our emphasis). This observation resonates with Anderson's (1991) well-established reflections about the role of the print media in shaping the nation as an 'imagined community' as well as Gal and Woolard's (2001) broader notion of 'publics' as communities of non-co-present individuals that are brought into being by way of some kind of textual mediation (see also Milani and Johnson 2008b). Put simply, the mass media do not simply *inform* or *educate* their audiences by mirroring societal arrangements in a neutral and objective way. Rather, they are 'centring institutions' (Silverstein 1998) that performatively bring into life and circulate a reality in which some *voices* are cited, grouped together and amplified, while others are downplayed or even sidelined (cf. Bakhtin 1981; Fairclough 1995; Talbot 2007). Furthermore, every performative act typically involves a series of 'interpellations' (Althusser 1971; Butler 1997). These are discursive acts of positioning whereby, say, the media attempt to establish some kind of ideological relationship with their audiences. It goes without saying that this per-formative process also includes the (re)production and propagation of language ideologies, understood as particular views and beliefs *about* languages and their *links* to social, political, moral and aesthetic values. Against this backdrop, the remainder of this section will explore the ways in which the BBC Voices home page can be viewed as a virtual stage on which certain aspects of language are *ideologized* (see Androutsopoulos, Chapter 10, this volume) by means of hypertext technology. In order to do this, we will focus on aspects of the flashing banner not just because this constitutes one of the most visually promi-nent ITEMS in the home page, but also because it provides us with an interesting micro-context in which to analyse a number of processes where by UK is *imagined* as a set of interrelated speaking communities.

As Figure 12.7 shows, the overall visual structure of the banner is similar for each of its five configurations: an arrow-like shape of bright, unsaturated colour partly overlaps with an image in which different social actors are on 'offer' (Kress and van Leeuwen 2006) to the gaze of an ergodist. The first element to note is the interrelation between verbal text and images. Here we agree with Kress and van Leeuwen (ibid.) that it is too simplistic to assume that, whenever verbal text is juxtaposed to an image, the former always explains the latter. Nonetheless, in the specific case of the banner, irrespective of whether an image precedes or follows verbal text, the text appears to function deictically by anchor-ing the image to a precise time, space and community as well as instan-tiating interpersonal relations with the ergodist.

To take the first screen shot as an example, without the caption 'The way we speak around the UK', it would not be possible to determine *where* the conversation amongst the three (seemingly quite cheerful) black teenagers might be taking place. Moreover, the use of the deictic expressions 'we' and 'the UK', in association with this particular image,

Figure 12.7 Complete sequence of banner changes (approx. 4.5 seconds intervals) (retrieved on 19 October 2007) (see colour plate section)

is not purely *descriptive* of an already existing reality. Rather, deixis and image work together in this context to bring into life the UK today as a community of speakers of which black teenagers are *foregrounded* as being a constitutive part. Of course, we do not want to convey that 'we' always functions as a token of national deixis. Moreover, according to Fairclough 'there is a constant ambivalence and slippage between exclusive and inclusive "we"' (2000: 35), whereby the deictic expression 'wanders' (Petersoo 2007) to encompass different referents at the same time. This is true in the case of the second screen shot, where the text 'How do we sound? Take an online audio-journey with the Voices recordings' is positioned next to the image of two smiling young white girls. Here it is quite difficult to determine with any degree of certainty the referent of 'we'. Does it relate specifically to the girls and their speech, as opposed to, say, *boys'* or *adults'* speech? Or does it refer to all those who have contributed to the Voices recordings? No less clear is whether the ergodist is included or excluded into this imagined speaking community. That said, analogous to what has been said about synthetic personalization above, the ergodist *is* directly addressed through the imperative form 'take' and thus encouraged to interact with the website and actively listen to the recordings.

By the same token, in the fourth screen shot, the script 'Voices in your area. Find out more in your part of the UK', together with a map of the British Isles, anchor a smiling black woman on a leafy background to a specific geographical context as well as establishing a direct relationship with the ergodist through the possessive adjective 'your'. Significant here is not just the recurrent acknowledgement of racial diversity, but also how the notion of the *local*, as opposed to national, is highlighted verbally ('your area' and 'your part of the UK') as well as visually through the black dots on a map of the British Isles. In this context, it is something of a truism that the interest in *local diversity* is but one of the components in the complex process of globalization (see Robertson's (1994) notion of 'glocalization' that aims to capture this global-local dialectic). No less undisputed is the fact that since the 1960s the UK has experienced a 'rise of the regional [. . .] into a position of newly fashionable prominence' (Mugglestone 2007: 279). This local/regional revival is not simply attested in the more liberal acceptance and use of regional accents in broadcast media (Talbot 2007: 25), but also in the overt policy of the BBC to foster its local radio stations. In this respect, it is important to highlight how 'Voices in your area' playfully alludes to both the BBC local radio stations and the actual recordings of dialectal variation within the Voices project. And it is interesting to note in this regard how the BBC has opted to visually signify local diversity through an (inaccurate) representation of the areas where the BBC local radios are situated as opposed to a map of the locations where the audio recordings were actually made (see http://www.bbc.co.uk/voices/recordings/index.shtml). This provides further support for Susan Gal's (2008) observation that maps – contrary to popular wisdom – do not in fact constitute objective icons of a pre-existing reality. Quite the contrary, maps are themselves socio-culturally and historically situated artefacts that authoritatively bring into being *one* view of geographical-spatial reality – a view that is particular in origin because it is invested with certain socio-cultural values, thereby privileging the interests of some groups (but not others). What is particularly relevant in the map

243

of the British Isles on the BBC Voices home page is that the black dots cluster almost exclusively within the geographical space that corresponds to England, leaving Northern Ireland, Scotland and Wales to appear almost empty or deserted, and therefore less visually prominent. Moreover, it is notable that the map is itself skewed. Whilst such tilting could be interpreted as disruptive of the habitual view of a map of the British Isles, it is also significant in relation to the trajectory of the gaze of the black woman. This is insofar as southern England is the point of intersection between (i) the oblique vector emanating from the frames of the woman's spectacles, and (ii) the horizontal axis along which her chin and the text 'Voices in your area' are aligned (cf. Kress and van Leeuwen 2006: 49)[9]. In sum, local diversity is recognized verbally and visually. However, the overall visual prominence of England relates to the verbal text as in a synecdoche where (southern) England is visually projected to stand for both 'your area' and the 'UK'. In this sense, our observations are not dissimilar to those of Anthony King, who emphasizes in the *BBC Trust Impartiality Report* (King 2008) how it is not uncommon for BBC presenters and newsreaders to inaccurately conflate England with the UK as a whole.

In order to further substantiate this point, we want to draw the attention to another semiotic item on the home page, namely the newsbite that informs us about the '620,000 words, supplied by you, mapped

Figure 12.8 Newsbite on the Word Map (see colour plate section)

across the UK' and encourages the ergodist to 'browse our Word Map of local language' (Figure 12.8). In the accompanying illustration the verb 'bung' – a dialectal variant of 'throw' – has been made prominent through bold typeface, and its use is represented spatially in the corresponding map.

The main feature in Figure 12.8 is that most of Scotland and a small portion of Northern Ireland are not included, which contributes to making England and Wales more central and visually prominent. The salience of southern England is further enhanced by the use of an unsaturated red colour. Again, we do not dispute the very fact that local diversity in the form of dialectal variation is being flagged up in this particular newsbite. Nevertheless, the choice of a lexical item most commonly occurring in southern England amongst the 620,000 words gathered through the survey, coupled with a map that visually highlights the southern part of Great Britain may be indicative of what Billig (1995) calls a 'syntax of hegemony'. In other words, we see how one part of a totality – southern England in both linguistic and geographical terms – is chosen and visually foregrounded to stand for the 'local language' and the 'UK' that appear in the verbal text of the newsbite.

Dialectal variation is also a key feature in the third screen shot, where a young white woman lying on a pebble beach is gazing happily in the direction of two stylized shoes positioned next to 'The Word Map. Plimmies, jimmies, daps, gutties or penny blacks? this is what you told us'. Here local diversity is evoked through the list of a few local/regional variants of the concept 'child's soft shoes worn for PE' (http://www.bbc.co.uk/voices/results/wordmap/). Most notably, dialectal variation is made salient by the way that the concept is evoked visually whilst the linguistic standard form ('plimsolls') is absent. Moreover, the choice of an image of a young woman in relation to dialectal forms is itself noteworthy insofar as it partly challenges the main assumption of dialectological research and folk linguistic perceptions alike that the 'typical' dialect speaker is an older non-mobile rural male. To this one could add that the use of lower-case 't' following a question mark in 'this is what you told us', coupled with the deictic expression 'you', may also be doing ideological work. On the one hand, such a non-standard orthographic practice could be either a typographical error or a subtle strategy through which to convey rapport and intimacy with the ergodist. On the other hand, through the pronoun 'you', the ergodist is here 'hailed' (Althusser 1971), that is, positioned, as a direct contributor to the pool of tokens on which the 'Word map' on lexical variation is based. In this way, the boundaries between the ergodist and the informant are blurred, and the former is called into being as a warrant of the 'vernacular authenticity' (Coupland 2003: 419) of the collected data.

Since 'Authenticity [. . .] requires an infrastructure of expert authenticators, monitors and recorders to establish and defend the status of authentic phenomena, and to ensure continuing consensus about this within a community' (ibid.), the ergodist is discursively constructed as a means through which to *validate* and *authenticate* the whole project (cf. Bucholtz 2003: 408). Put simply, the argument runs as follows: if you have contributed to the data collection, those data are attested. They are therefore 'ontologically real' and hence 'authentic' (see Coupland 2003: 421).

12.5 Concluding remarks

As the media theorist David Morley argues, 'public culture [. . .] is already an ethnic culture and has a colour which is only common to some of the citizens of the nation which it supposedly reflects, and which it attempts to address' (2000: 119–120) – an observation that could be broadened beyond race and ethnicity so as to encompass the linguistic dimension of culture (re)produced by mainstream national media. This is because the mass media 'give value and exposure to certain language codes, linguistic varieties, and discourse styles' (Spitulnik 1999: 149) in two ways: (i) through the deployment of such codes, varieties and style as shared means of communication, and (ii) through their meta-linguistic representations.

In this regard, the home page under investigation in this chapter represents the voice of the BBC in its most patent attempt to celebrate and thus materialize an ideology of linguistic diversity through representations of the UK as a set of happy and highly diverse speaking communities on the basis of race/ethnicity, gender, age, and locality. There is no doubt that the celebration of diversity has been an ideological thrust in the Voices project since its very inception (see introductory quote in Section 12.1). This is, in turn, falls within the BBC's broader remit to '(i) represent the different nations, regions and communities to the rest of the UK; (ii) cater for the different nations, regions and communities of the UK; (iii) bring people together for shared experiences; (iv) encourage interest in and conversation about local communities; (v) reflect the different religious and other beliefs in the UK; and (vi) provide output in minority languages' (BBC 2008).

That said, it remains incontrovertible how all semiotic choices inherently entail the *omission* of other possible ones (cf. Gal 2008), and this is no less evident on the Voices home page. First and foremost, it is important to note the absence of language varieties other than Standard English as linguistic codes employed in the home page – the only exceptions being a hyperlink in Welsh on the bottom right-hand side

246

and the dialectal lexical items in the banner. Second, ethnic and racial diversity is acknowledged, but only through images of what cannot be perceived as potentially destabilizing the socio-cultural and moral order in the UK. For example, there are no pictures of members of Asian (that is, Pakistani, Indian or Bangladeshi) minorities – a very hetero-geneous group that in recent years has been essentialized as a more or less uniform icon of social unrest and violence in the British media and political discourse (see e.g. Blackledge 2005; see also Chapter 8, this volume).

In conclusion therefore, our findings with regard to the Voices home page point in the same directions as those of King (2008) regarding BBC news reporting more generally. According to King (ibid.: 35), the BBC has failed to achieve its goal to fully reflect the UK's nations, regions and communities in favour of a focus on England and/or a fram-ing of the news from an Anglocentric perspective. Similarly, our analy-sis of the maps of the home page has shown that there is certainly a textual *tension* between an attempt to foreground local diversity, on the one hand, and the visual prominence of (southern) England as a meto-nymic representation of the UK, on the other. It remains to be seen in our future analyses whether there are more such absences, tensions and conflicts in the many other areas of the Voices website.

Notes

1 See http://www.bbc.co.uk/radio4/routesofenglish/index.shtml. Accessed 6/11/07.
2 For further details of the background to the BBC Voices project, see http://www.bbc.co.uk/voices/yourvoice/about_voices.shtml. Accessed 4/12/07.
3 We would like to express our gratitude to the Arts and Humanities Research Council (AHRC), who are funding a three-year project between 2007 and 2010 on language ideological debates on the BBC Voices website (ref. AH/E509002/1), from which this work is derived. We are also grateful to colleagues at the BBC, in particular Mandy Rose, for their support and coop-eration in this project as well as for permission to reproduce screenshots from the Voices website. We are particularly indebted to Bethan Davies, Misty Jaffe, Mark Sebba, Ann Thompson, Will Turner, and two anonymous reviewers for the CLSL Working Paper Series at Lancaster University for their comments on earlier drafts of this chapter, which have helped us to think through and unpack the complexity of the verbal/visual text of the BBC Voices home page. It goes without saying that any remaining shortcomings are entirely our own.
4 But see Johnson (2007) for an analysis of a *visual* image in relation to ideo-logical disputes around the reform of German orthography.
5 'Webpage' is a generic term to define any document on the World Wide Web. By contrast, 'home page' is used to identify a particular type of webpage that

functions as a gateway in order to welcome the user into a series of interrelated pages (Kok 2004: 140). From a web designer's perspective, the main function of a home page is 'to communicate what the company is, the value the site offers over competition and the physical world, and the products or services offered' (Nielsen and Tahir 2002: 2).

6 The term ergodicity derives from the Greek words *ergon* (work) and *hodos* (path).

7 For useful checklists of graphic and typographic features to be considered in multimodal analyses, see Lim (2004: 234–5). With regard to Lim's notion of the 'Space of Integration' in relation to the *visual*, we would argue that this could be usefully extended to the level of the *auditory*, that is, the relationship between the linguistic (spoken language) and the phonic (sound and music).

8 However, at the time of writing (June 2008), the logo and masthead have been changed.

9 We are grateful to Will Turner for pointing this out to us. See also the debate following the introduction of a new BBC weather map in May 2005, a move that infuriated many Scots because Britain was tilted in such a way that Scotland appeared as 'a pathetic pimple on top of England' (*The Observer*, 29 May 2005).

References

Althusser, L. (1971), 'Ideology and ideological state apparatuses', in L. Althusser (ed.), *Lenin and Philosophy*. New York: Monthly Review Press, pp. 85–126.

Aarseth, E. (1997), *Cybertext: Perspectives on Ergodic Literature*. Baltimore, MD: The Johns Hopkins University Press.

Agha, A. (2003), 'The social life of cultural value'. *Language and Communication*, 23(3-4), 231–73.

Anderson, B. (1991), *Imagined Communities: Reflections on the Origin and Spread of Nationalism*. London: Verso.

Bakhtin, M. (1981), *The Dialogic Imagination: Four Essays*. Austin, TX: University of Texas Press.

Baldry, S. (ed.) (2000), *Multimodality and Multimediality in the Distance Learning Age*. Campobasso, Italy: Palladino Editore.

Barthes, R. (1977), 'Rhetoric of the image', in R. Barthes (S. Heath, ed. and trans.), *Image-Music-Text*. London; Fontana, pp. 32–51.

BBC (2008), 'About the BBC: Purpose and values.' Retrieved at www.bbc.co.uk/info/purpose (23 April 2008).

Billig, M. (1995), *Banal Nationalism*. London: Sage.

Blackledge, A. (2005), *Discourse and Power in a Multilingual World*. Amsterdam/Philadelphia: John Benjamins.

Blommaert, J. (ed.) (1999a), *Language Ideological Debates*. Berlin: Mouton de Gruyter.

Blommaert, J. (1999b), 'The debate is open', in J. Blommaert (ed.) *Language Ideological Debates*. Berlin: Mouton de Gruyter, pp. 1–38.

Boardman, M. (2005), *The Language of Websites*. London: Routledge.

Bucholtz, M. (2003), 'Sociolinguistic nostalgia and the authentication of experience'. *Journal of Sociolinguistics*, 7(4), 398–416.

Butler, J. (1997), *Excitable Speech: A Politics of the Performative*. New York: Routledge.

Coupland, N. (2003), 'Sociolinguistic authenticities'. *Journal of Sociolinguistics*, 7(4), 417–31.

Coupland, N. (2007), *Style: Language Variation and Identity*. Cambridge: Cambridge University Press.

Coupland, N. and Jaworski, A. (2004), 'Sociolinguistic perspectives on metalanguage: reflexivity, evaluation and ideology', in A. Jaworski, N. Coupland and D. Galasiński (eds), *Metalanguage: Social and Ideological Perspectives*. Berlin: Mouton de Gruyter, pp. 15–51.

Coupland, N. and Bishop, H. (2007), 'Ideologized values for British accents'. *Journal of Sociolinguistics*, 11(1), 74–93.

Elmes, S. (2000), *Routes of English*. Vols. 1 and 2. London: BBC Factual and Learning.

Elmes, S. (2001), *Routes of English*. Vol. 4. London: BBC Factual and Learning.

Elmes, S. (2006), *Talking for Britain: A Journey through the Nation's Dialects*. Middlesex: Penguin. (Reprinted in paperback as *Talking for Britain: A Journey through the Voices of a Nation*).

Elmes, S. and Bragg, M. (2001), *Routes of English*. Vol. 3. London: BBC Factual and Learning.

Ensslin, A. (2007a), *Canonizing Hypertext: Explorations and Constructions*. London: Continuum.

Ensslin, A. (2007b), 'Of chords, machines and bumble-bees: the metalinguistics of hyperpoetry', in S. Johnson and A. Ensslin (eds) *Language in the Media: Representations, Identities, Ideologies*. London: Continuum, pp. 250–68.

Fairclough, N. (1995), *Media Discourse*. London: Arnold.

Fairclough, N. (2000), *New Labour, New Language?* London: Routledge.

Fairclough, N. (2001), *Language and Power* (2nd edn). London: Longman.

Gal, S. (2008), 'Language and space/place: implications for linguistics minorities'. Keynote address at the Research Conference on Language Planning and Policy, Saltsjöbaden, Sweden, 8–9 June 2008.

Gal, S. and Woolard, K. A. (2001), *Languages and Publics: The Making of Authority*. Manchester: St. Jerome Publishing Ltd.

Iedema, R. (2003), 'Multimodality, resemioticization: extending the analysis of discourse as multi-semiotic practice'. *Visual Communication*, 2(1), 29–57.

Jaffe, A. (2006), 'Diverse voices, public broadcasts: sociolinguistic representations in mainstream programming'. Paper presented at the 2006 meeting of the American Anthropological Association (AAA), San José, USA.

Jaworski, A., Coupland, N. and Galasiński, D. (eds) (2004), *Metalanguage: Social and Ideological Perspectives*. Berlin: Mouton de Gruyter.

Johnson, S. (2007), 'The iconography of orthography: representing German spelling reform in the news magazine, *Der Spiegel*', in S. Johnson and A. Ensslin (eds) *Language in the Media: Representations, Identities, Ideologies*. London: Continuum, pp. 91–110.

249

Johnson, S. and Ensslin, A. (eds) (2007), *Language in the Media: Representations, Identities, Ideologies*. London: Continuum.

Kerswill, P., Llamas, C. and Upton, C. (1999), 'The first SuRE moves: early steps towards a large dialect database', in C. Upton and K. Wales (eds), *Dialectal Variation in English: Proceedings of the Harold Orton Centenary Conference 1998*. Leeds Studies in English Vol. 30.

King, A. (2008), *The BBC Trust Impartiality Report: BBC Network News and Current Affairs Coverage of the Four UK Nations*. http://www.bbc.co.uk/bbctrust/assets/files/pdf/review_report_research/impartiality/uk_nations_impartiality.pdf (Retrieved on 19 June 2008).

Knox, J. (2007), 'Visual-verbal communication on online newspaper homepages'. *Visual Communication*, 6(1), 19–53.

Kok, K. C. A. (2004), 'Multisemiotic mediation in hypertext', in K. I. O'Halloran (ed.), *Multimodal Discourse Analysis: Systemic Functional Perspectives*. London/New York: Continuum, pp. 131–59.

Kress, G. (2003), *Literacy in the New Media Age*. London: Routledge.

Kress, G. and van Leeuwen, T. (2001), *Multimodal Discourse: The Modes and Media of Contemporary Communication*. London: Edward Arnold.

Kress, G. and van Leeuwen, T. (2006), *Reading Images: the Grammar of Visual Design* (2nd edn). London: Routledge.

Lemke, J. (1999), 'Discourse and organizational dynamics: website communication and institutional change'. *Discourse & Society*, 10(1), 21–47.

Lemke, J. (2002), 'Travels in hypermodality'. *Visual Communication*, 1(3), 299–325.

Levine, P. and Scollon, R. (eds) (2004), *Discourse and Technology: Multimodal Discourse Analysis*. Georgetown: Georgetown University Press.

Lim, F. V. (2004), 'Developing an integrative multi-semiotic model', in K. I. O'Halloran (ed.), *Multimodal Discourse Analysis: Systemic Functional Perspectives*. London/New York: Continuum, pp. 220–46.

Machin, D. (2007), *Introduction to Multimodal Analysis*. London: Hodder Arnold.

Machin, D. and van Leeuwen, T. (2007), *Global Media Discourse: A Critical Introduction*. London: Routledge.

Mazzarella, W. (2004), 'Culture, globalization, mediation', *Annual Review of Anthropology*, 33, 345–67.

McCrum, R., Cran, W. and MacNeil, R. (1986), *The Story of English*. London/Boston: Faber and Faber/BBC Books.

Milani, T. M. (2008), 'Language testing and citizenship: a language ideological debate in Sweden'. *Language in Society*, 37(1), 27–59.

Milani, T. M. and Johnson, S. (2008a), 'CDA and language ideology: towards a reflexive approach to discourse data', in I. H. Warnke and J. Spitzmüller (eds), *Methoden der Diskurslinguistik: sprachwissenschaftliche Zugänge zur transtextuellen Ebene*. Berlin: Mouton de Gruyter, pp. 365–88.

Milani, T. M. and Johnson, S. (2008b), 'Language politics and legitimation crisis in Sweden: a Habermasian approach'. *Language Problems and Language Planning*, 32(1), 1–22.

Morley, D. (2000), *Home Territories: Media, Mobility and Identity*. London: Routledge.

Mugglestone, L. (2007), *Talking Proper: The Rise of Accent as Social Symbol*. Oxford: Oxford University Press.

Nielsen, J. and Tahir, M. (2002), *Homepage Usability: 50 Websites Deconstructed*. Indianapolis, IN: New Riders.

Norris, S. (2004), *Analyzing Multimodal Interaction: A Methodological Framework*. London: Routledge.

O'Halloran, K. I. (ed.) (2004), *Multimodal Discourse Analysis: Systemic Functional Perspectives*. London/New York: Continuum.

Pennycook, A. (2004), 'Performativity and language studies'. *Critical Inquiry in Language Studies: An International Journal*, 1(1), 1–19.

Peters, J. D. (1997), 'Seeing bifocally: media, place, culture', in A. Gupta and J. Ferguson (eds), *Culture, Power, Place: Explorations in Critical Anthropology*. Durham: Duke University Press, pp. 75–92.

Petersoo, P. (2007), 'What does "we" mean? National deixis in the media', *Journal of Language and Politics*, 6(3), 419–36.

Robertson, R. (1994), 'Globalization or glocalization?' *The Journal of International Communication*, 1(1), 33–52.

Rose, A. and Mowbray. F. (no date), The UK Speaks (working title). BBC Nations and Regions. BBC Cymru Wales.

Silverstein, M. (1998), 'Contemporary transformations of local linguistic communities'. *Annual Review of Anthropology*, 27, 401–26.

Spitulnik, D. (1999), 'Media'. *Journal of Linguistics Anthropology*, 9(1-2), 148–51.

Stöckl, H. (2004), 'In between modes: language and image in printed media', in E. Ventola, C. Charles and M. Kaltenbacher (eds), *Perspectives on Multimodality*. Amsterdam: John Benjamins, pp. 9–30.

Talbot, M. (2007), *Media Discourse: Representation and Interaction*. Edinburgh: Edinburgh University Press.

The Observer (29 May 2005), Robin McKie, BBC forecasts a greater Scotland.

Upton, C. and Llamas, C. (1999), 'Two large scale and long term language variation studies: a retrospective and a plan'. *Cuadernos de Filología Inglesa*, 8, 291–304.

Upton, C., Parry, D. and Widdowson, J. D. A. (1994), *Survey of English Dialects: The Dictionary and Grammar*. London: Routledge.

Upton, C. and Widdowson, J. D. A. (2006), *An Atlas of English Dialect*. 2nd edn. London: Routledge.

van Leeuwen, T. (1999), *Speech, Music, Sound*. London: Macmillan.

van Leeuwen, T. (2002), 'Colour as a semiotic mode: notes for a grammar of colour'. *Visual Communication*, 1(3), 343–68.

van Leeuwen, T. (2004), *Introducing Social Semiotics*. London: Routledge.

van Leeuwen, T. (2005), 'Typographic meaning'. *Visual Communication*, 4(2), 137–43.

van Leeuwen, T. (2007), 'Sound and vision'. *Visual Communication*, 6(2), 136–45.

13 'It's not a telescope, it's a telephone': encounters with the telephone on early commercial sound recordings

Richard Bauman

13.1 Introduction

The turn of the twentieth century in the U.S. was a period of burgeoning development in the domain of communicative technologies. In the decades bracketing 1900, for example, the telephone greatly expanded its subscriber base and its range of application (Fischer 1992: 43–50; Marvin 1988: 64); motion pictures emerged as a commercially successful form of popular entertainment (Bowser 1994; Gomery 1992); and the phonograph was re-fashioned from a business tool to a medium of entertainment, based upon the mass marketing of commercial recordings (Gelatt 1977; Kenney 1999; Millard 1995; Welch and Burt 1994). Developments such as these have been the focus of increasing attention on the part of social historians and historians of the media in recent years, with specific attention to such themes as the history of science and technology, the growth of entrepreneurship and commodity culture, the re-figuration of public culture, and the recasting of social theory and ideologies of modernity (Briggs and Burke 2002). This is all rich and productive work, of great relevance to media anthropology and to social anthropology more generally. As a linguistic anthropologist, however, I am especially interested in how the advent of new communicative technologies is attended by transformations in communicative practice and experience, that is, in the production and reception of discourse or in the dynamics of communicative interaction. On these matters, there is still relatively little in the scholarly literature. What does mediation mean in terms of communicative practice? How is mediated communication actually managed by participants? How is it experienced? How do neophyte participants engage with new communicative technologies? (See also Ensslin, Chapter 11, this volume, for a look at related issues in the context of computer games.)

All of these questions, of course, are amenable to ethnographic investigation in contemporary societies. When it comes to the study of historical cases, however, a key problem is the identification of sources that will yield the kinds of data we need to reveal the processes and relationships and experiences with which we are concerned and the language ideologies that gave them shape. One especially illuminating source, I have discovered, is early media culture itself, in particular, early commercial sound recordings. The formative period in the development of commercial sound recording in the U.S. was marked by a high degree of reflexivity, as producers and consumers explored the capacities of the new medium and its attractions as a commodified form of popular entertainment. Vernacular entertainments are by their very nature a rich outlet for the expression of popular consciousness, and the social and cultural and ideological resonances of new communicative technologies at the turn of the twentieth century made them attractive symbolic resources for exploitation in popular culture. Accordingly, we find in the catalogues of early record companies recordings portraying people's engagements with the phonograph itself, with motion pictures, and with the telephone. I will deal in this chapter with one small set of these reflexive recordings, that is, phonographic performances of first experiences, or first experiences under novel conditions, with the telephone. I will look in particular at three revealing examples, one involving an Irish protagonist, the second a Jewish immigrant, and the third a rural New Englander in the city, as they try to come terms with this new medium of communication.

13.2 Casey at the telephone

Let me begin with the earliest example I have, a recording entitled 'Casey at the Telephone,' recorded by Russell Hunting around 1896. Hunting was a specialist in Irish dialect humor, known for his virtuosic ability to voice several characters in a single performance (Gracyk 2000: 180–83). He recorded a fascinating range of sketches featuring Michael Casey, an Irish immigrant apparently from Cork, judging by his accent. Casey is thus doubly marked as a clodhopper: Cork men are stereotyped as backward in Ireland, and Irish immigrants were stereotyped as ignorant greenhorns in the U.S. The opening announcement, typical of recordings from this period, informs us that the performance will represent Casey's 'first experience in using the telephone.'[1]

> **(i) Russell Hunting, 'Casey at the Telephone,' (ca. 1895), Columbia wax cylinder 9618**
>
> **Announcer** Michael Casey's first experience in using the, uh, telephone. A selection by Russell Hunting.

```
          [Knocking 9 raps]
          Clerk          Come in.
          [More knocking 9 raps].
          Clerk          Come in, sir, come in.
5                        [Door latch clicks]
          Casey          Heh heh. Good mahnin', sir
          Clerk          How d'you do?
          Casey          Yes, and I am, uh, would like to ask ye if I'd be let
                         speak in yer thermometer.
          Clerk          What's that?
10        Casey          Could I speak in yer thermometer?
          Clerk          Wh-wh-what do you mean?
          Casey          I mean that little electrical wire thing there on the wall.
          Clerk          Oh, the telephone!
          Casey          That's it. Yes, that's the thing.
15                       Would I be let speak in it?
          Clerk          Why, certainly.
                         Ah, do you know how to operate the telephone?
          Casey          Operate? Faith, I drove an ice wagon for three years.
          Clerk          Hah hah hah hah hah. That's all right, go ahead.
20        Casey          Yes, I'm much obliged.
                         Now I, I take, I just ring the bell here, and . . . and
                         speak in the little hole there.
          Clerk          Yes, that's right.
          Casey          All right, here she goes.
          [Ringing]
25                       I don't hear a thing but some b'iling water.
                         Just say whatever, must be a little girl [?].
                         Hello, little girl. Hello lit-
                         Whose place?
                         What do I want?
30                       I want to speak with Denny Murphy, in South Bend.
                         South Bend, Indiany.
                         Yes, he's a little man with red whiskers and overalls,
                         and 'e wears shoes.
                         Hmm? What number?
                         Right on the main street, he's in the, by the drugstore
                         there.
35                       The second door from the Truegood [?] Apothecary.
                         Eh? All right, I'll wait.
                         Spell it out: South Bend.
                         C-O-U-T-H South, B-U-I-N-D Bend
                         Yes, I'll wait here, all ri- . . . I'll not go 'way, certainly,
                         yes
40        Operator       I have that number: twenty-two  thirty-six
          Casey          Eh?
          Operator       Twenty-two thirty-six.
```

	Casey	Ah, no, South Bend. What's the matter with you?
		Denny Murphy.
45	**Angry voice**	Get off the wire!
	Casey	Who, who, who's a liar?
		Listen [agitated]: Look through this place here [?]
		Who says that?
		Some man says that I'm a liar.
50		I can lick the man who said that.
		Oh, no, that's a mistake.
		I'll bet you two dollars it's a man.
		Never mind, here's Murphy now.
		[Shouting] Hey! hey!
55		Murphy! Are you there?
		Casey's on the other end talkin'!
		Mike Casey.
		Yes! Am I speaking too loud for you?
		Yes! Why haven't you been to work for the last two days?
60		Yes, why haven't you been to work?
		What?! You don't tell me!
		Ohhh, hah hah hah hah hah.
		When was this?
		Tuesday night.
65		Ah, what is it, a boy or a, or a child?
		A little girl.
		Ten pounds, ahhh!
		Well, well, well, well, well, yer the sly devil.
		Hah hah hah hah hah!
70		Yes, certainly, I'll be over.
		I'll come right over now.
		I'll walk over in a hack [?]
		Yes, good bye to you.
		Oh, some Hageny water? Yes.
75		Beer and oysters!
		Good! Heh hah hah.
		That's great air there in South Bend, ain't it?
		Hah hah hah hah hah!

Now, what does this little enactment suggest to us about users' first encounter with the new communicative technology of the telephone? One striking element, I would suggest, is the sheer extent and complexity of the effort required to make it do what it is supposed to do, namely, put you into spoken contact with a distant interlocutor across a spatial gap. Note that Casey doesn't connect with the person he's calling, Denny Murphy, until line 53. Before he can talk with his friend, he has to negotiate a complex array of mediational barriers, and it is illuminating to trace his trajectory through the levels of mediation he has to traverse. For the purposes of this analysis, I follow Parmentier (1985: 25) in defining mediation as 'any process in which two elements are brought into articulation by means of or through the intervention of some third element that serves as the vehicle of medium of communication between them.'

First, Casey has to gain access to the telephone itself, which alone is no easy task, especially if you don't have a phone of your own and you've never done it before. In order to use the phone, Casey has to be authorized to do so by the gatekeeper on the premises where the phone is located, unspecified here, but probably a pharmacy, which is where most public phones were located in this early period (Aronson 1977: 32; Marvin 1988: 105–6). Again, the identity of the gatekeeper is unspecified, but I have called him a clerk, for convenience. There's a big status asymmetry here and Casey is accordingly very tentative and deferential: his speech is full of hesitation phenomena, false starts, repairs, and politeness forms. He doesn't even know the proper name for the telephone, committing the gaffe of calling it a thermometer. It is apparent to the clerk that Casey is a rank neophyte, so he asks him whether he knows how to use the telephone. Casey has a bit of an idea, likely from observation of others, and when the clerk confirms the technique, he gathers himself up and tries it: 'All right, here she goes.' Having rung the bell, however, Casey is not at all sure whether 'she goes' or not: all he hears is the hissing on the line, which he takes for boiling water.

But then it does work, and Casey has negotiated the second barrier, only to encounter the third level of mediation in his effort to make a telephone call: the operator. Yet again, he doesn't know quite how to manage the interaction. He greets her warmly, but she's all business; she wants from him the kind of identifying information that is necessary to put through his call: the identity of the person he wants to reach, his location, his phone number. Casey does his best, offering a physical description of Denny Murphy and the location of his house, taking the number requested by the operator to be Murphy's street address. Both are potentially useful guides to finding Murphy on the ground, but neither is at all relevant to making contact by telephone. He goes on to misspell South Bend as well, but the operator manages to find Denny Murphy's telephone number nevertheless. But now Casey has no idea what that number means and angrily falls back on Murphy's city and name: South Bend, Denny Murphy. In all, it's a difficult, vexed interaction – confusing and frustrating for Casey.

But it's not over yet. While Casey is still fussing with the operator, a fourth obstacle appears: a testy voice telling him to get off the wire, perhaps a wrong number, perhaps someone on a party line – it's not entirely clear. In any event, because of the technical limitations of the telephone, its lack of acoustic clarity and fidelity, perhaps compounded by Casey's own state of annoyance, he mishears the instruction to get off the wire as someone calling him a liar – fighting words. Or, Casey decides, calming down a bit, maybe not – maybe it's a mistake. But then, at last, he finally makes contact with Denny Murphy.

Let's take stock for a moment, considering all the layers of mediation Casey has had to go through to connect with his friend, Denny Murphy. The first level of mediation is the pharmacy clerk, the gatekeeper of access to the telephone. The difficulties at this level stem from the status asymmetry between Casey and the clerk, from Casey's supplicant position as the party who wants access to a material resource controlled by someone else, and from his own insecurities concerning his competence actually to use the thing. The second layer of mediation is the telephone mechanism itself, an esoteric technology which has to be manipulated by the proper technique to make it work. Once he has activated the telephone and worried about whether he has done it right, since all he hears is the hiss of the circuit noise, he encounters the next point of mediation, in the person of the operator. Casey doesn't quite know what she wants of him, and gets worked up by the mixed signals of their interaction. While he's in that disgruntled state, some irate party seems to get in his face by calling him a liar – or so he hears the injunction to get off the wire. And it's not until he gets past that impediment, which would short-circuit his call, that he finally connects with Murphy. The recorded performance is thus in effect a compendium of anxieties, obstacles, problems, vulnerabilities to which a neophyte approaching the telephone is susceptible.

The conversation with Murphy goes smoothly enough once the connection is made. The principal feature that shows Casey to be a neophyte telephone user is his tendency to shout into the phone, understandable both as a compensation for the limitations of the technology he has already encountered in talking to the operator and as a reflex action stimulated by the spatial distance between Murphy and himself. Perhaps the most noteworthy thing about the mediated conversation is that it winds up in the service of setting up an unmediated visit between the two friends, as Casey arranges to go 'right over' to Murphy's house (cf. Fischer 1992: 238).

To this point, we have focused our attention on the structures of mediation involved in the task of making a telephone call and the attendant difficulties experienced by a neophyte user in his first encounter with the new communicative technology. In the course of our considerations, however, we have been drawn to take note of various sociocultural factors implicated in Casey's effort to call his friend.

257

Let's turn more closely to this aspect of the recording, reading what we can out of the interactions enacted in the performance. What can we tell about Casey and his interlocutors from what they say, how they behave, and the interactions in which they engage?

The first person to speak in this recorded enactment is the clerk, responding to the knock on the door with an invitation to enter the premises: an innocuous, polite access ritual, including the generic honorific term of address, 'sir'. When Casey returns the greeting, though, the social contrast between the two men is immediately manifest. The clerk speaks standard English, well modulated and polite; Casey speaks with the broad accent of an Irish immigrant from Cork. The status asymmetry indexed by their respective speech styles is marked further by Casey's deferential manner: the hesitation phenomena, the false starts, the indirection of his initial request to use the phone, framed in the passive voice (Brown and Levinson 1987: 57, 94, 194–97), including Casey's malapropism – 'if I'd be let to speak in your thermometer.' Casey is the supplicant in this encounter, having to petition the socially superior clerk for access to a technological resource that the latter controls, and to thank him for the favor when the access is granted. Moreover, Hunting casts Casey as subordinate in knowledge and competence as well, calling the telephone a thermometer and being tentative about how to use it. And of course, the status asymmetry is further manifest in Casey's menial occupation – driving an ice wagon – as against the white-collar profession of the clerk and in his marginal literacy, evidenced by his misspelling of South Bend.

Consider also Casey's demeanor, equally heavily marked with diacritics of class. Most importantly, he is vividly emotional and mercurial in his mood swings. Look, for instance, at the affective profile of his interaction with the operator: coy in his initial greeting, brusque when she asks him what he wants, submissive when she interrupts him, impatient when he believes she's not attending to the identifying information he has given her for Denny Murphy, belligerent and ready to fight when he thinks he's being called a liar. Then, when he finally makes contact with Murphy, he's excited, loud, boisterous, given to outbursts of laughter. He is, in other words, the antithesis of the decorous, calm, measured model of bourgeois respectability (Agha 2003).

All in all, then, Casey is heavily, redundantly marked as lower class: by ethnic origin, language, occupation, marginal literacy, ignorance, deference, demeanor, all linked to his awkwardness and incompetence in using the telephone. He is impressively contrasted with the urbane, confident, clerk, and even with the operator – young and female, but sharply competent and very much in control of the technology she serves.

258

13.3 Cohen at the telephone

For comparative purposes, let us turn to another recorded representation of an immigrant's first encounter with the telephone, this one dating from 1916. The protagonist is a European Jew, Mr. Cohen, performed by Barney Bernard, a stage actor and one of many comic performers to record this sketch (Corenthal 1984: 6–7). In fact, 'Cohen at the Telephone' was enormously popular; Michael Corenthal (1984), who has done the most to document the Cohen oeuvre, lists more than twenty recordings of the piece, by nine performers, issued between 1913 and 1928. Bernard's is one of the earliest. In addition to the multiple recordings of this telephone sketch, Cohen figured in an extended array of additional performances, as he navigated and negotiated his way through the vagaries of immigrant life in America. But it all started with 'Cohen at the Telephone.'

(ii) Barney Bernard, 'Cohen at the Telephone,' (March 17, 1916), Victor 18029-A

Announcer: A description of the efforts of Mr. Cohen to use the telephone for the first time. Mr. Cohen is trying to call up the manager of a certain bank, who happens to be his landlord. The conversation is as follows.

> **Cohen:** Hello, are you dere?
> Hello, hello, vat?
> Vat number do I vant?
> Vat numbers have you got?
> 5   Huh! 'scuse me, my fault.
> I vant Central 248, please.
> Yes, dot's right.
> 248.
> I say, Miss,
> 10   am I supposed to keep on saying "are you dere?" und hello" till
>   you come back again?
> Vell, don't be long.
> Hello, und are you dere?
> Oh, yes, are you the bank*er*?
> I vant to see the manager, please.
> 15   I vant to see . . .
> Vat do you say?
> This is not a telescope, it's a telephone.
> You're very clever dis morning, ain't you?
> Vell do me a favor:
> 20   Hang a small piece of crepe on your nose – your brains are dead.
>   Und if I have any more of your impertinence, I'll speak to the
>   manager about you.

259

Richard Bauman

I say, I'll speak to the . . . Oh, you're the manager.
I beg your pardon.
I'm much obliged.
25 Say, Mr. Manager, I rang up to say I'm your tenant, Cohen.
I say, I'm your tenant, Cohen.
I ain't goin', I'm sittin' here.
[louder] I'm your tenant, Co-
Not Lieutenant Cohen.
30 I vant to tell you that last night de vind came and blew down the shutter outside of my house,
und I vant you to send . . .
I say, last night de vind came and . . . de *vind*, de *vind*!
V-I-N-D, vi-
Not de devil.
35 De *vind*! de *vind*!
Don't you know vat [fsssh], like dot.
Vell, dot blew mye shutter down outside o' my house,
und I vant you to . . .
I say, it blew de shutter out, de shutter!
40 No, I didn't say "shut up."
No, de shutter, de ting vot goes down de front of de shop.
I vant you to send a car*pen*ter to mend de shutter.
I say, I vant you to send a car*pen*ter to mend de shutter.
To mend de . . .
45 Not de tremendous shutter, no.
Hello, are you dere?
Last night de vind came and blew down de shutter outside of my house,
und I vant you to send a car*pen*ter.
[loud] A car*pen*ter!
50 A voiking man.
Yes, you know.
One of dose fellows vot hits de hammer vit de nail.
Dot's it: a voikman I vant you to send . . .
a voikman to mend de damaged shutter.
55 I say, I vant you to send a voikman to mend . . .
[loud] To mend!
Not two men, no!
One man to mend . . .
One man to mend de damaged shutter, to mend de damaged . . .
60 I ain't swearing at you.
I'm only telling you.
Are you dere?
[slowly and deliberately] Last night, de vind came and blew down de shutter outside of my house,
und I vant you to send a car*pen*ter, a car-, a carp-
65 Oy, never mind.
I'll have it fixed myself.

260

Again, as with Casey, an announcement sets the stage: 'A description of the efforts of Mr. Cohen to use the telephone for the first time. Mr. Cohen is trying to call up the manager of a certain bank, who happens to be his landlord. The conversation is as follows.' In this recording, however, there is no larger dramatic frame; the entire sketch consists of the phone call itself, though we know in advance from the announcement that Cohen will be interacting with a figure of status and power, both bank manager and landlord, a formidable combination. All we hear, though, is Cohen's voice, marked by his Jewish accent. A significant number of his utterances are double-voiced, to be sure, but Cohen is the only speaker we actually hear.

As with Casey, Cohen's efforts to accomplish his phone call are complicated by a number of impediments. All of the problems are grounded in the medium, though some are compounded by other factors as well. The very opening line of the monologue points toward one of the principal difficulties Cohen experiences in trying to make sense of the mediated communication of the telephone as a communicative technology. While 'Hello, are you there?' is a compound form of conventional telephone greeting routine, established very early in the history of the medium (Feaster 2006), 'are you there?' is deeply grounded in the nature of telephonic communication: the spatial separation of the interlocutors and the absence of any other means of establishing co-presence and communicative accessibility. It is a phatic monitoring device, a way of determining whether contact has been accomplished. Cohen, experiencing the telephone for the first time, already knows the appropriate opening, but he is nevertheless uncertain about the connection whenever his interlocutor – the operator or the party he has called – isn't speaking. Thus, in lines 9–10, Cohen is impelled to ask the operator for guidance, both about proper usage and about the maintenance of communicative contact. And then it happens twice more, during his conversation with his landlord, in lines 46 and 62: 'Are you there?' These phatic checks occur at what are, for Cohen, turn-transition points in the conversation. When his landlord doesn't respond, Cohen feels the need to confirm verbally – in the absence of other cues – that he's still connected and engaged.

Part of what is missing, of course, are the visual cues of engagement that are available in situations of physical co-presence. Telephone contact relies solely on the acoustic channel, and that takes some getting used to. This realignment of sensory modalities is another expressive device exploited in the performance. Still oriented primarily to face-to-face interaction, and not yet attuned to the technological limitations of the telephone, Cohen – in lines 14–17 – tells the person who answers the phone at the bank that he wants to '*see* the manager.' His interlocutor

261

corrects him: 'This is not a telescope, it's a telephone,' that is, it is about sound, not sight.

The biggest, and ultimately the most frustrating, problem that Cohen encounters in using the telephone is making himself understood. Time and again, in the course of the conversation, his banker-landlord mishears what he says: 'going' for 'Cohen' (line 27), 'Lieutenant Cohen' for 'your tenant Cohen' (line 29), 'devil' for 'de vind' (line 34), 'shut up' for 'shutter' (line 40), 'tremendous shutter' for 'to mend de shutter' (line 45), 'two men' for 'to mend' (line 57), 'damned shutter' for 'damaged shutter' (line 60), and so on. One basis for the miscommunication, we are to assume, is Cohen's heavy Yiddish accent. There is another recorded routine of Cohen on the telephone in which his interlocutor tells him to 'speak more distinctly' (Corenthal 1984: 55), suggesting that we are meant to attribute at least part of the disjunction to Cohen's accent. The early telephone, though, enhances the capacity for confusion, its lack of acoustic fidelity and clear transmission of sound exacerbating the inherent lack of clarity in Cohen's accented speech. Several of the misunderstandings are especially disruptive, insofar as the landlord takes them as insults or improprieties, in the same vein that Casey hears 'liar' for 'wire' and takes it as a challenge.

Compounding Cohen's travails still further is his landlord's propensity for interruption – eleven times in all, in this brief routine. Nine of the interruptions seem to be occasioned by his landlord's failure to understand what he is saying and to ask for repetition or clarification. We might take these nine instances as power-neutral, insofar as a lack of comprehensibility is an impediment to efficient communication and a request for clarification is in the interest of accurate comprehension. Still, the interruptions come at such a frequent and insistent rate that Cohen experiences them as intrusive, disruptive, and frustrating. We get the feeling that Cohen is trying hard to make himself understood and the landlord isn't making much of an effort. For Cohen, the relentless interruptions add up to a power move on the part of a higher-status individual to a social subordinate, both in terms of ethnicity and class (Goldberg 1990).

The status asymmetry between Cohen and his interlocutor is manifest in the exchanges in lines 14–24. When the person at the other end of the line makes the snide comment about how it's not a telescope, it's a telephone, Cohen has a quick rejoinder, an injunction to 'Hang a small piece of crepe on your nose, your brains are dead' and his threat to report the impertinence to the manager. On finding out that his interlocutor *is* the manager, however, Cohen quickly retreats, offering an apology, thanks when it is apparently accepted, and addressing the landlord respectfully as 'Mr. Manager.'

Note that Cohen is also deferential to the operator at the beginning of the sketch. Echoing Casey's confusion about what kind of number the operator is asking for, Cohen responds with 'Vat numbers have you got?' But then he realizes what is at issue, and quickly turns on the politeness, with an apology and a 'please' in the course of giving her the telephone number he wants to reach. Clearly, the idea of having a telephone number as an identificational and locative device was a novel idea and also took some getting used to.

Ultimately, however, in an intriguing contrast with 'Casey at the Telephone,' Cohen's phone call is an interactional and communicative failure. Whereas Casey does get past the rough spots in using the telephone, reaches Denny Murphy, has a cordial conversation with him, and ends up arranging a face-to-face celebratory visit, Cohen despairs of ever making himself understood. Giving up on his final, slow, deliberate, carefully enunciated effort to get across to his landlord what he wants, he resolves to fix the damaged shutter himself and terminates the call. He is defeated both by the telephone and by the opacity of his banker-landlord.

13.4 The old country fiddler at the telephone

The final example I will take up here is a bit different from the others. It is not a representation of a first encounter with the telephone, but rather, of the relationship between the telephone and various aspects of social transformation in early twentieth-century America. The recording is 'The Old Country Fiddler at the Telephone,' performed by Charles Ross Taggart, who styled himself as 'the man from Vermont'. Like Casey and Cohen, the Old Country Fiddler was a show-business persona sustained over an extensive range of recorded performances (University of Iowa Traveling Culture website). He was the homespun rustic from a small rural town, one variant of a broader symbolic type that ranged from the country rube – ignorant, backward, credulous – to the cracker-barrel philosopher, an object of fond nostalgia. These rural and small-town characters were an important symbolic vehicle for constructing and charting the advent of modernity, the urbanization and bourgeoisification of the U.S., the advent of new technologies, the growth of consumerism, the transformation of subjectivities and social relations, and other correlates of massive social change. Only the first part of 'The Old Country Fiddler at the Telephone' relates specifically to the telephone as a communicative technology; that portion of the record is as follows:

> (iii) Charles Ross Taggart, 'Old Country Fiddler at the Telephone,' (June 21, 1916), Victor 18148-A

Hellooo, Central?
Say, I want to talk with my son.
Eh?
My son.
5   Yes, he's here in New York City,
been here a year and a half.
Number?
Oh, just one, all the rest are gals.
What?
10   His number?
Whose?
My son's?
Heavens to Betsy, he ain't in jail, is he?
What's that?
15   Information?
What about?
Oh, his name is, uh, John Jackson.
1500 West 86th Street.
What's that?
20   H. O. J. Hollins?
Who's that?
Oh, that's prob'ly the man he works for.
Hello. Hello! Who's this?
Oh, Central, got back to you, have we?
25   Well, say, Central, I want to talk with Mr. H. O. J. Hollins.
Hello, is this Mr. Hollins?
Oh, this is you, is it, John?
Hello, John.
Say, this is me, Dad.

The entire opening segment of this recording, transcribed above, is taken up with the interaction – by now familiar to us – of the caller and the operator, here addressed as 'Central,' a common designation in this period. Listeners of the day would have recognized that the Old Country Fiddler is engaging with the operator in a rural mode. Rural and small town operators knew everyone in the network they served, how they were related, where they could be reached (Fischer 1992: 168). So, when the Old Country Fiddler tells the operator that he wants to speak with his son, he is assuming that she will know who he's talking about and readily make the connection. But then, in lines 5–6, we discover that he's not at home in Vermont, but in New York City, where his son now lives, and the frame of reference shifts.

The operator, once again in a manner we've seen before, asks for a number. Unfamiliar with the system of telephone numbers as identifiers, the Old Country Fiddler thinks she's asking how many sons he has. When it becomes apparent that that's not the information she wants, and she repeats the request, the Old Country Fiddler comes up with the only other basis on which his son might have a number, and fears that he is in prison. Again, a wrong assumption.

Still looking for identifying features that might serve in the large urban setting of New York City, the operator asks for 'information,' but our rustic caller still doesn't get it. Finally, he produces his son's name and an address, and the latter ultimately yields a phone listing in the name of the son's employer, H. O. J. Hollins. The Old Country Fiddler is ready to settle for that possibility, asks to talk to Mr. Hollins, and greets him when he answers. But it's not Hollins after all, but the Old Country Fiddler's son – the sought-after party – who answers the phone. This problem of misidentification is similar to the problem Cohen had in recognizing who was on the other end of the line. When you can't see your interlocutor, it's difficult to identify him.

Altogether, fully one-third of the recording is taken up with the Old Country Fiddler's effort to make the telephone connection, in a social and communicative environment that is unfamiliar to him. Urban identities and identifiers, together with the mediated nature of telephonic communication, represent impediments to interactional access.

13.5 Recorded performances

Thus far, we have considered what the enacted representations on the recordings reveal to us about neophytes' engagement with the telephone as a mediated technology of communication. Our examination has revealed a range of problems, dimensions of awkwardness and anxiety in managing the technology, making contact with the person one is trying to call, and carrying off the conversation. We have not yet, however, confronted the problem of how these encounters with the telephone are symbolically represented. What we are dealing with are recorded performances about telephone use, in which engagement with the new medium serves as an expressive resource. The performances are symbolic enactments. How are these enactments constructed, and what does their form and performance reveal not only about the telephone, but about the phonograph as communicative technologies?

One basic problem in representing mediated communication in performance lies in establishing a vantage point for the audience, an alignment to the represented action. Mediation – for the telephone and other communicative technologies we consider as 'media' – involves spatial separation. In practical terms, there is no inherent reason why sound recordings could not devise some means of representing both sides of a telephone conversation; we have seen some gestures in that direction in Casey's exchanges with the operator and with the person who tells him to get off the line. For listeners to early recordings, though, in the period we are considering, the default orienting framework for engagement with a performance was established by live, embodied, co-present, situated performance, in which you could not be in two places at the same time. This default expectation, I suggest, impelled the performative representation of telephone conversations toward alignment with one end of the mediated conversation, toward one party. The person at the other end of the line is physically removed, and his or her voice is audible only to the person performatively before us with the receiver to his ear. In addition, I believe that the very strangeness of overhearing only one end of a mediated conversation was itself a significant part of the contemporary fascination with the telephone. Most importantly, however, I would suggest that representation of only one side of the telephone conversation is a very effective device for the elicitation of participative engagement on the part of the audience. It calls for special interpretive work, the effort of trying to reconstruct mentally what is elided when one is shut off from one side of an ongoing conversation. To draw listeners into this more intensive interpretive work is to draw them more strongly into participative involvement in the performance. How, then, to represent the dialogic nature of the conversation from only one side? Let us consider the performative devices employed on our recordings to manage this task.

Consider, for example, lines 14-17 from 'Cohen at the Telephone.'

> I vant to see the manager, please.
> I vant to see . . . .
> Vat do you say?
> This is not a telescope, it's a telephone.

These four utterances, spoken by Cohen, are what we hear in the performance. But let's try to reconstruct the other side of the conversation. What does the bank manager/landlord say? Well, in line 14, we hear Cohen start to repeat what he has said in line 13, from which we can infer that his interlocutor has solicited the repetition, perhaps something to the effect of 'What did you say?' or 'I didn't hear you.' Then, in line 15, Cohen himself solicits a repetition: 'Vat do you say?' Note that both of these solicited repetitions are well motivated in terms of the performance routine itself, which revolves part around imperfections in the carrying capacity of the technology. 'Cohen at the Telephone' is replete with solicited repetition, often indexed by Cohen's 'I say . . . ' preceding his reiteration of his antecedent utterance (e.g., lines 25, 31, 38, etc.). Cohen's echo utterance in line 16, makes clear that the manager has said 'This is not a telescope, it's a telephone,' both between

Cohen's lines 15 and 16 and lines 16 and 17. Thus, we can reconstruct the conversation as follows; the italicized lines represent the side of the conversation we do not hear:

Cohen:	I vant to see the manager, please.
Manager:	*What did you say?*
Cohen:	I vant to see . . . .
Manager:	*This is not a telescope, it's a telephone.*
Cohen:	Vat do you say?
Manger:	*This is not a telescope, it's a telephone.*
Cohen:	This is not a telescope, it's a telephone.

Echo utterances in these performances often take the form of echo questions, as in Casey's 'What do I want?' (line 30) or 'What number?' (line 34), or the Old Country Fiddler's 'His number?' (line 10) or 'Who's that?' (line 21). After echoing the question originally posed by the absent interlocutor, the party we can hear – Casey or the Old Country Fiddler or whomever – can then supply the answer.

Consider another passage: lines 36–41 from 'Casey at the Telephone,' part of Casey's interaction with the operator prior to being connected with Denny Murphy:

36 Eh?
All right, I'll wait
Spell it out: South Bend.
C-O-U-T-H South, B-U-I-N-D, Bend.
40 Yes, I'll wait here, all ri- . . .
I'll not go 'way, certainly, yes.

We encounter in this passage some of the same devices we have already observed: for example, the request for repetition ('Eh?' line 36) and the echo statement ('Spell it out,' line 38). In lines 40 and 41, however, Hunting makes use of another cohesion device in conjunction with echo statements, namely rejoinders of assent and denial. 'Yes,' 'all right,' 'I'll *not* go 'way,' and 'certainly, yes' tie these utterances to antecedent ones we can't hear by assuming a positive or negative alignment to them. We can infer, then, that the operator has said 'Wait there' or 'Wait a moment' or something akin to those commands before Casey's 'All right, I'll wait,' and 'Wait there, don't go away' before 'Yes, I'll wait here, all ri- . . . I'll not go 'way, certainly, yes.'

These various cohesion devices, in which the audible utterances of the performance index the unheard antecedent utterances of the person at the other end of the telephone line, should suffice to suggest how the absent party, separated from the speaker we can hear – and from us – by the mediation of the telephone is restored to presence. The double-voicedness of Casey's and Cohen's and the Old Country Fiddler's utterances allows us interpretively to reconstruct both sides of the mediated encounter.

To consider the interpretive work of the audience in filling in the unheard side of the telephone conversations represented in these recordings is to open yet another dimension of mediation. Our focus on the telephone notwithstanding, we must not lose sight of the fact that what we are actually engaging with is phonograph recordings. How is this dimension of mediation managed?

The earliest of our recordings, 'Casey at the Telephone,' opens with an announcement: 'Michael Casey's first experience in using the, uh, telephone. A selection by Russell Hunting.' This announcement provides a contextualizing frame for what is to follow, by offering a summarizing precis, an abstract of the action. By calling the representation 'a selection,' the announcement also marks it as a text, a bounded stretch of represented discourse, extracted and set off from its discursive surround. And by naming the performer, Russell Hunting, the announcement further marks the recording as an enacted representation: Hunting is not Michael Casey, but assumes his persona and animates him in performance. Finally, note that the announcement frames the recording as a quintessentially public text, addressed to anyone and everyone among whom it may circulate, but to no one in particular. We as audience members activate the address and become the addressees by playing the record.

Immediately following the announcement, however, with the onset of the performance, we are recast from addressees to overhearers of the represented action, a dramatic skit in which the protagonist negotiates access to a telephone, makes his call, and engages in conversation with interlocutors on the other end of the line. The use of the telephone is inset into a larger enactment, contextualized by a larger dramatic frame. In the recording, however, the represented action is only accessible to us through the sensory modality of sound. Accordingly, Hunting has to find acoustic means of setting the scene, differentiating the dramatis personae, and representing their actions. In 'Casey at the Telephone,' he employs sound effects, such as the knocking and the clicking of the door latch, in conjunction with verbal access routines – 'Come in, sir, come in' and the greeting exchange – to do some of the scene-setting work, and takes on contrastive voices to differentiate the dramatis personae. Although we cannot see the setting in which the action takes place, Hunting helps us to visualize it and some of the action by such descriptive and deictic devices as 'I mean *that* little electrical thing there on the wall,' and 'I just ring *the bell here*, and . . . and speak in the *little hole there.*' For the most part, though, sound suffices. What is represented to us on the recording is primarily talk, an acoustic phenomenon, and we can get along fine as overhearers.

Like 'Casey at the Telephone,' 'Cohen at the Telephone' also opens with a contextualizing announcement: 'A description of the efforts of Mr. Cohen to use the telephone for the first time. Mr. Cohen is trying to call up the manager of a certain bank, who happens to be his landlord. The conversation is as follows.' 'Description' (or 'descriptive sketch') was the generic label for humorous skits in the popular entertainments of the period, so listeners knew immediately the kind of performance they were about to hear. The abstract identifies and describes the dramatis personae and the kind of action to be portrayed, specifying that the focal actor, the one who will provide our vantage point on the conversation is Cohen. And the final sentence informs us that the represented action will be an enactment of the telephone conversation itself, of which we will again be overhearers.

The switch from announcement to performance launches us right into the conversation itself, with a conventional formula for opening a telephone conversation. We know from the announcement that the speaker is Cohen. No framing drama, no, multiple voices, no sound effects: the whole performance consists of Cohen's talk. Note, then, that notwithstanding the announcement's assertion that 'The conversation is as follows,' what we overhear is only Cohen's side of the exchange. But, as we have seen, that's enough. Cohen's talk is so fully double-voiced that we can fill in the missing side of the conversation by hearing only what he has to say.

And finally, 'The Old Country Fiddler at the Telephone,' completely stripped down to the performance itself, without a framing announcement or other contextualizing information. There is one small break out of the telephone conversation, later in the recording, but it's a very minor bit of dramatic business. With this small exception, the entire performance consists of the Old Country Fiddler's side of the telephone conversation, framed by telephonic opening and closing formulae, and – as with the others – allowing us to reconstruct interpretively the other side of the conversation we cannot hear.

13.6 Conclusion

In one of the few sociolinguistically informed examinations of communicative technologies in relation to communicative practice, Ian Hutchby (2001: 30) urges attention specifically to users' practical engagement with such technologies in everyday life. For Hutchby, productively enough, that is a problem for empirical investigation: the examination of how to do things with communicative tools, subject to their inherent capacities.

My essay is obviously sympathetic to that orientation, but I'm interested in a further dimension of the problem. Communicative practices are historical and experiential emergents. No communicative technology is immediately, perfectly, transparently accessible to its users from the moment of its availability. When a tool first appears on the scene, people have to figure out what it can do, learn to use it, work at acquiring competence in its use (Gitelman and Pingree 2003). The first encounter with a new communicative technology is a richly interesting moment in the historical and experiential process, a formative moment, illuminated with regard to the telephone by the early recordings I have examined, themselves shaped by popular entertainments from the period in which the telephone was established as a widely accessible communicative technology. Analysis of the representations on the recordings illuminates the problems, difficulties, vulnerabilities, anxieties that users encountered in their efforts to deal with the technology and with the mediation involved in its use. It also reveals elements of the sociocultural affordances of the telephone, both with regard to access and to use.

To be sure, as symbolic representations of telephone use, the recorded enactments cannot be taken as fully transparent to reality; they are burlesques, built on exaggeration and caricature. But that is their virtue as well. To be so popular, the recordings must have struck a responsive chord of recognition in the audiences that listened to them, foregrounding popularly perceived elements of the experience of using a telephone for the first time. Significantly, though, the difficulties, infelicities, and displays of incompetence are projected in these recordings onto particular social categories: immigrants and rural people. In the early days of the telephone's commercial promotion as a means of communication, as Claude Fischer (1992: 81, 92, 97, 117) reveals, it was a widely held article of faith in the nascent industry that it wasn't fit for immigrants and rural people. Rather, the telephone was marketed to the middle and upper classes, and its assimilation became a diacritic of bourgeois modernity, linked to ideologies of communicative competence that valorized standard language, decorous comportment, and facility with technological innovations. Having a telephone and being competent in its use was a basis of distinction, and the purported incompetence of immigrant and rustic people was constructed as an object of amusement. And we must bear in mind that the marketers of commercial

270

sound recordings sought mainstream, middle-class audiences, those who could afford phonographs and records.

Some interpreters have suggested that this was all in good-natured fun, and that members of the very groups portrayed as incompetent users of the new technologies enjoyed the performance as good-humored representations of their own and their parents' earlier naivety. There is certainly a solid warrant for this interpretation (e.g. McLean 1965: 41–43; Nasaw 1993: 51–53). It is also important to acknowledge that notwith-standing their travails, our novice users of the telephone can neverthe-less ultimately succeed in connecting with the people they are trying to call and having a satisfying conversation; witness Casey and the Old Country Fiddler. And in Cohen's case, it is clear that a significant por-tion of the trouble he encounters is not his fault, stemming rather from the rudeness and indifference of his banker-landlord. That is to say, whatever apprehensions and difficulties they may encounter in using the telephone, Casey, Cohen, and the Old Country Fiddler do make a good effort, and we can well imagine that the next time they attempt a phone call, the process will be smoother and their efforts more assured. In any event, whether we hear the mocking laughter of non-members or the uneasy laughter of the already assimilated, the recorded representa-tions we have examined helped to define fields of communicability, in Charles Briggs's sense of the term (Briggs 2005), that is, structures of differential access to the production, circulation, and reception of dis-course and to the power and social capital that may accrue to author-ized and competent users. They illuminate not only the communicative mediation of the telephone and the phonograph, but the ways in which these new communicative technologies mediate structures of inequal-ity in society more generally.

Acknowledgments

I have presented earlier versions of this paper at the University of Michigan, New York University, Indiana University, and George Washington University. I am grateful to Misty Jaffe, Marilyn Merritt, and Lesley Milroy for valuable comments on those early drafts. Special thanks to Patrick Feaster for aiding and abetting my engagement with early commercial recordings in many ways, both material and intellectual.

Notes

1 In the transcriptions that follow, I have had two principal concerns in mind: (1) I intend the transcripts to convey that they are representations

of *spoken* language. The chief means I have employed to this end is non-standard spelling to capture features of pronunciation. I have not, however, resorted to eye-dialect. One of the recurrent problems in transcribing oral speech, especially oral speech in non-standard, vernacular dialects, is the danger of making the speakers appear to be unsophisticated bumpkins. I should make explicit, then, what will be even more obvious in my chapter, that those stereotypes are precisely what the *performers* are trying to convey, and if my transcriptions evoke them yet again, so much the better. (2) I have endeavored to represent by graphological means some of the significant formal patterning principles that organize the performances. Line breaks mark breath units, intonational units, and/or syntactic structures, which are usually – though not always – mutually aligned.

Primary sources

The original recordings of the extracts analysed are accessible online, through IU ScholarWorks, as follows:

'Casey at the Telephone,' https://scholarworks.iu.edu/dspace/handle/2022/3170.
'Cohen at the Telephone,' https://scholarworks.iu.edu/dspace/handle/2022/3172.
'Old Country Fiddler at the Telephone,' https://scholarworks.iu.edu/dspace/handle/2022/3171.

References

Agha, A. (2003), 'The social life of cultural value'. *Language and Communication*, 23(3–4), 231–73.
Aronson, S. H. (1977), 'Bell's electrical toy', in I. de Sola Pool, (ed.), *The Social Impact of the Telephone*. Cambridge, MA: MIT Press, pp. 15–39.
Bowser, E. (1994), *The Transformation of Cinema, 1907–1915*. Berkeley and Los Angeles: University of California Press.
Briggs, A. and Burke, P. (2002), *A Social History of the Media, from Gutenberg to the Internet*. Malden, MA: Polity Press.
Briggs, C. L. (2005), 'Communicability, racial discourse, and disease'. *Annual Review of Anthropology*, 34, 269–91.
Brown, P. and Levinson, S. C. (1987), *Politeness: Some Universals in Language Usage*. Cambridge: Cambridge University Press.
Corenthal, M. (1984), *Cohen on the Telephone: A History of Jewish Recorded Humor and Popular Music, 1892–1942*. Milwaukee: Yesterday's Memory.
Feaster, P. (2006), *'The Following Record': Making Sense of Phonographic Performance, 1877–1908*. Ph.D. dissertation, Folklore and Ethnomusicology, Indiana University, Bloomington.
Fischer, C. S. (1992), *America Calling: A Social History of the Telephone to 1940*. Berkeley and Los Angeles: University of California Press.

Gelatt, R. (1977), *The Fabulous Phonograph, 1877–1977*. New York: Macmillan.

Gitelman, L. and Pingree, G. B. (eds) (2003), *New Media, 1740–1915*. Cambridge, MA: MIT Press.

Goldberg, J. A. (1990), 'Interrupting the discourse on interruptions: an analysis in terms of relationally neutral, power- and rapport-oriented acts'. *Journal of Pragmatics*, 14(6), 883–903.

Gomery, D. (1992), *Shared Pleasures: A History of Movie Production in the United States*. Madison, WI: University of Wisconsin Press.

Gracyk, T. (2000), *Popular American Recording Pioneers, 1895–1925*. New York: Haworth Press.

Hutchby, I. (2001), *Conversation and Technology: From the Telephone to the Internet*. Malden, MA: Polity Press.

Kenney, W. H. (1999), *Recorded Music in American Life: The Phonograph and Popular Memory, 1890–1945*. Oxford: Oxford University Press.

Marvin, C. (1988), *When Old Technologies Were New: Thinking About Electric Communication in the Late Nineteenth Century*. Oxford: Oxford University Press.

McLean, A. F., Jr. (1965), *American Vaudeville as Ritual*. Lexington, KY: University of Kentucky Press.

Millard, A. (1995), *America on Record: A History of Recorded Sound*. Cambridge: Cambridge University Press.

Nasaw, D. (1993), *Going Out: The Rise and Fall of Public Amusements*. New York: Basic Books.

Parmentier, R. J. (1985), 'Signs' place *in medias res*: Peirce's concept of semiotic Mediation', in Elizabeth Mertz and Richard J. Parmentier (eds), *Semiotic Mediation: Sociocultural and Psychological Perspectives*. Orlando, FL: Academic Press, pp. 24–48.

University of Iowa website on Traveling Culture: Circuit Chautauqua in the Twentieth Century (http://sdrcdata.lib.uiowa.edu/libsdrc/details.jsp?id=/taggart/7&ui=1), accessed 15 December 2007.

Welch, W. L. and L. B. S. Burt (1994), *From Tinfoil to Stereo: The Acoustic Years of the Recording Industry, 1877–1929*. Gainesville, FL: University of Florida Press.

EPILOGUE

14 Media, the state and linguistic authority

Monica Heller

14.1 The media as discursive space

The underlying questions in this volume are not so much about the media (what it does, how it works) as about the media as discursive space for examining language ideological debates. As a great deal of recent work has pointed out, language is a terrain for working through struggles over the regulation of resources, that is, over how to organize ourselves and make that organization legitimate in the eyes of involved social actors. We may not be able to say that we don't really want immigrants in our workplaces; we can say, however, that we will only hire people whose linguistic 'skills' meet a certain set of criteria, determined, as it happens, by us. The bourgeoisie of Revolutionary France may not have been able to say that they were not willing to share property with peasants, but they were able to say that only those who mastered standard French merited full participation in the spaces where the resources of the State were distributed (Higonnet 1980). Educated white males of post-Revolutionary Europe may not have been able to say that they didn't want to give women the vote, but they could say that women's discourse is emotional and not rational, and therefore not suited to democratic deliberations (Outram 1987; Bauman and Briggs 2003).

How we define what counts as legitimate language, how we define what counts as an authoritative performance of linguistic competence, and who we define as a legitimate speaker, all are ways of constructing social boundaries (Bourdieu 1982). Language ideological debates (Blommaert 1999) can therefore occur around any of the dimensions of category construction where boundaries matter and operate: what the resources are which get produced and distributed by participants; what value those resources have and who attributes that value; what activities are involved in resource evaluation, production, distribution; and how access to those activities is regulated. Which of these dimensions matters to whom, under what circumstances, is historically contingent; as is, of course, the extent to which debate is even possible at all.

The construction, reproduction, contestation and modification of language ideologies is also work that gets done in real time by real people. A further empirical question is then when and where that happens, and who gets to participate in the process. I think it is useful to think in terms of *discursive spaces*, activities in which social actors, whatever else they may be doing, also define (again and again, or anew) what counts as legitimate language and who counts as legitimate speakers. We can think of the media as one of these, and ask questions about the kind of discursive space it is, who controls it, what kinds of interest they may have in defining linguistic competence the way they do, and what consequences this may have for ranges of speakers who control diverse arrays of linguistic resources.

Most importantly, it seems to me, we need to come to terms with the nature of the relationship between the media and the State. The construction of the liberal democratic European nation-State was achieved through the invention and extension of bureaucratized institutions. These institutions served as discursive spaces for the construction of what Anderson famously called 'imagined community' (Anderson 1983), that is, for the construction of modes of participation in and legitimation of activities controlled by the State; through the same process, they constructed, and still construct, the citizen (Weber 1976). Through education, members of the population learn what counts as legitimate knowledge, how to function in specific kinds of social order, and how to internalize the naturalness of their 'country' (and, sometimes, of its Empire or its imperial centre); those forms of knowledge are distributed on the basis of specific understandings of citizenship. Military service, civil service, even transportation offered similar opportunities. The media has played a key role in this joint process of constructing nation, State, Empire, citizen and subject, and in producing the legitimating ideologies of the social order. We can understand 'language ideologies and media discourse' in precisely these terms, namely as a field in which the media serves as one institution for the construction of citizens, one dimension of which is their linguistic practice.

It matters, then, what relationship specific media spaces bear to the State, or what kinds of regulation may operate there. What communities are imagined, in the service of what sets of interests? Who is constructed as a producer of discourse, and who as public (Gal and Woolard 2001) or even as consumer? This imagining is observable in all kinds of ways: not only in the content and form of the *discourses* produced there, but also in the institutional *practices* which assemble the resources on which it is based, which it creates and distributes, and which organize the selection of participants and their positioning in institutional roles.

278

What this amounts to is a call for broadening and anchoring our understandings of media discursive practices. The media are not disembodied (although they have resources for making the bodies which produce and consume disappear, a move which serves to naturalize media discourse in powerful ways); they are not timeless or free-floating. It does matter how specific spaces came into being, and how they relate to other spaces of discursive production on the subject of citizenship and consumption. It matters who makes decisions about how they operate, and how participants engage with the institutional constraints on their production. This dimension of media discourse has received little attention; we have yet to see full-scale ethnographies of media institutional discursive production, or of State, private sector or civil society engagement with the media in the production of discourses of identity and belonging, or of production and consumption. We know little as yet of what kinds of social actors, from what positions, regulate the resources of media discourse (but see Bell and Garrett 1998; Cotter 2001; Hannerz 2003).

Despite a widely shared set of assumptions about the 'effects' of media discourse on publics the media construct, from utopian visions of the full democracy of cyberspace to dystopian images of Big Brother, we know equally little about how publics are concretely constructed, how their actions are constrained by the structured relations obtaining between media institutions and civil society. We have little idea of what consequences engagement with the media actually have for actors' socialization into ideologies of language, nation, gender, class, sexuality, ableness, race or anything else that serves as a major organizing principle of the social order (let alone how it orients their action), or of how engagement with the media actually works to produce those effects. We may in fact be barking up the wrong tree by talking in terms of 'effects' at all; if we understand the media as a discursive space, we may be better off thinking in terms of discursive flows, and seeking ways to discover how specific discursive forms circulate from one space to another, as well as how actors are positioned, as producers, regulators, subjects and objects in terms of those discursive formations. Who takes up what in the way of communicative resources and discursive opportunities, with what consequences for the regulation of access to and further circulation of resources? That is, with what kinds of durable structuring effects (Giddens 1984)?

Finally, we need to think through the various ways in which we understand ourselves to be looking at language. What counts as legitimate language for an imagined community, who counts as a legitimate speaker (and thereby member of that community), what counts as a legitimate linguistic product (and mode of production and consumption),

279

all these are questions about the ways in which language serves as a terrain for the construction of community, and for the legitimization of specific regimes of authority. But our interest clearly also includes a general concern for how discursive resources are mobilized in the service of constructing community on other grounds, both in terms of defining criteria of inclusion and exclusion, and in terms of legitimizing the deployment of those criteria. I do want to insist that while they overlap, they are not the same thing, and that we have to consistently ask questions about the conditions under which language itself, as a field, is brought into play, and when it is not, as well as how it relates to the other forms of structuring of regimes of authority which are in play in historically and socially contingent ways.

Historically, language has been one of the means of unifying nation-States, conducting their business, and creating their citizens, and media has been one of the bureaucratized institutions mobilized in this project, both to construct and authorize language standardization and linguistic hegemony specifically, but also as a space for other dimensions of building States and citizens. We see the traces of that strongly across all the chapters here. But they also engage with more contemporary problems having to do with the destabilization of that relationship under current conditions of social change. What new challenges are presented to how the media works with and on the terrain of language to legitimize authority? What opportunities arise to imagine community differently?

14.2 Globalization, diaspora, commodification

Language ideological debates and the media as discursive space, or site of discursive construction, occupy us now, it seems, as windows into contemporary processes of social change. Perhaps we can think of this issue as the second in the series of defining moments of bourgeois liberal democracy and its realization in the form of the capitalist nation-State. The first would have been in the period of construction of the State, as manifested in the active work of construction of nationalist language ideologies and of bureaucratic, centralizing institutions and their enabling technologies. We are now in that phase of late capitalism, it appears, when the question of how that assemblage might work is once again on the table.

Many authors have provided accounts of why that might be. For my purposes here it is probably Castells' argument that is most useful, insofar as he argues that information technology in the service of the expansion of capital makes State regulation more difficult than perhaps it used to be, or at least opens up the possibilities of imaginaries that cut across or even replace the nation-State (Castells 2000). The question then becomes one of what kind of citizen is constructed in what kinds of media discursive space: who actually controls those spaces? What are they trying to do with them?

In some cases it seems clear that we are witnessing what Bourdieu might call saving the market, that is, using an existing instrument of nation-State construction to hang on to that way of doing things, to bolster the nation-State as it currently exists, even as compromises may be made with the flows and extended markets which push the boundaries of what it can reasonably be expected to do, or of how its action can be beneficial to capital. But we also see the exploration of practices which test out the affordances of the zones of expansion or traversal, and maybe even new imaginaries, whether immediately realizable under current conditions or not. Perhaps this is best thought of as using the discursive frames we have inherited to think about whether they are laying the groundwork for their own transformation, or whether we are simply tweaking them to fit what we experience as conditions which are new but still, in the end, recognizable.

How then to make sense out of what we see, whether in the form of discourse practices in older, established media forms anchored in the history of State formation, or in the emergence of new channels, and, possibly, new practices? This book lays out some approaches to charting this terrain, that is, to grasping the nature of what needs both description and explanation. I would argue, however, that in order to fully appreciate the nature of the beast, we have to pay more attention to what it does over the course of a period of time, who or what it interacts with, what conditions provide obstacles or opportunities and how it navigates them. We need both to understand the trajectory of the discursive space itself (who constructs it, in what shape, around what resources), and the trajectories of those who participate fully, marginally or maybe not at all. We need to discover what discourses are constructed there, what activities are rendered legitimate or even authoritative, and what subjects are produced. Finally, we can ask how these spaces are connected to others, in some form of organization of discursive flows, and we can ask how they are regulated and by whom.

Language is a doubly-useful lens for such interrogations. It is one terrain for the construction of the imagined community, and imagined citizen, of the nation-State, and our ways of understanding it are currently as challenged as are any of the central terrains on which nation-States were built, including culture, geography and history. At the same time it provides the raw material for re-defining and re-imagining, for opening up or closing down social relations, for debating legitimizing ideologies and their authority. The media is a space where we can see

281

these two threads interweaving, and perhaps come to some new appreciation of how we call ourselves into being.

References

Anderson, B. (1983), *Imagined Communities*. London: Verso.

Bauman, R. and C. Briggs (2003), *Voices of Modernity: Language Ideologies and the Politics of Inequality*. Cambridge: Cambridge University Press.

Bell, A. and P. Garrett (eds) (1998), *Approaches to Media Discourse*. Oxford: Blackwell.

Blommaert, J. (ed.) (1999), *Language Ideological Debates*. Berlin: Mouton de Gruyter.

Bourdieu, P. (1982), *Ce que parler veut dire*. Paris: Fayard.

Castells, M. (2000), *The Information Age: Economy, Society and Culture* (3 volumes). Oxford: Blackwell.

Cotter, C. (2001), *Discourse and Media*, in D. Schiffrin, D. Tannen and H. E. Hamilton (eds), *The Handbook of Discourse Analysis*. Oxford: Blackwell, pp. 416–36.

Gal, S. and Woolard, K. A. (eds) (2001), *Languages and Publics: The Making of Authority*. Manchester, UK: St. Jerome Publishing Ltd.

Giddens, A. (1984). *The Constitution of Society*. Berkeley, LA: University of California Press.

Hannerz, U. (2003). 'On being there . . . and there . . . and there! Reflections on multi-site ethnography'. *Ethnography*, 4(2), 201–16.

Higonnet, P. (1980), 'The politics of linguistic terrorism and grammatical hegemony during the French Revolution'. *Social Theory*, 5(1), 41–69.

Outram, D. (1987), 'Le langage mâle de la vertu: women and the discourse of the French Revolution', in P. Burke and R. Porter (eds), *The Social History of Language*. Cambridge: Cambridge University Press, pp. 120–35.

Weber, E. (1976), *Peasants into Frenchmen*. Stanford, CA: Stanford University Press.

Index

ABC (Spanish newspaper) 50
  commodification of Spanish 55, 56
  'culture' section 52
  projection and promotion of
    Spanish as unitary language
    53, 54
Abisheganaden, Jacintha 127
accents
  Hollywood and Disney movies 9,
    205, 211, 217
  loyalty 211
  Singapore's news presenters 138n. 3
  TV Globo news presenters 85,
    99n. 6
  video/computer games 9–10, 206,
    211–15, 216–17, 218n. 3
AILA *see* International Association
  for Applied Linguistics
Akamas (film) 116
Akanthiotis, K. 116
América Legal (TV show) 99n. 5
  language practices 84, 93–7, 98
Anglicisms
  German print media 20, 26, 28–9,
    35, 36
  threat to Spanish language 50
ANTENNA (TV channel) 101
Apsan, Moisés 93–7
argumentation strategies 104, 106–7,
  112, 147, 159, 175
Aristophanes 116
ASALE *see* Association of Spanish
  Language Academies
Association of Spanish Language
  Academies (ASALE) 48, 49
  representative voices in Spanish
    print media 52–3, 54

attitude hegemony 217
audience design 83
authoritative entextualization 104, 106

Baek Seungju 76n. 4
BAFTA Games Awards 219n. 10
Baleunmal Gounmal ('Correct
    Language, Beautiful Language')
    (TV show) 63
BB (TV show) *see* Big Brother
  (TV show)
BBC (British Broadcasting
  Corporation) 223
  Anglocentric perspective news
    reporting 247, 248n. 9
  language and symbolic racism in
    news programme 8–9, 150–8
BBC 2 224
BBC Nations and Regions/Asian
  Network 224
BBC Radio 4 224
BBC Trust Impartiality Report 244
BBC Voices project 10, 223–4
BBC Voices website homepage 10,
  224–5, 231–2, 246–7
  credibility, interactivity and
    playfulness 238–40
  general composition and
    individual items 232–7
  ideologized language 241
  relevance of British Isles map
    on 243–4
BBVA 57
Bernard, Barney 259
Big Brother (BB) (TV show) 164–5
  see also Celebrity Big Brother
  (TV show)

283

colour
  modality marker 228, 233–4
comedies 102
  business viability 109, 110, 111
  Cypriot Greek language 102, 114–15
  ethnic 192, 196
  ethnic speech styles and 187–8
  prime-time TV viewing
    suitability 111
  Singapore TV 127–8
commercial sound recordings
  performances of telephone use 10,
    253
  see also 'Casey at the Telephone';
    'Cohen at the Telephone'; 'The
    Old Country Fiddler at the
    Telephone'
Commission on Integration and
  Cohesion *see* United Kingdom.
  Commission on Integration and
  Cohesion
commodification of language 83
  Cypriot Greek 108
  globalization, diaspora and 280–2
  Spanish 7, 55–6, 57
common miscognitions 156
common-sense discourse 43, 143,
  144, 145
communicative technologies
  developments in US 252
  impact on communicative
    practices and experiences 252–3,
    270–1
comparative discourse analysis 18
  see also German and Greek
    newspaper language comparative
    analysis
complementarity
  Singlish 122, 125, 131
compositional coherence and
  cohesion
  BBC Voices homepage 237, 238
computer games *see* video/computer
  games
Computerspielemagazin GEE
  219n. 10
constatives 24, 206

context of discourse 146
Corenthal, Michael 259
corporeal double situatedness 210
correctives 18, 23, 26
  definition 23
  German and Greek newspaper
    languages compared 23–35
  major categories 27
Corsican broadcast media
  language activism and
    practices 89, 115–16, 116–17
  prescriptivism 72
Cosmopolitan (magazine) 82
critical discourse analysis (CDA) 5,
  51, 102–4, 224
  RAE discourse in press 56–7
critical paradigms
  debate on linguistic meaning 163
Croft, Lara (fictitious character) 209
cultural practices
  British Muslims 145–6
*Cybertext: Perspectives on Ergodic
  Literature* (Aarseth) 207
Cypriot Greek language 117n. 1
  limited usage in Cypriot TV
    112–13, 117
  non-serious language variety 102,
    106, 112–15, 117
  status 116
  usage in Cypriot TV series 8,
    101–2, 104–5, 115
  usage in Cypriot TV series, critique
    of 107–8
  see also standard Greek language
Cypriot television
  audience as 'producer' or 'origin' of
    series 104, 106–7
  audience viewing patterns 102
  channel and local programmes
    proliferation 101, 111
  content and language of
    series 101–2, 104–6, 107
  content and language of series, TV
    politics impact on 109–12, 117
  mirror of sociolinguistic
    practices 102, 104, 106–8, 117
  unique selling point 110